Jesus as a Figure in History

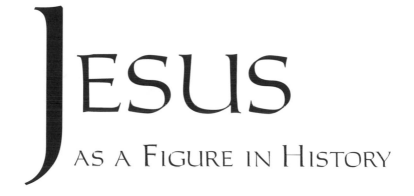

JESUS

AS A FIGURE IN HISTORY

How Modern Historians
View the Man from Galilee

Mark Allan Powell

Westminster John Knox Press
Louisville, Kentucky

For information, address
Westminster John Knox Press,
100 Witherspoon Street,
Louisville, Kentucky 40202-1396.

Scripture quotations, unless otherwise noted, are from the New Revised
Standard Version of the Bible, copyright © 1989 by the Division of
Christian Education of the National Council of the Churches of Christ
in the U.S.A., and are used by permission.

Book design by Sharon Adams
Cover design by Alec Bartsch
Cover illustration: Christ in the Temple, *artist unknown.*
  Courtesy of SuperStock.

First Edition
Published by Westminster John Knox Press
Louisville, Kentucky

This book is printed on acid-free paper that meets the
American National Standards Institute Z39.48 standard. ∞

PRINTED IN THE UNITED STATES OF AMERICA
99 00 01 02 03 04 05 06 07—10 9 8 7 6 5 4 3 2

Library of Congress Cataloging-in-Publication Data

Powell, Mark Allan, 1953–
    Jesus as a figure in history : how modern historians view the man
from Galilee / Mark Allen Powell.
        p.   cm.
    Includes bibliographical references and index.
    ISBN 0-664-25703-8 (alk. paper)
    1. Jesus Christ—Historicity.   2. Jesus Christ—Person and office.
I. Title
BT303.2.P68   1998   98-24284
232.9' —dc21

for Brandon Paul Curtis

Regardless of what anyone may personally think or believe about him, Jesus of Nazareth has been the dominant figure in the history of Western culture for almost twenty centuries. If it were possible, with some sort of super-magnet, to pull up out of that history every scrap of metal bearing at least a trace of his name, how much would be left?

—Jaroslav Pelikan, Professor of History, Yale University
Jesus through the Centuries:
His Place in the History of Culture
(New Haven, Conn.: Yale University Press, 1985), p. 1.

CONTENTS

Introduction   1

  1. Historians Discover Jesus   11

  2. Sources and Criteria   31

  3. Snapshots: Contemporary Images of Jesus   51

  4. The Jesus Seminar   65

  5. John Dominic Crossan   83

  6. Marcus J. Borg   101

  7. E. P. Sanders   113

  8. John P. Meier   131

  9. N. T. Wright   149

10. The Quest Continues: Issues and Concerns   167

Notes   185

Bibliography   209

Indexes

  Scripture and Ancient Sources   233

  Authors   237

INTRODUCTION

He comes as yet unknown into a hamlet of Lower Galilee. He is watched by the cold, hard eyes of peasants living long enough at subsistence level to know exactly where the line is drawn between poverty and destitution. He looks like a beggar, yet his eyes lack the proper cringe, his voice the proper whine, his walk the proper shuffle. He speaks about the rule of God, and they listen as much from curiosity as anything else. They know all about rule and power, about kingdom and empire, but they know it in terms of tax and debt, malnutrition and sickness, agrarian oppression and demonic possession. What, they really want to know, can this kingdom of God do for a lame child, a blind parent, a demented soul screaming its tortured isolation among the graves that mark the edges of the village? Jesus walks with them to the tombs, and, in the silence after the exorcism, the villagers listen once more, but now with curiosity giving way to cupidity, fear, and embarrassment. He is invited, as honor demands, to the home of the village leader. He goes, instead, to stay in the home of a dispossessed woman. Not quite proper, to be sure, but it would be unwise to censure an exorcist, to criticize a magician.

—John Dominic Crossan[1]

On a spring morning in about the year 30 C.E., three men were executed by the Roman authorities in Judea. Two were "brigands" . . . the third was executed as another type of political criminal. He had not robbed, pillaged, murdered, or even stored arms. He was convicted, however, of having claimed to be "king of the Jews"—a political title. Those who looked on . . . doubtless thought that . . . the world would little note what happened that spring morning. . . . It turned out, of course, that the third man, Jesus of Nazareth, would become one of the most important figures in human history.

—E. P. Sanders[2]

Wake up Sunday morning and travel about your town or county. No matter where it is in America, you will find churches—churches of all different sizes and structures, historic denominations and recent innovations, major "name brands" and generic community fellowships, sects, cults, and anonymous gatherings of people who haven't yet figured out what sort of organization, if any, they want to employ. You will find people meeting in towering cathedrals and in rented-out storefronts, in spacious auditoriums and in ranch-style sanctuaries. You will see stained glass and paraments, expensive commissioned artwork and tacky homemade banners. And the people are as diverse as their furnishings. Look around long enough and you will see every sort of person in America: Democrats and Republicans, liberals and conservatives, men and women, old and young, rich and poor, executives, laborers, citizens, refugees, illegal aliens, the educated, the illiterate, the aged, the infirm, the mentally retarded, gays, lesbians, Asian Americans, African Americans, Hispanic Americans, Native Americans, and so forth.

The most amazing thing about this is that all of these people have gotten out of bed and gathered with others on Sunday morning because of one person—a Jewish man who was born on the other side of the world over two thousand years ago.

Listen! You will hear congregations singing:

> Jesus shall reign where'er the sun
> Does its successive journeys run . . .

> What a friend we have in Jesus
> All our sins and griefs to bear . . .

> All hail the power of Jesus' name
> Let angels prostrate fall . . .

You will hear groups reciting a creed:

> We believe in one Lord, Jesus Christ
> the only Son of God,
> eternally begotten of the Father,
> God from God, Light from Light
> true God from true God,
> begotten not made,
> of one Being with the Father.

You will hear an evangelist exhorting individuals to accept Jesus as their personal Lord and Savior, inviting them to ask him into their hearts to cleanse them from sin. You will hear inspired worshipers claiming that Jesus has spoken to them this very morning and given them a word of direction for others who are present. If you are not one of these people—if you are not a Christian—all of this may seem bizarre. Even if you are a Christian, *some* of this may seem bizarre, for you probably have some ideas about which groups of Christians have got this Jesus stuff down right, and which have got it wrong.

What could we say about Jesus that everyone would agree is right? What could we possibly say that all the different types of Christians and even the non-Christians would accept? That he lived and died? Anything else?

Studying Jesus as a figure in history is different from studying him as the object of religious devotion or faith. This is clear, but just how is it different? Many may think that religion should be concerned with *beliefs* about Jesus, and history with *facts* concerning him. For example, if I say, "Jesus died by crucifixion," that is a historical fact, but if I say, "Jesus died for our sins," that is a religious belief. We would expect for good history to confine itself to the facts. Historians should do history and theology should be left to the theologians.

If it were only that simple. The line between facts and beliefs is not always as clear as in the example just cited. In a sense, nothing can ever be proven absolutely to have happened. History, especially ancient history, deals with degrees of plausibility. Some matters do come to be regarded as facts after careful analysis of evidence, but the standards by which this evidence is evaluated are grounded in beliefs. Honest historians readily admit to the role that ideology plays in their discipline. At the very least, they approach their task with ideas about what is intrinsically likely or unlikely and about what constitutes good evidence. Such ideas are inevitably debatable.

With regard to Jesus, the task of defining what constitutes a historical approach can be especially difficult. For one thing, most scholars who study Jesus are likely to have personal investment in the outcome of their work. In itself, this problem is not unique, since historians do not usually study people about whom they care nothing. But with Jesus, the level of investment tends to be especially pronounced. Paul Hollenbach admits that he pursues the Jesus of history "in order to overthrow, not simply correct, the mistake called Christianity."[3] Frederick Gaiser maintains that "historical investigation is part and parcel of biblical faith," that one should study the historical Jesus precisely as a way of understanding better "the incarnational God who took the risk of making himself the object of historical study."[4] What do we make of such biases? Some may think Hollenbach and Gaiser are likely to be bad historians because they are so blatantly prejudiced. Others may think they could be good historians because they are aware of their prejudices and state them outright. In any case, the mere fact that they *have* biases does not invalidate their research. If they uncover significant points about Jesus, they deserve to have these considered (and tested) by the academic guild of their peers as surely as do scholars who do not pursue their work with an admitted agenda.

Jesus studies can also be complicated by the exceptional character of the incidents reported. Various sources (biblical and otherwise) claim that Jesus was known for doing extraordinary things—working miracles, knowing the thoughts of others, predicting the future, and so on. Historians are accustomed to dismissing such reports. Some sources attribute miracles to Julius Caesar, for instance, but no reputable modern biography would claim that the Roman emperor possessed supernatural powers. Rather, historians realize that such legends often accrue around figures of renown and they are not reticent to refine primitive superstition in light of modern consciousness. But the connection of Jesus to events that would be considered exceptional (if not impossible) is hardly peripheral. Many would claim that apart from some such events (for instance, his resurrection from the dead), he would not be remembered at all. So what is the historian to do? To claim that something happened that historical science regards as impossible seems by definition to be bad history. But to dismiss a claim that something ordinarily impossible happened by saying, "It could not have happened because it is impossible," is clearly an exercise in circular reasoning. As we shall see, the historians discussed in this book deal with this philosophical problem differently.

So the distinction between historical and theological studies of Jesus is neither absolute nor clear. Apart from these problems, however, at least two points of agreement can be stated.

✴ First, studying Jesus as a figure in history means studying the person who lived on this earth in the early decades of what we now call the first century (because of him, in fact). It does not involve studying the heavenly or spiritual figure whom Christians worship, or the mystical figure who Christians say dwells in the midst of their assembly or lives in their individual hearts. It does not involve studying the second Person of the Holy Trinity, whom Christians identify as "begotten not made"—a person who, they claim, has been present since before the creation of the cosmos and, indeed, was responsible for its creation. Theology connects all of these figures with Jesus, but historical science does not.

❧ Over a century ago, a scholar named Martin Kähler made a distinction between "the Jesus of history" and "the Christ of faith."[5] The former is the subject of historical study; the latter, of theological reflection and religious devotion. The distinction proved both useful and problematic. Most Christians would reject the notion that the Jesus who now sits on the right hand of God to hear their prayers is a different person than the Jesus who lived and worked in Galilee. Recently, Marcus Borg has tried to offer a more neutral distinction: historians study the "pre-Easter Jesus" while Christians not only revere this person but also worship and claim to experience the reality of a "post-Easter Jesus."[6] Christians may believe the post-Easter Jesus is the same person as the historical figure if they wish, but historians do not have to believe in this post-Easter figure to study the man who lived before Easter.

Christians who find this distinction unsettling may take comfort in recognizing that it is made in the New Testament by Jesus himself. In the Gospel of Matthew, Jesus (before Easter) tells his disciples, "You will not always have me [with you]" (Matt. 26:11). Then, a few days later (after Easter), he tells those same disciples, "I am with you always" (Matt. 28:20). This is not a contradiction. Rather, Matthew's Gospel promises that Jesus will always be present with his followers while recognizing that he will not be present with them after Easter in the same way that he was before Easter.

Second, studying Jesus as a figure in history means treating all of the ancient sources regarding him as historical documents rather than as privileged or inspired literature. Historians may of course believe that the writings about Jesus in the Bible are Holy Scripture, but they cannot simply assert that claim to justify what they say about him as historians. None of the people discussed in this book will say, "I think this is true about Jesus because the Bible says this and I believe everything the Bible says is true." Such a statement might be regarded as good theology in some camps, but in no quarter would it be regarded as good history. Those who study Jesus as a figure in history are not trying to summarize what the Bible says about Jesus (which would be a relatively simple task). They are trying to sift through that material, as well as other nonbiblical materials, to find content that can be judged reliable from the perspective of modern historical science.

Christians need to keep this point in mind when evaluating historical treatments of Jesus. There may be a subconscious tendency to evaluate positively anything a historian asserts that accords with biblical content and negatively anything that contradicts it. To take an example, when historian John Meier says that Jesus baptized people,[7] we should not think that he erroneously derived this from John 3:22 without paying attention to the correction offered in John 4:1–2. Meier knows these verses, as well as John 3:26. He bases his claim that Jesus baptized people on a critical decision that John 4:1–2 does not seek to correct a misunderstanding but to refute a correct understanding (that Jesus was in fact baptizing). Those who understand Meier's position may nevertheless think that he is wrong; they might decide that his historical judgment is flawed and that a different conclusion makes better sense of the evidence. This is quite different from saying Meier is wrong because he doubts the accuracy of a statement in the Bible. In the latter instance, the argument cannot be pursued on historical grounds. Unless we recognize these ground rules, arguments can quickly become silly as the dialogue partners discover (or, worse, fail to discover) that they are speaking different languages.

These two points are only exemplary of the sort of concerns that emerge when scholars decide to study Jesus as a figure in history. Other issues will come to the fore as we proceed. For now, I suggest that readers consider a question that sometimes helps to bring some of these points into focus: What should be taught about Jesus in the public schools? In the United States, it is considered inappropriate if not illegal for a public school teacher to instruct students in matters of religious faith. Most Americans, including Christians, would consider a teacher out of line if he or she spoke of Jesus as a living reality today ("Jesus loves you and he will answer your prayers") or affirmed the authority of the Bible as a divinely inspired source for learning about Jesus. Most would probably also think it inappropriate for a teacher to tell public school children that Jesus worked miracles or that he rose from the dead. Then what *would* be appropriate for the teacher to say? What is there about Jesus that *all* children—be they Christian, Jewish, Muslim, Buddhist, or atheist—ought to know?

By almost any account, Jesus is one of the most significant persons ever to have lived. Recognizing this, the public schools have not ignored him completely. Chart 1 on page 6 presents everything that two widely used high school textbooks have to say about Jesus. Supposedly, all of this information is based on solid historical research, apart from presuppositions of faith. Still, all of the historians discussed in this book would regard the information presented in these texts as rather skimpy. Fear of controversy, perhaps, assures Jesus of receiving less attention in the curriculum than his influence on world history would commend. Ironically, public school students in countries where the presence of Christianity is minimal often learn more about Jesus than do students in the United States.

Chart 1. Jesus in the Public Schools

Exhibit 1.

Around A.D. 1, when religious fervor and political discontent were rising in Palestine, a Jew named Jesus was born in Bethlehem, near Jerusalem. Most of what is known of his life comes from the Gospels, the first four books of the New Testament of the Christian Bible. According to the Gospels, Jesus grew up in Nazareth, where he studied his religion in the synagogue and learned carpentry from his father.

Jesus began his public life of preaching when he was about 30 years old. His teachings were based on traditional Hebrew beliefs. For example, Jesus taught people to obey the Ten Commandments. He condensed the ten into two: People should love God with all their hearts, and they should love their neighbors as they love themselves.

Jesus also taught that God was loving and forgiving. He urged people to ignore wealth and fame and concentrate on helping others. To those who followed these teachings, Jesus promised eternal life.

Some people saw Jesus as a political leader—the King of the Jews who would free his people from the Romans. Jesus, however, claimed that his kingdom was a spiritual one—the Kingdom of God.

Jesus gathered around him a group of followers, 12 of whom he named as apostles. Jesus and his apostles spent three years traveling through Palestine, bringing his message to the people. According to the Gospels, Jesus attracted many followers and drew large crowds wherever he preached.

About A.D. 33 Jesus and the apostles arrived in Jerusalem to celebrate the Jewish holiday of Passover. The arrival of Jesus upset both the Roman authorities and the Jewish leaders in the city. The Romans were convinced that Jesus was a political agitator who wanted to start a rebellion. Some Jewish leaders were convinced that Jesus was attacking Judaism.

Jesus was arrested as a dangerous rebel, brought before Pontius Pilate, the Roman governor, and convicted of treason, or crimes against the state. He was executed in a customary Roman way called crucifixion, in which a prisoner was tied to a huge cross and left to die of exposure. Sometimes, as in the case of Jesus, a prisoner was nailed to the cross in order to speed death.

With the death of Jesus, his followers at first lost hope. Then the rumor spread that Jesus had risen from the dead on the third day after his crucifixion and had been seen by some of his apostles. Jesus' followers now believed he was truly a divine being. With more enthusiasm than ever, they began preaching the teachings of their leader to Jews in Palestine. Jesus became a symbol and an inspiration to his followers because he had died for the cause. He also became identified with the Hebrew belief in a messiah.

—from Peter Stearns, Donald R. Schwarz, and Barry K. Beyer,
World History: Traditions and New Directions
(Reading, Mass.: Addison-Wesley Publishing Co., 1989), 141–42.

Exhibit 2.

A few decades before the revolts of the Jews—at about the time Augustus had established the Roman province of Judea—a Jew named Jesus grew up in the town of Nazareth. After a traditional Jewish education, Jesus traveled through Judea from about A.D. 26 to 30, preaching a new message to his fellow Jews and winning disciples, or followers.

Proclaiming that the kingdom of God was close at hand, Jesus urged people to repent their mistakes and change their behavior. He said that God was loving and forgiving toward all those who repented, no matter what evil they had done or how lowly they were. Addressing people of every class, he often used parables, or symbolic stories, to get his message across. With the parable below, Jesus urged his followers to give up everything so that they would be ready for God's kingdom:

The kingdom of heaven is like treasure lying buried in a field. The man who found it, buried it again; and for sheer joy went and sold everything he had, and bought that field. (Matthew 13:44)

Jesus' disciples began to believe that he was the long-awaited messiah. Other Jews, believing that the messiah had not yet come, did not think Jesus deserved to be called messiah and so viewed him as an impostor. This disagreement soon became a fiercely debated controversy.

The controversy troubled Roman officials in Palestine. They believed that anyone who aroused such strong feelings in the public could jeopardize Roman authority. In about A.D. 33, the Roman governor arrested Jesus as a political troublemaker and ordered that he be crucified—hung from a cross until dead. This was the customary Roman way of punishing criminals.

After the death of Jesus, his disciples claimed that he had been resurrected, or had risen from the dead, and had appeared to them. They pointed to this as further evidence that he was the messiah. His followers began preaching that Jesus was the Son of God and the way of salvation.

—from Mounir Farah and Andrea Berens Karls,
World History: The Human Experience,
3d ed. (New York: Glencoe/McGraw-Hill, 1992), 157–58.

We can make two further observations about the information presented in chart 1: On the one hand, nothing is asserted here that would necessarily prove the legitimacy of the Christian faith; on the other hand, nothing is asserted that would expose it as a mistake. As we will see, the historians discussed in this book go beyond the observations offered in these schoolbooks in ways that defy both of these points. Sometimes, those who study Jesus as a figure in history do offer assertions that, if valid, would either confirm or challenge tenets of faith. If beliefs affect how one determines facts, then facts may also affect what one determines to believe.

The historical study of Jesus has progressed for two centuries now and the results are starting to come in. In the past decade, they have come *pouring* in, with an avalanche of published tomes on Jesus written by a variety of historical scholars. Sometimes the results of these studies are sensationalized in media reports; more often, they remain hidden in academic literature not accessible to the general reader. In any case, it seems appropriate now, at the turn of the millennium, to provide a simple, sober, and sincere report of this quest in its current stage. We should not expect unanimity, but we will discover broad areas of agreement. We will also see, in sharp focus, what remain the "hot topics" for debate, the questions on which even the most reputable historians do not agree.

Chapter 1 will offer a brief tour of the discipline up to the present, focusing on some of the key players and the contributions they have made to defining the questions that must now be addressed. Those who want to skip this and jump right into the main part of the book can probably do so without severe penalty, but the chapter does provide a good context for understanding how we got to where we are.

Chapter 2 describes principles and procedures that are widely accepted by those who do this sort of work. In particular, we will identify the key sources for studying Jesus (not just the Bible) and list key criteria that scholars use in making historical judgments on particular matters. Unless you are familiar with this material already, this chapter is probably a prerequisite for making sense of the rest of the book.

Chapter 3 presents what I call "snapshots," brief descriptions of images that some scholars have suggested may apply to Jesus. Some of these are controversial; some are pretty traditional. In no case does one image or snapshot offer a full picture of Jesus. Rather, these are proposed aspects of who Jesus was, or suggestions of how he appeared to some people some of the time. I suspect that many readers will find the material in this chapter quite fascinating.

Chapters 4 through 9 offer in-depth descriptions of what I consider to be the six most important studies of Jesus produced in the last few years. These may be read in any order, depending on interest. In each case, I present (1) an overview of the method or approach used by the particular scholar or team of scholars, (2) a summary of the results that have been obtained (a portrait of who Jesus was according to this view), and (3) a summary of the criticisms of this work that have been offered by other historians.

Finally, Chapter 10 offers some summary, cross-referencing topics on which these scholars agree and disagree.

I strive to offer unbiased reports throughout, yet I do not wish to feign objectivity, to pretend that I myself am somehow free of that element of personal investment that affects those I describe. I think, therefore, that I must now state what I believe. I shall intrude so blatantly in this manner only once now, and then, again, at the very end. You will have to be the judge of my success at keeping my prejudices in check the rest of the time.

I trust my life and destiny to what I call "the Jesus of story." This Jesus, I believe, is wholly compatible with all, but not identical to any, of the following:

- Kähler's "Jesus of history" and "Christ of faith" (page 4)
- Borg's "pre-Easter Jesus" and "post-Easter Jesus" (page 4)

- Fiorenza's "historical Jesus" and "Jesus of piety" (page 29)
- Meier's "historical Jesus" and "real Jesus" (page 133)
- Witherington's "Jesus that we can recover by means of the historical-critical method" and "historical Jesus" (page 202, note 13)
- Bultmann's "kerygmatic Christ" and Graham's "personal Lord and Savior" (pages 18–19).

By identifying Jesus with a story, I certainly do not mean to indicate that I regard him as a fictional character in literature. I think I would have to be a bigger fool than I am to trust my life or destiny to a cipher. No, I mean that for me the identity and significance of Jesus is inextricably caught up with a story, and that the Jesus of this story is given meaning and content by the effect and impact that he has upon his readers, his audience. Every reaction to him, positive or negative, may become part of the story.

The distinction between what I call the "Jesus of story" and the "Jesus of history" is not chronological, as are Kähler's and Borg's distinctions. The story of Jesus begins before anything that can reasonably be identified as historical and continues long after everything that can be identified as historical. The Jesus of story is the larger entity of which the Jesus of history is but a part. History *is* a part of the story, so understanding Jesus as a figure in history remains significant to anyone who wants to believe the story and trust the Jesus it reveals. Still, for me, trusting the Jesus of this story has come to mean more than knowing history. Over the years, it has come to mean recognizing the story to be grounded in the witness of the Spirit, in the testimonies of saints and martyrs, and in my own life experience.

People say this Jesus is found in the Bible and in the church. So many say it that I think it must be true, but for me the experience has not been one of finding him anywhere. For me, Bible and church, liturgy and creed, word and sacrament, have not served to facilitate a human quest through which we might recover Jesus and restore history. Rather, they have served to disclose a divine quest through which Jesus himself redeems history and recovers humanity. In short, I never once have felt as though I were finding Jesus in any of this, but I frequently feel as though I am being found. I think of the story that way: not as the place where I look for Jesus but as the place where he finds me.

I hope this book proves as useful and significant as its subject matter warrants. If you appreciate it, you will want to join me in thanking Trinity Lutheran Seminary for providing a community that encourages and facilitates such contributions on the part of its faculty; Aid Association for Lutherans for funding travel expenses; Westminster John Knox Press (with editors Jon Berquist and Nick Street) for helping me to develop the manuscript, improve it, and bring it to publication; and Melissa, David, Michael, Brandon, and Jillian—my lively, loving family—for filling my life with the joy that, I hope, pervades everything I do.

1

HISTORIANS DISCOVER JESUS

He comes to us as one unknown.

—Albert Schweitzer (1906)[1]

I do indeed think that we can now know almost nothing concerning the life and personality of Jesus.

—Rudolf Bultmann (1926)[2]

No one is any longer in the position to write a life of Jesus.

—Günther Bornkamm (1956)[3]

We can know quite a lot about Jesus; not enough to write a modern-style biography, including the colour of the subject's hair, and what he liked for breakfast, but quite a lot.

—N. T. Wright (1996)[4]

Historians search for Jesus for a variety of reasons. Some may be intellectually curious or intrigued by the challenge. Some hope to facilitate dialogue between religion and secular society. Some may wish to substantiate the Christian faith while others may want to discredit it. Many, no doubt, just want to submit their faith to honest scrutiny in the belief that only then can it be confessed with integrity. For whatever reason, the historian's quest for Jesus has been proceeding by fits and starts for two centuries now, though never with more vigor than today. Although this book is primarily concerned with the flood of Jesus scholarship produced in the last decade of the twentieth century, we should begin with a survey of what has come before.

Gospel Harmonies

Prior to the Enlightenment, Jesus was not studied as a historical figure in the modern sense. Non-Christian scholars took little or no interest in him and Christian scholars simply regarded the biblical accounts as straightforward historical records of his life. One problem, however, was noted early on: The Bible presents four different records of Jesus' life and they do not always seem to agree on what they report concerning him. Thus, for many centuries, creating a historical biography of Jesus was basically a matter of harmonizing the four Gospel narratives. This was actually done for the first time less than a hundred years after the Gospels themselves were written. A Mesopotamian Christian named Tatian wove the four Gospel accounts together into one continuous narrative, which he called the *Diatessaron* ("four-in-one"). The work was translated into several languages and was widely used for three hundred years. The Syriac version appears to have replaced the four individual Gospels in some churches.

We can only imagine what sort of decisions Tatian and others like him had to make as they sought to harmonize the Gospels. First would be the simple question of chronology: Even if we grant that Jesus did all of the things reported in all of the Gospels, we will still have to ask in what order he did these things. Creating one story from four forces the scholar to place some events ahead of others. In addition, we would have to ask about repetition. All four Gospels contain stories of Jesus turning over tables in the Jerusalem temple (Matt. 21:12–17; Mark 11:15–19; Luke 19:45–48; John 2:13–17). Do we assume that these are four reports of the same event? In the first three Gospels, the account comes near the end of the story, but in John it comes near the beginning. Did Jesus turn over tables in the temple twice? Some thirteen hundred years later, Martin Luther, confronted with precisely the same problem, would write, "The Gospels follow no order in recording the acts and miracles of Jesus, and the matter is not, after all, of much importance. If a difficulty arises in regard to the Holy Scripture and we cannot solve it, we must just let it alone."[5]

There also would be the question of contradiction. In Matthew 8:5–13, a centurion comes to Jesus in Capernaum and asks that Jesus heal his servant, while in Luke 7:1–10, the same centurion sends Jewish elders to ask Jesus to heal his servant. The words attributed to the centurion (Matt. 8:8–9) or to his friends (Luke

7:6–8) are almost identical. Assuming these are two reports of the same story, how are they to be harmonized? It seems very unlikely that these are separate reports of two events, that Jesus healed this poor man from a distance twice, saying the same things both times (once to the centurion's representatives and once to the centurion himself). The latter view has actually been tried[6] and is still sometimes asserted by fundamentalists,[7] but for the most part has been found wanting. But if the two stories report the same event, should a Gospel harmony such as Tatian's have the centurion go to Jesus in person, send a delegation, or both? Some scholars, notably John Calvin, despaired of producing a continuous narrative like the *Diatessaron* and simply presented similar stories from different Gospels side by side in parallel columns.[8]

In producing Gospel harmonies, scholars were already asking historical questions about Jesus, but they did so within a context of faith, not skepticism. All this changed with the Enlightenment, the European movement that exalted the use of reason as the best means for discovering truth. The Enlightenment emphasized the orderliness of nature and so encouraged disciplined scholarship that adhered to well-defined methods for testing and verifying hypotheses. It furthered the acquisition of knowledge and the development of critical thinking. Though initially a philosophical movement (featuring such luminaries as Descartes, Locke, Rousseau, and Voltaire), the new orientation led to tremendous advances in science and mathematics. Eventually, its effects were felt on politics and on religion. One legacy of the Enlightenment for Western thought was a lasting distrust of assertions that cannot be verified. The distinction between religious faith and superstition appeared to be no more than a matter of perspective.

"Lives" of Jesus

During the period following the Enlightenment, scholars embarked on what came to be known as "the quest for the historical Jesus." They went beyond the production of Gospel harmonies to write biographies, called *Lives* of Jesus. A Life of Jesus might draw heavily upon harmonization of the Gospel accounts but it differed in at least three ways. It would (1) typically impose some grand scheme or hypothesis upon the material that allowed everything to be interpreted in accord with a consistent paradigm (for example, "Jesus was a social reformer" or "Jesus was a religious mystic"), (2) exclude material in the Gospels that did not fit with this paradigm, submitting the biblical record to the author's critical judgment of what seemed most likely to be correct, and (3) include reflection about Jesus not derived from the Gospels, attempting to fill in gaps in the biblical record with the author's own projections concerning Jesus' motivations, goals, or self-understanding.

Hundreds of these Lives of Jesus were produced, mainly during the nineteenth century. Below is a sampling of some of the most influential.

Hermann Samuel Reimarus (1694–1768) believed Jesus was an unsuccessful political claimant who thought it was his destiny to be established by God as king of the restored people of Israel. Reimarus was a respected professor of Oriental languages at the University of Hamburg and his works on Jesus were not published until after his death. Apparently, he feared retribution for his controversial views during his lifetime. In any case, fragments of a large unpublished manuscript were printed between 1774 and 1778, and these mark what many consider to be the beginning of the quest for the historical Jesus.[9] The audacity of Reimarus's claims flew in the face of traditional pious scholarship and demanded engagement on historical grounds. Reimarus interpreted all of the passages in the New Testament where Jesus speaks of "the kingdom of God" or "the kingdom of heaven" as references to a new political reality about to be established on earth. Thus, Reimarus said, Jesus believed he was the Messiah (or "Christ"), but he meant this in a worldly sense. He thought that God was going to deliver the people of Israel from bondage to the Romans and create a new and powerful kingdom on earth where Jesus himself would rule as king. This is why he was executed, charged with the crime of claiming to be the King of the Jews (Matt. 27:37). This is also why, when he died, he cried out, "My God, my God, why have you forsaken me?" (Matt. 27:46). He realized in his last moments that God had failed him, that his hopes had been misplaced. His disciples, however, were unable to accept this outcome. Not wanting to return to their mundane lives in Galilee, they stole his body from its tomb, claimed he had been raised from the dead (see Matt. 28:11–15), and made up a new story about how Jesus had died willingly as an atonement for sins. The message of the kingdom was spiritualized and the teaching of the failed religious fanatic was transformed into a religion promising salvation after death to those who joined an organization led by his followers. Thus, "the new system of a suffering spiritual savior, which no one had ever known or thought before, was invented only because the first hopes had failed."[10] Despite its radical (and ultimately untenable) ideas, Reimarus's work raised questions and issues that had not been examined previously. Albert Schweitzer, who completely disagreed with the main thesis, nevertheless hailed its publication as "one of the greatest events in the history of criticism." As a side note, he also called it "a masterpiece of general literature," reflecting on the passion with which Reimarus spewed his venom against Christian religion: "It is as though the fires of a volcano were painting lurid pictures upon dark clouds. Seldom has there been a hate so eloquent, so lofty a scorn."[11]

Heinrich Eberhard Gottlob Paulus (1761–1851) was a veteran rationalist who became best known for offering naturalistic explanations for miracle stories reported in the Gospels. As professor of theology at the University of Heidelberg he published a two-volume work on the life of Jesus in 1828.[12] In essence, it was a Gospel harmony with explanatory notes. Paulus accepted the miracle stories as reports of historical events, but reasoned that a primitive knowledge of the laws of nature led people in biblical times to regard as supernatural occurrences what the advancement of knowledge has rendered understandable. For example, Jesus may have appeared to walk on water when he strode along the shore in a mist and he may have received credit for stilling a storm when the weather coincidentally improved after he awoke from sleep on a boat trip. Jesus healed people by improving their psychological disposition or, sometimes, by applying medicines mixed with mud (John 9:6) or saliva (Mark 8:23). Likewise, his disciples were provided with medicinal oil to use for curing certain ailments (Mark 6:13). The story of the feeding of the five thousand recalls a time when Jesus and his disciples generously shared their own provisions with those who had none, inspiring others in the crowd to do the same until everyone was satisfied. Paulus's book evoked a good deal of opposition at the time of its appearance, but its ideas continued (and still continue) to resurface, especially in writings of those who do not otherwise know what to do with the miracles.

David Friedrich Strauss (1808–1874) appealed to modern understandings of mythology to steer a middle course between naive acceptance of Gospel stories and the sort of simplistic explanations for these stories offered by Paulus. In 1835, Strauss published *The Life of Jesus Critically Examined,* a two-volume work over fourteen hundred pages in length.[13] He called for unbiased historical research to be done on the Gospels, establishing an orientation for scholarship that is still followed by many today. He discerned, for instance, that the stories in the first three Gospels are less developed than those in John which, accordingly, is the least valuable book for historical reconstruction. Still, Strauss regarded most of the stories in all of the Gospels as myths, developed often on the pattern of Old Testament prototypes. The point of such tales is not to record a historical occurrence but to interpret it in light of the religious ideas put forward by Jesus. For example, the story of Jesus' baptism includes references to the Spirit descending as a dove upon Jesus and a voice speaking from heaven. These things did not actually happen in the strict historical sense, but they interpret the significance of something that did occur. Jesus really was baptized by John and his sense of mission was somehow related to what he experienced on that occasion. Strauss's view of the Gospels as history interpreted through myth evinced a growing recognition on the part of scholars that these books describe "the Jesus of history" from a perspective that regards him as "the Christ of faith," a perspective that (supposedly) unbiased historians cannot endorse. Nevertheless, in its own day Strauss's work was highly controversial, and the publication of this influential book caused him to lose his position at the University of Zurich.

Ernst Renan (1823–1892) combined critical scholarship with novelistic aesthetic appeal to create what was probably the most widely read Life of Jesus in his day.[14] Published in 1863, the book broke with rationalism in its attempt to discern the emotional impact of the Jesus tradition and to trace the reasons for this to the passions, individuality, and spontaneity of Jesus himself. Regarding the Gospels as "legendary biographies," Renan sought to uncover the personality that inspired the legends while also displaying his own penchant for poetic, even sentimental, description. For example, since Jesus is said to have ridden into Jerusalem on a mule (in modern translations, an ass or a donkey), Renan imagines that he typically traveled about the countryside seated upon "that favorite riding-animal of the East, which is so docile and sure-footed and whose great dark eyes, shaded with long lashes, are full of gentleness," (see Schweitzer, *Quest of the Historical Jesus,* 184). Renan also attempted to fit the Gospel materials into an overall chronology for the life of Jesus. He described the initial years as "a Galilean springtime,"[15] a sunny period in which Jesus was an amiable carpenter who rode his gentle mule from town to town sharing a "sweet theology of love" that he had discerned through observation of nature. Eventually, however, Jesus visited the capital city of Jerusalem, where his winsome message met with opposition from the rabbis. This led him to develop an increasingly revolutionary stance with a harsher tone, to despair of earthly ambitions, and at last to invite persecution and martyrdom. Renan's book was a bestseller, going through eight printings in three months. Still, its imaginative reworking of biblical materials invoked the wrath of traditional Christians (he suggested the raising of Lazarus was a "staged miracle," a deliberate hoax designed to win acclaim for Jesus), while its sentimental features brought scorn from other historical Jesus scholars.[16] Like Strauss, he was fired from his university professorship, in this case from a position at the Collège de France that he had held for less than a year.

What lessons are to be learned from these Lives of Jesus, aside from the observation that such scholarship can be deleterious to one's career? While Reimarus's writings were overtly hostile to Christianity, the other three authors all viewed themselves as Christian theologians who sought to discover or salvage something in the biblical tradition that could be recognized as universally true. All four were skeptical of the miracle stories, displaying a reluctance to accept anything that deals with the supernatural as a straightforward historical account. All questioned the accuracy of the Gospels at certain points and sought to supplement the stories with what they thought were reasonable conjectures at other points.

The most important lesson, perhaps, was noted with verve by Albert Schweitzer in 1906. These authors, and numerous others, all managed to produce portraits of Jesus that they personally found appealing. For the non-Christian, the historical Jesus rather conveniently turned out to be a fraud. For the Christian, the historical Jesus seemed in every case to end up believing things that the author believed and valuing whatever the author valued. The scholars, Schweitzer claimed, had modernized Jesus, dressing him in clothes of their own design. Their interest, whether conscious or not, was in discovering a figure who would be relevant for their time, and this interest prevented them from seeing Jesus as a figure in his own time, as a figure of the past, a figure *in history*. One sign of this was that the Christian studies tended to present Jesus in a fairly generic ethnic guise—there was little about him that seemed specifically Jewish.

The so-called quest for the historical Jesus had tended in fact to become a quest for the relevant Jesus. Historical accuracy and relevance are not, of course, *necessarily* mutually exclusive, but the Christian scholars apparently failed to reckon with the possibility that they *might* be. In the final analysis, Schweitzer concluded, the quest had yielded only negative results. Indeed, he said, "there is nothing more negative than the result of the critical study of the Life of Jesus."[17] Did that stop Schweitzer himself from trying? No way! His survey of failed attempts serves as a prelude to his own description of the historical figure of Jesus, a portrait that at least avoids the trap of modernizing him, a portrait that until recently has been considered the most important study of Jesus ever produced by a modern historian.

Albert Schweitzer (1875–1965) identified the missing element in most of the Lives of Jesus as *eschatology*. The word *eschatology* literally means "study of last things"; in theology, it usually refers to what one believes regarding the future — life after death, the final judgment, the end of the world, and so forth. Schweitzer studied the Gospels through a discipline called form criticism to determine which parts of the written material had been preserved in a form most similar to that used for oral transmission.[18] He concluded that the numerous sayings of Jesus regarding the future belong to the oldest and best-preserved stratum of material. This material, neglected by most Jesus scholars today, is as close to the original, primitive setting of Jesus as we get. It records Jesus saying things that were hardly relevant when the Gospels were written, much less today. And what does this material reveal? It reveals Jesus to be a prophet who announced the end of the world, who declared that the kingdom of God was about to arrive (Mark 1:15). Especially in the first three Gospels, Jesus talks more about the kingdom of God than he does about anything else. Drawing heavily on the work of another scholar, Johannes Weiss, Schweitzer claimed that Jesus' beliefs about this coming kingdom were in no way tangential but in fact held the key to understanding everything that he said and did.[19] This realization could be embarrassing to Christian scholars, Schweitzer realized, because in the modern world people who go about declaring, "The end is near!" tend to be regarded as crackpots. Furthermore, we are left with the unsettling conclusion that if Jesus did claim this, he was wrong.

Jesus was wrong, Schweitzer concluded — twice. In the early period of his ministry, Jesus apparently believed that God was about to send a supernatural figure whom he called "the Son of Man" to establish the kingdom. At one point, he sent his disciples out on a brief preaching tour, telling them, "You will not have gone through all the towns of Israel before the Son of Man comes" (Matt. 10:23). But, of course, the disciples completed their mission and the Son of Man did not come. At this point, Jesus seems to have reconsidered the matter and come to a dark but startling conclusion. He decided that he himself was to become the Son of Man, and that he could do this only through suffering (see Mark 8:31–33). Previously, he had told his disciples that *they* would have to suffer before the Son of Man arrived (Matt. 10:17–22); now he realized that he must bear the suffering alone. He set in motion processes that would be sure to bring persecution and even death, believing this would prompt God to act, to bring in the kingdom and exalt him as the glorified Son of Man. Schweitzer's description of this plan has become famous:

[Jesus] lays hold of the wheel of the world to set it moving on that last revolution which is to bring all ordinary history to a close. It refuses to turn, and He throws Himself upon it. Then it does turn; and crushes Him. Instead of bringing in the eschatological conditions, He has destroyed them. The wheel rolls onward, and the mangled body of the one immeasurably great Man, who was strong enough to think of Himself as the spiritual ruler of mankind and to bend history to his purpose, is hanging upon it still. That is His victory and His reign.[20]

The kingdom did not come. Jesus was wrong again. His death, as noble and inspiring as his life, did not effect the change that he believed it would.

Schweitzer's portrait of Jesus as a misguided eschatological prophet stripped him of relevance for the contemporary age. As one scholar puts it, he "tore down sentimental portraits of Jesus and, like a revolutionary replacing the monarch's portrait on the schoolroom wall with that of the new leader, put up instead the sharp, indeed shocking, drawing of Jesus the towering prophetic genius."[21] Yet this mistaken genius remained a foreigner. "The historical Jesus," said Schweitzer, "will be to our time a stranger and an enigma."[22] Schweitzer himself seems to have decided the historical Jesus may be a subject best left alone. Even before his monumental book was published, he left theological studies to enter medical school, which he thought would better prepare him for service to humanity. He became one of the twentieth century's most brilliant doctors, serving as a medical missionary in West Africa, and was eventually awarded the Nobel Peace Prize. He also earned renown as one of this century's great organists, publishing a number of preludes and fugues, previously unavailable to the public, by Bach, about whom he also wrote a biography. He also wrote on the philosophy of Goethe and on the development of Indian thought. A remarkable man, Schweitzer lived and worked for sixty years after writing *The Quest of the Historical Jesus* without taking up the subject in earnest again.

Schweitzer's book was a bombshell, effectively immobilizing historical Jesus research for decades. Even scholars who thought Schweitzer had gotten it wrong were unable to find a way of avoiding the stigma of bias, that is, of being suspected that they were modernizing Jesus for the sake of contemporary relevance. Schweitzer's book had created what we might call a catch-22 in historical Jesus studies: The mark of unbiased scholarship was that it did not try to establish Jesus as relevant for today, but if the historical Jesus is *not* relevant for today, then why study him in the first place? Meanwhile, Christian theology moved decidedly in another direction, that of twentieth-century existentialism for which questions regarding the historical Jesus became increasingly insignificant. The foremost proponent of this movement was Rudolf Bultmann, who believed that "the Christ of faith" alone is significant for theology. The only thing that matters regarding the Jesus of history, Bultmann said, is that Jesus was a historical figure. His existence is important for theology; what he actually did is not.[23] Christian theology is developed out of the stories and traditions concerning him, inspired in various ways by his life and work. For example, the message of the kingdom that Jesus proclaimed came to be understood as a promise not of worldly intervention by God but of a power to be experienced here and now. We see this already in the writings of the apostle Paul (Rom. 14:17). Whether Jesus himself saw it this way or whether others built upon his initial proclamation, developing his ideas in ways that gave them eternal relevance, is inconsequential for Christian theology.

Indeed, Paul, the most important theologian of the early church, displays very little interest in the historical Jesus. He did not know the man Jesus, but believes he is in a living relationship with the risen Christ. He develops his theological doctrines and offers ethical advice to Christian communities without mentioning the words or deeds of Jesus—except, that is, for those associated with the last week of Jesus' life: the meal he shared with his followers, his death, and his resurrection. For Paul, the current reality of the living Christ is what matters. This reality Schweitzer himself continued to acknowledge:

> The truth is, it is not Jesus as historically known, but as spiritually risen within [people], who is significant for our time and can help it. Not the historical Jesus, but the spirit which goes forth from Him and in the spirit of [people] strives for new influence and rule, is that which overcomes the world.[24]

This lack of interest in the historical Jesus has been characteristic of Christianity at a popular level as well. One of the most visible exponents of Protestant Christianity in the twentieth century has been the American evangelist Billy Graham. As a conservative Christian, Graham has always insisted that all of the stories about Jesus in the New Testament should be accepted as straightforward historical accounts. Jesus really did do and say all the things reported of him in the Bible. But in his preaching, Graham summons individuals to be born again, to enter into a personal relationship with Jesus, to ask him to come into their hearts as their personal Lord and Savior. The focus of his faith, in other words, appears to be the risen, spiritual Christ that Schweitzer and Bultmann also confessed. Despite Graham's insistence that the biblical accounts are historically accurate, one has to wonder whether it would ultimately make much difference for his theology whether they were or not.

According to one scholar's analysis, a modern emphasis on the benefits of Christ for us has deflected interest in the specific, unrepeatable character of Jesus' historical life. For many Christians it would be "sufficient if Jesus had been born of a virgin (at any time in human history, and perhaps from any race), lived a sinless life, died a sacrificial death, and risen again three days later."[25] Granted this, the assurance of theologians that questions about the historical Jesus do not matter "formed an alliance with the fears of ordinary people as to what might happen to orthodox Christianity if history was scrutinized too closely."[26] For half a century, the quest for the historical Jesus was regarded as both methodologically impossible and theologically unnecessary.[27] Then it began again, initiated, ironically, by students of Rudolf Bultmann.

The New Quest

On October 23, 1953, Ernst Käsemann gave a lecture on "The Problem of the Historical Jesus" to an alumni gathering of academics who, like him, had studied with Bultmann.[28] Rarely has a lecture been so influential. Käsemann argued that theology about Jesus must be thoroughly grounded in a historical reality or else Jesus can be used to support anything. Most likely, Käsemann and his German colleagues were particularly concerned about what had happened recently in their homeland, as Nazi leaders had presented Jesus (whom historians know was Jewish!) as a proponent of anti-Semitism. Käsemann also affirmed that it is methodologically possible to discover a historical grounding for Jesus. For one thing, a great deal had happened in the years since Schweitzer's book was published. Archaeology and other disciplines had greatly enhanced academic knowledge of the ancient world, and refinement of methods for historical research had brought scholars closer to a consensus regarding the ground rules for such study. Käsemann, furthermore, did not project the writing of any more Lives of Jesus, but simply advocated the affirmation of what could be regarded as facts concerning him. Historical scholars could determine whether individual sayings or deeds attributed to Jesus are likely to be authentic without engaging in speculation regarding the chronology or psychological motivations behind such matters.

The New Questers, as these scholars came to be called, produced numerous historical studies of Jesus in the 1950s and 1960s. We will note two that have been especially influential.

Günther Bornkamm published a volume exactly fifty years after Schweitzer's tome that represented a fulfillment of what Käsemann wanted to see. It was called, simply, *Jesus of Nazareth*.[29] Unlike his nineteenth-century predecessors, Bornkamm displayed almost no interest in chronology of events or in Jesus' motives, goals, or self-understanding. He developed a list of historically indisputable facts about Jesus, all derived from the first three Gospels: He was a Jew from Nazareth, his father was a carpenter, he spoke Aramaic, he was baptized by John, and so forth. The real focus of Bornkamm's study, however, was on the message of Jesus, which he described in essence as making "the reality of God present."[30] The kingdom of God, Bornkamm claimed, had both a future and a present dimension for Jesus. The latter is brought out in many of his parables and in the significance of such customs as dining with outcasts. As a teacher, furthermore, Jesus challenged traditional interpretations of the law in favor of a new radical way of life that he held to be the will of God. That he could do this is an indication that he must have been a person of extraordinary authority. This is also evident from his calling of disciples and from the miracle stories which, though largely legendary, reveal the degree of authority attributed to him by his contemporaries. Finally, Jesus was crucified after his processional entrance to Jerusalem and act of overturning tables in the temple were perceived as a threat to the religious and social order.

Norman Perrin published a volume called *Rediscovering the Teaching of Jesus* in 1967, followed a decade later by *Jesus and the Language of the Kingdom*. He applied the discipline of redaction criticism to sayings of Jesus recorded in the first three Gospels to determine which of them were historically authentic. The method of redaction criticism (a mainstay of Bornkamm's work also) attempts to distinguish material that would have reflected Jesus' own thinking from that which appears to reflect the aims of the Christians who compiled and edited (redacted) the Gospels. Perrin helped to define many of the criteria for historical judgments that we will review in our next chapter. His own preference was to err on the side of caution: "the nature of the synoptic tradition is such that the burden of proof will be upon the claim to authenticity."[31] This philosophy came to be expressed through the popular motto "When in doubt, discard," meaning that nothing will be affirmed as authentic unless it is absolutely certain. Thus, Perrin was able to claim that while a great deal more of the Gospel material about Jesus' teaching is *possibly* authentic, the strictest canons of historical research allow us to affirm only selected items as an "irreducible minimum" (see chart 2).[32]

Chart 2. Norman Perrin's
"Irreducible Minimum" List of Authentic Sayings

1. Kingdom Sayings

the kingdom has come:	Luke 11:20
the kingdom is among you:	Luke 17:20–21
the kingdom suffers violence:	Matt. 11:12

2. The Lord's Prayer: Luke 11:2–4

3. Proverbial Sayings

binding the strong man:	Mark 3:27
a kingdom divided:	Mark 3:24–26
those who want to save their life:	Mark 8:35
a hand to the plow:	Luke 9:62
wealth and the kingdom:	Mark 10:23b, 25
let the dead bury the dead:	Luke 9:60a
the narrow gate:	Matt. 7:13–14
the first will be last:	Mark 10:31
what truly defiles:	Mark 7:15
receiving the kingdom as a child:	Mark 10:15
those who exalt themselves:	Luke 14:11 (compare 16:15)
turning the other cheek:	Matt. 5:39b–41
love your enemies:	Matt. 5:44–48

4. Parables

hidden treasure and pearl:	Matt. 13:44–46
lost sheep, coin, son:	Luke 15:3–32
great supper:	Matt. 22:1–14; Luke 14:16–24; Thomas 92:10–35
unjust steward:	Luke 16:1–9
workers in the vineyard:	Matt. 20:1–16
two sons:	Matt. 21:28–32
children in the marketplace:	Matt. 11:16–19
pharisee and tax collector:	Luke 18:9–14
good samaritan:	Luke 10:29–37
unmerciful servant:	Matt. 18:23–35
tower builder and king going to war:	Luke 14:28–32
friend at midnight:	Luke 11:5–8
unjust judge:	Luke 18:1–8
leaven:	Luke 13:20–21; Thomas 97:2–6
mustard seed:	Mark 4:30–32; Thomas 85:15–19
seed growing by itself:	Mark 4:26–29; Thomas 85:15–19

sower:	Mark 4:3–8; Thomas 82:3–13
wicked tenants:	Mark 12:1–12; Thomas 93:1–18

Perrin claims that more material attributed to Jesus is likely to be historical, but this is a rock-bottom list of what "competent scholarly opinion would recognize as authentic."

As the examples of Bornkamm and Perrin indicate, the New Questers tended to emphasize the teaching of Jesus over his deeds. Skepticism regarding the historicity of miracles and supernatural events remained, a legacy from the Enlightenment. Most of their studies also downplayed any specifically Jewish attributes of Jesus. In addition, they tended to discount any attribution of imminent eschatology to Jesus, preferring to interpret Jesus' sayings about the kingdom of God symbolically (Bornkamm said that the "making-present of the reality of God signifies the end of the world in which it takes place").[33] In some ways, the work of the New Quest seemed to come full circle, defying Schweitzer to affirm (with more rigorous methodology) the noneschatological, generically ethnic portrait of Jesus that he had critiqued.

Their work was deliberately spotty, evaluating each individual tradition on its own merits rather than considering the whole corpus of material in light of some grand hypothesis. They sought to obtain isolated insights regarding the historical figure of Jesus rather than to construct full biographies concerning him. And, regardless of whether they subscribed to Perrin's motto, most of the New Questers required even greater evidence of certainty for what they affirmed than would usually be expected for historical research in the secular academy. This scaled-back version of the quest paid off, restoring academic respect to a discipline that had become the object of ridicule. Bornkamm's book, in particular, became a standard text at colleges, universities, and seminaries. It tended to be relegated to courses on religion rather than world history in general, but in 1974 Bornkamm contributed the article (basically, an abbreviated version of his book) on "Jesus Christ" for the *Encyclopedia Britannica* (15th ed.). In academic circles, at least, scholarship concerning the historical Jesus was being taken seriously again. After the initial landmark publications, however, attention to the matter quieted down. Articles and seminar papers continued to be published, but the overall sense was that, save for some fine tuning, what could be done had been accomplished. Then, suddenly, in the last decade before the turn of the millennium, a veritable explosion of Jesus scholarship revealed the topic to be hotter than ever.

Third Quest?

N. T. Wright coined the term *Third Quest* in 1992 to refer to another type of historical Jesus research that emerged in the late twentieth century, one that did regard Jesus as an eschatological prophet and did emphasize his location in first-century Judaism.[34] In Wright's view, the Third Quest and the New Quest coexist, as two major streams of research that need to be distinguished because they differ on these fundamental points. Wright lists twenty major scholars who belong to this Third Quest, including Marcus Borg, Richard Horsley, John Meier, E. P. Sanders, Geza Vermes, and Ben Witherington—all of whom are discussed in this book.[35]

The lines for such categorization, however, get fuzzy. Borg's placement on the list of Third Quest scholars is questionable, since he explicitly denies attribution of an eschatological perspective to Jesus (part of the problem, as we will see, lies in defining what is meant by "eschatological perspective"). Other scholars complain that Wright's terminology implies some evolutionary development, as though what he calls Third Quest scholars are to be seen as embodying a more advanced stage of the discipline while other scholars are still pursuing a trend that is now out-of-date.[36] Recently, many writers have begun using the phrase "Third Quest" as a way of referring to all of the recent studies of Jesus, whatever their focus. The distinction, then, between Third Quest and New Quest is simply chronological.

In any case, this book is devoted to studying the most significant of all the recent works, regardless of classification. All of the scholars examined here have benefited from those who have gone before, either because these predecessors offered insights worthy of further development or because they took wrong roads and so saved attentive followers the humiliation of duplicating their errors. A lesson here may be drawn from Albert Schweitzer's comments regarding the fourteen-hundred page book of David Strauss. Schweitzer ultimately found the book to be short-sighted, but thought its chief virtue was that it completely destroyed the rationalizing explanations for miracle stories put forward by scholars like Paulus. If such ideas "continue to haunt present-day theology," said Schweitzer, "it is only as ghosts, which can be put to flight simply by pronouncing the name of David Friedrich Strauss, and which would long ago have ceased to walk if the theologians who regard Strauss's book as obsolete would only take the trouble to read it."[37] Such was the regard Schweitzer had for a very long, short-sighted book that was already eighty years old. And such is the regard that all of the most significant scholars today would have for Schweitzer and Strauss and Paulus and countless others besides.

HOW DID JESUS GET LOST?

The Gospel of Luke relates a rather charming story of how Jesus at age twelve was separated from his parents when his family visited Jerusalem. His parents sought diligently for him, finding him at last in the Jewish temple (Luke 2:41–51). In a corresponding fashion, some scholars aver that the Jesus of history got lost — not in the Jewish temple but in the Christian church. This claim has formed the background for much of the Jesus scholarship mentioned above and discussed below.

Even traditional Christians will sometimes complain that doctrines and dogmas developed by churches over the years can obscure the image of Jesus. They want to get back to the Jesus of the Bible, to see him as he is there, apart from religious trappings that have made him serve various interests. Some Jesus scholars have taken this a step further. Even the Jesus of the Bible needs to be freed from these trappings, since by the time the Gospels were written the development of Christian doctrine and dogma was already well underway. Even the Jesus of the Bible has been made to serve various interests — some spiritual, some political. Even the Jesus of the Bible needs to be distinguished from the Jesus of history.

Scholars who recognize discontinuity between the Jesus of history and the Jesus of the Gospels would disagree as to its extent and significance. We will look briefly at the work of three scholars who think the divergence is great. Their studies are controversial but, whatever one makes of them, they offer a background for historical research on Jesus. If these scholars are right, then the work of historical reconstruction becomes absolutely essential for anyone who wants to know the truth about Jesus. If they are wrong, then only the work of historical reconstruction will reveal their errors.

William Wrede

Five years before Schweitzer's book on the quest for the historical Jesus was published, a New Testament scholar at the University of Breslau in Silesia (now Poland) produced a volume on the Gospel of Mark that remains one of the twentieth century's most influential works. Called *The Messianic Secret* (1901), the volume analyzed what by any account is one of the most peculiar features in Mark's work — the propensity throughout the Gospel for Jesus to keep his identity as Messiah a secret. In Mark, for instance, Jesus silences demons because they know who he is and might make him known (1:23–25, 34; 3:11–12). He tells those who benefit from his miracles not to say anything to anyone about what he has done for them (1:43–44; 5:43; 7:36; compare 9:9). He describes his teaching about the kingdom of God as a mystery (4:11) and claims that he teaches in parables to prevent people for whom the message is not intended from understanding. When Peter identifies him as the Messiah, he rebukes his disciples, ordering them not to tell anyone about him (8:30). Scholars had long noted this theme and tried to explain it in various ways, such as that Jesus had to be circumspect about his claims to avoid being arrested too soon or to avoid being accosted by unmanageable crowds (see 1:45). But these explanations were never completely satisfying and in 1901, William Wrede offered a solution that did seem to make sense — with disturbing implications.

Basically, Wrede proposed that Mark had invented the scheme of a "messianic secret" to facilitate a presentation of Jesus that was not historically accurate. Mark's Gospel was the earliest one to be written, and at the time of its writing people who knew Jesus might still be alive. As Wrede saw it, Mark wanted to describe a messianic life, but memories of the actual nonmessianic life were still so fresh that he could not do this without maintaining that what he wrote about Jesus was a secret known only to a few. That way, if someone were to say, "Wait a minute! I was there and I don't remember Jesus ever working all these miracles or claiming to be the Messiah," Mark could respond, "He did say and do these things, but they were a secret. You were not among those privileged to know about them."

Wrede's thesis was actually much more profound than this description may indicate, and his arguments struck many at the time as persuasive. Even so, most New Testament scholars today would view the secrecy motif as a literary device intended to further some theological or pastoral point rather than to facilitate deception.[38] Wrede seems to have regarded Mark as unnecessarily devious and his assumption that Mark would be so concerned about historical credibility may be anachronistic. Most likely, Mark's readers already knew the stories that the Gospel relates and did not have to be convinced that these things happened. Still, Wrede introduced a suspicion that the earliest Gospel—the one historians regard as most reliable—might in fact be a fabrication, an account created by an author whose agenda was not simply to report the facts. Long after the specifics of Wrede's provocative thesis fell out of favor, the suspicions it engendered remained. Among historians, at least, the Gospels were never read in quite the same way again.

Burton Mack

If we flash forward some ninety years from the work of Wrede, we discover not too dissimilar views being expounded—for different reasons—by Markan scholars today. One of the most visible of these has been Burton Mack, professor of New Testament at the School of Theology in Claremont, California. His influential but controversial book, *A Myth of Innocence,* lays out a process for how the historical Jesus was transformed by early Christians into a very different figure who was to be the object of faith.[39] Mack finds evidence within the New Testament for two competing strains.[40] The first is the Jesus movement, whose adherents "kept the memory of Jesus alive and thought of themselves in terms of Jewish reform,"[41] and the second is the Christ cult, in which Jesus became "the Lord of a new religious society that called for abrogation of the past."[42]

The Jesus movement, composed initially of Jesus' own followers, attempted to proselytize their Jewish neighbors by spreading their master's teachings, but they were largely unsuccessful. Meanwhile, in northern Syria and across the Mediterranean basin, adherents of the Christ cult—Paul and others who had never actually known Jesus—had great success developing a religion loosely based on this same figure. In this non-Jewish, Greco-Roman environment, the notions of resurrection and ascension were first applied to Jesus. A ritual meal to facilitate social formation was introduced and invested with sacral meaning. A new notion of conversion as personal transformation emerged. The new religion had wide appeal to Gentiles, as "Jesus came to be imagined as the patron deity of . . . a new religion on the model of the Hellenistic cults."[43] But as Jesus became a divine being, the historical image of Jesus as a simple sage was largely erased.

As a second-generation Christian, Mark drew on the traditions of both strains identified above to create a "foundation myth" that would serve the needs of his specific social situation. The Jesus movement had essentially run its course by now, bequeathing to Mark a legacy of confusion over mission, hostility toward Jewish opponents, and a desire to withdraw from the world. The Christ cult was thriving but had become almost completely divorced from any narrative of Jesus' life and ministry. Mark's accomplishment was to retell the story of Jesus in light of these developments, for the benefit of the beleaguered remnants of the Jesus movement, but also from a perspective informed by the Christ cult. The Markan Jesus is a contentious rabbi who bests his Pharisaic opponents at debate. He is an authoritative Son of God who overcomes evil spirits and works fantastic miracles.

He is the apocalyptic Son of Man who announces the imminent end of the world and founds a sect composed of those privileged to know the secret of the coming kingdom. And he is the innocent redeemer whose death provides atonement for those who believe in him. All of these images made sense in Mark's social setting but none of them, says Mack, has much to do with the Jesus of history.

Most of Mark's Gospel, then, is fiction. The stories of Jesus' conflicts with the Pharisees were crafted to address arguments between early Christians and their Jewish opponents. (Mack questions whether there were many Pharisees in Galilee in Jesus' day and doubts whether Jesus ever had any significant contact with them.) The miracle stories were designed to present Jesus as a semidivine figure, on a par (at least) with other Hellenistic wonder workers. (Mack does not think that Jesus worked miracles or that he was even said to work miracles during his own lifetime.) Above all, the passion narrative was created to provide a myth to accompany the Christ cult's representation of Jesus' significance as "the innocent redeemer of the world." Of course, Mark had access to some early sources and oral traditions concerning Jesus, but he was also highly creative. In other words, much of the time he just made things up. With regard to the passion narrative, only the actual fact of crucifixion can be regarded as historical. Beyond this, only the account of the meal (the Last Supper) appears to have been present in pre-Markan tradition. The rest—the cleansing of the temple, the betrayal by Judas, the arrest at Gethsemane, the three denials by Peter, the trials before Caiaphas and Pilate, the mocking of Jesus, the crowning with thorns, the consignment of Simon to carry the cross, the darkness at noon, the division of Jesus' garments, the cry of dereliction ("Why have you forsaken me?"), the rending of the temple veil—all come from the creative mind of Mark:

> Mark's Gospel was not the product of divine revelation. It was not a pious transmission of revered tradition. It was composed at a desk in a scholar's study lined with texts and open to discourse with other intellectuals. . . . The story was a new myth of origins. A brilliant appearance of the man of power, destroyed by those in league against God, pointed nonetheless to a final victory when those who knew the secret of his kingdom would finally be vindicated for accepting his authority.[44]

Mark created this story for the benefit of his little apocalyptic sect, a group that had little need for a simple sage, but craved the approval of a god who would shortly bring this cruel world to an end in a way that would vindicate them and them alone. Mack suggests that the Roman destruction of the Jerusalem temple in 70 C.E. may have been the cataclysmic event that sealed this sect's view of reality. Their Jewish enemies had been punished by God in a way that could only signal the ultimate end of all things. Thus, the message of Jesus concerning how to live in this world was exchanged for a mythology that condemns the world and defers real life to a realm beyond death. Mark "gave up on imagining a society fit for the real world."[45]

One implication of Mack's theory of Christian origins is that the New Testament offers very little that can be deemed historically authentic with regard to

Jesus. Mack does not regard as historical events any number of occurrences for which the earliest witness is the Gospel of Mark: that Jesus was baptized by John, that he opposed or in some way demonstrated against practices in the temple, that he practiced or attempted to practice works of healing or exorcism. All that we have, basically, are a few scattered sayings that represent Jesus' teaching and depict him as a sort of wandering philosopher. This, Mack thinks, should be enough:

> Jesus ought to be ranked among the creative minds of the Greco-Roman age. . . . His importance as a thinker and a teacher can certainly be granted, and even greatly enhanced once we allow the thought that Jesus was not a god incarnate but a real historical person.[46]

Apocalyptic sects come and go, says Mack, but this one produced a work that became the foundational document for one of the world's major religions. Mark's fictional account of Jesus' life, ministry, death, and resurrection was taken up by the other Gospel writers and came to be regarded as narrative history, indeed as sacred scripture. The myth was relatively harmless when it functioned to empower an oppressed minority struggling to hold their own on the edge of the empire. But eventually the myth became the charter for the official religion of the empire with disastrous consequences. In a broad sense, Mack thinks the crusades, the Holocaust, colonial imperialism, even the Vietnam War can be blamed on the Gospel of Mark, as societies informed by this mythology have decided their destiny is to assume the role of innocent redeemer of the world: "the Markan myth is no longer good news."[47] Mack concludes the main text of his book with these words:

> The church canonized a remarkably pitiful moment of early Christian condemnation of the world. Thus the world now stands condemned. It is enough. A future for the world can hardly be imagined any longer, if its redemption rests in the hands of Mark's innocent son of God.[48]

Criticisms of Mack's daring thesis abound. His work is often regarded as speculative, lacking the kind of support from what historians would usually regard as evidence. He has been said to approach the story of Jesus the way filmmaker Oliver Stone has approached such subjects as the Kennedy assassination and the Vietnam War, rejecting any authoritative or official version of events if a motive can be posited for its creation.[49] Specifically, his assumption that diverse social groups must stand behind the different forms of biblical material and his attempts to date accounts on the basis of their perceived relationship to the process of social formation often seem arbitrary. Critics also think he sets up false alternatives. "Casting out demons is difficult to imagine for one adept at telling parables," Mack asserts.[50] So Jesus must have either been an exorcist or a teacher who taught in parables, but not both. Likewise, Mack assumes that either the wisdom sayings or the eschatological pronouncements of doom that are attributed to Jesus must be deemed unauthentic because the same person would not have said both.[51] Adela Collins, perhaps, goes to the very heart of the matter by suggesting that Mack's proposal is "weakened by a rigid dichotomy between historical report and literary fiction."[52]

Another common critique is that Mack's thesis rests on a minimalist portrait of Jesus that simply leaves too many gaps to be credible. Perhaps the most significant of these gaps is the motivation for Jesus' crucifixion. If the controversy stories and the passion narrative are all to be regarded as fiction, if Jesus was essentially just a philosopher who talked about an alternative way of life, then why would anyone want to kill him? More to the point, why did the *government* want to kill him? Why was he crucified? The best answer Mack has been able to propose so far is that Jesus' death might have simply been "accidental," which led to a flurry of jokes among scholars, such as one about Mack's Jesus being killed in a car crash on the Los Angeles freeway.[53] What Mack means, of course, is that Jesus could have just been caught up in the Roman pogroms against the Jews, especially if he looked or sounded at all unconventional. In this view there is no need to suppose that his earliest followers related his death in any meaningful way to his life.

Mack himself admits that *A Myth of Innocence* "is an essay, not a monograph."[54] It lacks the sort of detailed argumentation and scholarly documentation that build an airtight case point by point. It seeks, rather, to propose a different way of viewing the whole matter of Christian origins by suggesting a way that makes "social sense" of the materials at hand. Mack does not prove that the church *did* come quickly (before the writing of the Gospels) to view Jesus as something very different from what he was, but for some scholars his essay has described a plausible process of development that explains how the church *could* have done so. It is enough to keep alive the sort of suspicions that Wrede introduced almost a century ago.

Elisabeth Schüssler Fiorenza

Doubt regarding the historical accuracy of the Gospels has also been brought from another quarter, namely, feminist theologians who argue that a male-dominated church shaped the story of Jesus in ways that represent its own sexist perspective. Preeminent among these scholars is Elisabeth Schüssler Fiorenza, whose book *In Memory of Her* presents a feminist reconstruction of Christian origins. She uses models drawn from sociology of religion to reconstruct the social reality that lies behind the androcentric biblical texts. The reality that comes to the fore is a movement initiated by Jesus that defied the hierarchical structure of patriarchal society. In Fiorenza's view, Jesus denounced the Jewish social system based on purity and holiness, which correlated well with masculine dominance, in favor of another stream of Jewish consciousness, that of the wisdom tradition evident in the apocryphal book of Judith. He also attacked the patriarchal family system by insisting that no one except God should be viewed with the authority given to a father (see Matt. 23:9). Instead, Jesus encouraged a "discipleship of equals," creating an alternative community structure based upon "a vision of inclusive wholeness." Women were especially prominent in this community, as were other frequently disenfranchised people such as the poor, the sick, and those considered to be outcasts because of their occupation or behavior. In fact, Fiorenza theorizes, Jesus understood himself to be the representative of divine wisdom (see Luke

7:35), which is personified in the Old Testament as a woman (for example, in Proverbs 1—9). Fiorenza calls this woman "Sophia" (which means "wisdom") and suggests that Jesus encouraged people to worship God as Sophia. He thought of himself as the child or prophet of Sophia and so, even though he was biologically male, Jesus came to be viewed by his earliest followers as the incarnation of the female principle of God.[55]

What is most pertinent for our concern is that Fiorenza alleges that the egalitarian aspect of Jesus' message and ministry did not comport with the political agendas of the emerging church. His idea that men and women should have equal status and roles was particularly troublesome as the church tried to establish its place in a patriarchal society. The church introduced, for instance, the notion that Jesus appointed twelve male disciples to occupy a position of leadership over the rest. The Gospels, Fiorenza contends, must be studied with a "hermeneutics of suspicion," that is, with a strategy that involves reading between the lines of texts that we know to have been written, edited, and preserved by men. The Bible itself alludes to controversies in the early church concerning appropriate roles for women; the mere fact that some writers try to restrict these roles indicates that others must have wanted to expand them (see 1 Cor. 14:34–35; 1 Tim. 2:11–15). Church history reveals who the winners of this controversy were. By the second century the Christian church had become an extremely patriarchal institution, dominated by an all-male clergy. As every critical scholar knows, history is usually written from the perspective of winners, who naturally relate matters in ways that reflect their own agenda. This, Fiorenza says, is what happened with the Gospels. They offer an androcentric description of what was in reality far more egalitarian.

Fiorenza's view is criticized by people who think she is trying to modernize Jesus, to turn him into an exponent of contemporary thinking that may be politically correct today but would have been anachronistic for his own place and time. Her reconstructions are said to be based more on wishful thinking than solid historical evidence.[56] Nevertheless, she has been extremely successful in sensitizing modern scholars to an awareness of the social and political context in which the Gospels were produced and to consideration of ways in which this might have influenced the stories they relate. We may note that her evaluation of these writings is by no means as negative as that of Wrede or Mack; she allows for far more of the Gospel material to be accepted as historical than they do. She is also careful to distinguish between the historical Jesus and what she calls "the Jesus of piety." As a Roman Catholic, she urges Catholic Christians to take historical reconstructions of Jesus seriously, but not to allow them to be the sole norm or source for Christian identity. Interpretations of Jesus in the lives of saints, in scripture, and in liturgy all contribute to the image of Jesus that she favors.[57]

In conclusion, let me reiterate that many historians who study Jesus have much more respect for the historical reliability of the New Testament Gospels than these whom we have just mentioned. I call attention to the works of Wrede, Mack, and Fiorenza not because they are representative of the scholarly guild as a whole but because they exemplify the challenges that all historians must take into consideration if they want their work to be taken seriously. It will no longer do in an academic setting to summarize what the Gospels say about Jesus and present this as a historical record. The historical Jesus may have gotten lost somewhere in the theology and politics of the church before those Gospels were written. Whether he did or not is one of the questions historians hope to answer. The story in Luke's Gospel tells of Mary and Joseph seeking diligently only to discover that Jesus had never really been lost in the first place (Luke 2:41–51). That might, of course, turn out to be the case here as well. Eventually, we shall hear from several scholars who have sought diligently for the historical Jesus and who think that they have now found him. They will of course let us know whether the search was necessary, or whether the Jesus they discovered had been right there in the Gospels and in the church all along.

Jaroslav Pelikan, longtime professor of history at Yale University, asks us first to consider the following description:

> There was a great teacher, and gathered around him was a small group of faithful followers. They listened to his message and were transformed by it. But the message alienated the power structure of his time, which finally put him to death but did not succeed in eradicating his message, which is stronger now than ever.

As Pelikan observes, "That description would apply equally to Jesus and Socrates. But nobody's ever built a cathedral in honor of Socrates."[58] Part of the historian's task is to explain what there was about Jesus that inspired those cathedrals (and churches and storefronts and hospitals and colleges) to be built.

2

SOURCES AND CRITERIA

In the 1990s, the [historical quest for Jesus] has tried to be more sophisticated in its methodology, more self-aware and self-critical in dealing with a given author's preconceptions and biases, and more determined to write history rather than covert theology or christology. The quest benefits from recent archaeological discoveries, a better knowledge of the Aramaic language and the cultural context in 1st-century Palestine, a more differentiated view of the Judaisms developing around the turn of the era and new insights arising from sociological analysis and modern literary theory.

—John P. Meier[1]

It falls to the lot of the historian to be the person who subjects the gospels to rough handling. The historian may or may not assent to the theology of the gospels, the view that God acted through Jesus. In either case, he or she . . . has a professional obligation to subject sources to rigorous cross-examination.

—E. P. Sanders[2]

It is impossible to avoid the suspicion that historical Jesus research is a very safe place to do theology and call it history, to do autobiography and call it biography.

—John Dominic Crossan[3]

How do historians study Jesus in a way that will retain the respect of their academic peers? The most important scholars usually work out their own method and are fairly explicit in explaining how it operates. When we get to chapters 4 through 9, we will devote a major section of each chapter to the particular method of operation employed by each individual or group under discussion. Some matters, however, are basic and instead of repeating these six times later, it seems advisable to discuss them all in one place. We will begin with an overview of the sources available to historians who wish to study Jesus and then move on to a survey of key criteria that are applied to these sources in historical research.

THE SOURCES

Historical scholars are ultimately interested not only in materials that teach us about Jesus himself but also in those that reveal the world in which he lived. Insights drawn from archaeology and the social sciences have become especially valuable for modern reconstructions of Jesus' life and work.[4] For now, however, we will limit ourselves to sources in the narrow sense — ancient writings that mention Jesus. References to Jesus in such works are not numerous but they are quite varied. Historical scholars are interested in anything concerning him that they can find. Sometimes even the most meager reference can become significant in surprising ways.

Roman Literature

The three most important Roman historians for the first-century period are Tacitus, Suetonius, and Josephus. All three mention Jesus, as do a couple of other Roman writers. Only Josephus, however, has much to say about him. In general, the Romans were much more interested in Christianity than in Jesus himself.

Josephus is by far the most significant of the non-Christian writers who mention Jesus. He was not only Roman, but Jewish. Born in 37 C.E., just after the death of Jesus, Josephus wrote long, detailed descriptions of the events in Palestine. It is impossible for any historian to predict which current events or trends will prove to be significant in the long run, and Josephus certainly missed the mark with regard to the emergence of Christianity. He actually gives more space to describing the Essenes, a community of monastic Jews who were wiped out by 70 C.E., than he does to the Christians, who in a few centuries would be running the Roman Empire. But he does mention the Christians, as well as John the Baptist, Pontius Pilate, Herod, and other persons known to us from the Bible. He mentions Jesus twice.

One of these references doesn't offer much. In describing the illegal execution of James, the leader of the Christian church at Jerusalem, Josephus identifies him as "the brother of Jesus, who was called Christ" (*Antiquities* 20.9.1). Yet it is intriguing that a Jewish writer who is not a Christian would refer to Jesus with the term *Christ*.

The second reference is more detailed, but there is a problem with it. We have no original manuscripts of Josephus's work and some of the ones that we do possess have been edited by later Christians who added their own description of Jesus to what the Jewish historian originally wrote. In the quote as it appears below, I have omitted words that most scholars think are editorial additions, citing them only in the accompanying note.

> At this time there appeared Jesus a wise man.[a] For he was a doer of startling deeds, a teacher of people who receive the truth with pleasure. And he gained a following both among Jews and among many of Greek origin.[b] And when Pilate, because of an accusation made by the leading men among us, condemned him to the cross, those who had loved him previously did not cease to do so.[c] And up until this very day the tribe of Christians (named after him) has not died out. (*Antiquities* 18.3.3)[5]

Even without the Christian interpolations, this quote is surprisingly friendly. Josephus obviously thought well of Jesus, regarding him as one who taught the truth. Though not a Christian himself, he respected Jesus as "a wise man" and as a "doer of startling deeds." Both of these appellations are topics for discussion among historians. Does Josephus mean to use the adjective *wise* as a generic compliment, or by calling Jesus "a wise man" does he mean to describe his vocation, that is, indicate that he was by profession a philosopher or sage? And when Josephus says Jesus did "startling deeds" does he mean that Jesus performed what we might call "extraordinary (if unconventional) good deeds" or does he mean to say that Jesus worked miracles?

Tacitus (56–117 C.E.), a Roman senator, records that Jesus was "executed in Tiberius's reign by the governor of Judea, Pontius Pilate" (*Annals* 15.44). The context for this remark is to introduce the Christians, who were followers of this executed man and who suffered greatly under the cruelty of Nero. Tacitus continues:

> Nero had self-acknowledged Christians arrested. Then, on their information, large numbers of others were condemned. . . . Their deaths were made farcical. Dressed in wild animals' skins, they were torn to pieces by wild dogs, or crucified, or made into torches to be ignited after dark as substitutes for daylight. . . . Despite their guilt as Christians and the ruthless punishment it deserved, the victims were pitied, for it was felt that they were being sacrificed to one man's brutality rather than to the national interest.   (*Annals* 15.44)

Tacitus gives no indication that he knows anything about the beliefs of these Christians (whom he regards as "notoriously depraved"), much less about the life or teaching of Jesus himself.[6]

Suetonius reports in a writing from around 120 C.E. that the emperor Claudius expelled Jews from Rome because of trouble arising over "Chrestus" (*Twelve Caesars* 25.4). Most scholars think this is a mangled spelling of the Latin for "Christ." The event, then, would be the same as that reported in the book of Acts, which records that Jews were expelled from Rome by Claudius (Acts 18:2). Suetonius, however, displays no knowledge of the man Jesus who lived in Palestine. He is interested only in the figure who came to be at the center of Christian religion in Rome.

Pliny the Younger writes about Christians in a letter to the emperor Trajan around 111–113 C.E. He comments that they "chant verses to Christ as to a god" (*Letter to Trajan* 10.96) but does not otherwise mention Jesus.

Lucian of Samosata (115–200 C.E.) writes a mocking satire about Christians who are said to worship a "crucified sophist" from Palestine and to live "under his laws," because he "introduced this new cult into the world" (*The Passing of Peregrinus* 11, 13). The reference to Jesus as a sophist is interesting, but otherwise, again, he is known only because of his followers.

Jewish Writings

▪ Scholars debate whether there may be obscure references to Jesus in some of the collections of ancient Jewish writings, such as the Talmud, the Tosefta, the targums, and the midrashim.[7] Occasional polemical comments in these writings are sometimes thought to be veiled references to Jesus, but since he is not mentioned by name, no one knows for sure. The text that is most often accepted as referring to him comes from the Babylonian Talmud. The main problem here is that the materials that make up this work were collected over a long period of time, finally coming together around 500–600 C.E. Thus, there is no way of knowing how early (or how reliable) the reference may be. Nevertheless, here it is:

> On the eve of Passover, they hanged Yeshu [= Jesus?] and the herald went before him 40 days saying "[Yeshu] is going forth to be stoned, since he practiced sorcery and cheated and led his people astray. Let everyone knowing anything in his defense come and plead for him." But they found nothing in his defense and hanged him on the eve of Passover.   (*Sanhedrin 43a*)

Later this same text also says, "Jesus had five disciples: Mattai, Maqai, Metser, Buni, and Todah." This of course is neither the traditional list of names nor the traditional number.

New Testament Epistles

Surprisingly, the letters of Paul preserved in the New Testament tell us little more about Jesus than the non-Christian writings. The great Christian missionary did not know the earthly Jesus but says the risen Christ appeared to him (1 Cor. 15:8). Paul's thoughts are clearly guided by the belief that he and other Christians remain in a dynamic relationship with the Lord Jesus Christ who lives now in heaven with God but interacts with his followers on earth and will someday return to consummate their salvation. Most of Paul's references to Jesus are couched in present or future tenses. When he does use the past tense to refer to what we are calling the Jesus of history, he almost always refers to what he regards as the final events of that life—his death and resurrection. Once, he also describes Jesus' last meal with his followers (1 Cor. 11:23–25).

Even though Paul does not explicitly relate stories about the life or ministry of Jesus or pass on much of his teaching, he may at times allude to sayings of Jesus.[8] The command of the Lord prohibiting divorce that Paul refers to in 1 Corinthians 7:10 might be a reference to the historical teaching of Jesus (compare Mark 10:2–9). Likewise, Paul's claim that "the Lord commanded that those who proclaim the gospel should get their living by the gospel" (1 Cor. 9:14) may recall a saying of Jesus such as that reported in Matthew 10:10. Occasionally, Paul offers moral advice that may reflect the influence of words attributed elsewhere to Jesus without actually citing Jesus as his source (for example, the exhortation to love one's enemies in Rom. 12:14, 17–20 and Matt. 5:38–48). In other instances, however, Paul claims authority to give instructions "through the Lord Jesus" (1 Thess. 4:2), which may indicate that he believes he has received revelations from the risen Lord, and that people are to regard these words as similar to those spoken by Jesus when he was on earth. Whether or not this is the case, historians are cautious about taking everything Paul presents as "words of the Lord" as representative of the actual teaching of the historical Jesus.

Nevertheless, Paul's letters are regarded as an important source for what little they do reveal. This is primarily true because the letters are so early. By most estimates, Paul's letters were written some twenty to thirty years before the Gospels. Furthermore, despite the apparent lack of interest in Jesus' earthly life and ministry, details sometimes turn up almost by accident. For instance, Paul refers in 1 Corinthians 15:5 to "the twelve," confirming the (later) report in the Gospels that some of Jesus' disciples were known by this designation. Elsewhere, he lets slip that Jesus was of Davidic descent (Rom. 1:3).

Other New Testament letters offer even less. Again, scholars note passages that may be reworked sayings of Jesus, such as the prohibition of oaths in James 5:12 (compare Matt. 5:34–37), but the epistles themselves do not attribute these sayings to Jesus. The anonymous letter to the Hebrews mentions that Jesus was of the tribe of Judah (7:14) and refers to an agonized prayer reminiscent of that which the Synoptic Gospels say he offered in Gethsemane (Heb. 5:7–8; Mark 14:32–42). These letters, however, are probably not as early as Paul's, and may even be dependent on the Gospel traditions. Even the meager information they offer about Jesus is not deemed very valuable.

The Synoptic Gospels

The first three Gospels (Matthew, Mark, and Luke) are called the Synoptic Gospels because they have many parallel passages, that is, passages that are very similar if not identical in wording (the word *synoptic* means "parallel"). Most scholars do not believe that any of these three works were written by disciples of Jesus or by eyewitnesses to the events that they report. The Gospels themselves are anonymous. Church tradition that the first Gospel was written by Matthew the tax collector who became a disciple of Jesus is almost universally rejected by modern scholars. Traditions that the second Gospel was written by John Mark and the third by Luke the physician are also challenged, but in any case neither John Mark nor Luke was a person who had met Jesus.[9]

From early on, Christian scholars have believed that one of these Gospels served as the prototype for the others. Augustine, for instance, believed that Matthew's Gospel was written first and that the other two copied material from Matthew, adding or subtracting information relevant to their own situations. For historians, the question of which Gospel served as the prototype is extremely important because that work would stand closest to the actual events it relates and, so, would tend to be viewed as the most reliable source for historical information. But which is it?

The matter gets complicated, but the short answer is that the great majority of scholars now believe the Gospel of Mark was the earliest of these three books. Matthew and Luke both had copies of Mark and took much of their material from him. They did not, however, just copy stories from Mark word for word but edited them, changing details in the process. For a rather extreme example, see the story of Jesus and the scribe in chart 3. In Mark, the scribe agrees with Jesus, who then declares that he has answered wisely; in Matthew, there is no indication of agreement and the very question is posed as an attempt to test Jesus (to see what Luke does with this story, see Luke 10:25–28). If Mark's Gospel contains the original form of this story, then historians will be more likely to accept his version of the encounter as authentic. In this instance, at least, they will be inclined to believe that Jesus had a friendly encounter with a scribe rather than a hostile one in which he was put to the test.

Chart 3.

Mark 12:28–34

One of the scribes came near and heard them disputing with one another, and seeing that he answered them well, he asked him, "Which commandment is the first of all?" Jesus answered, "The first is, 'Hear O Israel: the Lord our God, the Lord is one; you shall love the Lord your God with all your heart, and with all your soul, and with all your mind, and with all your strength.' The second is this, 'You shall love your neighbor as yourself.' There is no other commandment greater than these." Then the scribe said to him, "You are right, Teacher; you have truly said that 'he is one, and besides him there is no other'; and 'to love him with all the heart, and with all the understanding, and with all the strength,' and 'to love one's neighbor as oneself'—this is much more important than all whole burnt offerings and sacrifices." When Jesus saw that he answered wisely, he said to him, "You are not far from the kingdom of God."

Matthew 22:34–40

When the Pharisees heard that he had silenced the Sadducees, they gathered together, and one of them, a lawyer, asked him a question to test him. "Teacher, which commandment in the law is the greatest?" He said to him, "You shall love the Lord your God with all your heart, and with all your soul, and with all your mind.' This is the greatest and first commandment. And a second is like it: 'You shall love your neighbor as yourself.' On these two commandments hang all the law and the prophets."

But things get more complex. Most scholars also believe that Matthew and Luke had copies of another early Christian document, one that has since been lost to us. For convenience, this work is called *Q*. The label seems odd, especially to American students, for whom references to Q likely summon images from James Bond or *Star Trek*. It may help to know that the letter is probably short for the German word *Quelle* (which means "source"), though nobody really remembers for sure how this designation was chosen. In any case, Q was apparently an early collection of sayings attributed to Jesus. Both Matthew and Luke copied these sayings into their Gospels, altering them perhaps as they did the material they took from Mark. The historian's dream would be for archaeologists to dig up a copy of Q somewhere, but that is not likely to happen. The next best thing from a historian's point of view is to reconstruct what Q probably said based on comparisons of what is found in Matthew and Luke.

Thus, even though Mark was probably the earliest Gospel, Matthew and Luke continue to be treasured by historians because they preserve sayings from Q, which was probably even earlier than Mark. In addition, Matthew and Luke incorporated other material into their Gospels that they may have derived from any number of sources. The extra material that is found in Matthew is called *M* and the extra material found in Luke is called *L*. Most scholars, including almost all historical Jesus scholars, follow this paradigm. We should note that a minority of scholars dispute this construal altogether, arguing instead that Matthew's Gospel was written first, that Luke used Matthew as a source, and that Mark produced his Gospel last as an abridgment of the other two.[10]

The upshot of all this is that when historians deal with the Synoptic Gospels, they do not so much think of the material as coming from three Gospels (Matthew, Mark, and Luke) as from four source strata (Mark, Q, M, and L). An appendix at the end of this section (pages 39–42) lists the material that is usually ascribed to Q, M, and L.

Mark is usually thought to have been written sometime around 70 C.E., either just before or just after the temple in Jerusalem was destroyed by Roman armies. A minority position places Mark about ten years earlier than this.[11] Some scholars think that the author might have had access to Peter and learned some of the stories he relates from this disciple of Jesus. This is by no means certain, however, and cannot be accepted by historians as a guarantee of authenticity. Even so, Mark is generally regarded as the most historically reliable of the four Gospels in terms of its overall description of Jesus' life and ministry. This is why theories posited by scholars such as William Wrede and Burton Mack (see pages 24–28) are potentially devastating to the historical quest for Jesus. If, as these scholars contend, the Gospel of Mark is largely fiction, then our main source for the historical reconstruction of Jesus' life is lost. As we pursue the work of historians in the next few chapters we will see that a determining factor for the outcome of their work is the value that they place on the Gospel of Mark. Some scholars, including Crossan and others associated with the Jesus Seminar, rely very little on Mark; others, such as Sanders, Meier, and Wright, make Mark foundational for their work.

Even those who do use Mark for historical research may press the further question of whether everything in Mark is of equal value. Part of this question involves the issue of whether Mark used sources for his Gospel, material that had already been memorized or put into writing before his Gospel was produced. Some scholars discern (1) a collection of controversy stories, including those found now in Mark 2:1–3:6, (2) a collection or, possibly, two collections of miracle stories, including many of those now found in chapters 4—8, (3) an apocalyptic tract containing much of what is now in chapter 13, or (4) an early version of the passion narrative, the story of Jesus' death and resurrection now found in Mark 14—16. Of course, such theories are by nature tenuous and always evoke debate.

Q is the most controversial of the early sources. Some scholars doubt that it ever existed. Others propose that it was a written document, perhaps a collection of notes taken by one of Jesus' own disciples. Still others think it may have been only a memorized collection of sayings that Christians passed on to one another in an age when most people were still illiterate. Despite the arguments, however, there is broad agreement on certain points. The great majority of scholars, including all of the historians discussed in this book, believe that the material attributed to the Q source is among the oldest and most reliable material found in the Gospels. This material is considered especially valuable in describing the teaching of Jesus.

Beyond this near-consensus lies breakdown over details. Scholars have tried to define the theology of the Q source and to determine the nature of the community that would have produced it. A number of scholars even believe that layers of recension can be discerned within their reconstructed version of Q. In other words, they believe that some of the Q material is earlier than the rest. The best-known version of this theory is that of John Kloppenborg, who divides Q material into three recensions: Q^1, Q^2, and Q^3. Burton Mack (see pages 25–28) claims that all we can really know of Jesus comes from the earliest recension of Q. Notably, the sayings of Jesus preserved there do not include eschatological concerns involving the future, nor do they present Jesus as engaging what would be specifically Jewish concerns. We recall from the discussion in chapter 1 that the New Quest scholars have tended to deemphasize precisely these two aspects of Jesus' ministry, presenting him as noneschatological and as generic in his ethnic appeal. They would maintain that this is justified by claiming that this is how the community of Christians that preserved the earliest collection of Jesus' sayings understood him. Mack goes on to stress that early Q (that is, Q^1) is valuable precisely because it is pre-Christian. The Christian church had not yet come into being:

> The remarkable thing about the people of Q is that they were not Christians. They did not think about Jesus as a messiah or the Christ. They did not take his teachings as an indictment of Judaism. They did not regard his death as a divine, tragic, or saving event. And they did not imagine that he had been raised from the dead to rule over a transformed world. Instead, they thought of him as a teacher whose teaching made it possible to live with verve in troubled times. Thus they did not gather to worship in his name, honor him as a god, or cultivate his memory through hymns, prayers, and rituals.[12]

But these theories regarding Q are complex and controversial. Charlotte Allen notes, "This entire edifice—building from hypothesis to document to Gospel to theology to community—is either a marvel of perceptive scholarship or a showy sandcastle."[13] But which is it? One major scholar has actually proposed the opposite of what Kloppenborg suggests with regard to layers of tradition: Siegfried Schulz thinks that the Jewish tradition presenting Jesus as the eschatological Son of Man constitutes the original Q and the more generic wisdom materials are later additions.[14]

Most scholars remain cautious about any attempt at discerning layers of tradition in a source for which we have no extant manuscripts.[15] John Meier, whose work is discussed in chapter 8, says, "I doubt that we have the data and the methods sufficient to answer questions about the community, locality, tradition process, and coherent theological vision that supposedly produced Q."[16] Piqued at the confidence in Q theories evinced by some of his colleagues, he adds:

> I cannot help thinking that biblical scholarship would be greatly advanced if every morning all exegetes would repeat as a mantra: "Q is a hypothetical document whose exact extension, wording, originating community, strata, and stages of redaction cannot be known."[17]

M and L are regarded as ambiguous collections of material that is of unknown origin and is difficult to date. In most cases this material is unparalleled, that is, found nowhere else. An example would be the famous story of the Good Samaritan, which Jesus tells in Luke 10:30–37. The tale is ascribed to the L material and no reference to it is found anywhere else in the Bible. Most scholars think that the Gospels of Matthew and Luke were completed around 85 C.E. A more conservative position dates them along with Mark to the sixties.[18] In either case, materials from M and L could be from an earlier time or they could be as late as the Gospels themselves. Since it is difficult to tell, most scholars are reluctant to rely too heavily on this material when constructing their portraits of the historical Jesus.

Contents of Q, M, and L[19]

Q

Preaching of John the Baptist (Luke 3:7–9; Matt. 3:7–10)

Temptation of Jesus (Luke 4:1–13; Matt. 4:1–11)

Beatitudes (Luke 6:20–23; Matt. 5:3–12)

Love for enemies (Luke 6:27–36; Matt. 5:39–48; 7:12)

On judging others (Luke 6:37–42; Matt. 7:1–5; 10:24; 15:14)

On bearing fruit (Luke 6:43–45; Matt. 7:15–20)

The house built on rock (Luke 6:47–49; Matt. 7:24–27)

Healing of a centurion's servant (Luke 7:1–10; Matt. 8:5–10, 13)

John the Baptist questions Jesus (Luke 7:18–35; Matt. 11:2–19)

The would-be disciples (Luke 9:57–60; Matt. 8:19–22)

Jesus' missionary discourse (Luke 10:2–16; Matt. 9:37–38; 10:9–15; 11:21–23)

Thanksgiving to the Father (Luke 10:21–24; Matt. 11:25–27; 13:16–17)

The Lord's Prayer (Luke 11:2–4; Matt. 6:9–13)

Asking and receiving (Luke 11:9–13; Matt. 7:7–11)

Jesus identified with Beelzebul (Luke 11:14–23; Matt. 12:22–32)

Return of an evil spirit (Luke 11:24–26; Matt. 12:43–45)

The sign of Jonah (Luke 11:29–32; Matt. 12:38–42)

On light (Luke 11:33–36; Matt. 5:15; 6:22–23)

Woe to the Pharisees (Luke 11:37–52; Matt. 23:4–7, 13–36)

Fear of humans and God (Luke 12:2–12; Matt. 10:19, 26–33; 12:32)

Do not worry about life (Luke 12:22–34; Matt. 6:19–21, 25–33)

Be ready for the master's return (Luke 12:39–46; Matt. 24:43–51)

Divisions in the family (Luke 12:51–53; Matt. 10:34–36)

Signs of the times (Luke 12:54–56; Matt. 16:2–3)

Settle out of court (Luke 12:57–59; Matt. 5:25–26)

Mustard seed and leaven (Luke 13:18–21; Matt. 13:31–33)

The narrow door (Luke 12:23–30; Matt. 7:13–14, 22–23; 8:11–12)

Lament over Jerusalem (Luke 13:34–35; Matt. 23:37–39)

Parable of the banquet (Luke 14:15–24; Matt. 22:1–14)

Carrying the cross (Luke 14:26–27; Matt. 10:37–38)

Parable of the lost sheep (Luke 15:1–7; Matt. 18:12–14)

On serving two masters (Luke 16:13; Matt. 6:24)

Role of the law and prophets (Luke 16:16–17; Matt. 5:18; 11:13)

Rebuking and forgiving sin (Luke 17:1–6; Matt. 18:6–7, 15, 20–22)

The day of the Son of Man (Luke 17:23–27, 33–37; Matt. 24:17–18, 26–28, 37–41)

Parable of the talents (Luke 19:11–27; Matt. 25:14–30)

M (all from Matthew)

Genealogy of Jesus (from Abraham)	1:2–17
Birth of Jesus (with focus on Joseph)	1:18–25
Visit of the magi	2:1–12
Flight to Egypt	2:13–21
On fulfilling the law	5:17–20
The antitheses	5:21–24, 27–29, 31, 33–38, 43

On practicing piety	6:1–15, 16–19
Pearls before swine	7:6
Coming persecutions	10:21–23
Invitation to rest	11:28–30
Parables: weeds, treasure, pearl, net	13:24–30, 36–52
Peter tries to walk on water	14:28–31
Blessing of Peter	16:17–19
Peter pays the temple tax	17:24–27
Recovering the sinful member	18:15–20
Peter asks about forgiveness	18:21–22
Parable of unforgiving servant	18:23–35
Parable of laborers in vineyard	20:1–16
Parable of two sons	21:28–32
Prohibition of titles	23:2–5, 7–12
Denunciations of Pharisees	23:15–22
Parable of bridesmaids	25:1–13
Description of last judgment	25:31–46
Death of Judas	27:3–10
Pilate washes his hands	27:24–25
Resuscitation of saints	27:52–53
Guard at the tomb	27:62–66; 28:11–15
Great Commission	28:16–20

L (all from Luke)

Dedication to Theophilus	1:1–4
Promised birth of John	1:5–25
Announcement of Jesus' birth to Mary	1:26–38
Mary's visit to Elizabeth	1:39–56
Birth of John the Baptist	1:57–80
Birth of Jesus (with shepherds, manger)	2:1–20
Presentation in the temple	2:21–38
Childhood visit to Jerusalem	2:41–52
John's reply to questions	3:10–14
Genealogy of Jesus (to Adam)	3:23–38
Good news to the poor	4:14–23, 25–30
Miraculous catch of fish	5:1–11
Widow's son at Nain	7:11–17

Encounter with homeless woman	7:36–50
The ministering women	8:1–3
Rejection by Samaritan village	9:51–56
Return of the seventy	10:17–20
Parable of Good Samaritan	10:29–37
Mary and Martha	10:38–42
Parable of friend at midnight	11:5–8
Parable of rich fool	12:13–21
Parable of barren tree	13:1–9
Healing of woman on sabbath	13:10–17
Healing of man with dropsy	14:1–6
Lessons for table guests and hosts	14:7–14
Counting the cost	14:28–33
Parable of lost coin	15:8–10
Parable of lost son	15:11–32
Parable of dishonest steward	16:1–12
Parable of rich man and Lazarus	16:19–31
Cleansing of ten lepers	17:11–19
Parable of widow and judge	18:1–8
Parable of Pharisee and tax collector	18:9–14
Story of Zacchaeus	19:1–10
Jesus weeps over Jerusalem	19:41–44
The reason for Peter's denial	22:31–32
The two swords	22:35–38
Jesus before Herod	23:6–12
Pilate declares Jesus innocent	23:13–16
Sayings associated with Jesus' death	23:28–31, 34, 43, 46
Appearance on the road to Emmaus	24:13–35
Appearance to the disciples	24:36–49
The Ascension	24:50–53

The Gospel of John

The fourth Gospel is almost universally regarded as the latest of the New Testament witnesses to Jesus. Like the other Gospels, it is anonymous. Notably, however, the book claims that some of the things it records are based on the testimony of a mysterious figure called "the disciple whom Jesus loved." Indeed, it says that this disciple is the one "who is testifying to these things and has written them"

(John 21:24). Some scholars doubt the legitimacy of this claim, but even for those who accept it many questions remain: Which things reported in the Gospel go back to the testimony of this beloved disciple, and who was this person? Was he John the son of Zebedee, the fisherman who became a disciple of Jesus, as church tradition has often maintained? Theories abound but the questions remain unanswered.

Most scholars believe that the Gospel of John was composed in stages. As with the Synoptic Gospels, some of the material would then be earlier than the rest. One theory is that the current Gospel might include a collection of remembrances of the beloved disciple, dealing mostly with the last week of Jesus' life. Another is that material underlying the great speeches attributed to Jesus in the Gospel might derive from sermons given to the community by this beloved disciple. Even more significant, potentially, is yet another proposal, that John's Gospel has incorporated an earlier document called the "Signs Gospel." This work would have recorded seven or eight miracle stories (2:1–12; 4:46–54; 5:1–9; 6:1–13; 9:1–7; 11:1–44; 21:1–6; maybe 6:15–25) and might also have included an account of the passion and resurrection.[20] This theory of an early Signs Gospel, however, has found less acceptance among scholars than proposals concerning the existence of a Q source that was used by Matthew and Luke.

The bottom line is that historians are unsure of the date and origin of most of the material in John's Gospel, and so do not rely on it as strongly as they do on Mark or on the material attributed to Q. In one sense, this means that when images of Jesus in John and the Synoptics differ, the latter is usually preferred by historians. For example, the Synoptic Gospels repeatedly present Jesus as a teller of parables, but Jesus never tells a single parable in the Gospel of John. Historians do not allow the Johannine portrait to cast doubt on the image of Jesus as a parable-teller, but assume that the Synoptic portrait is accurate and that John just missed this point (or omitted it because it did not serve his interests). Again in John's Gospel Jesus talks a great deal about himself, claiming to be "the light of the world" (8:12) and "the way, the truth, and the life" (14:6). He does not make such grandiose claims about himself in the other Gospels. Historians are reluctant to admit the authenticity of such claims on the testimony of John's Gospel alone.

Apocryphal Gospels

Many other Gospels besides Matthew, Mark, Luke, and John were written in the first few centuries of Christianity.[21] Those that did not ultimately become part of the New Testament are called *apocryphal gospels* to distinguish them from the four *canonical Gospels* that Christians regard as scripture.[22] Many of these works have only recently been discovered and some exist only in fragmentary form. A few are completely lost to us and are known only through quotations in the writings of church leaders, who often did not approve of them.

Historians, of course, are concerned not with the theological question of which books should be considered to be divinely inspired, but with the historical question of whether these books accurately reflect upon the life and teaching of Jesus.

Except for the notable exceptions discussed below, however, the verdict of historians with regard to these apocryphal gospels has been overwhelmingly negative. Most of the books claim to have been authored by someone close to Jesus—one of his twelve disciples or closest friends—but in no case is such a claim accepted by historical scholars. Rather, almost all of the apocryphal gospels appear to have been written in the second or third centuries. Their real value to historians lies not in what they reveal about Jesus but in what they disclose about the early church.[23] Many of them reflect an effort by some believers to claim the story of Jesus in support of different political or theological agendas from those that were sanctioned by the representatives of what eventually became known as "orthodox Christianity." Specifically, many of the works reflect the influence of gnosticism, a pervasive religious philosophy that was the subject of much controversy in the developing church.[24] Other apocryphal gospels seem to have been motivated by no more than curiosity at a popular level—they offer fanciful stories that fill in gaps left by the New Testament Gospels, relating, for instance, tales of miracles performed by Jesus when he was a small child.

The exceptions may be the Gospel of Thomas and the Gospel of Peter. These two books, especially the former, are often distinguished from the other apocryphal gospels as offering credible historical information about Jesus.

The Gospel of Thomas is a collection of sayings attributed to Jesus, similar in form to what is assumed for the Q document. Scholars had known of this ancient book for some time, since it is referred to by certain early church leaders, but no copy of it was known to have survived. Then, in 1945, a complete manuscript was unearthed in the Egyptian city of Nag Hammadi. The text was written in Coptic, and was recognized to be a translation of a Greek document, some fragments of which had been found previously. The book is thought to have been written originally in Edessa in Syria.

Often regarded as harboring a gnostic orientation, the Gospel of Thomas emphasizes wisdom motifs and the possibility of experiencing Paradise here and now. Jesus is presented as promoting radical asceticism, demanding, for instance, celibacy on the part of his followers. These themes may be reflected in the following quote, though the language is admittedly mysterious:

> Jesus said to [his disciples], "When you make the two into one, and when you make the inner like the outer, and the upper like the lower, and when you make male and female into a single one, so that the male will not be male nor the female be female . . . then you will enter the Father's domain."
>
> *(22:4–7)*

The Gospel of Thomas claims to be the work of Didymus Judas Thomas who was not only one of Jesus' twelve disciples but in fact the twin brother of Jesus! No historian takes this claim seriously, but many do think that the book records some authentic sayings of Jesus. The group of scholars known as the Jesus Seminar has identified three sayings in Thomas that they are certain go back to Jesus and another forty sayings that they think are likely to be authentic. All three of the certain sayings, however, are almost exact parallels to words of Jesus found in the

Synoptic Gospels (Thom. 20:2–3 = Matt. 13:31–32; Thom. 54 = Luke 6:20; Thom. 100:2 = Mark 12:17). The same is true for most of the sayings deemed likely to be authentic also, but here are two exceptions, brief parables that have no parallel in the New Testament:

> The Father's imperial rule is like a woman who was carrying a jar full of meal. While she was walking along a distant road, the handle of the jar broke and the meal spilled behind her along the road. She didn't know it; she hadn't noticed a problem. When she reached her house, she put the jar down and discovered that it was empty.
>
> *(Thom. 97:1–4)*

> The Father's imperial rule is like a person who wanted to kill someone powerful. While still at home he drew his sword and thrust it into the wall to find out whether his hand would go in. Then he killed the powerful one .
>
> *(Thom. 98:1–3)*

In other cases, the version of a saying from Thomas is decidedly different from what is found in the New Testament. Compare the parable of the treasure from Thomas and Matthew:[25]

The Father's imperial rule is like a person who had a treasure hidden in his field but did not know it. And when he died he left it to his son. The son did not know about it either. He took over the field and sold it. The buyer went plowing, discovered the treasure, and began to lend money at interest to whomever he wished. (Thom. 109:1–3)	Heaven's imperial rule is like a treasure hidden in a field: when someone finds it, that person covers it up again, and out of sheer joy goes and sells every last possession and buys that field. (Matt. 13:44)

As we will see in the chapters that follow, evaluation of the Gospel of Thomas is a matter of great controversy in historical Jesus research. The key issue, perhaps, is the question of when it was written. Some scholars, including many associated with the Jesus Seminar, have placed it firmly in the first century, around the same time as the four canonical writings.[26] The majority of historians, however, think that the Gospel of Thomas belongs to the second century and that it is probably dependent upon the canonical Gospels for much of its material. If that is the case, its value as a historical source is greatly diminished, though, even then, the possibility that it preserves some authentic sayings of Jesus that are not found elsewhere does not have to be completely discarded.

The Gospel of Peter offers an account of Jesus' death and resurrection attributed to Jesus' premiere disciple. Discovered in 1886, only fragments of the work remain, but these provide an account of Jesus' passion and resurrection different from the accounts found in the New Testament Gospels. In general, the account here seems to be more imaginative, describing events in nonliteral language intended to bring out their theological significance. An obvious example would be its most famous passage, the account of the walking, talking cross:

> They see three men leaving the tomb [two angels plus Jesus], two supporting the third, and a cross was following them. The heads of the two reached up to the sky, while the head of the third, whom they led by the hand, reached beyond the skies. And they heard a voice from the skies that said, "Have you preached to those who sleep?" And an answer was heard from the cross, "Yes!"
>
> *(10:2–4)*

Needless to say, historians are not impressed by the accuracy of such fanciful reports. Recently, however, one of the most important historical Jesus scholars has advanced a controversial thesis regarding the Gospel of Peter. John Dominic Crossan does not believe that the overtly theological tone of this narrative necessarily marks it as later than the canonical Gospels. Indeed, he argues for the opposite—the earliest accounts of the passion and resurrection were the most obviously theological. Only later did Gospel writers try to give the story the appearance of a historical record. Thus, Crossan, supported by Helmut Koester of Harvard University, argues that the Gospel of Peter drew upon a primitive version of the passion narrative (which he calls "the Cross Gospel") that also served as a source for what is found in other Gospels.[27] This view has not yet attracted wide support, but it has at least raised the possibility that the Gospel of Peter might have been composed in stages, with some of the material extending back to an early time.

CRITERIA OF AUTHENTICITY

As historical scholars review these sources, they apply a variety of criteria to determine which matters ought to be accorded the most legitimacy. Obviously, the date and derivation of a source is a primary consideration. As we have indicated, there is not always unanimity on these points, but scholars will usually rely most heavily on those sources that they determine to be the earliest. Even then, however, individual points that the source recounts will be put to various tests. In the chapters that follow, we will see that some scholars rely more heavily upon certain criteria than others. Some also modify the criteria that are defined here, in an attempt to apply them with more precision than their peers. For now, though, let us list six factors that, in one way or another, come into consideration for almost all researchers studying the historical Jesus.

Multiple Attestation

Matters are more likely to be accepted as historically accurate if they are attested by more than one source. For example, Jesus is portrayed as telling parables (though not the same ones) in Mark, Q, M, L, and Thomas. Thus, historians are inclined to accept as a well-attested fact the premise that Jesus taught in parables.

The significant point here is to find sources that are independent of each other, and, as we have seen, scholars do not always agree on which sources these would be. The story of Jesus feeding a multitude of five thousand people is found in Matthew, Mark, Luke, and John. The assumption of most scholars is that Matthew and Luke got the story from Mark and, so, these do not count as separate sources. But scholars are divided as to whether John had access to any of the Synoptic Gospels. If he did, then the feeding miracle is really only attested by one independent source. If he did not, then it has two sources in its favor.

Though all scholars make use of this important criterion, most do not think it essential for determining that an event is historical. Wright observes that the number of times that something "happens to turn up in the records is a very haphazard index of its likely historicity."[28] In other words, no matter is to be judged nonhistorical simply because it is mentioned only once.

Dissimilarity

Material is more likely to be deemed historically reliable if its contents and ideology are dissimilar to those most relevant to the source itself. Historical scholars are by nature suspicious. They must ask whether the Gospel writers are reporting what Jesus actually said and did or whether they (or the sources they drew upon) are attributing to Jesus things that *they* want to convey. If, therefore, Jesus is presented as saying or doing things that seem almost out of place for both Palestinian Judaism and early Christianity, the likelihood of the presentation being accurate seems great. For example, Jesus is described as calling God by the rather personal name "Abba," an informal term for father (Mark 14:36). Most historians accept this as historical because the address does not appear to have been used by Jews in Palestine, nor did it become part of the early Christian liturgy. If Jesus didn't really use this term, where would Mark or his sources have derived it? Another example would be the stories in the Gospels that present Jesus as eating with tax collectors and other social outcasts (Mark 2:13–17, for example). We have no record of anyone else doing this, nor was the practice continued in the early church.

Related to this criterion is what is sometimes called evidence for "awkwardness" or "embarrassment." Matters that are reported in the Gospels might be judged historically accurate if they are likely to have caused some discomfort among the early Christians who treasured these stories and wrote them down. The point, quite simply, is that Christians would not have made up stories that caused problems for the church. The most oft-cited example is the fact that Jesus was baptized by John the Baptist. This was potentially embarrassing to Christians because (1) John's baptism was for those who repented of their sins, and Christians claimed Jesus was sinless; and (2) by submitting to John's baptism Jesus seems to have implied that he wanted to become the latter's disciple. Indeed, the story is told in Matthew's Gospel in a way that tries to address some of these concerns (Matt. 3:13–15). Some historians might think Matthew is doing a first-century version of "spin control" but few would doubt the basic fact that seems to need controlling: Jesus was baptized by John.

This criterion of dissimilarity is perhaps the most controversial of the criteria we are discussing. It seems logical, when used to support the inclusion of data. Some scholars, however, also use it as a negative criterion, deeming matters nonhistorical when they fail the test of dissimilarity. Other historians object strongly to this use, maintaining that common sense dictates that much of what Jesus said and did probably accorded well with his Palestinian context. The early Christians, furthermore, probably copied him in as many ways as possible. We should expect Jesus to be similar to both Palestinian Judaism and early Christianity in key respects. The counter-response is to claim that historical science is by nature a minimalist enterprise. We will never be able to ascertain everything about Jesus, but are able to determine only what was most distinctive about him. Historians, so this argument goes, are most interested in discovering what was unique about Jesus, what set him apart from others. The reply to that might be that historical appreciation for Jesus' accomplishments needs to recognize how innovations that originated with him were carried on by his followers. If he is defined only by those features of his life that were not continued, his significance and impact will appear necessarily slight. And so the argument continues. As time goes on, few scholars are adamant extremists for either position. Most recognize the need to use the criterion of dissimilarity, but to balance it with other concerns. Still, we will see this issue raised again in the chapters that follow.

Memorable Content or Form

• Material is more likely to be judged authentic if it is couched in terms that would have been easy to remember. The assumption here is that almost nothing concerning Jesus was written down during his lifetime. The culture in which he lived was given mainly to oral transmission, that is, to conveying information by word of mouth. Accordingly, historians think it more likely that people would have remembered short sayings, such as proverbs ("Prophets are not without honor, except in their hometown," Mark 6:4) or beatitudes ("Blessed are the meek, for they will inherit the earth," Matt. 5:5). Because stories are intrinsically memorable, parables tend to score high by this criterion also. Other factors that make material memorable include the use of humor, exaggeration, or paradox. In one instance, Jesus is said to have accused the Pharisees of straining out gnats and then swallowing camels (Matt. 23:24). In another, he bemoans hypocrites who worry about a speck in someone else's eye but don't notice the log that is in their own (Matt. 7:3–5). Sayings or deeds may also be judged memorable if their very content was shocking or unexpected, such as the call to "turn the other cheek" when anyone strikes you (Matt. 5:39). By contrast, long discourses such as those attributed to Jesus in John's Gospel are usually deemed too complex to have been remembered and passed on in the form that we now have them. This criterion, though, like all the others, is applied differently by different scholars. Some critics insist that people who live in a primarily oral culture develop keen memories and are capable of remembering vast quantities of information word for word.

Language and Environment

• Material is more likely to be deemed historical if it is compatible with the language and environment of the period it describes (the life of Jesus in Palestine) rather than the period of the source itself. The Gospels were probably written in various cities of the Roman Empire in settings different from that in which Jesus lived. If what they report of Jesus is accurate, historians say, it should be free of anachronism. Sayings of Jesus that would make more sense applied to Gentile merchants living in cities than to Jewish peasants in rural areas may be regarded with suspicion. For example, in Mark's Gospel Jesus says, "Whoever divorces his wife and marries another commits adultery against her; and if she divorces her husband and marries another, she commits adultery" (Mark 10:11–12). Under Jewish law, only husbands were allowed to initiate divorce. The second half of this saying, therefore, is anachronistic. Most historians would conclude that Jesus is not likely to have warned Jewish peasant women against divorcing their husbands, since in their culture such a thing was impossible. Under Roman law, however, either the husband or the wife could initiate divorce, which could explain why Jesus' saying was adapted to address the context in which Mark wrote his Gospel.

Explanation

Some scholars also appeal to an overriding criterion that judges material more likely to be authentic if it explains developments in the Jesus tradition and, so, helps to account for the impact of Jesus' life. Typically, this is not applied to isolated sayings or pericopes but to the portrait as a whole. As we observed in chapter 1, one criticism of Burton Mack's thesis that fictional stories in the Gospels turned the real Jesus (who was essentially a philosopher) into a mythical religious figure is that Mack has no adequate explanation for why this philosopher Jesus would have aroused so much opposition that the Romans would want to crucify him. The validity of this criterion, however, remains questionable. Many scholars (including Mack) allow that historical science is a minimalist discipline. Explanations are not always forthcoming and construals of data ought not be bent to obtain them.

Coherence

Finally, material that cannot be established as historical by such criteria as those given above may nevertheless be judged authentic if it is generally consistent with the information that is so derived. In Jesus studies, historical critics test the validity of uncertain elements in the tradition by comparing them with other elements that they have previously decided to be authentic. This criterion provides something of a catch-all category for broadening the circle of what is included. For example, some historians would accept the saying attributed to Jesus in Thomas 82 as authentic: "Whoever is near me is near the fire; whoever is far from me, is far from the Father's domain." Although nothing quite like it is found in the other Gospels, it sounds like the sort of thing that Jesus might have said (compare Mark 9:49; 12:34). Typically, what is determined to be authentic by this criterion is regarded as secondary, less certain than what proves true through other criteria. However, at least one scholar we will discuss, N. T. Wright, has developed a

method that makes "coherence with a workable hypothesis" a primary consideration for historical reconstruction.

Some observers contend that, in addition to these criteria, most historians operate with another, often unstated criterion: the adoption of a post-Enlightenment
worldview. In short, material is more likely to be regarded as historically reliable
if it does not require acceptance of ideas that contradict modern views of reality.
Some historians seem to operate with a prejudice that determines some things reported in the Bible not to have happened because they *could not* happen. An a pri-
ori judgment about what is possible transcends any consideration of how many
sources attest to the event, whether it was potentially embarrassing for the church
to report it, or anything else. The case is closed before it opens. Some readers of
this book will probably think that this is how history should be done, while others
may think such biases make the discipline a pseudoscience. Both types of readers
will meet friends and foes before we are done.

No matter how hard they work, no matter what attention they give to sources
and criteria, Jesus scholars have a hard row to hoe. The degree of personal investment alluded to in the introduction (page 3) affects not only the scholars but their
audience as well. Russell Shorto, a journalist who by his own admission is normally more at home in the world of *GQ* than Q, recently wrote a book on Jesus
scholarship for general readers. As he did the usual publicity tour associated with
such publications, he was amazed at the comments of average Americans:

> I'm Jewish, and we Jews have always known that Jesus received
> esoteric black magic . . .
>
> I think it's fascinating that these so-called scholars continue to re-
> press the known fact that Jesus was black . . .
>
> Any astronomer will tell you that the alignment of the planets at the
> time of the Nativity . . .
>
> Why are these experts afraid to admit that Jesus' bloodline passed
> to the Knights Templar . . . ?[29]

Everyone, Shorto says, seemed to think they had the inside scoop on Jesus. Perhaps he shouldn't have been surprised. Jesus still gets more headlines than Elvis
in supermarket tabloids, which regularly scream about signs of his return or the
appearance of his image on screen doors or tortillas. The Jesus of history can be a
hard sell.

And then there are those who will suspect something else is involved, that behind all the academic platitudes and scholarly research lurks a controlling sinister
force. Shorto recalls a question he received after explaining the attention Jesus
scholars give to Hellenism, the influence of Greek culture on the Roman Empire
during the time of Jesus. "Don't you think that it's just a little bit odd," a woman
inquired, "that the word *Hellenism* begins with *Hell*?"[30]

3

Snapshots:
Contemporary Images
of Jesus

Who was Jesus? That disarmingly simple question is . . . asked passionately by Christians—and non-Christians—of the most widely varying theological stances. While certainly not all of that interest is in touch with the academic quest for the historical Jesus, all who seek to answer the question have a vision of who Jesus was, whether that person is a television evangelist who talks about "JEE-sus" with every breath or is an Orthodox priest who almost shudders to say the name.

—Walter F. Taylor, Jr.[1]

I asked my class, "Who was Jesus?" Most said he was a religious figure. Some said philosopher, comparing him to Socrates. Then there was Jesus as political leader, with one student comparing him to Mao and Stalin.

—Tyler Roberts[2]

Remember that playground ditty sung out by children jumping rope?
  Rich man, poor man, beggar man, thief
  Doctor, lawyer, merchant, chief.
 Scholarly theories about the historical Jesus have by now multiplied to a tangled mass ever bit as disparate:
  Wandering preacher, zealot, activist, magician
  Cynic peasant, prophet, wisdom-logician.
 (The rhythm works out after about a dozen tries.)

—Robert W. Yarbrough[3]

In chapters 4 through 9, we will examine six major biographical studies of Jesus that have been produced (or are being produced) by historical scholars. First, however, we will examine a few of the images for Jesus that have been suggested by modern scholars. The studies discussed in this chapter are not intended to be comprehensive; the scholars who present them do not necessarily claim that the image they describe offers a complete picture of who Jesus was. In most cases, they are calling attention to an aspect that they find especially significant or one that they may feel has been neglected. All of these studies have been influential. That is, the scholars presented in the following chapters have had to wrestle with the ideas presented in this chapter. They have either had to incorporate these aspects of Jesus into their overall portraits or explain why they think particular images are not fitting.

JESUS THE SOCIAL PROPHET
(RICHARD A. HORSLEY)

According to Richard Horsley, Jesus stood in the classic tradition of Israelite prophets, which is to say that he must be understood as one who was fundamentally concerned with the social and political circumstances of his day. Popular Christianity attempts to view Jesus in "religious" terms rather than "political" ones, but these categories are artificial and do not do justice to the social context or sacred tradition that informed Jesus' ministry. Horsley is professor of religion at the University of Massachusetts and is the author of *Jesus and the Spiral of Violence* (1987), in which his main views concerning the historical Jesus are set forth. For a full appreciation of his ideas, however, this volume must be read along with *Bandits, Prophets, and Messiahs* (1985) and *Sociology and the Jesus Movement* (1989), two works in which Horsley discusses the world with which Jesus and his followers were engaged.

Horsley uses models drawn from the social sciences to reconstruct a portrait of the political and social circumstances in Palestine at the time of Jesus. Put simply, the situation was one of colonial class struggle. About 90 percent of the population consisted of rural peasants who were dominated and oppressed economically by a minority of urban elites. Horsley details multiple layers of taxation that helped those in power to maintain their status while guaranteeing that the poor would only get poorer. This situation created a "spiral of violence" as oppression led to protest, which would evoke counterrepression, which would, in turn, inspire revolt. In this context, social bandits and popular prophets arose, including Jesus.

Jesus himself was a peasant and, within his social environment, his ministry may be understood as fomenting a social revolution on behalf of peasants. He blessed the poor and condemned the rich (Luke 6:20, 24). He talked about forgiveness of debts (Matt. 18:23–33; Luke 11:4), and lending without expectation of profit (Matt. 5:42; Luke 6:34–35).[4] He spoke of abolishing hierarchical and patriarchal relationships (Matt. 10:37; 23:8–9; Mark 3:35; 10:43–44).[5] He threatened the temple, which the elite priestly establishment had turned into "an instrument of imperial legitimation and control of a subjected people."[6] It is a solid historical fact, says Horsley, "that Jesus was executed as a rebel against the Roman order."[7] The charges against him, furthermore, were valid. Jesus *was* stirring up the people. From the perspective of the political authorities, the crucifixion of Jesus was not a mistake. He was not just a religious teacher concerned with only spiritual matters; he posed a genuine threat to the social order of his day.[8]

Horsley distinguishes the *social* revolution he believes Jesus wished to foment from what is often called a *political* revolution. A political revolution, he says, is "top down," involving a replacement of leadership. Jesus had no plans to overthrow political authorities, to drive the imperial forces out of Palestine, or to effect any other change of this order. He probably believed, says Horsley, that God would do this, and do it soon, but he recognized it as something only God could do.[9] Rather, Jesus sought to change society from the "bottom up." His aim was to reorganize and renew peasant society in a way that would respect the covenantal traditions of Israel.

Jesus did not practice, organize, or advocate armed resistance, but Horsley refrains from calling him a pacifist. He maintains that Jesus did not commend or insist upon nonviolence either. The famous "turn the other cheek" passage (Matt. 5:39) referred to nonretaliation against other members of the peasant community. Likewise, the command to love one's enemies (Matt. 5:44) referred to local enemies, not foreign military powers. Jesus counseled peasants to work out their differences peacefully and stick together, but he did not seek to dissuade resistance to Roman oppression.[10]

One of the more controversial but far-reaching aspects of Horsley's construction is that he regards the kingdom of God in Jesus' preaching as a social and political phenomenon. As a metaphor for God's transforming action, it refers always to the liberating use of power within history: "It is important to keep in mind that the 'kingdom of God' is a political metaphor and symbol. In Jesus' preaching and action the kingdom clearly includes the social-economic-political substance of human relations as willed by God."[11] Horsley, then, does not think that Jesus spoke much, if at all, about life beyond death. He offered no vision of life other than that which is to be found in this world. Salvation for Jesus meant peace and justice, here and now.

Horsley is usually praised by other scholars for trying to interpret Jesus in relation to his social and political environment. "More than any other North American scholar," writes Marcus Borg, "Horsley has made Jesus' engagement with his social world central to his portrait of Jesus."[12] Borg, Crossan, and Wright all make use of Horsley's insights in developing their portraits of Jesus (though of these three, Wright is the most cautious and critical).[13] A number of modern scholars, however, think he overplays the this-worldly nature of Jesus' concerns, failing to account for Jewish eschatological expectations. Sanders and Meier in particular offer this critique. Ben Witherington thinks he overestimates the revolutionary climate of Galilee in Jesus' day and gives too little attention to the influence of "the literate." Furthermore, Witherington sees no reason to presume Jesus was involved in reforming village structures; the Gospels all portray his teaching as directed to the community of his own disciples, not to villagers in general or, for instance, to local village author-ities.[14] Wright thinks Horsley's "frequent suggestion that the real impetus for revo-lution came from social rather than theological factors" poses a false antithesis that misunderstands the fundamentally religious milieu of first-century Palestine.[15]

Some of Horsley's minor points have not fared well. The notion that love for enemies is intended only as a local ethic without more general application is crit-icized by Walter Wink.[16] Horsley thinks the Gospel accounts of Jesus associating with tax collectors are not historically accurate.[17] Such persons, he says, were Jew-ish traitors, collaborators with the Roman powers, and Jesus would not have com-promised his solidarity with the oppressed by making friends with oppressors. But Horsley is probably the only historical Jesus scholar to deny the historicity of this part of the tradition, which most find well attested and established by the criterion of dissimilarity (there is little evidence that either Palestinian Judaism or early Christianity viewed association with such outcasts as commendable).

These critiques aside, the main contours of Horsley's projection of Jesus as a social prophet are widely accepted. Most historical Jesus scholars today view Jesus as one whose ministry must be understood at least on some level as a re-sponse to the political situation of his day. A major study by R. David Kaylor builds noticeably upon Horsley's contributions. Kaylor attempts to interpret much of Jesus' teaching in ways that address the sort of political situation described by Horsley. Some of these interpretations are innovative, if not surprising. For ex-ample, Kaylor suggests that the story of a farmer who lets weeds and wheat grow together until the harvest (Matt. 13:24–30) is not an illustration of how God with-holds judgment until the end time, but a joke depicting the poor agricultural strate-gies of large estate owners who buy up the land of local farmers but don't know how to care for it properly.[18] In many such ways, Horsley's basic attempt to relate Jesus' ideas to concrete social situations rather than to spiritualized religious themes has been influential in historical Jesus scholarship.

JESUS THE CHARISMATIC JEW
(GEZA VERMES)

When Geza Vermes published his book *Jesus the Jew* in 1973, the very title seemed to foretell a new day in historical Jesus research. No one doubted, of course, that Jesus was Jewish, but the trend in historical studies up to that point had been to play down his connections to Judaism and emphasize the conflicts, the features that set him apart as the forebear of a new religion. Vermes' book pre-sented Jesus as more Jewish than Christian, a shift that seemed to parallel moves the author had made in his own life. Raised a Roman Catholic in Eastern Europe, Vermes discovered as an adult that he was of Jewish origin. This recognition sent him on a spiritual pilgrimage that culminated in his conversion to the faith of his ancestors.[19] As a scholar, Vermes became professor of Jewish studies at Oxford, wrote prolifically on the Dead Sea Scrolls, and followed his groundbreaking book on Jesus with additional volumes: *The Gospel of Jesus the Jew* (1981), *Jesus and the World of Judaism* (1983), and *The Religion of Jesus the Jew* (1993).

There are many aspects to Vermes' work, but the most enduring contribution has been the connections he draws between Jesus and other charismatic, pious Jews who are reputed to have been miracle workers. Vermes calls Jesus a *hasid,* a type of holy man in first-century Judaism who claimed to draw upon the power of God in ways that transcended the usual channels of religious authority. Two such persons are especially important: Honi the Circle Drawer and Hanina ben Dosa. According to the Talmud, both of these men were miracle workers who operated in Galilee. Honi was active shortly before Jesus and Hanina shortly after him. Both are said to have healed the sick and exercised power over demons. Hanina is credited with healing the son of Gamaliel from a distance (*b. Ber.* 34b; *y. Ber.* 9d; compare the story of Jesus in Luke 7:1–10). In a series of remarkable passages from the Babylonian Talmud, Hanina is referred to as "my son" by a heavenly voice (*b. Taan.* 24b; *b. Ber.* 17b; *b. Hul.* 17a; compare Mark 1:11). Both Hanina and Honi are regularly compared to Elijah, as is Jesus in the Gospels.

Vermes concludes that "a distinctive trend of charismatic Judaism existed during the last couple of centuries of the Second Temple" period and that it "is likely to have had Galilean roots."[20] The "unsophisticated religious ambiance" of Galilee and the relatively "simple spiritual demands" of the people there provided an atmosphere for men such as Honi, Jesus, and Hanina to flourish:[21]

> These holy men were treated as the willing or unsophisticated heirs to an ancient prophetic tradition. Their supernatural powers were attributed to their immediate relation to God. They were venerated as a link between heaven and earth independent of any institutional mediation.[22]

The logical inference is that Jesus can be understood as one in a series of such Galilean holy men, as perhaps the paramount example of *hasidim* produced by this Jewish charismatic movement.

Vermes' thesis has been sharply criticized by scholars who think he overlooks significant differences between Jesus and these other Jewish figures and relies on inadequate sources to establish the connections he does make. The problem is that the Talmudic writings, though difficult to date, are definitely later than the Gospels, and may in some cases be hundreds of years later. The accuracy of their representation of Honi or Hanina is thus even more questionable from a historical perspective than the New Testament's representation of Jesus. The earliest references to Honi and Hanina, furthermore, do not present them as miracle workers but as righteous men whose prayers were answered by God. And Josephus (writing in the first century C.E.) locates Honi in Jerusalem, not Galilee. The suspicion of many historians, then, is that legends about these men grew over time, possibly in response to the stories Christians told about Jesus. The late traditions regarding Honi and Hanina contain accounts similar to those in the Gospels precisely because Jewish writers wanted to create Galilean holy men of their own who would be on a par with Jesus. John Meier is one scholar who has considered Vermes' thesis carefully only to dismiss it: "Ultimately, Vermes' acritical use of sources undermines his whole argument."[23]

Others are much more friendly. John Dominic Crossan and Marcus Borg both make ample use of the parallels to Honi and Hanina in their studies of Jesus, and Borg makes Vermes' category of "charismatic holy man" a dominant model in his own portrait of Jesus.[24] Sanders also appreciates the deep connection of Jesus with Judaism emphasized by Vermes and thinks the stories of Honi and Hanina offer insightful parallels for understanding how Jesus' miracles might have been perceived.[25]

Another historical Jesus scholar, Graham Twelftree, has made observations that are sometimes cited as corrections of Vermes' view. In his book *Jesus the Exorcist,* Twelftree notes first that Jesus' healings and exorcisms are not connected with prayer (as are those of Hanina and Honi) or with the use of mechanical aids as were the exorcisms of other persons of this period. Thus, "Jesus' technique of exorcism, if not innovative, would have at least been very conspicuous."[26] Jesus casts out demons and declares people healed rather than asking God to do it. Second, Twelftree notes that the Gospels link Jesus' exorcisms closely to his proclamation of the kingdom of God. Jesus is presented as claiming that his exorcisms are a demonstration that Satan's power is being restricted and God's rule is being established (Matt. 12:28; Mark 3:27). Thus, "the unique and unprecedented aspect of Jesus' exorcisms is that he gave a profound meaning to the relatively ordinary event."[27]

JESUS THE MAGICIAN
(MORTON SMITH)

In 1978, just five years after Vermes' study of Jesus from a modern Jewish perspective appeared, Morton Smith published a book that identified Jesus with the image assigned to him by early Jewish opponents of Christianity: *Jesus the Magician.* At the time, Smith was professor of ancient history at Columbia University. His claim that Jesus could legitimately be regarded as a magician was and still is controversial, indeed offensive to many Christians. Smith had to argue against the witness of the New Testament and allege that much significant evidence had been suppressed.

Before we look at his argument, we should be clear what is meant by the term *magician.* In modern parlance, the word may refer to an entertainer, to someone who does "magic tricks," or, in other words, to someone who pretends to make things happen through magical forces, which we know do not really exist. Obviously, this was not the view of the first century. It was then widely believed that supernatural powers were at work in the world. Different cultures might attribute these to gods, angels, demons, or other types of spirits, but, in any case, magic was the art of accessing these powers. Magic in the broadest sense involved "private dealings with supernatural beings."[28]

Smith surveys the writings of ancient opponents of Christianity, which he claims almost unanimously present Jesus as a magician. Most of these writings are now known only through references and quotations found in the writings of Christians who wished to refute them. The works themselves "were destroyed in antiquity after Christians got control of the Roman empire."[29] There are two sides to every argument, Smith maintains, and the counterclaims of Jesus' opponents deserve to be heard.

The Gospels themselves admit that Jesus' reputed miracles were controversial even during his own lifetime. Some religious leaders believed he performed exorcisms with the aid of an evil spirit (Mark 3:22). Others may have thought he had called into himself the spirit of the murdered John the Baptist (Mark 6:14). Smith's own study of the Gospels reveals an attempt to cover up aspects of Jesus' activity that would support the charge that he was a magician.[30] For example, the earliest tradition found in the Gospel of Mark portrays Jesus as using techniques that his contemporaries would have regarded as indicative of magic: He uses spittle to effect healing of blindness (8:22–26) and speaks Aramaic words or phrases that effectively function as magic formulas ("Talitha cum" in 5:41 and "Ephphatha" in 7:34). Notably these stories are dropped or revised in the later Gospels of Matthew and Luke. Such tendencies make Smith suspicious that there was originally far more to the tradition that Jesus was a magician than we are now privileged to see.

Despite suppression and coverup, though, Smith finds abundant evidence of Jesus working magic throughout the Gospels. He compares numerous passages to quotations from ancient magical papyri and compares the stories of Jesus extensively to those of another famous miracle worker, Apollonius of Tyana. The account of a spirit entering Jesus and a bird resting upon him at his baptism describes "just the sort of thing that was thought to happen to a magician."[31] Jesus' teaching is often revelatory; the call to hallow God's name (Matt. 6:9) has a background in magic, says Smith, for the magician would make the name of a deity famous by applying it in his craft.[32] Reliable tradition credits Jesus with the institution of the Eucharist, which Smith calls "an unmistakably magical rite."[33] Finally, Jesus is even shown to work what is called "black magic" when he sends evil spirits into things or people. He sends demons into pigs (Mark 5:13) and, according to Smith, sends Satan into a piece of bread so that Judas will be invaded by the devil when he eats the morsel (see John 13:21–30).[34]

Lest his description of Jesus as a magician seem too polemical, Smith indicates that the distinction between a religious miracle worker and a magician is largely one of perspective. The same man may be called a divine man, or Son of God by his admirers, and a magician by his enemies:

> "Jesus the magician" was the figure seen by most ancient opponents of Jesus; "Jesus the Son of God" was the figure seen by that party of his followers which eventually triumphed; the real Jesus was the man whose words and actions gave rise to these contradictory interpretations.[35]

Smith indicates that the Gospels themselves recognize that there were exorcists and miracle workers who were not accused of using magic or demonic power (see Matt. 12:27). Jesus, however, claimed to be able to do the things that he did because he was possessed of a spirit, a spirit that he and his followers called divine, but others might just as well call demonic.

Smith's study has not found wide acceptance among historical Jesus scholars, but it has accented the need for considering the perspective of opponents in composing a historically responsible portrait of Jesus. Furthermore, John Dominic Crossan has recently revived Smith's work and made the image of Jesus as magician a major component of his own sketch. We will look at that in more detail in chapter 5.

One of the most informed critiques of this view has come from John Meier, who offers an extensive study of magic and miracles in the ancient Near East and argues that the two phenomena must be differentiated:

> At one end of the spectrum, the ideal type of magic involves the elements of (1) automatic power possessed by a magician (2) in virtue of secret formulas and rituals, with (3) the resultant coercion of the divine powers by humans (4) in search of quick solutions to practical problems. Also, magic is usually marked by (5) a spirit of individualism or entrepreneurship as opposed to a perduring community of faith. At the other end of the spectrum, miracles belong in general to a context of (1) faith in a personal God to whose will one submits one's own will in prayer, (2) a perduring community of belief, and (3) a public manifestation of God's power (4) that is not dependent on a set ritual or formula.[36]

JESUS THE JEWISH SAGE
(BEN WITHERINGTON III)

Ben Witherington III, professor of New Testament at Asbury Theological Seminary, has suggested that Jesus be thought of as a sapient figure. Witherington's first study on Jesus carried the provocative title *The Christology of Jesus* (1990), and sought to explain what Jesus thought and taught about himself. The initial proposal presented there was expanded in a later work, *Jesus the Sage* (1994). A busy author, Witherington has also written *The Jesus Quest* (1995), which relates his views to other proposals about Jesus, including most of those discussed in this book.

Witherington's understanding of Jesus is informed by the reading of numerous Jewish writings that were well known at the time of Jesus and which belong to what is called the wisdom tradition. These include the biblical books of Ecclesiastes, Job, Proverbs, and Daniel, as well as such apocryphal writings as the Wisdom of Solomon, Sirach, and the *Parables of Enoch*. A number of features in these writings have parallels with what is attributed to Jesus in the Gospels:[37]

- Jesus' use of Father language for God is not characteristic of the Old Testament, but such language is frequently found in the wisdom materials (Sir. 23:1, 4; 51:10; Wis. 14:3);
- The phrase "kingdom of God," frequently on Jesus' lips in the Synoptic Gospels, is rarely found in the Old Testament, but Wisdom 10:10 portrays Solomon being granted a vision of the kingdom of God;
- Jesus' use of Son of Man language echoes the book of Daniel as well as the *Parables of Enoch;*
- Jesus' exorcisms may be understood in light of first-century traditions that regarded Solomon (the favorite figure of the wisdom tradition) as an exorcist;

- Jesus' willingness to portray himself with female imagery (Matt. 23:37–39) may be related to personifications of Wisdom as a female figure in Proverbs 8—9 and Wisdom of Solomon 8—9;
- Jesus' parables about banquets and his practice of eating with outcasts exemplify classic wisdom themes that encourage the enjoyment of life, often with feasting as a prime symbol of such celebration.

In light of such parallels, Witherington thinks *sage* is a more precise description of Jesus than *prophet*. Most Bible readers are aware that prophets were regarded as people filled with the Spirit of God who spoke God's word to Israel. But the wisdom tradition also claimed the inspiration of God's Spirit. Isaiah describes the descendant of David who would later be called the Messiah as one whom the Spirit of God instills with wisdom, knowledge, understanding, and the fear of the Lord—characteristics most valued in wisdom literature (Isa. 11:1–3). Later Talmudic writings claimed that God took prophecy from the prophets and gave it to the sages.[38]

Jesus, Witherington notes, never uses the classic formula of prophets, "Thus says the Lord . . ."[39] He speaks on his own authority, as does the Teacher of Ecclesiastes and the author of Proverbs. The form of his speech is not oracles but riddles, parables, aphorisms, personifications, and beatitudes. The content of his message draws often on "creation theology," extolling God's providence as evidenced in nature (Matt. 6:25–33) and decrying divorce as contrary to God's original intent (Matt. 19:3–9). In all these ways, he presents himself as a sage with deep roots in the wisdom tradition of Israel.[40]

A couple of key passages fit Witherington's proposal especially well. First, Jesus contrasts himself with John the Baptist, whom he calls a prophet. He notes that whereas John is an ascetic, he has come "eating and drinking." Then he concludes, "Wisdom is vindicated by her deeds" (Matt. 11:16–19).[41] Second, Jesus claims that he is the only one who knows the Father, that all things have been handed to him by the Father, and that no one can know the Father unless he reveals the Father to them (Matt. 11:25–27). Many historical scholars would doubt the authenticity of this latter saying, since it smacks heavily of the developed theology of the early church. But Witherington argues that it does go back to Jesus and presents him as claiming for himself the role elsewhere ascribed to the Wisdom of God (Prov. 8:14–36; Wis. 2:13, 16; 4:10–15).[42]

Witherington does not think the label *sage* captures the whole truth about the historical Jesus, but he does think it offers an important category, perhaps the dominant one, for understanding him. He thinks it may be best to describe Jesus as "a prophetic sage" or even as "a prophetic and eschatological sage." In his later book *Jesus the Sage,* Witherington goes so far as to suggest that Jesus believed he was Wisdom made flesh, the personification of God's wisdom. In Matthew 11:19, he seems to refer to himself as Wisdom and to claim that his actions vindicate him as such. Thus, he sees the rejection of him as the rejection of God's wisdom (Matt. 23:37–39). Traditional writings had already personified the Wisdom of God as a heavenly figure entrusted with the secrets of God and with the task of revealing these to humans (Job 28; Prov. 1, 3, 8, 9; Sir. 1, 24). Jesus may have believed that he was this figure, descended to earth in human form. As such, he saw himself as "the revealer of the very mind of God."[43]

The image of Jesus as a Jewish sage is one significant component of Marcus Borg's treatment of Jesus, presented in chapter 6 of this book. Borg emphasizes the subversive nature of Jesus' teaching, a point Witherington also develops, though in different ways.[44] Borg parts company from Witherington in that he takes the emphasis on Jesus as a teacher of wisdom (which is present-oriented) as an indication that Jesus did not speak much about the future.[45] N. T. Wright and E. P. Sanders object to any subordination of prophet to sage. They both regard the former category as the dominant model for Jesus (thus, he was not so much a prophetic sage as a prophet who sometimes drew upon wisdom traditions). Sanders complains that an emphasis on Jesus as a sage can end up presenting him primarily as a teacher whose ideas were "striking in manner but not especially in matter."[46] Most wisdom teaching, after all, deals with general advice that would apply in almost any time or place. Likewise, Wright insists that the image of a sage must not be taken to imply that he "did not address the urgent state of affairs within Israel," but he praises Witherington as one who does not push the model to that extreme.[47]

JESUS THE CYNIC PHILOSOPHER
(F. GERALD DOWNING)

Probably the single most influential of the nontraditional images associated with Jesus in recent scholarship has been that of the Cynic philosopher.[48] This is, in fact, the controlling image of Jesus for the work of Burton Mack described in chapter 1 (see pages 25–28) and, in later chapters, we will see that this becomes a dominant concept in the work of the Jesus Seminar and of John Dominic Crossan.

Many scholars have noted similarities between traditions about Jesus and those concerning Cynic philosophers,[49] but none so persistently as F. Gerald Downing. The author of numerous books on theology and faith, Downing serves as vicar at the Anglican parish of St. Simon and St. Jude in Bolton, England. Several of his writings reflect appreciation for the social movement in ancient Greece and Rome involving an eccentric spectrum of people called Cynics.

To understand the Cynics, we must first expunge negative connotations that derive from the English word *cynical*. Cynics were not pessimistic people who tended to expect the worst. Rather, they were radical individualists who advocated the avoidance of worldly entanglements and defiance of social convention. The Cynic movement is usually traced to Diogenes of Sinope (400–325 B.C.E.), although it took on a variety of forms after him.[50] Diogenes embraced a simple, natural lifestyle free of hypocrisy or pretense. By living simply, he claimed to achieve self-sufficiency, which freed him from the need to impress others. So liberated, he could do as he wished, which was to accept whatever was "natural" without shame.

By the time of Jesus, Cynics are known to have traveled throughout many countries, practicing their eccentric lifestyle and propagating the ideas that it entailed. Stories known as *chreiai* were told about and by Cynics.[51] Typically, these are brief accounts that recall a memorable aphorism or describe a symbolic action. One *chreia* recounts how Alexander the Great visited Diogenes when he was sunbathing and asked if there was anything he could do for him. No respecter of authority, Diogenes replied, "Just now, you can get out of my light" (Cicero, *Tusculan Disputations* 5.92). Other stories record that Diogenes would defecate or engage in sexual acts in public to demonstrate the shamelessness of these natural deeds (Laertius, *Lives* 6.69).[52] This, in fact, explains the derivation of the word *Cynic;* it comes from the Greek word for dog (*kyōn*), and Aristotle commented that Diogenes behaved "like a dog" when he acted shamelessly in public.[53]

The Cynics loved being described as antisocial and deliberately sought such an identification. As John Dominic Crossan is fond of saying, "They were hippies in a world of Augustan yuppies."[54] They dressed as beggars with a cloak, bag, and staff, wore their hair long and kept their beards untrimmed. And they went barefoot. "Wearing sandals is next to being bound," wrote one Cynic, "but going barefoot gives the feet great freedom" (Musonius Rufus, Fragment XIX). Another summarized his lifestyle this way: "a cloak serves as my garment, the skin of my feet as my shoes, the whole earth as my resting place" (*Pseudo-Anacharsis* 5). Seneca reports that Diogenes "on seeing a boy drink water from the hollow of his hand, forthwith took his cup from his wallet [bag] and broke it, upbraiding himself with these words: 'Fool that I am, to have been carrying superfluous baggage all this time!'" Then Seneca exhorts his readers, "If mankind were to listen to this sage, they would know that the cook is as superfluous as the soldier. . . . Follow nature, and you will need no skilled craftsmen" (Seneca, *Epistulae Morales* 90.14–16).[55]

In 1988, Downing published *Christ and the Cynics,* which was not so much a monograph as a compilation of materials from Cynic writings arranged side by side with quotations from the New Testament. Here are but two of the 289 examples he adduces:

"Lots of people are praising you," Antisthenes was told. "Why?" he asked. "What have I done wrong?" (Laertius, *Lives* 6.8)	Woe to you when all speak well of you, for that is what their ancestors did to the false prophets. (Luke 6:26)
Where do the little birds go to get food to feed their young, though they're much worse off than you are—the swallows and nightingales and larks and blackbirds? Do they store food away in safekeeping? (Musonius 15)	Look at the birds of the air; they neither sow nor reap nor gather into barns, and yet your heavenly Father feeds them. Are you not of more value than they? (Matt. 6:26)

Downing admits that similarity in wording need not entail agreement in meaning, and he recognizes differences between the early Jesus tradition and Cynicism.[56] Nevertheless, on the basis of the numerous parallels, he proposes that "Christians who shared publicly the teaching and stories that go to build up our first three Gospels must have been entirely happy to sound as well as look like Cynics. . . . They focussed on the same topics, very often pressing the same conclusions, and that in very similar language."[57]

As such, Downing's study focuses more on the history of early Christianity than on the historical Jesus. We might assume that the evangelists who wrote the Gospels cast Jesus' words in ways that reflected Cynic influence in order to appeal to the Gentile world they wanted to evangelize. But in his next major work, *Cynics and Christian Origins,* Downing came to insist that Cynics exercised a direct influence on Jesus himself.[58] Though Jewish, Jesus deliberately emulated these Gentile philosophers. The implication of such a proposal is that Jesus and his Jewish audience were thoroughly Hellenized, that is, acclimated to Greco-Roman culture.

Essential to this thesis is Downing's analysis of Gospel material assigned to the Q source. Here he finds the greatest abundance of parallels, such that he claims the very genre of Q may have been that of "a Cynic life," comparable to those found in a work by Diogenes Laertius (*Lives of Eminent Philosophers,* Book 6). Laertius offers brief biographical sketches of Cynic philosophers with a primary interest in collecting their more memorable sayings. Downing notes several similarities between Q and these "Lives" of Cynics, but we should note that this part of his proposal has been sharply contested by other Q scholars.[59] Still, Downing concludes that "Q would have seemed akin to Cynic teaching in its choice of topics, conclusions urged, vocabulary, and imagery used."[60] Common features in the teaching of the Cynics and that of Jesus include rejection of wealth (Mark 10:17–26; Epictetus, *Diss.* 2:14.14, 18–24), advocacy of simple living (Mark 6:8–9; Dio, *Orat.* 6:15), approval of begging (Luke 6:30; Laertius, *Lives* 6:29), and the expectation of persecution (Matt. 5:11–12; Lucian, *Demonax* 11). Furthermore, Downing says, Q presents Jesus as teaching in his own name as did the Cynics, not as the representative of a school as did rabbis, or in the name of God as did the prophets (Jesus does not say, "Thus says the Lord").

The Cynics, in Downing's view, were not just cavalier vagabonds. They were "friends of freedom," outspoken and courageous protesters who stood up for individual liberty in an oppressive society.[61] Like Jesus and his followers, they mingled with the lower classes, teaching the ordinary people rather than restricting their insights to lectures at the salon. Their philosophy was termed "popular," and yet it strangely appealed to many aristocrats who sensed the emptiness of life in the higher reaches of imperial Roman society.

Some scholars have questioned whether all of the parallels Downing cites for Cynicism and Christianity are legitimate. This issue is complicated by difficulty in dating Cynic materials (most extant writings are later than the New Testament) and by the spectrum and diversity of views that can be attributed to Cynics.[62] The parallels he cites are, in any case, drawn from a period of over five hundred years, and many concern persons who might not technically be classed as Cynics. Both

Musonius Rufus and Epictetus, cited above, are usually regarded as Stoics, though the distinction between Stoicism and Cynicism is admittedly ambiguous.[63] Downing's response is to claim that "the niceties of intellectual definition" are of little importance, but rather "how things appeared to the populace at large."[64]

Downing claims "to show not only that there are many similarities between Cynics and Christians but also that over all (and often in detail) these similarities are quite distinctive."[65] The latter part of this claim has been disputed by some who maintain that the similarities between Jesus and the Cynics can be explained in other ways (for example, by analogy to Jewish prophets or wisdom teachers). Moreover, critics of Downing's hypothesis point out key areas of contrast. In Luke 9:3, Jesus explicitly forbids his disciples from taking a staff or a bag with them when they go out as missionaries, perhaps because he wanted to *avoid* any identification of his followers with Cynics.[66] But Downing indicates that even the Synoptic tradition is varied on this. In Mark 6:8–10, the disciples are allowed a staff though no bag. In Matthew 10:9–10, they are not allowed either, yet now they are required to go barefoot (like Cynics)! So if the early Christian tradition allowed variation on these minor points, why not assume that Cynic tradition did as well? The whole point, for Downing, is nonconformity with society, not imposition of a new set of regulations.[67]

Other differences seem more substantive. Cynics were Greeks and lived in the cities; Jesus was Jewish and wandered the countryside. Cynics had a strong this-worldly attitude; Jesus is represented as preaching about a coming kingdom of God, about life after death and the final judgment. Cynics were noted for embracing asceticism; Jesus, for avoiding it (Mark 2:18–19; Luke 7:33–34). Cynics advocated dependence on self; Jesus, dependence on God (Matt. 6:25–33).[68] And, notes Henry Chadwick, we hear no stories of Christian missionaries copulating in the streets.[69] On these points, Downing appeals to the diversity of themes, behaviors, and commitments that could be attributed to particular Cynics at particular times. He maintains that the "shamelessness" of Diogenes' antics had ceased to be an identifying factor for Cynics by the time of Jesus. And he claims that some Cynics did employ eschatological language; they at least took the imagery of afterlife and of judgment and applied it to life on earth.[70]

Perhaps the most sharply challenged aspect of Downing's proposal, however, has been his suggestion that Jesus was directly influenced by Cynics. Some scholars wonder where Jesus would have even encountered them. There is no sure sign that Cynics were ever in Galilee, particularly in the villages that Jesus knew. Downing supposes that Jesus could have seen Cynics in the Roman city of Sepphoris, which was only three miles from Nazareth. Cynics might have been there, and Jesus might have visited there, but all this is speculation, for neither Cynics nor Sepphoris are ever mentioned in the Bible or in any of the other Jesus traditions. On surer ground, Downing points out that notable Cynics were located in Gadara both the century before and the century after Jesus' ministry. Gadara was a city of the Decapolis, a region visited by Jesus according to the New Testament Gospels.[71] And if Cynics were there, it is not unlikely that they were elsewhere too. Leif Vaage observes that this is not essential; the remarkable similarity of certain Cynics and some early Christians helps to inform our understanding of Christian origins regardless of whether the two movements are "genealogically related."[72]

All these images of Jesus come into play for historical researchers, and eventually, affect perception at a popular level as well. The work of academicians has a way of trickling down to the people in the pews. "Every time we preach on a Gospel passage," seminary professor Walter Taylor tells Christian ministers, "we are stating our understanding of Jesus—is he a revolutionary, a pious teacher, a charismatic leader, or a misguided fool?"[73] Preachers are shaped by what they read, and they, in turn, shape their congregations. Just lately, furthermore, historical Jesus studies have been bypassing preachers altogether. Major news magazines run cover stories on the subject (usually at religious times of the year such as Christmas and Easter), offering a curious public a glimpse at what is going on.

Still, sometimes, the scholarship does not trickle down at all. A few years ago, *Life* magazine took a different tack and published a compendium of quotes from prominent people about Jesus, informed or not.[74] Here's a sample:

- "There was no such person in the history of the world as Jesus Christ. There was no historical, living, breathing, sentient human being by that name. Ever." (Jon Murray, president of American Atheists)
- "Jesus . . . never once yielded to sin, nor was he at any time susceptible to injury or harm or hurt from anything, mortal or otherwise. He explored creation, although he was at the same time the creator." (Jerry Falwell, pastor of Thomas Road Baptist Church, Lynchburg, Virginia)
- "In only three years, he . . . organized Christianity, which today has branches in all the world's countries and a 32.4 percent share of the world's population, twice as big as its nearest rival. . . . Jesus was the most effective executive in history. The results he achieved are second to none." (James F. Hind, author and motivational speaker)

All three of these perceptions are snapshots of a different sort than those described in this chapter: an imaginary Jesus (Murray), a docetic Jesus (Falwell),[75] an entrepreneurial Jesus (Hind). They exemplify an almost stubborn ignorance of academia, a triumph of personal predilection over historical evidence. I do not believe there is a single scholar discussed in this book who would regard any of these three statements as compatible with knowledge that the historical quest for Jesus has brought to the fore. But, of course, the scholars have their own predilections also. Let's find out what they are.

4

THE JESUS SEMINAR

Jesus is one of the great sages of history, and his insights should be taken seriously but tested by reference to other seers, ancient and modern, who have had glimpses of the eternal, and by reference to everything we can learn from the sciences, the poets, and the artists. Real knowledge, divine knowledge, is indiscriminate in the vessels it elects to fill.

—Robert W. Funk, founder of the Jesus Seminar[1]

Jesus taught that the last will be first and the first will be last. He admonished his followers to be servants of everyone. He urged humility as the cardinal virtue by both word and example. Given these terms, it is difficult to imagine Jesus making claims for himself—I am the Son of God, I am the expected One, the Anointed—unless, of course, he thought that nothing he said applied to himself.

—The Jesus Seminar[2]

[The work of the Jesus Seminar] will put both Jesus and the Bible "in the news." By so doing, it opens a window of opportunity for significant consciousness raising and education within the church, as well as more broadly in our culture. Together with biblical scholarship generally, it can provide a way for people to be both thoughtful and Christian, rather than having to choose between the two.

—Marcus Borg[3]

The most noteworthy and controversial research on Jesus in recent years has been conducted by a group of scholars who call themselves "the Jesus Seminar." Describing their work as "noteworthy" does not imply that it is valid or correct any more than describing it as "controversial" implies that it is invalid or wrong. Rather, the significance of this group's accomplishments may be measured in terms of their influence. Some of the authors described in subsequent chapters of this book are members of the Jesus Seminar and have relied on the group's findings in their own descriptions of Jesus as a historical figure. Others are opposed to the Seminar's work and their own research has been motivated at least in part by an attempt to present credible alternatives. In any case, no student of Jesus as a figure in history can afford to ignore the Jesus Seminar.

This group of scholars has also succeeded in capturing the attention of popular culture. Publications by and about the Jesus Seminar may be found in bookstores across America. Members have appeared on televised talk shows, and such magazines as *Atlantic Monthly, Newsweek, Time,* and *U.S. News and World Report* have devoted cover stories to their work. Hollywood producer Paul Verhoeven (known for such films as *Robocop, Basic Instinct, Total Recall, Showgirls,* and *Starship Troopers*) is a member of the Seminar and is making a movie about Jesus based on the group's work.[4]

THE WORK OF THE JESUS SEMINAR

The Jesus Seminar was founded in 1985 by Robert Funk, a prominent New Testament scholar who has taught at Texas Christian, Harvard, and Emory Universities and who served for many years as a leader of the Society of Biblical Literature. Often a figure of controversy, Funk has been described by Claremont University professor James M. Robinson as "the most brilliant, the most creative, though, understandably, the most alienated American New Testament scholar of our time."[5] The Seminar is officially sponsored by the Westar Institute, an organization directed by Funk. Originally, the Seminar's intention was "to examine every fragment of the traditions attached to the name of Jesus in order to determine what he really said."[6] Eventually, their work transcended this goal to include study of deeds and actions attributed to Jesus as well.

For this undertaking, Funk assembled an impressive array of scholars. Over two hundred were involved at different points in the Seminar's history, though usually only thirty to forty would take part in a single meeting. The group's most widely published rosters list seventy-four to seventy-nine persons, most of whom have earned doctorates and positions at respected academic institutions (even Verhoeven has a Ph.D. in mathematics).[7] From the outset, the Seminar sought to involve a wide spectrum of participants, insisting that its qualifications for membership involved academic ability, not ideological commitment. The presence or lack of religious faith was deemed irrelevant to the project.

Phase One

To meet the original goal of investigating the sayings of Jesus, the Seminar first compiled a numbered list of everything that Jesus is reported to have said in any document prior to 300 C.E. This list included all of the words attributed to Jesus in the Bible, as well as quotations found in apocryphal gospels and in other writings of early Christians. Notably, no sayings of Jesus are found in non-Christian literature; though Jewish and Roman writings occasionally mention Jesus, they contain no records of his speech or teaching.

The next task of the Seminar was to examine these sayings of Jesus to determine whether they were historically authentic or whether they had been attributed to him by Christians for one reason or another. Group members circulated papers arguing various positions and met twice a year to discuss the results of their research. Finally, they voted on whether a given saying ought to be regarded as authentic. The results of this voting were presented by classifying sayings according to a color scheme: red, pink, gray, or black. The "red" sayings were the ones deemed most likely to be authentic and the "black" sayings were those deemed least likely to be authentic. "Pink" and "gray" represented degrees of uncertainty. When scholars voted, they would indicate what color they thought the saying should be; the weighted average of all votes cast determined the final classification.

After six years, the group completed this phase of its program and published its results in a book called *The Five Gospels*. The name of this book reflects the conclusion that all pink and red sayings may be found in only five books, the four New Testament Gospels and the apocryphal Gospel of Thomas. Numerically, the results break down as follows:[8]

	Total Number of Sayings	Red Sayings	Pink Sayings	Gray Sayings	Black Sayings
Matthew	420	11	60	115	234
Mark	177	1	18	66	92
Luke	392	14	65	128	185
John	140	0	1	5	134
Thomas	201	3	40	67	91

This color scheme was one aspect of the Jesus Seminar's project that caught the attention of the popular press. Early on, Seminar members actually voted on sayings by placing colored beads into a hopper. The practice proved cumbersome and was discontinued, but the image of scholars "blackballing Jesus" proved irresistible to journalists. Also, comparisons were drawn to popular red-letter Bibles published in the twentieth century, in which the words of Jesus were printed in red type. Now, reporters would point out with glee, Bibles could use four colors for Jesus' words, depending on whether he really said them or not. In short, media reports almost always focused on the Seminar's negative conclusions.

Many of the findings *are* negative. Popular Bible verses classed as black sayings include Jesus' words regarding the salt of the earth (Matt. 5:13), bearing the cross (Mark 8:34), and being born again (John 3:3). All seven of his words from the cross are regarded as unauthentic (Mark 15:34; Luke 23:34, 43, 46; John 19:26–30), as are most of his sayings about himself, including his claim to be the Messiah (Mark 14:62) and "the way, the truth, and the life" (John 14:6). All sayings in which Jesus spoke of the end of the world or of a final judgment are black. Monologues by Jesus to which there could have been no witness are considered to be counterfeit, as are all verses in which Jesus expresses foreknowledge of events after his death.

In general, sayings recognized as red or pink tend to be ones that are not specifically Christian in tone. These include wisdom sayings that offer common sense observations about life in a memorable way and moral aphorisms that provide what might be regarded as good ethical advice apart from any specific religious doctrine. The only pink saying in John's Gospel is Jesus' lament that prophets have no honor in their own country (John 4:44) and the only red saying in Mark's Gospel is Jesus' suggestion to "give to the emperor the things that are the emperor's, and to God the things that are God's" (Mark 12:17).

Of all the sayings examined by the Jesus Seminar, the five that garnered the most votes for authenticity were

1. "If anyone strikes you on the right cheek, turn the other also" (Matt. 5:39);
2. "If anyone wants to sue you and take your coat, give your cloak as well" (Matt. 5:40);
3. "Blessed are you who are poor, for yours is the kingdom of God" (Luke 6:20);
4. "If anyone forces you to go one mile, go also the second mile" (Matt. 5:41); and
5. "Love your enemies" (Luke 6:27).

Notably, all five of these are found in material derived from the Q source. The majority of red and pink sayings also come from this early collection of Jesus' sayings. The next largest number of authentic sayings are found in the Gospel of Thomas, which is similar to Q in form, that is, a collection of sayings rather than a narrative account of Jesus' life. The significance of this point can be exaggerated, however, for only two of the Thomas sayings colored red or pink have no parallel in the canonical Gospels (Thom. 97 and 98; see page 45).

There has been some confusion over how to interpret the Seminar's findings. Popular reports usually build on the assertion that red means "definitely yes" and black means "definitely no" to assume that pink means "probably yes" and gray means "probably no." This seems logical, but may not be correct. The Seminar itself struggled to define exactly what was meant by the various colors. Two different official interpretations were offered to guide members in their voting and one member, Leif Vaage, offered a third colloquial interpretation that also became quite popular (see chart 4). There appears to have been confusion especially over the meaning of a gray vote. The official introduction to *The Five Gospels* declares that gray was intended to

Chart 4. What Do the Colors Mean?

*Sayings and Deeds: Option 1
(Official)*

*Sayings: Option 2
(Official)*

Red: I would include this item (or "narrative information") unequivocally in the database for determining who Jesus was.

Red: Jesus undoubtedly said this or something very like it.

Pink: I would include this item (or "narrative information") with reservations (or modifications) in the database.

Pink: Jesus probably said something like this.

Gray: I would not include this item (or "narrative information") in the database, but I might make use of some of the content in determining who Jesus was.

Gray: Jesus did not say this, but the ideas contained in it are close to his own.

Black: I would not include this item (or "narrative information") in the primary database.

Black: Jesus did not say this; it represents the perspective or content of a later or different tradition.

Deeds: Option 2 (Official)

Third Option (Colloquial)

Red: The historical reliability of this information is virtually certain. It is supported by a preponderance of evidence.

Red: That's Jesus!

Pink: This information is probably reliable. It fits well with evidence that is verifiable.

Pink: Sure sounds like Jesus.

Gray: This information is possible, but unreliable. It lacks supporting evidence.

Gray: Well, maybe.

Black: This information is improbable. It does not fit verifiable evidence, or it is largely or entirely fictive.

Black: There's been some mistake

Based on information from Robert W. Funk et al., *The Five Gospels*, 36–37, and *The Acts of Jesus*.

signify "a weak form of black"[9] but some have observed (based on the interpretations offered) that gray seems to be more of a weak form of pink. At issue is whether gray really does mean "probably no" or whether it means "maybe yes." For some, such a distinction comes down to splitting hairs; for others, the difference is considerable.

In practice, Seminar member Marcus Borg alleges that "gray frequently functioned as an 'I'm not sure' vote." Furthermore, when the voting on a controversial saying was divided, black votes would tend to cancel out pink and red ones so that the saying would end up being classed as gray. For example, the parable of the two sons in Matthew 21:28–31 ended up being printed in gray type even though only 11 percent of the voters actually cast gray votes for it (32 percent voted black and 58 percent either red or pink). The large number of gray sayings, then, do not necessarily represent material that is "probably unauthentic." Rather, according to Borg, the gray sayings are those on which "the verdict is not clear."[10] This perspective leads to a less negative interpretation of the overall results than that which has been popularly reported.

Given the mandates of the Seminar's research, its results can be read in a way that is surprisingly positive. Historical scholars tend to be very skeptical, especially when dealing with literature as tendentious as the Gospels. The Jesus Seminar embraced such methodological skepticism as a working principle, adopting a new version of an old motto: "When in sufficient doubt, leave it out" (compare page 20).[11] In other words, they were encouraged to err on the side of exclusion rather than inclusion, to discover a bare minimum of material that could be regarded as almost unquestionably authentic. Some members, it is said, voted black virtually all the time.[12] Even a few black votes could pull down the weighted average of a saying's final score in a way analogous to the effect a few Fs can have on a student's overall GPA. Granted this, the proportion of sayings that were deemed pink or red is impressive. The story that, by and large, went unreported was this: two hundred historians, relying on investigative techniques of critical scholarship, affirmed the authenticity of some 18 percent of the sayings attributed to Jesus in books that were written a generation after his death by people who made no pretense of being objective or unbiased in what they wrote. The media, however, missed this story, reporting instead the rather bland and predictable instances in which critical scholarship was unable to affirm convictions of religious piety.

Phase Two

The second phase of the Jesus Seminar's work involved investigation of propositions concerning the life and work of Jesus. Reading through stories about Jesus in the Bible and elsewhere, the Seminar developed lists of propositions such as the following:

> • Jesus was born in Bethlehem.
> • Jesus was of Davidic descent.

• Jesus cured Simon's mother-in-law.
• Jesus was crucified.

After discussion, the Seminar voted on each proposition, using once again the system of four colors (the above propositions were deemed black, gray, pink, and red, respectively).[13] They now defined these color codes as reflecting a sliding scale of reliability, from "virtually certain" (red) to "improbable" (black).[14] Sometimes the Seminar would also vote on how to color code a biblical passage "as a whole." This was to facilitate publication of their next volume, *The Acts of Jesus,* which would print all of the Gospel stories about Jesus in color type that reflected their reliability as historical accounts.[15]

Often the Seminar would vote on several different propositions regarding the same event. When considering the proposition "Mary conceived Jesus without sexual intercourse with a man" (black), they also voted on about a dozen related suggestions, such as "Jesus was conceived while Mary and Joseph were betrothed" (gray), "Mary conceived of Joseph" (gray), and "Mary conceived of some unnamed man by rape or seduction" (gray). The goal was to be thorough, to consider, as it were, every conceivable option. They even stopped to ask whether Mary was really the name of Jesus' mother (red).[16]

The language of these propositions was often worded carefully. For instance, a proposition derived from Mark 5:1–20 reads, "Jesus exorcized a man who thought he was demon-possessed" (gray).[17] So stated, members might regard the event as historical without thereby affirming that an exorcism of an actual demon occurred. Again, rather than polling members to determine whether they believe Jesus rose from the dead, the Seminar asked them to vote on whether "Jesus' resurrection from the dead involved the resuscitation of his corpse" (black) and on whether "the resurrection of Jesus was an event open to empirical verification" (black).[18] Such careful wording was necessary because some persons might claim that Jesus did rise from the dead in a sense other than that which these propositions meant to test. Theologian Rudolf Bultmann, for instance, used to claim that Jesus rose from the dead "in the kerygma [preaching] of the church."[19]

When *The Acts of Jesus* appeared in 1998, it color coded 387 reports of 176 separate events. Of these, ten events were rated red and nineteen pink. Thus, 16 percent of the events reported in the Gospels were deemed authentic, slightly less than the 18 percent of the sayings deemed authentic in *The Five Gospels.*

Phase Three

The Jesus Seminar has decided to publish yet another book, one that will describe the man Jesus as Seminar members see him. Such a collective witness may be difficult to produce. "There could be hopeless disagreement" cochair John Dominic Crossan says. "Bob Funk's Jesus is quite different from mine."[20] Still, those who have analyzed the Seminar's voting patterns believe that some consensus will be reached regarding general parameters for a Jesus biography. When Seminar members met in October 1997 and in March 1998, each submitted his or her own profile of who Jesus was. These will be compared and either correlated or published side by side.

According to work published so far, the Jesus that the Seminar envisions began as a disciple of John the Baptist, but he eventually rejected both the ascetic life that his mentor advocated and the apocalyptic message of a coming judgment that was supposed to motivate people to repent and adopt such a lifestyle. Instead, Jesus said the kingdom of God was already a reality, here and now, and he made a deliberate practice of eating and drinking in what was considered a profane style to celebrate this. An iconoclastic poet, he fraternized shamelessly with social outcasts and caricatured the empty values on which human behavior can be based. Favorite targets for his wit included reliance on wealth, uncritical respect for blood relatives, and the pomposity of religion. For Jesus, temples, priests, and all other accoutrements of religion were unnecessary, as were, ultimately, earthly possessions and family.

Jesus had a knack for telling parables and for coining paradoxical aphorisms that challenged usual ways of thinking. He also recalled and used secular proverbs but probably did not quote the scriptures. He became a traveling sage who wandered from village to village offering his eccentric brand of teaching to people in exchange for handouts. He did not call on people to repent or fast or observe the sabbath, nor did he make any theological statements about God. His message, if one can call it that, was primarily a challenge to social convention. He was a social critic, but not one who had any program or prescription for solving the world's ills. He ridiculed those who claimed to have answers and did not claim to have any answers himself. Otherwise, he was reticent and unassuming, neither enlisting followers nor initiating debate. He did not speak of himself at all, nor did he have any particular vision of the future.

He attracted attention all the same. Apparently, dozens of people began to follow him about. They (and others) would ply him with questions, to which he would never give direct answers. They also maintained that he was able to exorcize demons and cure diseases. Jesus went along with this, effecting some psychosomatic cures and accepting this as demonstrative that, indeed, life here and now can be all that it ought to be. Eventually, he made his way to Jerusalem, where he instigated some kind of incident in the temple area during a festival. He was arrested and quickly executed without a trial.[21]

The completion of this third phase of the Seminar's work does not necessarily signal its demise. The group continues to meet, discussing other projects, such as the attempt to discern the layering of traditions in the Gospel material, to determine in a rough chronological sense which material is most original and which was added at various stages of accretion. The Westar Institute has also begun related programs: a "Canon Seminar" that is revisiting the question of which documents ought to belong in the Bible, and a "Paul Seminar" that focuses on discerning the historical words and deeds of the famous first-century missionary. There is also talk of a "Creed Seminar" that will address implications of historical research for creeds and confessions of the church. With a stated agenda of "advocacy for religious literacy," the Westar Institute also sponsors a number of other projects. For example, it recently published a volume analyzing the presentation of Jesus in films.[22] Another goal involves the eventual publication of the Westar Institute's own version of the New Testament (tentatively titled "The *New* New Testament"). This volume will include some noncanonical material and will exclude material in the present New Testament thought to be unauthentic.

The Seminar and the Media

Observer Charlotte Allen describes the figure who emerges from the Seminar's work as "a dirt-poor, illiterate peasant sage from Galilee influenced perhaps by Greek Cynic philosophers."[23] He is also a "non-Christian Jesus"—a man who displays no interest in the end of the world, resurrection, or redemption—and a "no-frills" Jesus—a Jesus with little supernatural baggage but much respect for cultural diversity. This makes him very contemporary and potentially popular, with the world at large if not with the church. The Jesus of the Jesus Seminar, Allen muses, is "a Jesus for the America of the third millennium."[24] Allen is a journalist, not a historian or theologian, and some Seminar members may think her pithy comments trivialize the group's serious academic agenda. Nevertheless, the comments seem to capture the way this work has been perceived at a popular level.

Seminar members themselves are often cited in the media as describing Jesus in unconventional terms. Leif Vaage thinks Jesus was "a party animal, somewhat shiftless, and disrespectful of the fifth commandment: Honor your father and mother."[25]Arthur Dewey says, "There is more of David Letterman in the historical Jesus than Pat Robertson."[26] Funk agrees: "Jesus was perhaps the first stand-up Jewish comic."[27] Was he even religious? Not in the conventional sense. The Bible presents him as alienated from the religious institutions of his day, the temple and the synagogues. For the Jesus Seminar this was not because he wanted to start a better religion, but because he was adverse to institutional religion, period. "Starting a new religion," Funk says, "would have been the farthest thing from his mind."[28] But did he believe in God? Did he, for example, pray? "I think he prayed," Hal Taussig says, "but I don't think he made a big deal out of it."[29]

IMPLICATIONS OF THE
JESUS SEMINAR'S WORK

Robert Funk believes the Jesus Seminar is laying the foundations for a new reformation. "Christianity as we have known it is anemic and wasting away," he says. "It is time to reinvent Christianity, complete with new symbols, new stories, and a new understanding of Jesus."[30] He lays out the agenda for such a reformation in his book *Honest to Jesus*. Christian faith can continue, but it must become secularized spirituality rather than institutionalized religion.

Funk contrasts the development of "creedal Christianity" with the faith that inspired Jesus:

Popular creedalism insists on a miraculous birth, accrediting miracles, death on a cross understood as a blood sacrifice, a bodily resurrection, and Jesus' eventual return to hold cosmic court. We need only ask, Which of these doctrines derives from what we know of the historical Jesus? Which of them depends on Jesus' authorization? Or are they part of the mythological overlay invented by Jesus' early admirers?[31]

He contends that, indeed, Christianity as we know it was not inaugurated by Jesus, but by people like Peter and Paul. It is "a second-hand faith," not the religion *of* Jesus but a religion *about* him.[32] Jesus himself pointed people to something he called God's domain. Instead of looking to see what he saw, his followers tended to "stare at the pointing finger."[33]

Making Jesus the object of faith is certainly ironic, Funk says, since "the Jesus of whom we catch glimpses in the gospels may be said to have been irreligious, irreverent, and impious."[34] The church has had to ignore this "real Jesus" in order to perpetuate its religious views regarding the mythological figure. To illustrate, Funk cites the historic Apostles Creed:

> He was conceived by the power of the Holy Spirit
>   and born of the virgin Mary.
> He suffered under Pontius Pilate,
>   was crucified, died, and was buried . . .

What's missing? The *life* of Jesus! The framers (and confessors) of such a creed, Funk fumes, apparently believe that nothing worth mentioning lies between the miraculous birth of Jesus and his death on the cross. "The creed," he says, "left a blank where Jesus should have come."[35] And the Jesus that it leaves out is one who would not have approved of its content or even of the basic idea of having authoritative creeds in the first place. With the development of Christianity into a formal religion, Funk says, "the iconoclast became an icon."[36]

Funk goes on to outline his understanding of a faith that is based on the vision of Jesus rather than on the proclamations of others concerning him.[37] Many cherished doctrines, including blood atonement, resurrection, and apocalyptic promises of reward and punishment, will have to go. In their place will be an ethical spirituality that includes and nourishes. Jesus prioritized inclusivity and reciprocal forgiveness and advocated an "unbrokered relationship with God." He condemned the public practice of piety and made it clear that all rewards and punishments are intrinsic. If Christianity can be reconstituted as the faith *of* Jesus rather than as faith *in* Jesus, Christians will also have to abandon all sense of privilege, including the notion that they can be distinguished from others as "saved" or "redeemed" people who occupy a favorable position in God's eyes.

Marcus Borg interprets the implications of the Jesus Seminar's work in a less radical way.[38] Essentially, he believes, the Jesus Seminar has helped people to distinguish between "the pre-Easter Jesus and the post-Easter Jesus," that is, between the historical person who lived on this earth for a short time and the enduring figure who remains the subject of Christian tradition and experience. Borg makes this distinction with fewer value judgments than Funk does. Insights that came from early Christians are not necessarily less valuable than those that can be attributed to Jesus himself. For Borg, then, the color scheme reflects only the origin of the material, not its veracity. Some of the material in black he finds "quite wonderful." Even if the historical Jesus did not actually say, "I am the light of the world" (John 8:12), the early Christians who put these words on Jesus' lips believed he was the light of the world, and consideration of the experiences that led them to believe this may be as important for contemporary faith as is analysis of words that the Seminar prints in red type.

Why bother with a distinction at all then? For one thing, Borg says, the pre-Easter Jesus ceases to be a credible figure if attributes properly belonging to the post-Easter Jesus are ascribed to him. He ceases to be human, which is "neither good history nor good theology."[39] The problem for Borg is not that the church has developed confessional statements about Jesus based on post-Easter experiences, but that it has allowed these to eclipse its vision of Jesus as he was before Easter. He suggests that the Seminar's work may be understood as analogous to archaeology. It sorts out the layers of tradition, so that we may see what belongs properly to each layer (Jesus himself, the later church). Each layer is important, but each ought to be understood on its own terms. Christian faith, Borg continues, ought not be based solely on historical reconstructions of the pre-Easter Jesus any more than it should be based solely on creedal affirmations about the post-Easter Jesus. The goal should be to find "a dialogical and dialectical relationship between the two."[40]

Burton Mack is less interested in dialogue. An early member of the Jesus Seminar who dropped out before *The Five Gospels* was published, Mack embraces a radical skepticism regarding almost everything about Jesus that is not attested in the Q source (see pages 25–28). According to Mack, the effects of historical Jesus study such as that conducted by the Seminar should be devastating. It undercuts Christianity's claim to be the religion of Jesus. "It should bring to an end the myth, the history, the mentality of the Gospels," he avers.[41] The people behind the Q document did not view Jesus as the Messiah or Son of God, nor did they have any idea that his death offered them atonement for their sins. Nor did they believe he rose from the dead. "It's over," Mack concludes, without pity. "We've had enough apocalypses. We've had enough martyrs. Christianity has had a two-thousand year run, and it's over."[42]

CRITIQUE OF THE JESUS SEMINAR

The Jesus Seminar has its foes. Roused by the audacity of the group's claims, by the intensity of public response, and by awareness of what is at stake, critics across a wide spectrum have launched an unorganized counteroffensive. Craig Blomberg, a Baptist minister and professor of New Testament at Denver Seminary, appeals to the Christian doctrine that God's Spirit inspired the writing of the Bible, ensuring an accuracy that could not have been there otherwise.[43] Luke Timothy Johnson, a Roman Catholic layman and professor of New Testament at

Candler School of Theology (Emory University), advises people to ignore questions about the historical Jesus altogether and, if they need validation of their faith, to look at the quality of life demonstrated by those who confess it.[44] N. T. Wright, an Anglican priest and historian of the classical period, approves of the historical quest for Jesus but believes the Seminar's agenda was so shaped by opposition to fundamentalism as to foster a closed-minded caricature of scholarship that was itself ironically fundamentalistic.[45] Blomberg, Johnson, and Wright differ on their own ideas regarding Jesus as a figure in history, but they have this in common: they believe the Jesus Seminar is wrong, perhaps dangerously wrong. "Things of fundamental importance are being distorted," says Johnson.[46]

Rhetoric runs rampant. Boston University professor Howard Clark Kee calls the Jesus Seminar "an academic disgrace"[47] and Richard B. Hays of Duke University accuses them of "reprehensible deception."[48] Johnson charges Funk with "grandiosity and hucksterism" and derides the Seminar as "a ten-year exercise in self-promotion."[49] Some Seminar members can give as good as they get. Funk is reported to have had harsh words for other historical Jesus scholars, denouncing John Meier as "a blockhead" and dismissing N. T. Wright as "eccentric."[50]

Polemic runs the risk of derailing discussion from debate over issues worthy of consideration. For convenience, we may place criticisms leveled against the Jesus Seminar into seven broad categories. For what it is worth, I am presenting these according to what I personally regard as an ascending order of validity.

First, the *motives* of the Jesus Seminar are challenged. The group is often depicted in the media as comprising a goodly number of lapsed Christians. Journalist Charlotte Allen described the meetings as having "the air of a village atheists' convention," while also noting that "a favorite after-hours activity for members is to belt out the rousing evangelical hymns of their church-going childhoods."[51] Almost every media report mentions that Funk is a *former* evangelist who once led revival meetings in rural Texas[52] and that cochair Crossan is a *former* Roman Catholic priest (he left to marry, but admits his unorthodox views would have made an eventual departure unavoidable).[53] The implication may be that they and other Seminar members are simply working out frustrations born of their own crises, even getting revenge on institutionalized religion for not being more acceptable (or accepting). "Unfortunately," Wright observes slyly, "the attempt to escape from one's own past is not a good basis for the attempt to reconstruct someone else's."[54]

It seems unlikely, however, that all members of the Seminar would be so possessed or that Funk and Crossan would have been able to mold them so easily to their own designs. The academic credentials of the group and its founders are impeccable. No one bothered to question Funk's motives when he produced one of the most important Greek grammars of the twentieth century, or Crossan's when he did groundbreaking work on the literary genre of parables.[55] In any case, speculation regarding the psychological motives of scholars contributes little to evaluation of their work. Mixed or unclear motives do not invalidate research any more than pure motives (if such existed) would guarantee sound results.[56]

The *tactics* of the Jesus Seminar are disparaged, particularly the deliberate appeal to the media. Johnson says this is what provoked him to attack the group. Academic freedom allows scholars to say all kinds of outlandish things in restricted settings where the comments are open to critical scrutiny and debate. But when statements such as "Bible Scholars Say Jesus Didn't Promise to Return" become banner headlines or sound bites on the evening news, the context does not allow for caveats or counterarguments. "There was a deliberate decision to play to the media," Crossan admits, adding that he himself had to be persuaded by Funk that "there was an ethical necessity to let the public in on what we were doing."[57] The very purpose of the Westar Institute, according to Seminar member Vernon K. Robbins, was to get public attention for "serious religious scholarship" instead of allowing "the right-wing Christian community" to dominate all talk about religious matters.[58] "What's wrong with scholarly knowledge becoming common knowledge?" Funk asks. Heart surgeons and rocket scientists are adept at explaining their work to a general audience, at writing books and getting interviewed on television. Now it is time for the philosophers, theologians, and social scientists to do the same.[59] The debatable point, perhaps, is not whether the public ought to be brought in on such discussions, but whether in courting the media the Jesus Seminar opened the door for an inevitable sensationalism. Regardless of the Seminar's intentions, some would say that the media have oversimplified complex issues, presented minority views as consensus statements, and in other respects skewed the discussion in ways that the public is not able to detect or evaluate.

The *constitution* of the Jesus Seminar has been criticized and its claim to diversity rebutted. First, observers note that almost all members are white, male, and from North America. There was no apparent attempt to exclude others. Rather, the near homogeneity of race and gender is attributable to the current composition of the guild of biblical scholars as a whole, and participation of scholars from other countries was made difficult by location of the Seminar's meetings in North America. Nevertheless, a more diverse group may very well have reached different conclusions. Even given the location on this continent, the Jesus Seminar did not draw from as broad a pool of candidates as one might expect. As Hays has noted, no faculty members from Yale, Harvard, Princeton, Duke, Chicago, Union, Vanderbilt, Southern Methodist, or Catholic University were involved.[60] In terms of educational background, just five schools account for the doctorates of forty of the group's seventy-four rostered members.[61]

At the heart of this concern is a question regarding ideological diversity. Don A. Carson of Trinity Evangelical Divinity School describes the group as espousing "left-wing ideology,"[62] a charge that gains some credence when Seminar members contrast their work with that of "right-wing" Christians (see the quote by Robbins above). Johnson's charge that the group is "hostile to any traditional understanding of Jesus as defined by the historic creeds of Christianity"[63] is hard to rebut when its founder maintains that the *goal* of the Jesus Seminar is "to set Jesus free from the scriptural and creedal prisons in which we have entombed him."[64] But when Johnson claims that members of the Seminar were "self-selected" according to a prior agreement that they would portray Jesus as a countercultural figure who reflects the attitudes favored by liberal academics, we enter the realm of unprovable conspiracy theory. With regard to religious affiliation, the group has tried to be ecumenical, with partial success. About equal numbers of Protestants, Catholics, and nonreligious persons are involved. A few Jewish scholars take part. Even fundamentalists were invited to participate, but none accepted the offer. According to one report, "Southern Baptist scholars took part until pressure from within their denomination forced them to withdraw."[65]

The group's ideological slant, then, may have been unintentional, but it is also undeniable. The Jesus Seminar is not representative of the guild of New Testament historical scholarship today. Rather, it is representative of one voice within that guild, a voice that actually espouses a minority position on some key issues. Nevertheless, this voice is a chorus. The charge "They all think alike!" is not completely accurate but, in any case, begs the question "*Why* do they think alike?" The harmony of so many usually independent voices is precisely what demands that attention be given to this chorus of scholars.

The *content* of the Jesus Seminar's findings is dismissed as incredible. Blomberg maintains that "the Seminar's Jesus simply is not sufficiently Jewish to be a historically credible figure."[66] Wright echoes this concern but focuses on another. He finds the Seminar's noneschatological portrait of Jesus remarkable, since even they grant that eschatological elements were central to the thinking of John the Baptist and to the apostolic community. Are we really to believe that Jesus was "radically different from his predecessor and mentor and was radically misunderstood by almost all his followers from the very beginning"?[67] Numerous scholars complain that the Seminar has no adequate explanation for Jesus' death. If he was basically just a passive, witty spouter of aphorisms, why was he crucified? John Meier puts it this way: "Such a Jesus would threaten no one, just as the university professors who create him threaten no one."[68]

The Seminar has answers for all of these points. Some members suggest, for instance, that Jesus' death may have been more or less accidental. Perhaps, as indicated above, he pulled some kind of prank in the Jerusalem temple that got him labeled a subversive. Perhaps the Romans did not make fine distinctions between social critics and political revolutionaries. In any case, Jesus could have just said or done the wrong thing in the wrong place at the wrong time and been caught up in a somewhat cavalier Roman pogrom of potential insurgents. The Jesus Seminar, at any rate, maintains that its conclusions are based on more than a decade of hard work by competent scholars. The results ought not be dismissed just because they are untraditional or surprising. Rather, those who think the findings are incredible ought to review the process through which the Seminar came to these conclusions and consider the evidence on which the controversial findings are based. This leads us to the next point.

The Jesus Seminar's *methods of research* are subject to critique. First, the Seminar's application of criteria is criticized. They relied quite heavily on the criterion of dissimilarity, which grants historical authenticity to elements of the Jesus tradition that differ from what became normative in the Christian church and tends to deny the historical authenticity of elements that appear to have been Christianized (see pages 47–48). All historical scholars make some use of this criterion, but the Jesus Seminar is said to have used it so heavily as to guarantee a non-Christian Jesus. Ruling out sayings attributed to Jesus simply because they concur with later church tradition seems to assume that Jesus' followers did not learn anything from him. Other criteria are also challenged. The Jesus Seminar stressed "orality" as a test for the authenticity of Jesus' sayings, by which they meant that in an oral culture where few things were written down, the sayings most likely to be remembered were short, pithy ones such as aphorisms and parables. Critics claim that people in oral cultures have been known to memorize epics, such that the length of a quote alone ought not eliminate it from consideration.

The group accepted as basic operating assumptions a number of points that are debated within the field. For example, the Gospel of Thomas was understood to be a first-century work, contemporary with or earlier than the four New Testament Gospels. As indicated in chapter 2, many scholars date the composition of Thomas to the second century and regard it as dependent on the New Testament writings (see pages 44–45). The Seminar also relied more heavily on reconstructions of Q than many scholars would think appropriate. The Jesus that the Seminar finally presents is essentially the Jesus of Q, with eschatological elements expunged. Within the wider field of biblical scholarship, most writers would be more tentative regarding reconstructions and dating of Q material, and few would regard what derives from this source as having more intrinsic credibility than what derives from Mark, the earliest of the four Gospels.

The charge, essentially, is that many of the Seminar's conclusions were predetermined by its methodological presuppositions. We may see this with regard to the main finding about Jesus, namely, that he was a sage. Such a conclusion, it is said, was guaranteed by the Seminar's devotion to the criterion of orality. The process appears to critics to have gone something like this: the Seminar (1) started with the assumption that aphorisms are the type of material most likely to be authentic, (2) discovered that the material they deemed authentic on the basis of this assumption contained mainly aphorisms, and (3) concluded on the basis of this research that the authentic Jesus was a speaker of aphorisms, a sage.

A similar process of circular reasoning may have informed another of their findings: the conclusion that Jesus was noneschatological, that is, that he did not speak in apocalyptic language about the end of the world or a final judgment. Such a "discovery" appears to have been guaranteed by devotion to the criterion of dissimilarity. Apocalyptic language is attributed to Jesus in almost all of the early material (except Thomas), including the Seminar's much-vaunted Q source. But since the early Christian church was thoroughly eschatological in its views, the Seminar eliminated such material as too compatible with Christianity to fit its image of Jesus.

Within the academy of biblical studies, observers of the Jesus Seminar often recall a now-famous observation made by a promising member of the guild over a quarter of a century ago: "Methodology is not an indifferent net—it catches what it intends to catch."[69] The scholar who offered this comment was none other than Robert W. Funk.

In 1991, Funk listed sixty-four premises that the Seminar followed in its deliberation of material.[70] Though many were noncontroversial, statements such as the following were also included:

- Premise 10: The oral tradition exhibits little interest in biographical data about Jesus.
- Premise 29: John is a less reliable source than the other gospels for the sayings of Jesus.
- Premise 45: Only a small portion of the sayings attributed to Jesus in the gospels was actually spoken by him.

As Wright observes, statements such as these sound not like premises but conclusions.[71] Indeed, the media has often reported such statements as results of the Jesus Seminar's research. They were not results; they were presuppositions. In many instances, the Seminar itself has been forthright about saying this, but neither the press nor the public have appreciated the distinction.

Finally, the Jesus Seminar's *interpretation* of their own work is open to debate. Two points here are especially pertinent. First, the Seminar is inclined to equate "unverifiable" with "unauthentic." The project not only proceeds from an assumption that places the burden of proof upon authenticity (tradition is guilty unless proven innocent), but also dares to speak where historians would normally keep silent. Most scholars would grant, for instance, that the virgin birth of Jesus cannot be established as a historical event according to generally accepted criteria of historical science. The Jesus Seminar goes further. They claim that it is a historical fact that Jesus was conceived when his mother had sexual relations with a human male. For the Jesus Seminar, in other words, lack of support for a claim may be interpreted as evidence that the claim is false, and a post-Enlightenment historical-scientific view of reality is allowed to determine not only what is verifiable, but also what is believable. Such a stance turns a corner in the traditional understanding of the relationship that faith and philosophy bear to science and history. In America, for instance, a public school teacher would currently be regarded as violating constitutional separation of church and state for teaching in history class that Jesus was miraculously born to a virgin. History students should be taught only what is amenable to historical verification. The Jesus Seminar's vision, however, would empower public school teachers to tell their history students that Jesus was *not* born of a virgin, that the story of the virgin birth is a fictive tale composed by the church, that educated people should know it didn't really happen. Thus far, secular society does not seem to accept this vision but prefers the traditional pattern of respecting religious views when they are labeled as such.

Second, the Jesus Seminar has described its work in positivistic terms, claiming to offer "the assured results of historical-critical scholarship."[72] To some, this conveys a false impression of "objective" scholarship, according to which evidence is impartially weighed by academics who had no vested interest in the outcome. This was not the case. Funk says that Seminar members found the process of voting on Jesus' sayings to be as exciting as a sporting event, occasionally cheering or moaning the outcomes.[73] No scholar is ever completely objective, and those who composed the Jesus Seminar made no pretense at being such. Before the group was even a year old, Funk was announcing that its conclusions would combat the "pious platitudes of television evangelists and the doomsday writings of modern apocalyptists."[74] How did he know, already, what the findings would be? He didn't *know,* perhaps, but he certainly had a vision of what he hoped they would be! As Wright observes, the Jesus Seminar misrepresents its work if it claims to have conducted "a detailed objective study of individual passages, leading up to a new view of Jesus." Rather, it has worked through a detailed list of sayings in light of a particular view of Jesus to determine the extent to which this view is sustainable.[75]

The Jesus Seminar needs to be evaluated for what it is. It is not a collection of liberal apostates conspiring to undermine the Christian faith, nor is it a think tank of objective historians dispassionately following the strictures of academic research to see what they will reveal. It is a group of like-minded scholars testing a set of hypotheses regarding Jesus as a figure in history. The fact that they begin with hypotheses rather than with a blank slate does not invalidate their work. All serious historians do so, including all the historians of Jesus discussed in this book.

What marks the Jesus Seminar as unique — probably the *only* thing that marks them as unique — is that they are a group. Though other scholars may confer with colleagues, only the Jesus Seminar has invested the time, money, and energy to meet so regularly and under such circumstances that their publications can truly be termed the work of the whole group. This is not an inconsiderable accomplishment, and this fact alone earns them the attention they have received. Some have said that the Jesus Seminar represents only a small minority of New Testament scholars and, statistically, this is true. The number of persons with the academic and professional qualifications to have worked on *The Five Gospels* project would probably have been close to ten thousand in North America alone. Only seventy-four scholars consented to place their names on that volume. Still, that is seventy-three more names than are associated with any of the other positions described in this book. Although the group seems early on to have established parameters that limited their consideration to hypotheses that fit within a particular interpretative scheme, its research was genuine in terms of fine-tuning and revising those hypotheses in the crucible of critical debate. Thus, the group may represent only one of several available positions on the historical Jesus, but it represents that position well, having presented it with intense attention to detail. As the "Introduction" to *The Five Gospels* claims:

> The Fellows of the Seminar are critical scholars. To be a *critical* scholar means to make empirical, factual evidence — evidence open to confirmation by independent, neutral observers — the controlling factor in historical judgments. . . . Critical scholars adopt the principle of methodological skepticism: accept only what passes the rigorous tests of the rules of evidence. . . . Critical scholars practice their craft by submitting their work to the judgment of peers. Untested work is not highly regarded.[76]

5

JOHN DOMINIC CROSSAN

According to John Dominic Crossan, Jesus was a Jewish Cynic peasant with an alternative social vision.

—Marcus Borg[1]

Crossan's Jesus, whose role model seems to have been Stanley Kubrick's Spartacus, ate with outcasts and led a raggedy band of first-century hippies from village to village, preaching a message of radical egalitarianism to the oppressed denizens.

—Charlotte Allen[2]

For Crossan, the Jesus of history was the center of a Galilean Camelot, the halcyon days when Jesus and his band roamed the countryside, disregarding societal structures, defying hierarchical patterns, irritating elites and confounding the powerful, creating a grass-roots movement with nobodies while at the same time refusing to be its leader or mediator.

—Leander Keck[3]

Social revolutionary, Jewish Socrates, political troublemaker—this shocking, insightful portrait presents Jesus as a societal rebel who preached and practiced a message of radical egalitarianism.

—advertisement for John Dominic Crossan's
Jesus: A Revolutionary Biography

One thing can be said about John Dominic Crossan from the outset: no other scholar of the historical Jesus is more admired by his or her opponents. "Crossan is one of the most brilliant, engaging, learned, and quick-witted New Testament scholars alive today," opines N. T. Wright, before going on to conclude that the Irish savant's views about Jesus are nevertheless "almost entirely wrong."[4] Or, again, immediately after claiming that Crossan engages in "wild and insupportable conjectures," Ben Witherington notes that it will be unfortunate if this causes "the better parts of his work" to be dismissed.[5]

He has earned the praise through years of devotion to far-ranging scholarship. Archaeology, anthropology, sociology, source criticism, literary criticism—if a field has any usefulness for contemporary study of the New Testament, Crossan, it seems, has been there and left his mark. Now professor emeritus at DePaul University in Chicago, his knowledge of the ancient world appears to be encyclopedic. He has made seminal contributions to study of the parables and to research on apocryphal writings.[6] His name appears in bibliographies of books that have nothing to do with the historical Jesus and yet now, in retrospect, that topic seems to have been his primary concern all along.

Crossan engages in Jesus research for what he calls ethical and theological reasons as well as historical ones. As an avowed Christian, he is able, at times, to offer his somewhat disturbing conclusions "as a challenge within the Christian faith." He does not conceive of the task as a "search" or a "quest," which might imply the possibility of attaining a definitive answer once and for all. His preferred term for what he does is *reconstruction:* "something that must be done over and over again in different times and different places, by different groups and different communities, and by every generation again and again and again."[7]

In 1991, Crossan published *The Historical Jesus,* followed in 1998 by *The Birth of Christianity.*[8] Together, these studies represent a magnum opus of considerable stature. We will be concerned primarily with the first work, which according to a blurb on the jacket seeks to present "the first comprehensive determination of who Jesus was, what he did, and what he said." Whether it is "first" or "comprehensive," the book is certainly thorough. It devotes some two hundred pages to laying out an approach for understanding Jesus within his own historical context and then another two hundred to describing Jesus as Crossan envisions him. Complex methodological issues are engaged and yet the book remains informative and provocative throughout. Almost every reviewer comments on the "beauty" or "elegance" with which it is written, words not usually associated with theological tomes. "He seems incapable," says Wright, "of thinking a boring thought or writing a dull paragraph."[9] Indeed, Crossan has also released a series of popularized spin-offs from this project, designed to reach a wider audience:

> • *Jesus: A Revolutionary Biography* presents a synopsis of his more provocative ideas in a series of short vignettes tailored, it seems, for fans of *Reader's Digest;*

- *The Essential Jesus* offers a compendium of ninety-three quotes, Crossan's own translations of things he believes Jesus said, arranged one per page with illustrations and lots of white space;
- *Who Killed Jesus?* provides a popular account of his views on the crucifixion story and on the unjust slander of Jewish people as responsible for a crime in which (he believes) they were not actually involved.

The popular treatments, along with his involvement in the Jesus Seminar (which he cochairs), have brought a degree of celebrity to Crossan. It agrees with him. As comfortable chatting on *Larry King Live* as he is engaging in academic debates at meetings of the Society for Biblical Literature, he appears to have become to biblical studies what Carl Sagan was to astronomy. Unlike many scholars, he doesn't mind "being a personality," having his work interpreted with reference to his own life journey. Indeed, he invites it. In *The Historical Jesus,* he eschews objectivity as unobtainable and spurious, and offers in its place a more realistic credential for scholarship: honesty.[10] As an instance of such honesty, he maintains that he did not endeavor to find a Jesus whom he liked or disliked, and that, in fact, he found one whom he personally is unable to follow. He imagines this conversation with the historical Jesus:

> "I've read your book, Dominic, and it's quite good. So, now you're ready to live by my vision and join me in my program?"
>
> "I don't think I have the courage, Jesus, but I did describe it quite well, didn't I, and the method was especially good, wasn't it?"
>
> "Thank you, Dominic, for not falsifying the message to suit your own incapacity. That at least is something."
>
> "Is it enough, Jesus?"
>
> "No, Dominic, it is not."[11]

CROSSAN'S METHOD FOR STUDYING JESUS

Crossan's approach entails analysis at what he calls three levels of operation: the microcosmic, the mesocosmic, and the macrocosmic.

The microcosmic level involves *treatment of literary sources*. He provides a fairly comprehensive "inventory" of traditions about Jesus, assigning each element of tradition two numbers, separated by a slash. The first number indicates the age of the source in which the tradition first appears:

1 = 30 to 60 C.E.

2 = 60 to 80 C.E.

3 = 80 to 120 C.E.

4 = 120 to 150 C.E.

A second number indicates how many independent attestations to the tradition can be found in all of the sources considered. Thus, Crossan's program claims to rely heavily on the dating of sources and on what is usually called "the criterion of multiple attestation" (see pages 46–47). The value of a tradition for historical consideration is enhanced by a low first number and/or a high second number. Thus, various sayings of Jesus about "kingdom and children"[12] are given a 1/4 rating (very good), meaning that such sayings are attested in four independent sources (Thom. 22:1–2; Mark 10:13–16; Matt. 18:3; John 3:1–10), at least one of which dates from the earliest period. The tradition that identifies Jesus as the divine Word who "in the beginning was with God and was God" (John 1:1) gets a 4/1 rating (very bad) because it is found in only one source, one that Crossan dates to the latest of the four periods.

This system appears to be more scientific than the Jesus Seminar's color coding approach, which is said to have been influenced unduly by predilections of Seminar members and by an overreliance on the controversial criterion of dissimilarity. Still, Crossan's dating of sources has been sharply challenged.[13] He places a good deal of apocryphal material in the earliest layer, including most of the Gospel of Thomas and a "Cross Gospel" that he has reconstructed from the passion narrative of the Gospel of Peter. The main material from the New Testament to fall into this earliest layer is the Q source and a group of miracle stories found in both Mark and John. Wright observes that "all but a few within the world of New Testament scholarship would find this list extremely shaky, and all except Crossan himself would have at least some quite serious points of disagreement with it."[14] In his book *The Birth of Christianity,* Crossan lays out six "crucial decisions about sources" that are foundational for his work: (1) the priority of Mark, (2) the existence of the *Q Gospel,* (3) the dependence of John on the Synoptic Gospels, (4) the independence of the Gospel of Thomas from the canonical Gospels, (5) the independence of the *Didache* (an early Christian book of community rules), and (6) the existence and independence of the *Cross Gospel.* He admits that these presuppositions become increasingly controversial as the list proceeds, but he also offers fairly extensive reasons for holding to these views even when his position is a lonely one.[15]

The mesocosmic (second) level of operation involves *historical reconstruction of the place and time in which Jesus lived.* Crossan is extremely knowledgeable, with regard to both the Greco-Roman world and the specific Palestinian environment. He draws on a wide variety of sources, citing not only such obvious references as Josephus and Cicero but also little-known papyri, scraps of ancient manuscripts archived in various museums throughout the world. He attends, of course, to the political realities, but does not stop there. Every detail that can be ascertained must be taken into account as potentially relevant: how business was conducted, how homes were built, how medicine was practiced, and so forth. The goal at this level of investigation is to establish a context for understanding who Jesus was and what his words and deeds would have meant.

Two parts of this context that Crossan deems especially significant are the general situation of peasant unrest and the specific phenomenon of Cynic philosophers. As for the former, Crossan describes Palestine at the time of Jesus as being in a period of *turmoil,* a technical term here for the first of three stages that would lead ultimately to a disastrous war with Rome in 66–70 C.E. (the next two stages are conspiracy and open unrest).[16] The principal causes of this turmoil were oppressive taxation and social policies that continued to worsen from year to year. Within this context, Crossan describes various types of peasant resistance that could be found; tales of protesters, prophets, bandits, and messiahs are all recounted by the Roman historian Josephus. All this will serve as background to his presentation of Jesus as a somewhat different type of subversive, one that he thinks is best described by the term *magician.*

The phenomenon of Cynic philosophers has already been discussed in chapter 3. The Cynics, Crossan suggests, viewed life as a struggle of "nature against culture" and their allegiance was squarely with the former. From a religious perspective, they represent what anthropologist Bryan Wilson has called "an *introversionist* response to the world"—one that assumes the world is irredeemably evil such that people must abandon it (rather than amend it or wait for God to enact some radical reform).[17] This discussion too will serve as background for Crossan's presentation of Jesus, whom he calls "a peasant Jewish Cynic" who espoused a view he calls "ethical eschatology."

Crossan's work at this descriptive level of operation is the least controversial. It involves basic research common to all historical study. Few scholars would have major disagreements with his reconstruction of the historical world at the time of Jesus, though numerous fine points are debated. Indeed, even his opponents often rely on him as a resource for information in areas on which he is an obvious expert. What *is* sometimes debated, however, is the relevance of particular information for understanding Jesus. In other words, he is sometimes thought to cast his methodological net too far and wide, bringing into play information about Greco-Roman society that may not have had much bearing on life in the villages of Palestine.[18] At issue is the extent of the Hellenization of Galilee, and historical scholars are divided on their analysis of this point.

The macrocosmic (third) level of operation involves *analysis of the Jesus movement from the perspectives of social and cultural anthropology.* Crossan attempts to reconstruct the social dynamics and structure of the world in which Jesus lived and to compose likely scenarios that relate the nuggets of tradition about Jesus to this reconstructed world. He draws upon studies regarding preindustrial peasant societies, colonial protest movements, and so forth, illuminating the value such a culture would place on honor and shame and describing the tensions that would evolve from a system of patron-client relationships. The breadth of his knowledge in this regard is impressive. Many have noted that Crossan's work presents not simply a historical study of Jesus but a comprehensive, multidisciplinary study of Jesus as a historical person.

One aspect of sociocultural analysis is especially important for Crossan's work, namely, his understanding of the system of brokerage that held Mediterranean society together. Drawing on the work of anthropologist Gerhard Lenski, Crossan describes the Roman world as a society of "haves" and "have nots." About 10 percent of the population comprised aristocrats and their retainers, with the rest being artisans, peasants, or worse (beggars, bandits, and other "expendables"). In lieu of a middle class, society required brokers, clients of wealthy patrons who would themselves become patrons to others. The understanding of this system is so integral to Crossan's study of Jesus that it determines the very organization of his book. *The Historical Jesus* is divided into three main parts: (1) Brokered Empire, (2) Embattled Brokerage, and (3) Brokerless Kingdom. He presents Jesus' call for people to rely on God alone as a fundamental challenge to the fabric of his social world.

In general, Crossan's work at this level has been appreciated and accepted. The criticisms that have been offered tend to indicate that his use of materials is somewhat selective, not taking into account alternative possibilities. He has been said to confuse the social categories of "peasant" and "artisan,"[19] and some think he is too quick to follow Horsley in categorizing Jesus' affront to the traditional system as a form of banditry (see pages 52–54).

Crossan's method ultimately consists of an attempt to bring these three levels of operation together. He seeks to interpret the source material that he considers most likely to be historically authentic in light of what his historical reconstruction and interdisciplinary analysis reveals about Jesus' historical and social context.

CROSSAN'S PORTRAIT OF JESUS

As an initial observation, we may note that for Crossan the life and mission of Jesus are what counts in terms of historical significance. In this respect, he may be contrasted with Paul who maintained that the three things "of first importance" were the death, burial, and resurrection of Christ (1 Cor. 15:3–4). For Crossan, the first of these is less important than the so-called apostle thinks, and the second and third did not happen. As usual, Crossan is honest and clear: "My thesis . . . is that Christian faith is not Easter faith."[20]

Jesus and the Brokerless Kingdom

Jesus was a member of the peasant class, not the educated, scribal class. He was probably illiterate, and his message was one that would be meaningful primarily to peasants. Like the Cynics, he was concrete, not theoretical. He acted in ways that involved a shattering of convention with regard to matters that touched on the stuff of everyday life: dress, meals, family, and so forth. There were, however, differences. The Cynics were Greeks, they were usually associated with urban centers, and they were known to be individualists; Jesus was Jewish, kept to the villages and countryside, and had a social vision.

Jesus tried to inaugurate the "brokerless kingdom of God." He used the language of Israel's prophets to speak of the kingdom of God but presented this "not as an apocalyptic event in the imminent future but as a mode of life in the immediate present."[21] He tried to subvert the patron-client system of his day by encouraging everyone, especially the lowest classes, to have "unmediated physical and spiritual contact with God and unmediated physical and spiritual contact with one another."[22] He was opposed, in principle, to any form of hierarchy (including that of the traditional family system) that divides people along generational and gender lines. Drawing on such texts as Luke 11:27–28; 12:51–53; and 14:25–26, Crossan insists that Jesus would "tear the hierarchical and patriarchal family in two along the axis of domination and subordination."[23] By claiming that God's kingdom is for children (Mark 10:13–15), Jesus basically maintained that it is for anybody or—more to the point—for nobodies. He viewed himself and his companions as examples of such nobodies and told witty parables likening the group to impure leaven (Matt. 13:33) or uncontrollable weeds (13:24–30) whose influence cannot be contained.[24]

Jesus' vision of life informed by God's radical justice came to expression in his two most characteristic activities, which Crossan describes under the heading "Magic and Meal." The first term refers to what biblical scholars traditionally call miracles and the second to Jesus' practice of eating with outcasts.

First, the "magic." Crossan accepts as historically authentic a number of stories of Jesus' miracles, all ones that record him healing the sick or casting out demons. He appeals to a distinction some medical anthropologists make between disease and illness. Disease is the physical condition; illness the social meaning attributed to this condition.[25] Crossan emphasizes that the historical Jesus cured people of illness, even though he did not and could not cure disease. Through Jesus' actions, for instance, lepers were deemed clean and reintegrated into society. To ask whether their lesions actually closed would impose a modern notion of healing that misses the point. The lesions remained, but as far as people in the first century were concerned, Jesus was able to heal the sick.[26] Likewise, Crossan insists that Jesus did perform exorcisms in which both he and his observers believed a literal spiritual being that had invaded a person's body was forcibly ejected. But Crossan himself does not believe such spirit-beings exist; he assumes Jesus was delivering people from some sort of psychosomatic trauma similar to what might be diagnosed today as multiple personality disorder.[27]

What is most significant about Jesus' healing activity for Crossan is that he enacted these cures without official authorization and that he did so free of charge! Crossan uses the term *magic* advisedly, reserving the word *miracle* for acts of divine power that operates in accord with regular religious channels. Jesus enables people to access divine power apart from established religion. Thus, Crossan's identification of Jesus as a magician is similar to that of Morton Smith (see pages 56–58), but Crossan goes further in exploring the social meaning of that categorization. *Magic,* says Crossan, is the term religious leaders use to denigrate miracles done by the wrong sort of people. Magic is to religion what social banditry is to politics.[28] Jesus' unsanctioned miracles have social implications. As he hints in one story, those who are healed without going through the appropriate channels may conclude that they are forgiven as well (Mark 2:1–12). What need will they have for priests or scribes (religious brokers)?[29]

These stories can be read with a political slant also. Crossan views the prevalence of exorcism stories in the Gospel tradition through the lens of cultural anthropology, noting that widespread belief in demon possession is most typical for societies in which there is an occupying colonial power. The story in Mark 5:1–13 is particularly telling, for there the demons that possess the afflicted person are actually named "Legion," the term used to designate a contingency of Roman troops, such as those who had taken possession of the very territory where this tale is recounted. When the demons enter a herd of swine and rush into the sea, one can easily catch an image of Palestinian hope, an image of Roman soldiers-demons-pigs running back into the sea from whence they apparently came. Building on Mary Douglas's proposal that the physical body is a microcosm of the social body, Crossan suggests that exorcisms are a form of "individuated symbolic revolution."[30]

The second element of Jesus' mission that is essential for Crossan is the practice of open table fellowship, or what he prefers to call "open commensality." In Jesus' social setting, meals were governed by rules of conduct that went well beyond modern concern for etiquette. Strict guidelines determined who was allowed to eat with whom and where the participants were expected to sit (or recline, as was the custom). Meals, even more than an individual's body, were viewed as microcosms of society, and so were fraught with symbolic meaning. Mere participation in a communal meal implied a general endorsement of the other diners, and acceptance of one's specific place at the table implied recognition of one's social standing relative to that of the others (see Luke 14:7–11). In the face of such conventions, Jesus made a point of indiscriminately eating with anyone, including those who were regarded as outcasts. He told a parable likening the kingdom of God to a person who goes into the streets to invite the poor, the crippled, the blind, and the lame to his banquet (Luke 14:21–23). He openly flaunted propriety by ignoring the boundaries between slave and free, male and female, pure and impure, patron and client, rich and poor.[31]

The conjunction of these two activities, magic and meals, is significant for Crossan. In exchange for free healing, Jesus and his followers would often be given meals. But these meals were not just a means of supporting the mission, for that could have been accomplished in other ways. The meals themselves were integral to the mission, for they became occasions for actualizing what the magic was really about. No one could be excluded because they had been categorized as sick, sinful, demon-possessed, or unclean. Jesus' generosity with spiritual aid would inspire villagers to generosity with physical sustenance.

Together, these two activities challenged what was "normal" for Jewish religion and for Roman power. Jesus' vision of "shared egalitarianism" was an implicit attack on his social system, a system that depended on patronage and brokerage. Health care and nourishment are basic needs of earthly life. By demonstrating that people can receive these things directly from God and from each other, Jesus struck at the very heart of what made his social system work (though, of course, it worked better for some than for others). If people were actually to begin sharing with each other, they would have little need for patrons, much less brokers. With typical literary flair, Crossan describes why the enterprise Jesus started could be called a "movement":

> The mission we are talking about is not, like Paul's, a dramatic thrust along major trade routes to urban centers hundreds of miles apart. Yet it concerns the longest journey in the Greco-Roman world, maybe in any world, the step across the threshold of a peasant stranger's home.[32]

In his own way, Jesus the Jewish Cynic was a social and political reformer. The open sharing of healing and food presented a political threat to Roman society. It was no less than "a strategy for building or rebuilding peasant community on radically different principles than those of honor and shame, patronage and clientage."[33]

Two further points can be noted. First, Crossan emphasizes that Jesus spoke of God's kingdom in present terms only. He grants that early on, Jesus was a disciple of John the Baptist who used apocalyptic language to speak of a future consummation of all things to be enacted by God at the impending judgment. But Crossan regards Luke 7:28 as an authentic saying of Jesus and he interprets the latter part of this verse ("the least in the kingdom is greater than John") to mean that Jesus changed his mind about his mentor and rejected his apocalyptic message to espouse what Crossan calls "ethical eschatology." The latter view favors nonviolent resistance to systemic evil; it does not wait for God to act violently to judge the world but assumes God is waiting for us to act nonviolently to redeem it. The bottom line for Crossan is that Jesus "never spoke of himself or anyone else as the apocalyptic Son of Man" and he never spoke of God's kingdom as anything but a reality to be experienced here and now.[34]

Second, Crossan wants to make clear that Jesus did not want to be viewed as a mediator himself. The inherent danger in his mission as described above was that *he* would become the new broker of God's privileges (such as healing). To prevent this from happening, Jesus remained itinerant, moving from village to village so that no one place could ever be deemed his headquarters. He insisted that any who regarded themselves as his followers be itinerant also. The last thing he ever would have wanted would have been to be viewed as a mediator between God and God's people.[35] Eventually, Crossan decides against speaking of Jesus as having disciples at all. The better term is *companions*, and Jesus' relationship to these companions is one not of mediation but of empowerment: "The kingdom is not his monopoly. . . . He does not initiate its existence. He does not control its access."[36]

Jesus' Death and What Followed

What happened to this self-effacing proponent of justice and generosity? Crossan suggests the following scenario. He visited Jerusalem, where the act that had played so well in rural Galilee was met with swift and brutal resistance. His message of spiritual and economic egalitarianism created a disturbance at the temple ("the seat and symbol of all that was nonegalitarian")[37] and this time soldiers were on hand who were well trained at dealing with such disturbances. Jesus was hauled outside the city and crucified. He died. The soldiers then either left his body on the cross or threw it on the ground and covered it with dirt. In either case, it was eaten by dogs.

Most of this, Crossan admits, is guesswork—but that is his main point! A disturbance in the Jerusalem temple is well attested (Mark 11:15–19), as are the attribution of antitemple sayings to Jesus (Mark 14:58; Thom. 71). But since Jesus' followers all fled in terror when he was arrested no one knows what happened after that, except that Jesus was crucified. The fact of his crucifixion can be established by both Roman and Jewish sources in addition to Christian ones. But the elaborate passion narratives that the Gospels have constructed regarding this event are fiction. Crossan believes the stories were created years later through the conjunction of two processes. First, literate and sophisticated Christians scoured the Jewish scriptures to find texts that dealt with suffering and vindication. They created narrative incidents to correspond to such nuggets, which then came to be viewed as prophecies of what would happen. For example, the division of Jesus' garments by lot (Mark 15:24) derives from Psalm 22:18, and the noontime darkness at his crucifixion (Mark 15:33) comes from Amos 8:9.[38] The method was "hide the prophecy, tell the narrative and invent the history."[39] According to Crossan, these exegetically derived nuggets were then woven into a biographical story by women in the Jerusalem community as part of the traditional process of female lament and ritual mourning. This, of course, helps explain why much of the burial and resurrection story is told from the perspective of women. The "female lament tradition turned the male exegetical tradition into a passion-resurrection story once and for all."[40]

Thus, the passion narratives are "not *history remembered but prophecy historicized*."[41] They reveal more about the concerns of the early church than about the fate of the historical Jesus. The now lost "Cross Gospel" (see pages 45–46) turned the story into a narrative of a type Crossan calls "Innocence Rescued." Later, the Gospel of Mark revised this account according to another typological narrative format that Crossan calls "Martyrdom Vindicated." The essential difference between the two was that the first model used a resurrection motif to present Jesus being saved from death before the eyes of his enemies. The later version made the death itself salvific and, though keeping a resurrection, postponed vindication to the parousia. Salvation "was not from but through death, not in the here below, but in the imminent hereafter."[42]

Resurrection stories were created not only to provide closure (rescue or vindication) to an otherwise unbearable account but also to legitimate power claims in the developing church. Crossan thinks the earliest stage of tradition is represented by the Gospel of Thomas, which does not speak of resurrection at all, but of "unbroken and abiding presence."[43] In other words, Jesus' followers believed that in some sense he was still with them after he died, empowering them to continue his mission, to imitate his lifestyle, and to practice free healing and open table fellowship, what Crossan calls "open commensality." Paul represents a later stage, claiming to have experienced an apparition of the risen Jesus in some sort of a trance. Paul uses this claim, notably, to justify his position as "an apostle" (1 Cor. 15:1–11). Still later, we get the stories in Matthew, Luke, and John of Jesus walking about on earth after his death, appearing to people in a physical, tangible way. These, Crossan claims, are not "factual history" but "fictional mythology."[44] The point of the stories was not their proclamation that Jesus was raised so much as their identification of those to whom he chose to appear and commission. They are "deliberate political dramatizations of the priority of one *specific leader* over another, of this *leadership group* over that *general community*. . . . They detail the origins of Christian leadership, not the origins of Christian faith."[45]

The bottom line, at any rate, is that the passion and resurrection narratives reveal almost nothing about what really happened to Jesus in Jerusalem. Devoid of sources, minus his microcosmic level, Crossan attempts to postulate a reasonable synopsis of what may have happened based on knowledge of the world at that time. He accepts (as do most historians) that Jesus was arrested in response to an incident at the temple. What that was, we cannot be sure; Jesus probably did something (such as upsetting a table) to demonstrate symbolically that his egalitarian movement would "destroy" the temple. It makes sense within the parameters of that place and time to assume he would be arrested for this. After that, what makes most sense is a tale of "casual brutality":

> I do not presume at all any high-level consultations between Caiaphas or Pilate about or with Jesus. They would no doubt have agreed before the [Passover] festival that fast and immediate action was to be taken against any disturbance and that some examples by crucifixion might be especially useful at the start. I doubt very much if Jewish police and Roman soldiery needed to go too far up the chain of command in handling a Galilean peasant like Jesus.[46]

So there is no need, historically, for a trial, much less for the series of trials (before Caiaphas, Pilate, and even Herod) reported in the Gospels.

And there is no need for a burial either. The Romans crucified thousands of Jews, Crossan points out, and yet to date only one skeleton of a crucified person has ever been found. The reason: they weren't buried. Crucifixion was an act of state terrorism, and a good part of the terror lay in its aftermath. Being devoured by beasts was a supreme Roman penalty, and historians insist that this was typically the fate of crucifixion victims. "What we often forget about crucifixion," writes Crossan, "is the carrion crow and scavenger dog who respectively croak above and growl below the dead or dying body."[47]

Crossan knows, of course, that the Gospels claim Jesus was an exception to this policy, but their stories reveal desperate hope. The account that Crossan deems earliest says Jesus was taken down from the cross by his Jewish enemies (Gospel of Peter 6:21–22). The next layer of tradition has him being placed in a tomb (safe from the dogs) by a member of the Jewish Council (Mark 15:42–47). Later, we hear that the tomb was brand new and belonged to a rich man who was actually a disciple of Jesus (Matt. 27:57–61). Still later, we are told that this tomb was in a garden (John 19:38–42). Thus, the tradition grew "from burial by enemies to burial by friends, from inadequate and hurried burial to full, complete, and even regal embalming."[48] Crossan no doubt recalls his Shakespeare ("The lady doth protest too much, methinks") and like Queen Gertrude in Hamlet decides such apologetics serve only to underscore the intolerable nature of the truth. By Easter morning, no one who cared knew where the body of Jesus was. But everyone knew about the dogs.

For those who take such a "denial" of the resurrection as incompatible with Crossan's claim to be a Christian, he offers the following theological comment: "Bodily resurrection has nothing to do with a resuscitated body coming out of its tomb. . . . Bodily resurrection means that the *embodied* life and death of the historical Jesus continues to be experienced. . . . [It continues] to form communities of like lives."[49]

Crossan claims no interest in offending Christian sensibilities. His demeanor is decidedly different from those scholars who appear to delight in scandalizing the pious. He says his chapter on the passion narratives was the hardest one to write— *methodologically* hard because of the lack of sources, but also hard for another reason:

> It is hard not only for those who have faith in Jesus, but also for those who have faith in humanity, to look closely at the terror of crucifixion in the ancient world. . . . But since that world did in thousands what our century has done in millions, it is necessary to look with cold, hard eyes at what exactly such a death entailed.[50]

Birth of Christianity

In his second major tome on this subject, Crossan endeavors to show what happened in the first two decades after the execution of Jesus, before the developments that become evident in the writings of Paul. He considers the best witnesses to these "lost years" between Jesus and Paul to be Q and Thomas, and to a lesser extent, his reconstructed "Cross Gospel." The social backdrop for the story he finds there is one driven by Roman policies of urbanization and concomitant ruralization: the development of cities under Roman imperialism dislocated the peasant population in rural areas where indebtedness and taxation were on the rise and dispossession of the land became the rule. Against this backdrop, Crossan sketches two streams of earliest Christianity: the Life Tradition, centered in Galilee, where primarily rural Christians emphasized the sayings of Jesus, and the Death Tradition, centered in such places as Jerusalem, Damascus, and Antioch, where primarily urban Christians emphasized the death and resurrection of Jesus.[51]

As indicated above, Crossan sees the development of the Death Tradition as a conjunction of (male) scribal exegesis and (female) lament tradition. Much of *The Birth of Christianity,* however, is devoted to tracing the development of the Life Tradition, which Crossan thinks can be discerned in redactional emendations in the early collections of Jesus' sayings. He identifies, for instance, three types of eschatology in this early material: (1) ethical eschatology, which "negates the world by actively protesting and nonviolently resisting a system judged to be evil, unjust, and violent" (this is what Crossan thinks the historical Jesus espoused), (2) apocalyptic eschatology, which "negates this world by announcing that in the future, and usually the imminent future, God will act to restore justice in an unjust world" (this is found in what Crossan thinks is later material in Q), and (3) ascetical eschatology, which "negates this world by withdrawing from normal human life in terms of food, sex, speech, dress, or occupation" (this is found in what Crossan thinks is later material in Thomas). In short, Crossan claims that Jesus espoused ethical eschatology, but that this was transmuted into apocalyptic or ascetical varieties within the first two decades after his execution.[52] Yet another development of the Life Tradition can be seen in an early Christian document called the *Didache,* which recounts an attempt on the part of Christian "householders" to contain the more radical elements of the itinerant movement. Jesus' call for people to abandon their possessions, for instance, is translated into an encouragement of salvific almsgiving: "having nothing" becomes "sharing everything."[53]

Crossan finds one locus in which the Life Tradition and the Death Tradition come together in earliest Christianity: the Common Meal. This principal ritual act of the early Christians was interpreted with symbolic reference to Jesus' death and resurrection but also signified the inclusive, communal sharing that was a hallmark of Jesus' ethical eschatology. In those years, we must remember, the Eucharist was a full supper, not just the token sip and morsel distributed in most Christian churches today. In a society where food was scarce and hunger constant, even those who invested this meal with symbolic and sacramental significance could not have denied its fundamental meaning:

> The Common Meal Tradition may look to a Last Supper in the past, to a communal meal in the present, or to a messianic banquet in the future—or, quite validly, to all of those at the same time. But it can never get away from this: *it is in food and drink offered equally to everyone that the presence of God and Jesus is found.* . . . So the Lord's Supper is political criticism and economic challenge as well as sacred rite and liturgical worship. . . . Christians claim that God and Jesus are peculiarly and especially present when food and drink are shared equally among all.[54]

CRITIQUE OF CROSSAN'S STUDY OF JESUS

Many of the criticisms that have been leveled against Crossan's work are similar to those made with regard to the Jesus Seminar, which he cochairs.

First, his whole method of operation is criticized as idiosyncratic, tendentious, and circular. He is said to approach the materials with unwarranted skepticism, ignoring the basic biographical interest implied by the literary genre of the canonical Gospels, and assuming that Jesus' disciples would be quick to invent sayings for their teacher. Witherington bristles at his cute description of those disciples as "people not parrots," noting that "disciples in early Jewish settings were learners, and, yes, also reciters and memorizers."[55]

As already noted, very few (if any) scholars would accept his scheme for dating and classifying materials. Many think Mark is as reliable a source as Q and most think the bulk of material in the canonical Gospels predates almost everything in the apocryphal writings. The great majority of scholars believe that the passion narratives assumed a fairly fixed form early on rather than coming together at the tail end of the process, as Crossan has it.[56] If this is true, then we do have fairly reliable sources for this part of the story that he has not taken into account.

Thus, Crossan's reconstruction of the last week of Jesus' life (which he admits is guesswork) has not fared well in the world of scholarly critique.

Wright argues that Crossan's dating of materials is in fact the *result* of his understanding of the historical Jesus rather than the *grounds* for it. Spurning objectivity but extolling honesty, Crossan wants us to trust him to provide us with a worthy image of Jesus and to accept his views on source materials precisely because they will lead us there. For Crossan, history itself remains a matter of brokerage, with "the historian as patron and the reader as client."[57] But then the question has been raised as to whether Crossan's presentation is really dependent upon his idiosyncratic source theories. Among others, Robin Scroggs has questioned whether the appropriation of apocryphal materials has significantly affected the final portrait.[58] Many scholars have noted that Crossan does not always feel obliged to follow his own system when it does not take him where he wants to go. Sayings in which Jesus predicts his apocalyptic return are found in the first stratum and have multiple attestation but are regarded as coming from later tradition.[59] Similarly, Crossan insists that Jesus did not choose twelve disciples and that the Last Supper did not take place, despite early, multiple attestation for both traditions. Presumably, appointment of the twelve runs counter to Crossan's image of Jesus opposing hierarchies and the story of the Supper presents a somewhat exclusive meal, marred by talk of mediation ("my body given for you").[60] We may do best to say that Crossan tries to establish interrelationships between his proposals regarding source materials and his portrait of Jesus, while recognizing that the two are not necessarily interdependent.[61]

The situation most scholars face in evaluating Crossan's work, then, is almost the opposite of what the organization of the book may seem to present. Most scholars are not going to be persuaded initially to accept his novel dating of materials and proceed from there to accept the implications of such dating for historical Jesus research. Instead, the test will be whether Crossan's hypothesis about Jesus holds up on other grounds—basically, whether it makes sense within the context of the social and historical world brought to light through his other two levels of analysis (historical reconstruction and social/cultural anthropology). If it does, then scholars might be inclined not only to accept the portrait but also to reexamine their views regarding the dating of source materials, since much of the material that has traditionally been dated late or deemed apocryphal fits Crossan's portrait of Jesus better than that which has been considered early and canonical. The question is whether the portrait holds up apart from any dependence on his particular source theories.

The response to this question has been mixed. Even those who do not accept Crossan's source theories find much in his reconstruction of Jesus' life and ministry that is compelling. Still, leaving aside minor quibbles, at least five elements are disputed:

1. Some think that the analogy between Jesus and Cynic philosophers is strained. The same arguments are made as were discussed above with reference to the work of Downing (see pages 60–64). But Crossan's view is more tempered than Downing's, especially as it comes to expression in his later work. "We have

in the final analysis, no way of knowing for sure what Jesus knew about Cynicism, or whether he knew about it at all," Crossan writes. "Maybe he had never even heard of the Cynics and was just re-inventing the Cynic wheel all by himself."[62] For Crossan, the point of invoking the Cynics is not to determine the derivation of Jesus' ideas or to identify a conscious model for his ministry and lifestyle. The point, rather, seems to be to find a roughly contemporary historical analogy, to discuss a similar movement about which we know a good deal in order to help us form hypotheses about how Jesus' movement would have been perceived. Crossan is upfront about the differences between Jesus and the Cynics, but finds the similarities nevertheless to be instructive. When he is most clear on these points, his critics quiet down, only to raise their voices again when he persists in *calling* Jesus a Cynic, in saying he actually *was* a Cynic, albeit one of peculiar stripe ("a Jewish peasant Cynic").

2. Some scholars think Crossan's portrait underplays the Jewish dimension of Jesus and his world. Positively, Wright wants to ask how the social program Crossan attributes to Jesus would have related to the hopes of Israel. Negatively, he wonders why it would have offended those who saw themselves as guardians of Israel's sacred traditions. Crossan leaves all the controversy stories (over sabbath laws, for instance) out of his portrait, relegating them to a later stage of tradition. He shows us how Jesus offended people in authority but, Wright says, "he never explains why there would be hostility from Jews *qua* Jews."[63] Similarly, Witherington notes that for all the comparisons between Jesus' parables and Cynic *chreiai,* Crossan almost never compares them to the parables of Jewish sages.[64] Crossan responds by noting that Judaism at the time of Jesus was "richly creative, diverse, and variegated."[65] Furthermore, all Judaism was Hellenistic, and the most significant distinction between its various types was whether they embraced an inclusive or exclusive perspective toward Hellenism. He claims that his Jesus is thoroughly Jewish, but a representative of inclusive Hellenistic Judaism rather than of some sort of conservative, rabbinical variety. Jesus was more interested in adapting the customs of Israel than preserving them.[66]

3. Predictably, the specific representation of Jesus as a magician has suffered abuse. Crossan (like Morton Smith) intends this to be provocative and his readers have not disappointed him by remaining unprovoked. The same arguments cited above in our discussion of Smith (see pages 56–58) are applied to Crossan. Notably, in his later work, Crossan seems to back off from using the term *magic* to describe the miracles of Jesus or his companions. In *The Birth of Christianity,* he defines a miracle as "a marvel that someone interprets as a transcendental action or manifestation."[67] The earlier distinction connecting *miracle* to official religious channels and *magic* to unofficial ones seems to have been set aside.

4. Many scholars also challenge the likelihood of Crossan's completely non-apocalyptic portrait of Jesus. Here, again, the criticisms repeat those made of the Jesus Seminar (see pages 78–79). John Meier notes that the symbol of God's kingdom was used so prominently in eschatological contexts in the centuries immediately preceding Jesus that if Jesus wanted to use it in a different sense (to refer to a present mode of being) he would have had to make this semantic shift explicit.[68]

Meier's critique of Crossan at this point is so sharp that (we may note with some irony) it amounts to a final judgment:

> Future transcendent salvation was an essential part of Jesus' proclamation of the kingdom. Any reconstruction of the historical Jesus that does not do full justice to this eschatological future must be dismissed as hopelessly inadequate.[69]

Similarly, E. P. Sanders claims:

> If Jesus meant [*kingdom*] only symbolically, then we would have to conclude that he completely deceived his disciples, who continued to expect a kingdom. The view that Jesus was entirely deceptive and misled his disciples into false hopes, while spinning parables which can be unraveled only by twentieth-century literary analysis, must be rejected.[70]

To many, the assertion that Jesus was unconcerned with the end of the world or with life beyond death seems not only unlikely, but unnecessary. Crossan apparently thinks that inclusion of such an aspect in his portrait would contradict his image of a man concerned with this-worldly affairs. Witherington thinks he sets up false alternatives:

> Crossan . . . would have us choose between a Jesus who is a sage and a Jesus who is an apocalyptic seer, between a Jesus who is more like a Cynic and a Jesus who is more like John the Baptist. There are other options.[71]

Paul, for example, has no trouble speaking of the kingdom of God in both future (1 Cor. 15:50) and present (Rom. 14:17) terms, and a dynamic tension between "the already and the not yet" is prominent in all three of the Synoptic Gospels. If the future orientation of John and the present orientation of the Cynics are not mutually exclusive, then why must Crossan posit Jesus rejecting the former to embrace the latter?

5. Some scholars say that the historical Jesus presented by Crossan does not offer an adequate basis for understanding Christianity's development of ideas concerning him. Wright asks, "If Jesus' work concentrated on articulating and enacting a 'brokerless kingdom,' a 'kingdom of nobodies,' then why did he die, and why did the church come to attribute to his death the significance it did?"[72] The latter part of the question is most relevant. Crossan *does* have an explanation for why Jesus was killed. But why would the church come to interpret his death as an atonement for sin (Rom. 3:25; 1 John 2:2), as a ransom (Mark 10:45), or as a sacrifice (Heb. 9:11–14)? The closest Crossan comes to answering such a query is to suggest that scribal exegetes arrived at these interpretations by applying scriptural citations to Jesus (such as the "scapegoat" text in Leviticus 16:7–10, 21–22). But then the question becomes, What would motivate early Christians to interpret such texts with reference to Jesus if he had displayed no interest in the themes of atonement or ransom or sacrifice, if indeed the very concept of mediation that these terms imply ran counter to everything he stood for?

Redemption is but one topic on which this point can be made. The presence of an apocalyptic perspective, just noted, is another. And the examples can be multiplied: Crossan's Jesus had no messianic consciousness, yet early Christians (even Gentiles) soon hailed him as the Jewish Messiah. Crossan's Jesus was completely self-effacing, yet Christians (even those passionately committed to monotheism) began very early to worship him. Some such gaps are no doubt to be expected in the growth of a movement, but the magnitude of the chasm in this case seems to demand an explanation. Crossan's Jesus, like that of the Jesus Seminar, is *very* dissimilar from the Jesus in whom many early Christians believed and for whom many were willing to die.

We should note that this complaint, that Crossan does not account adequately for the disjuncture between his image of Jesus and the Christ of Christianity, was made in response to *The Historical Jesus*. The criticisms just described predate Crossan's second major tome, *The Birth of Christianity,* which describes his vision of the theological and political movements in the years following Jesus' death. In that volume, however, he shows little interest in explaining the divergences that he believes he is able to document. He simply lays out in even more detail developments evident in the earliest sources (as he construes them).

Already in the first book, we see Crossan agreeing with his critics that the differences between the Jesus of history and the Christ of Christianity are significant. Still, he refuses to accommodate the former to the latter. The other option, the one his critics don't want to consider, is to acknowledge that Christianity really did get it very wrong. He suggests that Christianity may have "lost its soul" in its efforts to convert the Roman Empire. This began, innocently enough, with a theological move that interpreted Christ as a mediator between God and humanity. In itself, and properly understood, such a move did not have to be devastating, but "most inappropriately and unfortunately," understanding Jesus as a broker (mediator) may have facilitated a later move away from inclusive service toward the accoutrements of power. The effects of such a move became evident by the time of Constantine, when Christianity became the official religion of the empire and the church's leaders (male bishops) now expected to be served by others:

> Christianity . . . when it attempted to define as clearly as it could the meaning of Jesus, insisted that he was "wholly God" and "wholly man," that he was, in other words, himself the unmediated presence of the divine to the human. I find, therefore, no betrayal whatsoever in the move from Jesus to Christ. Whether there were ultimate betrayals in the move from Christ to Constantine is another question. . . . Maybe, Christianity is an inevitable and absolutely necessary "betrayal" of Jesus, else it might have died among the hills of Lower Galilee. But did that "betrayal" have to happen so swiftly, succeed so fully, and be enjoyed so thoroughly? Might not a more even dialectic have been maintained between Jesus and Christ in Jesus Christ?[73]

6

MARCUS J. BORG

Jesus was a peasant, which tells us about his social class. Clearly, he was brilliant. His use of language was remarkable and poetic, filled with images and stories. He had a metaphoric mind. He was not an ascetic; he was world-affirming, with a zest for life. There was a sociopolitical passion about him—like a Gandhi or a Martin Luther King, he challenged the domination system of his day. He was a religious ecstatic, a Jewish mystic, if you will, for whom God was an experiential reality. As such, Jesus was also a healer. And there seems to have been a spiritual presence around him, like that reported of Saint Francis or the present Dalai Lama. And I suggest that as a figure of history, Jesus was an ambiguous figure—you could experience him and conclude that he was insane, as his family did, or that he was simply eccentric, or that he was a dangerous threat—or you could conclude that he was filled with the Spirit of God.

—Marcus Borg[1]

Borg has attempted to locate Jesus within models taken from a wider history of religions context, and at the same time to integrate his findings with a positive restatement of Christian experience and theology. . . . He is clear and positive about his own Christian commitment, which by his own account has grown stronger as his work on Jesus has progressed.

—N. T. Wright[2]

Marcus Borg prefers not to talk about "the historical Jesus" as a figure of the past who can be studied apart from religious or spiritual concerns. As indicated above, he suggests a change in terminology; instead of talking about "the Jesus of history" and "the Christ of faith," we should speak of "the pre-Easter Jesus" and "the post-Easter Jesus" (see page 4). Both are historical realities, subject to study and critique, and both are significant for theology and faith.

A prominent member of the Jesus Seminar, Borg is professor of religion and culture at Oregon State University. As the designation of his field implies, he is heavily invested in the relationship between matters of faith and sociopolitical realities. He has been a student of world religions, with particular interest in varieties of spirituality and mysticism. Although a confessing Christian, he admits that his own faith has been enhanced by studying Buddhism, the writings of Carlos Castenada, and the latter's Indian seer, Don Juan.

Of all the scholars whose views are described in this book, none has been so open or articulate about his personal level of engagement with these issues as Marcus Borg. His 1994 book, *Meeting Jesus Again for the First Time,* is on the way to becoming a classic of spiritual autobiography. He describes his childhood as a time marked by "precritical naiveté"; he worshiped Jesus and believed whatever authority figures said to believe concerning him. His adolescence, he says, was a time of intellectual struggle and doubt. In college, he was exposed to academic study of theology in a way that did not help him to believe but, he says, "provided a framework within which I could take my perplexity seriously."[3] He went off to seminary and then to graduate school, a "closet agnostic."[4] He learned to study the Gospels as developing traditions in early Christianity rather than as divine documents or straightforward historical records. "I found all of this very exciting," Borg reports, "though it also seemed vaguely scandalous and something I shouldn't tell my mother about."[5] He also learned to identify beliefs in Christian tradition as cultural products, developed to serve psychological human needs and to expedite certain social functions. With the recognition that such beliefs could be explained naturally, without recourse to God, came an increasing suspicion "that there probably was no such reality."[6] Then, Borg says, he had a number of mystical and ecstatic experiences that fundamentally changed his understanding of God, Jesus, religion, and Christianity. "It became obvious to me," he writes, "that God—the sacred, the holy, the numinous—was 'real.' God was no longer a concept or an article of belief, but had become an element of experience."[7] Not only God, but Jesus:

> Believing in Jesus does not mean believing doctrines about him. Rather, it means to give one's heart, one's self at its deepest level, to the post-Easter Jesus who is the living Lord, the side of God turned toward us, the face of God, the Lord who is also the spirit.[8]

It was with this awareness and within the context of this understanding of faith that he now approached the study of Jesus, working still as a trained historical scholar.

BORG'S METHOD FOR STUDYING JESUS

Borg is less explicit about methodological considerations than other scholars discussed in this book. Whereas some (Crossan, Meier, Wright) have devoted hundreds of pages—even entire books—to this subject, Borg offers only a few explanatory comments. Part of the attraction of his work is that it goes right to the task at hand, presenting a vivid and persuasive description of Jesus in fewer words than some expend on prolegomena.

In general, Borg tries to "go with the flow" of mainstream historical criticism, accepting what most scholars would regard as reliable without proposing novel theories regarding sources or criteria of authenticity. There is nothing in his presentation of Jesus that depends on acceptance of the apocryphal Gospels of Peter or Thomas, but there is probably nothing there that would be contradicted by those materials either. In keeping with the perspective of most historical scholars, he pretty much ignores the Gospel of John, relying most heavily on material in the three Synoptic Gospels. Unlike the Jesus Seminar as a whole, however, he does not radically elevate the Q sayings over the narrative material in Mark's Gospel.

Borg does not care so much about the specifics. He is more interested in determining what "kind of person" Jesus was than in whether he said or did particular things that are attributed to him.

> Though we cannot ever be certain that we have direct and exact quotation from Jesus, we can be relatively sure of the *kinds* of things he said, and of the main themes and thrusts of his teaching. We can also be relatively sure of the kinds of things he did: healings, association with outcasts, the deliberate calling of twelve disciples, a mission directed to Israel, a final purposeful journey to Jerusalem.[9]

All of the Gospel traditions, Borg grants, have been shaped by the church. Rather than "preoccupying ourselves with the question of whether Jesus said *exactly* the particular words attributed to him," we should notice what types of sayings and deeds are attributed to him. By doing this, "we can sketch a fairly full and historically defensible portrait of Jesus. . . . We can in fact know as much about Jesus as we can about any figure in the ancient world."[10]

Once the task is defined as determining what kind of person Jesus was, the major trajectory of Borg's method becomes clear. He uses an interdisciplinary approach to interpret the general tendencies of the Jesus tradition from a perspective informed by sociology, anthropology, and a study of the history of religions. Specifically, he compares the images for Jesus presented by this tradition to classic "religious personality types" that are known to appear cross-culturally and within the history of Israel.[11] Comparative studies of other religious and social figures offer analogies for understanding how Jesus related to his social world. At times, Borg also draws overtly on his own experiences or observations of contemporary religion. For instance, he offers the following as one reason for the unlikeliness of Jesus having prophesied the imminent end of the world:

> Most of us have heard street preachers (and others) whose message essentially is, "The end is at hand, repent!" In my experience, people who strongly believe

"the end is near" sound very different from what I hear in the Jesus tradition considered as a whole.[12]

In short, Borg's method for studying Jesus appears to be informed by an awareness of historical-critical study of the New Testament, an appreciation for analogies drawn from interdisciplinary studies of religion, and a good dose of common
sense.

BORG'S PORTRAIT OF JESUS

Borg's depiction of the historical Jesus has been laid out in *Jesus: A New Vision* (1987), though some of his preliminary research was presented in an earlier
work, *Conflict, Holiness and Politics in the Teachings of Jesus* (1984).[13] The later
book offers four images of Jesus: healer, sage, movement initiator, and social
prophet. He relates these four images to two focal points: social world and spirit.
Jesus' social world was the center of his concern (not just the background for his
activity) and the Spirit was the source of his sense of mission and of the perspective from which he spoke.[14] In effect, this latter focal point becomes yet another
category, albeit the transcendent one. Borg views Jesus fundamentally as "a spirit
person." This is the umbrella designation under which the other four descriptions
will fit, the glue that holds them all together.

Jesus as Spirit Person

The world in which Jesus lived was one that took for granted the existence of
a world of spirit, that is, "another dimension or layer or level of reality in addition
to the visible world of our ordinary experience."[15] Believing in this other reality,
Borg stresses, did not take what we may call "faith." It was virtually a universal
notion, accepted without question by all cultures prior to the modern period. This
other world was a reality to be experienced, but since it lay beyond sensory perception it could be known only through mediation. At certain places or times, the
world of spirit seemed to intersect with our ordinary world, allowing people to experience union or communion with it. In practically every culture, furthermore,
certain individuals experienced such communion more frequently or vividly than
most. Though they take a variety of forms (healers, prophets, lawgivers, shamans,
mystics), such charismatic "spirit persons" are found in almost every culture.[16]
Jesus, says Borg, was such a person.

The first episode regarding Jesus that can be regarded as a historical event is
one that places him squarely in charismatic religious tradition. He is baptized by
John, who was himself regarded as a spirit person (a prophet), and at this baptism
is said to have seen a vision of the heavens opening and the Spirit descending upon
him "like a dove" (Mark 1:10). Jesus is reported to have seen other visions as well;
the Q material speaks of three visions of temptation he experienced while fasting
in the wilderness (Matt. 4:1–11; Luke 4:1–13), and elsewhere Jesus claims to have
seen a vision of Satan falling from heaven like lightning (Luke 10:17–18).[17]

Borg also notes that Jesus is described as a man of prayer, and he calls attention to two aspects of this. First, Jesus is said to have prayed for long periods of time (Luke 6:12, "all night"), suggesting that the form of prayer was not just verbal expression but deep contemplation or meditation. Second, Jesus is said to have called God, "Abba" (Mark 14:36), an Aramaic word used by young children, similar perhaps to the English "Papa."[18] His use of this word implies an almost casual familiarity remarkable for a social world where the usual convention was to use circumlocutions that avoided using the name of God altogether (Mark 14:61). In short, Jesus' prayer life expressed an abiding sense of communion and intimacy with God.[19]

Jesus' spirituality also had an external dimension, affecting how he was viewed by others and how he interacted with them.[20] Like most spirit persons, Jesus is said to have evoked awe and amazement in those about him, not simply in response to things he said or did but as a general reaction to his very person. Mark 10:32 puts it vividly: "They were on the road, going up to Jerusalem, and Jesus was walking ahead of them; and they were amazed, and those who followed were [filled with awe]." Reports of incidents such as the Transfiguration (Mark 9:2–4) testify to how Jesus was viewed as an extraordinary Spirit-filled person, regardless of whether these events are accepted as actual occurrences. Jesus drew on such perceptions by speaking and acting as though he possessed some inherent divine authority. The mere fact that he called disciples testifies to this, as do numerous sayings attributed to him (for example, Matt. 12:28, which is from Q).

In developing this portrait, Borg does not rely as overtly on source criticism as do Crossan and other members of the Jesus Seminar. He speaks rather of "the cumulative impression created by the synoptic gospels":

> Matthew, Mark, and Luke all portray him as a Spirit-filled person through whom the power of the Spirit flowed. His relationship to Spirit was both the source and energy of the mission which he undertook. . . . Moreover, Jesus' relationship to the world of Spirit is also the key for understanding the central dimensions of his ministry: as healer, sage, revitalization movement founder, and prophet.[21]

Jesus as Healer

Parting company with the majority of his colleagues in the Jesus Seminar (but in agreement with Crossan), Borg regards the assertion that Jesus was a healer and an exorcist as "virtually indisputable" on historical grounds. He cites multiple attestation of accounts in the earliest sources and points out that "despite the difficulty which miracles pose for the modern mind," healings and exorcisms were "relatively common in the world around Jesus."[22] He cites the example of another first-century charismatic, Rabbi Hanina ben Dosa, who according to the Talmud was able not only to expel demons, but also to heal people from a distance and overcome the poison of serpents—powers attributed also to Jesus (Luke 7:1–10; 10:19). The Gospels freely grant that some of Jesus' opponents—the Pharisees—were able to cast out demons (Matt. 12:27; compare Mark 9:38–39). What's more, Jewish leaders who opposed the early Christians later in the first century did not even bother to claim that his healings were the result of fakery or that they had been misreported. They acknowledged the healings as authentic but attributed them to power drawn from an evil spirit (see Mark 3:20–30). In short, the healing ministry of Jesus loses its uniqueness in the light of historical study, but for that very reason gains in credibility.[23]

Borg avoids trying to explain how modern medical science might perceive "what really happened" when Jesus healed people or drove demons out of them. The tendency to find "a psychosomatic explanation that stretches but does not break the limits of our modern worldview" ultimately misses the point, which is that the healings and exorcisms were experienced as an incursion of otherworldly power.[24] Historically, we must acknowledge that Jesus presented himself as a person through whom such power could and did operate, and that those around him experienced him as a channel for such power. The fact that the power was said to operate for healing is also significant, for it indicates what sort of spirit person Jesus was. The world knew, for instance, of spirit-empowered warriors or of prophets who could curse their opponents in ways that would bring affliction upon them. Such stories are not found in reliable sources for Jesus.

Jesus as Sage

The image of Jesus as a sage is a popular one in modern historical study. We have already seen that this identification dominates the work of the Jesus Seminar and, in various ways, the work of Crossan, Downing, Fiorenza, Mack, and Witherington as well. For Borg, however, the category of sage is not dominant. It is but one expression of Jesus as a charismatic spirit person. Jesus taught specifically as a person who claimed to have intimate knowledge of God and the spirit world. The content of his teaching, therefore, revealed the true nature of God and reality. Borg does not appeal to the Cynics for an analogy of Jesus as sage, but to Buddha and to Lao Tzu.[25] He was similar to them in that he proclaimed a way of transformation based on insight into how things truly are.

Jesus' teaching was based on a vision of reality that challenged conventional wisdom. Borg defines conventional wisdom as "what everybody knows" in a given culture, that is, the "convictions and ways of behavior so taken for granted as to be basically unquestioned."[26] One aspect of conventional wisdom for Jesus' society was the understanding that reality was organized on a basis of rewards and punishments: life goes well for those who live in a way that is wise or "right" and poorly for those who live in a way that is unwise or "wrong." Jesus challenged this perception of reality. He pointed to nature as indicative of a cosmic generosity: God feeds birds who do no labor (Matt. 6:26) and provides sun and rain for the crops of good and bad people alike (Matt. 5:45). He likened God to a father who celebrates the return of an errant son (Luke 15:11–32) and to an employer who pays a full day's wage to people who had worked but a single hour (Matt. 20:1–16). Borg concludes: "What distinguished [Jesus] from most of his contemporaries as well as from us, from their conventional wisdom as well as from ours, was his vivid sense that reality was ultimately gracious and compassionate."[27]

Jesus was "neither anti-law nor anti-convention. He was a Jew who treasured his tradition."[28] The very forms of speech that he used (proverbs, parables, lessons from nature) belonged to the wisdom tradition of Israel. But "Jesus used the forms of traditional wisdom to challenge conventional wisdom."[29] Unlike the Cynics, he did not simply subvert a vision of the world; he affirmed another vision, offering "an alternative way of being and an alternative consciousness shaped by the relationship to Spirit and not primarily by the dominant consciousness of culture."[30] Jesus' teaching did not consist of instruction in doctrine or ethics, but took the form of "an *invitation to see differently.*"[31] Still, his new vision of reality did have practical consequences. Jesus contrasted the "broad way" of conventional wisdom with the "narrow way" of living in accord with his vision. Those who follow the broad way (most people) will see reality as hostile or indifferent and self-preservation will be the first law of their being. But for those who come to see reality as supportive and nourishing, another response to life becomes possible—trust.[32] Life that is grounded in trust involves a death to self-interest (Mark 8:34) and a centering in God.

Jesus as Movement Initiator

The way of transformation that Jesus taught had social and political implications. Ultimately, says Borg, Jesus was not simply calling individuals to a new perception of reality but was offering an alternative vision for society as a whole. His "concern was the renewal of Israel" and his "purpose was the transformation of the Jewish social world."[33] To effect such a transformation, he created a sectarian revitalization movement of itinerant followers who sought to emulate what life grounded in the new vision could be. His concern that this movement represented a new way *for Israel* is demonstrated in his identification of twelve followers as having a special calling. Borg regards this choosing of the twelve as "one of the most certain facts of Jesus' ministry" and interprets it as a symbolic reconstitution of the twelve tribes of Israel.[34] Thus, Borg rejects the extremely Hellenistic image of Jesus offered by some historians and affirms a specific commitment to Israel.

Still, Jesus' reform movement challenged the conventional wisdom of Israelite society. The repudiation of an understanding of life based on rewards and punishment would certainly have had social and political implications, but Borg focuses even more on a challenge Jesus offered to another aspect of his world's conventional wisdom, to the ethos that had created what Borg calls "a politics of holiness." At the very heart of the social world of Jesus, says Borg, lay a cultural paradigm that accepted holiness as its core value and sought to define what was holy and what was not. This paradigm was expressed through a purity system that established strict boundaries. Certain times, places, and things were declared holy and had to be treated in a special way. Similar categories were established with regard to people, and distinctions were made with regard to Jews and Gentiles, men and women, oldest sons and younger siblings, and so forth. These distinctions were inevitably hierarchical, leading to a rigid mindset concerning what roles were appropriate for whom and what status should be assigned to people occupying those roles.

Undergirding this whole system was the fundamental notion that holiness must be protected by *separation;* that which is holy, pure, or clean must be preserved from defilement through contact with what is unholy, impure, or unclean. This cultural dynamic was grounded in a concept of *imatio dei* (imitation of God), as expressed in Israel's holiness code: "Speak to all the congregation of the people of Israel and say to them: You shall be holy, for I the Lord your God am holy" (Lev. 19:2). This code was developed during the exile, where it served to preserve Israel's cultural identity. Under Roman rule, however, various Jewish movements intensified the strategy in ways that produced a system that was both unjust and instable. For example, large numbers of the population came to be regarded as "sinners" or outcasts, similar to the lower caste of "untouchables" in India.[35]

The movement that Jesus initiated was essentially a countercultural association that deliberately defied the politics of holiness. Jesus and his followers ate openly with outcasts and associated with women in ways that violated social expectations. They demonstrated concern for the poor that went well beyond almsgiving to suggest commitment to radical redistribution of resources. They also spoke and acted in ways that counseled peaceful nonresistance to the Roman oppressors. They did all these things in a spirit of joyful celebration, claiming that true purity was internal. The movement was decidedly charismatic; Jesus' followers performed healings and exorcisms as he did, claiming that God's Spirit was at work in and through them. Indeed, this movement was also based on a call to live in imitation of God. Because God was generous and compassionate, people should be also. Earlier, we saw that Jesus challenged the notion that God was selective in awarding blessings to people, claiming rather that God gives to good and bad alike. The social implication of this teaching was that Israel should be an inclusive people, an egalitarian society. Jesus was offering his world a new cultural paradigm, grounded as the old one was in the concept of *imatio dei*. But Jesus sought to replace "Be holy as God is holy" with "Be compassionate as God is compassionate."[36]

Jesus the Social Prophet

The image of Jesus as a social prophet is developed through analysis of conflict stories in light of Borg's understanding of the cultural dynamics of Jesus' social world. In these stories, which present Jesus in conflict with the various leaders of Israel, Jesus spoke and acted in ways similar to what we associate with the authors of the prophetic writings of the Old Testament. Like them, he identified a threat to his social world, presented an indictment of those responsible, and summoned people to repentance. Indeed, Borg claims that "of all the figures in his tradition, Jesus was most like the classical prophets of Israel."[37] The crisis that Borg thinks Jesus identified was not the imminent end of the world, but a potential destruction of Jerusalem and the temple. He predicted that such a catastrophe would occur "unless the culture radically changed its direction."[38] The politics of holiness had to be rejected in favor of a new politics of compassion.

As a prophet, Jesus' protest was not directed against Israel as a nation or against Jewish nationalism in general. Rather, it was directed quite specifically against what sociologists would call "the ruling urban elites." Like Crossan, Borg draws on the work of social anthropologist Gerhard Lenski regarding "pre-industrial agrarian societies."[39] According to Lenski, the single most striking characteristic of these societies was the "marked social inequality" between its two social classes: urban elites and rural peasants. The former were wealthy and owned or controlled most of the land; the latter worked the land, paid heavy taxes, and lived in poverty. As a social prophet, Jesus decried this system, pronouncing blessings on the oppressed peasants and woes on the rich (Luke 6:20, 24). In doing so, Borg claims, Jesus stood in line with the God-intoxicated prophets of the Hebrew Bible.[40] In fact, Borg maintains that the critique of the purity system discussed above was also aimed primarily at these ruling elites, not at Israel as an undifferentiated entity. Clear correlations between purity and class structure can be detected, indicating that "the purity system was the ideology of the ruling elites," intended to guarantee that "their place in society was divinely sanctioned."[41] The leaders of the temple cult, then, were as much a part of the ruling elite as the wealthy landowners. What we no longer know, Borg admits, is the extent to which the peasants Jesus addressed would have affirmed this ideology themselves. Had they bought into it? Was it *their* conventional wisdom? "Would peasants, for example, have viewed an untouchable as an untouchable?"[42] We cannot be sure whether Jesus the social prophet merely spoke aloud what many thought privately or whether he put into words a viewpoint most had never considered. Either way, he found an audience.

It was this role as prophet that got Jesus killed. Borg believes that Jesus brought his reform movement to Jerusalem to affect the heart of Israelite society. He performed two prophetic acts. First, he rode into the city on a donkey's colt, demonstrating that the society of which he spoke was to be a kingdom of peace, not war.[43] Then, he overturned tables of moneychangers in the temple as an act protesting "the sacred order of separation" that the temple cult with its sacrificial enterprise and ecclesiastical merchants manifested. In itself this act was no big deal; it was purely symbolic, "limited in area, intent, and duration, done for the sake of the message it conveyed."[44] But it was enough. What happened next, Borg admits, is difficult to reconstruct, but he theorizes: some of the Jewish authorities in charge of the temple, who no doubt did not appreciate "the message" Jesus was sending, interrogated him "and then handed him over to Pilate as a political claimant." He was charged with treason and summarily executed as an insurrectionist. The charge, Borg notes, was not entirely fair. As an advocate of nonviolence Jesus did not pose the sort of direct threat to the empire that such an execution could imply. But as a charismatic prophet, he did indeed pose a threat to the social order, as the Jewish leaders and, perhaps, Pilate rightly discerned.[45]

This concludes our survey of Borg's portrait of Jesus, save for two more points that should be made. First, Borg argues for a noneschatological Jesus.[46] In this way, his image of Jesus parallels that of the Jesus Seminar and others we have discussed.[47] He agrees with the Seminar, for instance, in assigning all of the sayings attributed to Jesus regarding the coming of the Son of Man to a later development of the tradition. These sayings (for example, Mark 13:24–30; Luke 12:8–9) are unauthentic. Jesus did not speak of a supernatural figure who would come with angels at the end of the world, much less identify himself with this figure. Rather, belief in a second coming of Jesus arose in the church after Easter and came to be expressed in apocalyptic terms. Borg grants that Jesus did speak about "the kingdom of God," but maintains that he used this expression as "a tensive symbol, that is, one with a number of nuances of meaning."[48] He suggests that it may refer to the world of spirit, which coexists with this material world and which will someday be united with it. Jesus, then, did believe in a final consummation, when the worlds of matter and spirit would be related to each other at the end as they were at creation, but he gave no indication that he believed such an occurrence was imminent. When Jesus spoke of the kingdom of God being near or at hand, he may have meant to articulate the possibility of knowing and experiencing that world of spirit here and now. Likewise, the tensive symbol can indicate (1) the power of God, (2) the experiential presence of God, (3) covenantal life under God's rule, which is radically different from other ways of living, (4) a community within which the reality of God's presence and way of life are experienced, (5) an ideal state of affairs. Sometimes the symbol may even function as a political metaphor, such as when the kingdom of God is contrasted with that of Herod or Caesar.[49]

Second, Borg offers some comments on the resurrection of Jesus. From a strict, historical perspective, he admits, not much can be said: "The story of the historical Jesus ends with his death on a Friday in A.D. 30." He insists, nevertheless, that the post-Easter Jesus is real: "The living, risen Christ of the New Testament has been an experiential reality (and not just an article of belief) from the days of Easter to the present."[50] The point, for him, is to separate the notion of resurrection from that of resuscitation of a corpse. The notion of resurrection implies that Jesus entered into another mode of being, that he is no longer limited by space and time, but is able to be present—as a living, experienced reality—with his followers in a new way. This notion does not require an empty tomb. Borg admits that the empty tomb stories are relatively late and confused, but dismisses their significance for accepting the truth of the resurrection.[51]

CRITIQUE OF BORG'S STUDY OF JESUS

Borg's view is more comprehensive than many. N. T. Wright has called him "a bridge," indicating that his description of Jesus has points in common with sketches offered by scholars whose views appear to be disparate if not irreconcilable.[52] The combined images of Jesus as healer and sage are similar to those that play heavily into Crossan's portrait (chapter 5), while the image of movement initiator parallels the work of Fiorenza (pages 28–29) and that of social prophet echoes concerns important to Horsley (pages 52–54). Even the characterization of Jesus as a charismatic spirit person resonates with contributions offered by Geza Vermes (pages 54–56). The upshot of all this is that practically every scholar finds things to praise in Borg's analysis, as well as points to dispute.

To put things a bit too simply, major historians of Jesus often seem to fall into

two camps: those who accent the Hellenistic matrix for Jesus and downplay his eschatological teaching (the Jesus Seminar, Crossan, Downing, Mack), and those
who accent the Jewish matrix for Jesus and emphasize his eschatological teaching
(Meier, Sanders, Witherington, Wright). If Borg is a bridge, it is because his Jesus
is very Jewish but also noneschatological. Thus, his views may be attacked from
both sides. According to Burton Mack, Galilee was such a Hellenized Roman state
that the Jewish concepts of holiness Borg describes as conventional wisdom would
not have played a significant role in Jesus' cultural environment.[53] According to E.
P. Sanders, appreciation for Jewish restoration theology prominent at the time of
Jesus demands that such actions as his selection of twelve disciples and symbolic
destruction of the temple be interpreted as eschatological acts that anticipated
God's establishment of a new age.[54] For Borg, the problem with being a "bridge"
is having it both ways.

On other points, Borg is actually criticized for ruling out options that need not
be mutually exclusive. Witherington complains that he sets concern for compassion and holiness against each other such that Jesus can only proclaim the one at
the expense of the other. A large amount of material, such as sayings on divorce
and adultery (Matt. 5:27–32), reveal that Jesus was concerned about maintaining
purity or holiness in a moral sense.

Another point of contention would be Borg's construal of conventional wisdom
regarding holiness. A number of recent scholars, including Sanders, have questioned whether purity codes were exercised in an oppressive manner. Sanders,
whose views we will discuss further in the next chapter, believes that the purity
codes were followed only by a select group of Jews (the *haberim*) who may have
been roughly equivalent with those the New Testament designates as Pharisees.
These were laity who, for theological reasons, chose to maintain themselves in the
relatively high state of ritual purity expected of priests. But the decision to do this
was completely voluntary. According to Sanders, the *haberim* did not consider
others sinful for not following this way, nor did they exercise enough power in
Galilee at the time of Jesus to have had much effect even if they had. Although he
does not criticize Borg directly, Sanders clearly wants to undermine the whole notion of "a politics of holiness" on which portions of Borg's presentation rest. Indeed, Sanders thinks such construals are Christian misrepresentations of Judaism
that smack of anti-Semitism.[55]

Despite the multifaceted nature of Borg's portrait of Jesus, some critics think
his view is too limited. What he leaves out is significant:

> [First], in all likelihood, the pre-Easter Jesus did not think of himself as the Mes-
> siah or in any exalted terms in which he is spoken of. Second, we can say with
> almost complete certainty that he did not see his own mission or purpose as dy-
> ing for the sins of the world. Third and finally, again with almost complete cer-
> tainty, we can say that his message was not about himself or the importance of
> believing in him.[56]

If many other Jewish categories can be applied to Jesus, why not messiah as well?[57]
Josephus tells about messianic claimants, some of whom are also mentioned in the

book of Acts (see 5:36–37; 21:38). Why is it unlikely that Jesus would have made such claims or at least interpreted his work in light of what was associated with messianic expectations? The notion may be absurd to some of Borg's colleagues in the Jesus Seminar who regard Jesus as belonging to a Hellenistic milieu that did not think in such terms, but once the Jewish matrix for Jesus' ministry is established, the rationale for excluding this category seems to disappear. Likewise, since Borg affirms that Jesus called God "Abba," then why deny that he would have identified himself as the Son of God in some specialized sense or that his teaching might have included reflection on the intimacy of his own (unique?) relationship with God?

Finally, Wright notes that Borg's Jesus must ultimately be considered a failure.[58] His charismatic movement to revitalize Israel by changing society's core value from holiness to compassion did not work. We must then ask historically, "Why did people continue to care about him after his death?" and theologically, "Why should people pay him any mind today?"

In response to the historical question, Borg would probably appeal to the experience of Jesus after Easter. This authenticated his movement for early and contemporary Christians in a way that success measured in social or political terms never could. And in response to the theological question, Borg insists that historical knowledge of the pre-Easter Jesus informs the vision of those who stand in relation to the post-Easter Jesus today. Put simply, it tells us something about what it means to be "a Christian":

> It means to see God as an experiential reality, not simply an article of belief. It means to live by an alternative wisdom, whose primary content is a relationship with the same Spirit Jesus knew. It means to actualize compassion in the world, both as an individual virtue and as the core value of the alternative social vision of Jesus. And it means to be a part of a community of memory that celebrates, nourishes, and embodies the new way of being that we see in Jesus.[59]

7

E. P. SANDERS

*I am a liberal, modern, secularized Protestant, brought up in a church domi-
nated by low christology and the social gospel. I am proud of the things that
my religious tradition stands for. I am not bold enough, however, to suppose
that Jesus came to establish it, or that he died for the sake of its principles.*

—E. P. Sanders[1]

*According to Sanders, Jesus was an eschatological prophet standing in the tra-
dition of Jewish restoration theology. Jesus believed that the promises to Israel
would soon be fulfilled . . . brought about by a dramatic intervention by God,
involving the destruction of the Jerusalem temple and the coming of a new (or
renewed) temple.*

—Marcus Borg[2]

*Jesus saw himself as God's last messenger before the establishment of the king-
dom. He looked for a new order, created by a mighty act of God. In the new
order the twelve tribes would be reassembled, there would be a new temple, force
of arms would not be needed, divorce would be neither necessary nor permitted, outcasts—even the wicked—would have a place, and Jesus and his disciples—the poor, the meek, and lowly—would have the leading role.*

—E. P. Sanders[3]

E P. Sanders made a name for himself over two decades ago with a treatise entitled *Paul and Palestinian Judaism*.[4] He quickly became established as a major Pauline scholar and, even more, as an expert on first-century Palestinian Judaism. After a brief stint at the University of Oxford, Sanders returned to North America, where he is now professor of arts and sciences in religion at Duke University. Though not Jewish himself, his numerous writings have had a profound effect on how scholars understand the Jewish world of the New Testament.[5] Even his critics will agree: few people alive today know as much about the life, practice, and religion of first-century Jews as E. P. Sanders.

Above all, Sanders describes Judaism as a religion of grace. This may be seen in its central doctrines of creation and election. God created the world and blessed it, then chose Israel and redeemed the people. In both instances, the fundamental view is "that God's grace preceded the requirement of obedience."[6] God's favor is not something that must be earned. Sanders realizes that many Christians do not think of first-century Judaism primarily as a religion of grace, but he credits this to caricatures produced by those who wished to promote the Christian religion at the expense of its Jewish parent. Such sentiments are found in the New Testament itself (see John 1:17) but do not stand up to critical historical scrutiny. Examination of Jewish literature that comes from this time reveals solid grounding in what Christian theologians would call a concept of "prevenient grace" (grace that comes first, that is freely offered, that precedes demand).[7]

Sanders develops this further in his explication of covenantal nomism, the understanding that God created a covenant with the Jewish people and sealed it through the divine revelation of the law:

> The "pattern" or "structure" of covenantal nomism is this: (1) God has chosen Israel and (2) given the law. The law implies both (3) God's promise to maintain the election and (4) the requirement to obey. (5) God rewards obedience and punishes transgression. (6) The law provides for means of atonement, and atonement results in (7) maintenance or re-establishment of the covenantal relationship. (8) All those who are maintained in the covenant by obedience, atonement, and God's mercy belong to the group which will be saved.[8]

Caricatures of first-century Judaism tend to focus on the fourth and fifth points above to present the faith as a legalistic religion to be contrasted with the Christian gospel of God's unmerited grace offered through Christ. But, says Sanders, the role of the law for the Jewish people must be understood in light of this whole paradigm.

The law was itself a gift of grace, offering people a guide to life, and the law provided ways for atonement that would keep people in God's grace when they failed to live as they ought. Furthermore, even though God was thought to reward or punish people based on their obedience to the law, the covenant itself did not depend on such obedience. God would be faithful to God's promises *despite* disobedience.[9] Or, to put it differently, "Obedience maintains one's position in the covenant, but it does not earn God's grace as such. It simply keeps the individual in the group which is the recipient of God's grace."[10] Sanders considers this concept of covenantal nomism to be "the common denominator which underlay all sorts and varieties of Judaism."[11] Contrary to Christian stereotypes, the Jews of the first century did not view obeying the law as something burdensome. Rather, they "understood obeying the law as the . . . appropriate response to the prior grace of God."[12]

Also pertinent to our concerns is Sanders' description of Jewish restoration eschatology, the belief that God was going to act decisively and soon to fulfill the covenantal promises to Israel.[13] This perspective was pervasive for first-century Jews who believed that they were living at the end of time. Different groups construed the restoration in different ways; for instance, some looked for political redemption, others apocalyptic salvation in another world. Still, there were recurring features. The restoration would include a new or renewed temple and a reconstitution of the twelve tribes of Israel. Those who spoke of this restoration typically described an impending judgment and issued a call for national repentance. Often, they predicted that Gentiles would finally be admitted to the full salvation enjoyed by Israel.

This restoration eschatology presupposes the covenantal nomism and its accent on grace that marked all varieties of first-century Judaism. Taking them together, Sanders lists three constitutive elements of the Jewish milieu in which Jesus lived: (1) the belief that God had graciously initiated a covenant with Israel and would be faithful to that covenant, no matter what, (2) the expectation that Israel would respond to God's grace with loyalty demonstrated through obedience to the law, and (3) the strong hope that God would act soon in history to restore the fortunes of Israel. "These three component parts," Sanders says, "are found widely in Jewish literature: chronologically from Ben Sira to the Rabbinic material" (that is, from the second century B.C.E. until at least the second century C.E.).[14]

At first Sanders applied his understanding of Judaism to interpretation of Paul. Then he turned his attention to Jesus. His description of Jesus is set forth in two books: *Jesus and Judaism* (1985) and *The Historical Figure of Jesus* (1993). The first was regarded as a monumental theological contribution upon its publication, receiving several prestigious book awards. The second volume offers a more popular account of Sanders's key ideas, updated somewhat as a result of further reflection and dialogue.

SANDERS'S METHOD FOR STUDYING JESUS

Sanders displays far more confidence in the authenticity of canonical tradition than any other historical Jesus scholar discussed so far. "We should trust this information," he asserts, "unless we have good reason not to do so; that is unless the stories in the Gospels contain so many anachronisms and anomalies that we come to regard them as fraudulent."[15] This attitude is diametrically opposed to that of the Jesus Seminar, which tends to regard Gospel tradition as guilty of fabrication unless proven innocent. At the same time, Sanders's work shows no influence from noncanonical writings about Jesus. While admitting to the possible authenticity for a few sayings in Thomas, he also claims to "share the general scholarly view that very, very little in the apocryphal gospels could conceivably go back to the time of Jesus. They are legendary and mythological."[16] Sanders does not use sources uncritically. He seems to regard traditions in John as suspect, and he often detects exaggeration or other editorial tendencies in the biblical tradition. Still, his Jesus looks quite a bit like the Jesus of the Synoptic Gospels.

Rather than beginning with an analysis of the sayings of Jesus (as the Jesus Seminar ostensibly does), Sanders begins with a list of virtually indisputable facts about Jesus. He thinks that if we start with matters on which almost everyone would agree, these will provide a framework for discussing individual points. Each of Sanders's two books about Jesus begins with such a list (as indicated in chart 5).[17] The later list is longer than the first.[18] Still, some points that Sanders regarded as "almost indisputable facts" in 1985 are no longer presented as such in 1993: that Jesus' ministry included healings, that he spoke of *twelve* disciples, that he confined his ministry to Israel, and that some Jews persecuted some parts of the movement. Sanders still believes all these points are verifiable, but in the later work he presents them more cautiously, with accompanying evidence.

For Sanders, the key to understanding Jesus as a historical figure is interpreting these facts about his life in light of what we know about his social world. By "social world" he does not mean primarily the Hellenistic world of the Roman Empire, the milieu within which the Jesus Seminar and John Dominic Crossan would interpret Jesus' life and ministry. He means the world of first-century Palestinian Judaism, which, as we have noted, is Sanders's specialty. Christians, Sanders says, have tended to describe Jesus over against Judaism rather than within Judaism, and in so doing they have reaped the fruit of the misconceptions about Judaism described above. Having caricatured the Jewish religion that Jesus himself espoused, Christians have ended up believing in a caricature of Jesus himself.

SANDERS'S PORTRAIT OF JESUS

Sanders finds that much of Jesus' life and ministry can be related to the perspective of restoration eschatology that was so prevalent in first-century Judaism. The facts about Jesus that are most certain identify him as a figure who "fits into the general framework of Jewish restoration theology" and as "the founder of a group that adhered to the expectations of that theology."[19] Two virtually certain facts are particularly significant: the action in the temple and the selection of twelve disciples, for these correspond to key components of restoration eschatology, namely, the renewal of the temple and the reconstitution of the twelve tribes. If "magic and meal" serve as an alliterative key to Crossan's understanding of Jesus (see page 89), "temple and tribes" may exercise a similar function for that of Sanders.

Chart 5. "Almost Indisputable Facts about Jesus" (E. P. Sanders)

Jesus and Judaism (1985)	*The Historical Figure of Jesus* (1993)
	Jesus was born c. 4 B.C.E., near the time of the death of Herod the Great;
	he spent his childhood and early adult years in Nazareth, a Galilean village;
Jesus was baptized by John the Baptist.	he was baptized by John the Baptist;
Jesus called disciples and spoke of there being twelve.	he called disciples;
Jesus confined his activity to Israel.	he taught in the towns, villages, and countryside of Galilee (apparently not the cities);
Jesus was a Galilean who preached and healed.	he preached "the kingdom of God";
	about the year 30 he went to Jerusalem for Passover;
Jesus engaged in a controversy about the temple.	he created a disturbance in the temple area;
	he had a final meal with the disciples;
	he was arrested and interrogated by Jewish authorities, specifically the high priest;
Jesus was crucified outside Jerusalem by the Roman authorities.	he was executed on the orders of the Roman prefect, Pontius Pilate;
	his disciples at first fled;
	they saw him (in what sense is uncertain) after his death;
	as a consequence, they believed he would return to found the kingdom;
After his death, Jesus' followers continued as an identifiable movement.	they formed a community to await his return and sought to win others to faith in him as God's Messiah.
At least some Jews persecuted at least parts of the new movement.	

The Action in the Temple

All four canonical Gospels contain accounts of Jesus creating a disturbance in the temple. Mark says, "Jesus entered the temple and began to drive out those who were selling and those who were buying in the temple, and he overturned the tables of the money changers and the seats of those who sold doves" (Mark 11:15). Most historians believe that some such incident did occur; indeed, most think it provided the immediate cause for Jesus' crucifixion.[20]

Historical knowledge sheds some light on how the incident is to be understood. When Mark says Jesus "entered the temple," he actually means that Jesus entered the temple area, not the building itself. Tables were set up in a large area surrounding the temple building called the "court of the Gentiles," where doves and other animals were sold to be used for sacrifices inside. This area was massive and Jesus' action appears to have been limited in scope. He did not surround the temple complex with an army and order all business transactions to stop. Apparently, he just turned over a few tables in one section of the area surrounding the temple — an area specifically designed for the sort of commerce that was being conducted there. Why would he do this? If it was not a determined attempt to shut down the entire enterprise or (as no scholar would suggest) simply a spontaneous tantrum on his part, then what did he expect to accomplish? Sanders insists, and most scholars would agree with this much, that the act was staged as a symbolic demonstration. The question is, What was it supposed to symbolize? Destruction, says Sanders. Not the need for reform, but the fact of impending doom. God was going to destroy the temple. This flies in the face of popular interpretations that present Jesus as opposing corrupt business practices or commercialization of religion in a rather generalized sense. Sanders argues that the point could not have been a simple "cleansing of the temple." Something more radical was intended. The main function of the temple was to facilitate the offering of sacrifices to God, and the money changers and dove sellers attacked by Jesus were integral to this. Jesus is described as challenging the very essence of the temple, questioning its continued existence.

Sanders thinks the symbolism of destruction is intrinsic to the imagery of overturning things, but he also notes that many sayings in the Gospels recall a tradition that associated Jesus with threatening to destroy the temple. The authenticity of this tradition is practically guaranteed by the discomfort with which the Gospels report it—crediting it to false witnesses (Mark 14:57–59), rendering it as a prediction rather than a threat (Mark 13:1–2), investing the saying with metaphorical meaning (John 2:18–22). Whatever Jesus actually said, observes Sanders, we can be relatively certain that Jesus' contemporaries believed he had publicly indicated that the temple was going to be destroyed. It seems natural to interpret the public act that led to his crucifixion in light of this.[21]

Christian reflection tended to interpret this tradition in ways that pitted Jesus against Judaism. For example, the destruction of the temple was viewed as a divine punishment on the Jews for rejecting Jesus or as a divine sign that the Jewish religion was false and the Christian religion true. Setting aside such post-Easter impositions, Sanders seeks to understand why Jesus—interpreted *within* Judaism—would have announced an imminent divine destruction of the temple. The most likely answer seems to be that he believed God was going to replace the old temple with a new one, an event that would attend the restoration of Israel.[22] Whether Jesus thought the new temple would be on earth or in heaven cannot be determined and is somewhat inconsequential. What is more important is that a new temple meant a new age; God was about to inaugurate the long-awaited kingdom, in which all covenant promises would be fulfilled.

The Twelve Disciples

In 1993, Sanders removed from his list of virtually indisputable facts about Jesus the assertion that Jesus had spoken of "the twelve" as some identifiable group among his followers (see chart 5). This is a testimony to his integrity as a scholar, for that item is very important to his argument. He removed it no doubt because some historians have disputed it.[23] Still, Sanders argues that the point is almost certain. It is attested by Paul (1 Cor. 15:5) who wrote much earlier than the Gospels and would have had no reason to invent such a tradition since, if anything, it tended to undermine his own authority as one who did not belong to the twelve (see 1 Cor. 15:8–10).[24] Sanders acknowledges that some parts of the tradition regarding the twelve are shaky; the various lists provided in the Gospels and Acts do not agree on their names, for instance. What is constant, however, is the number. The "conception of the twelve was more firmly anchored than the remembrance of precisely who they were."[25] Indeed, in his later study Sanders suggests that there may never have been a definitive list, that Jesus could have described his disciples as "the twelve" without meaning to imply that there were literally only twelve of them or that twelve of them were somehow more important than the rest.[26]

The number was primarily (if not exclusively) symbolic. In speaking of his followers as "the twelve," Sanders says, "Jesus intended to show that he had in view the full restoration of the people of Israel."[27] This corresponds to a key element in Jewish restoration eschatology. First-century Jews in Palestine had a strong sense of their history as portrayed in their scriptures. These told them that they were originally a kingdom of twelve tribes but that the kingdom split after David's rule and that ten of the tribes were subsequently lost. One great sign of God's faithfulness to the covenant would be the miraculous recovery of these lost tribes. Such a restoration would indeed be a miracle. No one expected the lost tribes simply to be found somewhere on earth. They had vanished from this world, decimated by the Assyrian conquests eight centuries before. That is what made the hope for restoration eschatological. The tribes would be reconstituted when the present world came to an end and a new kingdom was inaugurated by God.[28] Jesus is quoted in Matthew's Gospel as saying that his disciples will judge or rule the twelve tribes of Israel (Matt. 19:28). The saying must be authentic, Sanders reasons, for the tradition that one of the twelve was a traitor would have prevented the church from ever inventing such a prediction.[29] Jesus probably expected that he and his followers would rule from Jerusalem over all the earth.

Jesus the Eschatological Prophet

As a result of these and similar observations, Sanders determines that the best context for understanding Jesus is that of Jewish restoration eschatology:

> Jesus looked for the imminent direct intervention of God in history, the elimination of evil and evildoers, the building of the new and glorious temple, and the reassembly of Israel with himself and his disciples as leading figures in it.[30]

But there is more. Jesus did not just subscribe to this theological tradition; he believed that he was called as a prophet to Israel and as a prophet he functioned within this tradition.

When Jesus called his followers "the twelve" and overturned tables in the temple he was performing prophetic acts comparable to symbolic actions associated with prophets of old: Isaiah went naked for three years (Isa. 20:3), Jeremiah wore a yoke (Jer. 27:1–7) and broke a pot (Jer. 19:1–13). Sanders identifies other such acts in the life of Jesus, events that are probably historically authentic. The tradition of Jesus riding into Jerusalem on a donkey (Mark 11:1–10) may have been a staged fulfillment of prophecy (Zech. 9:9) in which Jesus assumed the role of king to demonstrate that the kingdom was coming. Likewise, the tradition of Jesus gathering his disciples the night before his death to eat a meal in anticipation of the coming kingdom (Mark 14:22–25; 1 Cor. 11:24–26) probably reflects another prophetic demonstration—a symbolic act proclaiming that the kingdom was at hand and that he and his disciples would share in it.

The fundamental message portrayed in all these acts of Jesus was that the divine restoration of Israel was near. This belief affected everything he said and did, but was especially manifest in two aspects of his ministry. The first is his preaching about the kingdom.[31] A large number of sayings attributed to Jesus concern the kingdom of God. Most, in Sanders's view, describe the kingdom as a realm in heaven that people may enter after death or as a realm on earth that God will establish at the final judgment. Some, he grants, speak of the kingdom as the ruling power of God that manifests itself on earth even now (Luke 17:20–21) and is being actualized through Jesus' own words and deeds (Matt. 11:2–6; 12:28). Sanders is willing to accept virtually all of these sayings as authentic, but he strongly emphasizes the former set. Especially prominent are those sayings in which Jesus says the Son of Man will come on clouds within the lifetime of his own disciples (Mark 13:24–30; Matt. 16:27–28). The authenticity of these sayings is practically guaranteed by the simple fact that this did not happen. The church would not have attributed predictions to Jesus that were not fulfilled.[32] Sanders does not think these "Son of Man sayings" anticipate the end of the world as such, but rather "a decisive act that will put the Lord or the Son of Man in charge and gather around him the elect."[33] Neither does he think that Jesus was referring to himself as the one who would initiate this action. Originally, Jesus said that God was about to inaugurate the new age by sending the Son of Man. After Jesus' death, his disciples identified him as this Son of Man and reinterpreted sayings about the coming of the Son of Man to imply a "second coming" of Jesus. But even this did not materialize within the lifetime of the first generation and the expectations had to be revised. It worked. Theological development allowed for an expanded understanding of eschatology (see 2 Peter 3:3–8) and "Christianity survived this early discovery that Jesus had made a mistake very well."[34]

The second aspect of Jesus' ministry that Sanders believes demonstrates Jesus' commitment to restoration eschatology is his performance of miracles and healing.[35] Sanders accepts the tradition that Jesus was renowned for working miracles, especially healings and exorcisms, and he is hesitant about attempting to explain these stories in light of modern scientific knowledge.[36] More to the point for him is determining the significance that Jesus and his contemporaries ascribed to events that they considered to be miracles. "Probably most Galileans heard of a few miracles—exorcisms and other healings—and regarded Jesus as a holy man, on intimate terms with God."[37] But people do not seem to have understood the miracles the way Jesus would have wanted. Jesus himself thought of his miracles as "signs of the beginning of God's final victory over evil."[38] They were acts of an eschatological prophet, signaling or foreshadowing the dawn of the imminent kingdom, in which pain, suffering, and death would be no more (see Luke 10:17–20). Jesus seems to have believed this but also to have recognized that, of themselves, miracles would not prove to anyone that he was the end-time prophet. Other miracle workers were known. Thus, he refused to work miracles as "signs" when challenged to do so (Mark 8:11–12).

The image of Jesus as an eschatological prophet may also be secured from another angle. It not only provides a framework that makes sense of much source material, but also establishes Jesus as the connecting link between two known entities. John the Baptist used apocalyptic language to speak of an imminent divine intervention in history (Matt. 3:10–12) and Paul expected the parousia to occur soon (1 Thess. 4:15–17). On either side of Jesus—his mentor and his followers—we find lively eschatological hope that the consummation of all things and the dawn of the new age is at hand. "To pull Jesus entirely out of this framework," says Sanders, "would be an act of historical violence."[39]

For Sanders, identifying Jesus as an eschatological prophet allows for reasonable explanation both of his own self-consciousness and of the identity attributed to him by the early church. "The clearest and possibly the most important point that can be made about Jesus' view of himself," says Sanders, is that "he regarded himself as having full authority to speak and act on behalf of God."[40] Jesus rejected the title Messiah (Mark 8:27–30). He did not speak of himself as the Son of God and even if he did refer to himself as the Son of Man, we can no longer determine in what sense he meant this.[41] He presented himself, instead, as "a charismatic and autonomous prophet" whose authority "was not mediated by any human organization, not even by scripture."[42] As an eschatological prophet, however, he viewed himself as the emissary of God's kingdom and so was able to present himself symbolically as "a king." The title most faithful to Jesus' own conception of himself, Sanders says, would be *viceroy:* "God was king, but Jesus represented him and would represent him in the coming kingdom."[43] This explains the origin of the church's later confession of him to be the Messiah. The transition after Jesus' death from king (of the messianic kingdom) to Messiah was an easy one for his followers to make.[44]

Jesus and Covenantal Nomism

We noted above (page 115) that Sanders identifies three elements as pervasive in Palestinian Judaism at the time of Jesus. So far, we have seen that he relates Jesus strongly to the last of these—the hope for divine restoration of Israel. But Sanders claims that this restoration eschatology actually assumes the other two elements, which are fundamental to what he calls covenantal nomism: the belief that God would be faithful to the covenant no matter what, and the expectation that Israel would respond to God's grace with obedience to the law. We should not be surprised, therefore, to find that Sanders relates Jesus' ministry and message to these elements as well. We might be surprised, however, when we see how he does this.

Let us take the second element first: obedience to the law.[45] Sanders argues that Jesus did not abrogate the Jewish law; in particular, he did not oppose laws governing sabbath, food, or purity. Prime evidence for this is the fact that Christians struggled to define what their attitude should be on such issues in the generations following Easter (see, for example, Paul's discussion in Romans 14). If Jesus had actually "declared all foods clean" (Mark 7:19), the later church would not have been embroiled in controversy over observance of dietary laws. Thus, Sanders thinks the controversy stories in the Gospels are told from the perspective of Christians who are now defining themselves over against Judaism. He doubts the authenticity, for instance, of stories in which Jesus and the Pharisees debate what is proper to do on the sabbath (Mark 2:23–28) but notes that "to debate details of Sabbath observance presupposes general acceptance of the law."[46] In fact, Sanders claims, modern "Jewish scholars do not find any substantial points of disagreement between Jesus and his contemporaries, and certainly not any which would lead to his death."[47]

Jesus also affirmed the unfailing nature of God's covenant with Israel. His acceptance of Israel's special covenantal status is seen in that "his mission was to Israel in the name of the God of Israel."[48] Indeed, we cannot be sure what his attitude toward Gentiles was, though Sanders is inclined to think that Jesus believed some Gentiles would participate in the coming kingdom, for no other reason than that "a good number of Jews expected this to happen" and "Jesus was a kind and generous man."[49] But with regard to Israel, Jesus appears to have proclaimed God's covenantal grace with shocking implications. He called sinners, whom Sanders takes to be not merely social outcasts but "the truly wicked." Christian interpretation sometimes "debases and falsifies Judaism" and "trivializes Jesus" by construing "the issue of 'Jesus and the sinner' as if it were 'Jesus and the common people *versus* the narrow, bigoted but dominant Pharisees.'"[50] Rather, the "sinners" are such people as dishonest tax collectors and prostitutes, people who flagrantly violate God's laws. Jesus too would have regarded such people as morally reprehensible, yet he promised them a place in the kingdom. He even told religious people (chief priests and elders) that "the tax collectors and the prostitutes are going into the kingdom of God ahead of you" (Matt. 21:31). "New ages by definition must alter the present," Sanders observes wryly. "Why offer the kingdom to those who are already running it?"[51]

Sanders finds no indication that Jesus demanded repentance on the part of the wicked. Very few of the sayings attributed to Jesus mention repentance and those that do are often either summary statements (Mark 1:15; Matt. 4:17) or edited versions of earlier material (compare Luke 5:32 to Mark 2:17). In either case, the later view of the church intrudes. Furthermore, Sanders argues, Jesus' friendship with sinners (Matt. 11:19) would not have been controversial if he had been requiring these persons to change. He would have been a national hero. But the tradition reveals that this was a major point of contention between Jesus and his contemporaries as well as a characteristic that distinguished him from John the Baptist (Luke 7:31–34): "'Change now or be destroyed' was not his message, it was John's. Jesus' was, 'God loves you.'"[52] Obviously, Jesus would not have been opposed to repentance, but he "thought that God was about to change the circumstances of the world. . . . Jesus did not want the wicked to remain wicked in the interim, but he did not devise a program that would enable tax collectors and prostitutes to make a living in less dubious ways."[53] Jesus seems to have thought (and taught) that "those who followed him belonged to God's elect, even though they did not do what the Bible itself requires."[54] This idea may provide the historical roots for the subsequent Christian doctrine of atonement. After Jesus' death, the fact that he "came to *call* the wicked was transformed into the belief that he *died to save* sinners from sin and to make them upright."[55]

Traditional Christian exegesis has held that Jesus rejected those parts of the Jewish law that have to do with purity codes but insisted on repentance and obedience with regard to moral behavior. Sanders challenges both points at once. Jesus favored the whole law, ritual and ethical prescriptions alike, but he did not demand repentance or obedience with regard to any of it. These two proposals, taken together or separately, have provoked more controversy and criticism than any other aspects of Sanders's work. Neither point, however, is really essential to his main thesis, that Jesus was a prophet of Jewish restoration eschatology. Indeed, as is often noted, these points seem to detract from that thesis, for Sanders himself says that a call to repentance was a typical feature of restoration eschatology. If he could show that Jesus (like John) called sinners to repent in face of the coming judgment, he would be able to set that element alongside his temple and tribe themes as yet another parallel with this first-century Jewish perspective. As it is, he is left to surmise that maybe Jesus omitted this because he thought that John had taken care of that part of the overall task.[56] The intriguing thing about Sanders's commitment to these controversial points, then, is that he clearly is not stretching evidence to fit his thesis. If anything, he seems to be admitting that the evidence is not strong enough to support these points, even though they would fit his thesis if it were.

Jesus' Death and Resurrection

While granting that Jesus' attitude toward sinners may have been controversial, Sanders sees no reason to believe it sparked the sort of opposition that would lead to execution. Similarly, the notion presented in the Gospels that "a series of good deeds by Jesus led the Pharisees to want to kill him" is "intrinsically improbable."[57] The common view that Jesus was killed because of his position on grace has been "manufactured out of whole cloth."[58] The idea presumes that the Jews had no appreciation for God as gracious the way Christians do and then retrojects this misconception of the theological controversy back into Jesus' historical life. For those who have an accurate picture of first-century Judaism, such a scenario portrays Jesus as being executed for espousing "things about as controversial as motherhood."[59] Such a line of thinking, Sanders suggests, "is basically opposed to seeing Jesus as a first-century Jew, who thought like other Jews, spoke their language, was concerned about things that concerned them, and got into trouble over first-century issues. It is thus bad history." Then he adds, "Though I am no theologian I suspect that it is bad theology."[60]

Sanders would be likely to fault others discussed in this book (Crossan, the Jesus Seminar) for failing to see Jesus as a first-century Jew. But he agrees with them that the incident in the temple was the immediate cause of Jesus' death. This simply makes sense, for it is the one thing Jesus is reported to have done that would have been most likely to get him in trouble with the Jewish and Roman authorities. Furthermore, it is something that he did in Jerusalem (*where* he was crucified) during Passover week (*when* he was crucified). For a historian, the trick is holding together the fact that Jesus was executed as a would-be king with the fact that his disciples were not subsequently hunted down and eliminated as followers of a political claimant. Sanders does not think that either Caiaphas the Jewish high priest or Pilate the Roman governor saw Jesus and his followers as posing any serious political threat. More likely, they thought he was a religious fanatic who nevertheless might create a disturbance. Thus,

> Caiaphas had Jesus arrested because of his responsibility to put down troublemakers, especially during festivals. . . . Jesus had alarmed some people by his attack on the Temple and his statement about its destruction, because they feared that he might actually influence God. It is highly probable, however, that Caiaphas was primarily concerned with the possibility that Jesus would incite a riot. He sent armed guards to arrest Jesus, he gave him a hearing, and he recommended execution to Pilate, who promptly complied.[61]

The biblical accounts of Pilate vacillating over what to do with Jesus and then acceding to the will of the mob are probably Christian propaganda to make Jesus look more innocent in the eyes of the Roman government (at the expense of the Jewish people, who become scapegoats). Most likely, Pilate sent Jesus to the cross without a second thought, as Josephus says he was wont to do. Indeed, Pilate was eventually dismissed from office as a result of the large number of executions without trial that took place on his watch.[62]

Did Jesus intend to die? Sanders notes that all the biblical material that attributes such an intention to Jesus is heavily infected with Christian doctrine. On the surface, it doesn't make much sense. The presumption would have to be that Jesus determined to be killed so that his death could be understood in some particular way and then set about accomplishing this by deliberately provoking the authorities. "It is not historically impossible that Jesus was weird," says Sanders, but "other things that we know about him make him a *reasonable* first-century visionary."[63]

If he did not intend to die, what did he think would happen? He thought the kingdom of God would come. He thought this when he entered Jerusalem, and he appears to have continued to think this even after the temple incident when he may have realized that his own days were now numbered. Sanders regards as authentic the saying attributed to Jesus at the meal with his disciples: "I will never again drink of the fruit of the vine until that day when I drink it new in the kingdom of God" (Mark 14:25). He takes this as indicating that Jesus believed God would intervene and bring the kingdom before he was arrested and executed. It is in this light, Sanders says, that we must consider the cry of Jesus from the cross, "My God, my God, why have you forsaken me?" Sanders regards these words as authentic—they represent Jesus' own reminiscence of Psalm 22, not just a motif inserted by early Christians:

> It is possible that, when Jesus drank his last cup of wine and predicted that he would drink it again in the kingdom, he thought that the kingdom would arrive immediately. After he had been on the cross for a few hours, he despaired, and cried out that he had been forsaken.[64]

In any case, "after a relatively short period of suffering he died, and some of his followers and sympathizers hastily buried him."[65]

Sanders considers the resurrection experiences of the early Christians in an epilogue to his study. He notes that they are varied and ambiguous, resisting the idea that the risen Jesus was a ghost but also resisting the idea that he was simply a resuscitated corpse. He dismisses rational explanations for these accounts (deliberate fraud, mass hysteria) as inadequate. The bottom line:

> That Jesus' followers (and later Paul) had resurrection experiences is, in my judgement, a fact. What the reality was that gave rise to the experiences I do not know.[66]

But then he adds:

> Without the resurrection, would [Jesus'] disciples have endured longer than did John the Baptist's? We can only guess, but I would guess not.[67]

CRITIQUE OF SANDERS'S STUDY OF JESUS

Of all the views discussed in this book, Sanders's is the most "traditional" in terms of historical scholarship. It is similar in many respects to that of Albert Schweitzer, which held sway for over fifty years (see pages 17–19).[68] The historical representation of Jesus as a (mistaken) eschatological prophet presented problems and possibilities that occupied many of the twentieth century's biblical and theological scholars. As we have seen, though, the movement in recent studies of the historical Jesus has been away from this model. As a return toward the former consensus, Sanders's study has been extremely influential, but has also been sharply attacked.

The first major point of contention is the degree to which Sanders locates Jesus within the world of Palestinian Judaism. Obviously, scholars such as Downing, Mack, Crossan, and most of those associated with the Jesus Seminar would consider this a false move, for they believe Jesus' social environment was much more influenced by the Hellenistic world of the Roman Empire. But even scholars who do stress the Jewish matrix for Jesus' life and ministry criticize Sanders for assuming too much continuity between Jesus and his Jewish contemporaries. John Meier thinks he takes "the criterion of dissimilarity and stands it on its head."[69] Sanders says that a saying of Jesus reported in Mark 7:15 cannot be authentic because it is "too revolutionary" for a first-century Jew.[70] Normally, discontinuity from the world of Judaism would count as evidence *toward* authenticity.

So, too, James D. G. Dunn applauds Sanders's concern to relate Jesus to the world of Judaism but questions whether he has "pushed the pendulum too far in the opposite direction."[71] And Borg complains that Sanders does little to indicate how Jesus differed from others. What was remarkable about him? What would have caused conflict?[72] Indeed, Sanders does not indicate how Jesus differed. In fact, Sanders concludes,

> We cannot say that a single one of the things known about Jesus is unique: neither his miracles, non-violence, eschatological hope, or promise to the outcasts. He was not unique because he saw his own mission as of crucial importance, nor because he believed in the grace of God. . . . We cannot even say that Jesus was a uniquely good and great man.[73]

But Sanders does not consider this a problem. He notes that history always has trouble with declaring anything unique and faults other New Testament scholars for exaggerating claims about Jesus in this regard.[74]

The second major point of contention with Sanders's work would concern his description of Jesus as one whose life and work was shaped by a radical eschatological expectation. Of all the historians discussed so far in this book, Sanders is the only one who thinks Jesus expected God would soon inaugurate a new age through some drastic disjuncture in history. The others will criticize him at exactly this point. Borg, again, can be their spokesperson. He thinks the linchpin of Sanders's position is the "connecting link" argument that Jesus must have held such a perspective because both John the Baptist and Paul did. This reasoning, Borg contends, is not as sound as it appears, for even Sanders grants that Jesus differed from these figures in other respects. Unlike John, Jesus did not speak much of judgment or repentance, and unlike Paul he did not identify the imminent eschatological event with his own return. Borg thinks it quite possible, then, that Jesus moved away from the apocalyptic perspective of John, and that the early Christians reverted to such a perspective as a result of their Easter experiences.[75] Without this "connecting link" argument, Sanders's desire to place Jesus in the context of Jewish eschatology loses its force, for such elements as the temple incident and the selection of "the twelve" can be explained in other ways. Borg also thinks that Sanders's location of Jesus within the milieu of Jewish restoration eschatology does not account for a great deal of the material concerning him, particularly the parables and aphorisms that evidence a sapiential or wisdom tradition:

> I find it very difficult to reconcile the mentality that we see at work in the subversive wisdom of Jesus with a mentality that could literally expect that God would miraculously (and soon) build a new temple on Mt. Zion and establish Jesus and the twelve as the rulers of the new age. They seem like two different mentalities; it is difficult to imagine them combined.[76]

Wright, Witherington, and others rush to Sanders's defense at this point. They think the "connecting link" argument is very strong, and do not find the coexistence of wisdom and eschatological anticipation to be incredible. But even Sanders's allies—notably John Meier—have criticized him for downplaying the significance of the "present kingdom" in Jesus' message, a tendency that he showed some signs of correcting in his second volume.[77] Witherington also wants to correct Sanders on another point. He believes that Jesus proclaimed God's eschatological salvation as being *possibly* imminent, not as *necessarily* imminent.[78] This allows more easily for inclusion of other concerns and also avoids the problem of having to explain how the Christian faith remained viable after Jesus was proved wrong in his central conviction.

On a related issue, many critics claim that Sanders's eschatological portrait of Jesus downplays his role as a social reformer. Sanders, they claim, relates Jesus to the world of ideas in a way that makes him an apolitical, abstract thinker. His Jesus is "so unconcerned about his social world that he is curiously other-worldly, or perhaps better, next-worldly."[79] This seems to be correct. But Sanders sees the objection as grounded in hopes and preferences rather than in solid research. Naturally, a politically correct Jesus would be more appealing to modern scholars than a mistaken prophet. Still,

> it is almost impossible to explain the historical facts on the assumption that Jesus himself did not expect the imminent end or transformation of the present world order. . . . As a desperate measure, people whom this makes uncomfortable can say that everybody misunderstood Jesus completely. He really wanted economic and social reform. The disciples dropped that part of his teaching and made up sayings about the future kingdom of God—which they then had to start retracting, since the kingdom did not arrive. . . . Such views merely show the triumph of wishful thinking.[80]

Meier appears to agree (see page 144), but others claim that there is authentic material in the Jesus tradition that does point toward social and economic reform. Scholars such as Richard Horsley, Gerd Theissen, and John Howard Yoder have exposed political overtones in many of the aphorisms and parables.[81] And Witherington wants to make his point about the distinction between necessary and possible imminence once again: "A person who believes the end *may* come soon is still likely to say and do a good deal about the interim."[82] Sanders yields little ground on this point. "It is a question of emphasis," he concludes. "Jesus doubtless had views about the social, political, and economic conditions of his people, but his mission was to prepare them to receive the coming kingdom of God."[83]

Other criticisms of Sanders's work concern minor arguments, and he is more flexible with regard to his own position. As indicated, many scholars have disputed the notion that Jesus did not require repentance of sinners. Crossan, for instance, thinks Sanders was "seduced" into reaching this "strange conclusion" by failing to identify the texts on which he draws as expressive of polemical invective: "There should never be serious historical debate on Jesus accepting unrepentant tax collectors, sinners, or prostitutes unless there is also serious historical debate on Jesus as a lunatic, a demoniac, a glutton, a drunkard, and a Samaritan."[84] Sanders himself notes a paradoxical tension within the tradition. Jesus apparently required high moral standards of his followers, for example, prohibiting divorce among them, and yet "the overall tenor of Jesus' teaching is compassion towards human frailty."[85] Jesus himself did not live a stern or strict life and his parables reveal God to be surprisingly generous (Matt. 20:1–16) and surprisingly undiscriminating (Matt. 22:1–10).[86] Meier, we should add, seems favorably disposed to Sanders's argument here, agreeing that Jesus offered a place in the kingdom to "the wicked" without requiring "the usual process of reintegration."[87]

Likewise, the argument that Jesus did not come into significant conflict with his contemporaries over matters of the law is disputed. Witherington claims that the very acceptance of sinners that Sanders attributes to Jesus would have entailed abrogation of purity laws prescribing cultic means for readmission to the community. If Jesus would ignore these laws, why dismiss the authenticity of Gospel accounts that indicate he transgressed sabbath rules and other purity codes?[88] Wright thinks Sanders's notion that Pharisees did not try to press their legal interpretations upon others is undercut by the personal testimony of the Pharisee Paul (1 Cor. 15:9; Gal. 1:13–14).[89] Furthermore, Wright argues that, on this point, Sanders ironically tries to interpret Jesus' relationship with the Pharisees "within the non-eschatological category of 'patterns of religion'" by insisting that Jesus and the Pharisees had only minor disagreements over matters of the law.[90] If Jesus was an eschatological prophet, says Wright, it is likely that he challenged the basic tenets of "religion as usual" and this would have brought conflict:

> If the synoptic scenarios are anything other than a complete fabrication, Jesus was not debating with the Pharisees on their own terms, or about the detail of their own agendas. Two musicians may discuss which key is best for a particular Schubert song. Somebody who proposes rearranging the poem for a heavy metal band is not joining in the discussion, but challenging its very premises.[91]

Reginald Fuller simply accuses Sanders of applying the criterion of dissimilarity inconsistently: Sanders rejects that criterion when he suspects the authenticity of anything that marks Jesus as different from the world of Judaism but then uses it to distinguish the authentic Jesus from the antilegal tradition of the early church.[92]

The last comment indicates that Sanders's method of operation may not be as precise as it could be. He has been criticized on this point by friends and foes alike. Meier, for instance, praises Sanders for breaking out of the narrow focus on sayings, parables, and aphorisms that seems to have characterized much of Jesus scholarship, but faults him for essentially equating actions and deeds with "facts" and then interpreting sayings in light of these.[93] Meier thinks the actions and sayings must be held together. He sees Sanders trying to do this with regard to the temple incident and he thinks his case could be strengthened elsewhere if he would demonstrate such meshing of traditions.[94] As we have seen, less friendly critics have been able to attack the very foundations of Sanders's system by taking up his lists of what are supposed to be virtually indisputable facts and then disputing them.

In his second book on Jesus, Sanders appears to be frustrated at times by what he must regard as obsessive tendencies of scholars to micromanage the tradition, by efforts to determine whether every individual saying or deed should be regarded as authentic. He prefers to note major trajectories and emphases in those parts of the tradition that are generally regarded as reliable. "We do not need to decide which of the 'antitheses' [the sayings recorded in Matt. 5:21–48] go back to Jesus," he writes at one point. "Let us say that they all do."[95] Such comments appear dismissive of the scholarly enterprise, of the painstaking deliberation on individual texts that characterizes the work of the Jesus Seminar on the one hand and (as we will see) that of Meier on the other. The criticism of Sanders has been that, in trying to paint the big picture, he has not paid enough attention to the details. He might claim, to use a different metaphor, that we have enough information already to describe the forest without making final decisions on the bark or root structure of every individual tree.

In conclusion, there are two points on which Sanders is quite certain—that Jesus must be interpreted as a representative of first-century Palestinian Judaism and that he expected an imminent eschatological restoration of Israel—and on these he is resolute. However, Sanders often appears to be more open to critique and to revision than any other scholar working on the historical Jesus today. The pages of his books are literally crowded with qualifiers: "maybe," "possibly," "likely," "perhaps." He frequently admits that he is guessing with regard to certain matters and that he simply does not know what to think about other ones. He acknowledges that he has been wrong about assessments in the past and yields to new interpretations. All this marks his projects with a winsome humility.

As usual, we let him have the last word:

Historical reconstruction is never absolutely certain, and in the case of Jesus it is sometimes highly uncertain. Despite this, we have a good idea of the main lines of his ministry and his message. We know who he was, what he did, what he taught, and why he died. Perhaps most important, we know how much he inspired his followers, who sometimes themselves did not understand him, but who were so loyal to him that they changed history.[96]

8

JOHN P. MEIER

*J*esus persists in veiling himself in indirect references and metaphors. . . . It is almost as though Jesus were intent on making a riddle of himself. . . . Whoever or whatever Jesus was, he was a complex figure, not easily subsumed under one theological rubric or sociological model.

—John Meier[1]

*M*eier labels Jesus a marginal Jew because in his own life he lived at the edge of the empire, traveled within a narrow range, identified with those on the margins of society, and held views and performed miracles that were out of the ordinary. . . . What made Jesus unique was a complex configuration of factors: he was teacher, he was miracle worker, he was prophet of the last days, and he was the gatherer of Israel. . . . Meier sees Jesus as some sort of messianic figure, however much Jesus eludes precise definition.

—Ben Witherington III[2]

John Meier wins the prize for length. His study of the historical Jesus is over sixteen hundred pages long and is only two-thirds done. Quantitatively, at least, he has exceeded all other Jesus scholars, ancient and modern.

A Catholic priest educated and ordained in Rome, Meier is now professor of New Testament at Notre Dame University in South Bend, Indiana. Though he has been known to be critical of his church's political and theological stances, he remains loyal. He has served as president of the Catholic Biblical Association and as editor of the prestigious journal *Catholic Biblical Quarterly*.

When *U.S. News and World Report* sought a catchy caption to distinguish Meier from other Jesus scholars they settled on the phrase "dogged digger."[3] And so he is. Meticulous in his scholarship, he examines every saying and fact about Jesus, rigorously applying a well-defined set of criteria for determining historical authenticity. For those who are not truly committed, the presentation can become tedious, but one thing is always clear: if, at the end of a discussion, you do not agree with Meier's conclusion, you can see exactly how he reached it and identify at what juncture you parted company, and why. This, his academic peers affirm, is traditional (his critics say "old-fashioned") historical criticism at its best.

Meier's study of Jesus began as a simple prelude to a commentary on Matthew, but as he kept finding questions that had not been adequately researched, the project took on a life of its own. The work is being published under the grand title *A Marginal Jew: Rethinking the Historical Jesus*. When it is finished, it will be "at least" three volumes. So far, only two have been published. The first is subtitled *The Roots of the Problem and the Person,* and the second, *Mentor, Message, and Miracles.*

A word may be said about the phrase "marginal Jew." Meier initially chose this phrase as a tease, a sort of riddle meant "to open up a set of questions" and to suggest "intriguing possibilities."[4] He did not mean for it to become the defining phrase for understanding his view of Jesus, though some commentators seem to take it that way. With that in mind, we may ask what some of the intriguing possibilities might be. Meier does not mean to imply that Jesus is marginal in his ultimate importance, but he does maintain that in his own day Jesus was "at most a blip on the radar screen" of the Greco-Roman world.[5] Roman historians such as Josephus, Tacitus, and Suetonius pay little attention to him. But Meier may also be trying to express something else with his book's title—the paradox of seeing Jesus within his Jewish world while also recognizing what made him distinct. We have seen other scholars struggle with this: for Crossan, Jesus seems hardly Jewish at all; for Sanders, Jesus is a typical Jew. Meier wants to steer a middle course: Jewish, but not typical—at least in key respects. Jesus appears to have remained celibate. He left his home and family to pursue an itinerant ministry. He eschewed fasting and prohibited divorce. His teaching evinced a style and content that "did not jibe with the views and practices of the major Jewish religious groups of his day."[6] This was not unrelated to his eventual fate:

> By the time he died [Jesus] had managed to make himself appear obnoxious, dangerous, or suspicious to everyone, from pious Pharisees through political

high priests to an ever vigilant Pilate. One reason Jesus met a swift and brutal end is simple: he alienated so many individuals and groups in Palestine that, when the final clash came in Jerusalem in 30 A.D., he had very few people, especially people of influence on his side.[7]

And again:

A poor layman from the Galilean countryside with disturbing doctrines and claims was marginal both in the sense of being dangerously anti-establishment and in the sense of lacking a power base in the capital. He could easily be brushed aside into the dustbin of death.[8]

MEIER'S METHOD FOR STUDYING JESUS

Meier is at the opposite end of the spectrum from John Dominic Crossan with regard to objectivity in scholarship. Crossan dismisses objectivity as "spurious" and "unattainable"; in its place he commends "honesty" with regard to one's own inclinations and presuppositions.[9] Meier is all for honesty, but he insists that a commitment to professional objectivity is fundamental to academic scholarship. Throughout his study, he employs the image of what he calls an "unpapal conclave" of scholars—a Catholic, a Protestant, a Jew, and an agnostic—who have been "locked up in the bowels of the Harvard Divinity School library, put on a spartan diet, and not allowed to emerge until they have hammered out a consensus document on who Jesus of Nazareth was and what he intended in his own time and place."[10] With regard to issue after issue Meier asks, What would this committee make of the evidence? For example, in his study of miracles, Meier concedes that one member might think that Jesus really did work miracles, while another might claim that this is intrinsically impossible. All four, however, could agree that Jesus did in fact do startling deeds that people in his day (friends and foes alike) considered to be miracles. This, then, is what the historian can affirm.

As such, the historical task is necessarily reductionist. The object of historical inquiry is not ultimately the "real Jesus" but only those aspects or facets of him that are amenable to academic study:

In contrast to the "real Jesus," the "historical Jesus" is that Jesus whom we can recover or reconstruct by using the scientific tools of modern historical research. The "historical Jesus" is thus a scientific construct, a theoretical abstraction of modern scholars that coincides only partially with the real Jesus of Nazareth, the Jew who actually lived and worked in Palestine.[11]

Meier has affirmed elsewhere that he personally does believe in the virgin birth, the miracles, and the resurrection of Jesus.[12] These matters would belong to the large portrait of what he regards as "the real Jesus," but they do not necessarily belong to the smaller portrait of what he regards as "the historical Jesus."[13]

Meier's claim to professional neutrality has been challenged more philosophically than practically. On the surface, it appears arrogant: Meier is only one person. How can he claim that his work faithfully represents what would be produced by a four-person committee? Meier is a Catholic. How can he claim to represent the perspective of a scholarly Protestant, Jew, or agnostic? But, in practice, critiques of his work have not faulted him at this point; the implications of his conclusions are at least as challenging to the Catholic faith as to the other three perspectives. Ironically, Meier's study of Jesus has been viewed as far less tendentious than that of the Jesus Seminar, a committee that *is* in fact composed of Catholics, Protestants, Jews, and agnostics. Still, the very notion that neutrality can be symbolized adequately by a convergence of perspectives regarding *religious* ideology (rather than with regard to social, political, ethnic, gender, or class distinctions) is revealing in a way that for some undermines the claim to detachment.[14]

Given Meier's commitment to objectivity, however, clarity about methodological procedures becomes a high priority. He devotes over two hundred pages to method in the first volume of his work. To summarize, we may note that he regards five criteria as especially useful: embarrassment, discontinuity, multiple attestation, coherence, and what he calls "the criterion of Jesus' rejection and execution."[15] The last of these is not widely used in historical Jesus studies; Meier and N. T. Wright are the two persons discussed in this book who give it most attention. Furthermore, we should note that Meier construes the criterion of multiple attestation in a distinctive way by indicating that the case for historicity is enhanced when there is a multiple attestation of *forms* as well as *sources.* To illustrate this point, let us consider once more the question of miracles. Most scholars note that multiple sources (Mark, Q, M, L, and John) attribute miracles to Jesus; Meier also notes that we have both *narratives* of Jesus working miracles and *sayings* about Jesus working miracles. The double attestation of multiple sources and multiple forms is a strong argument for authenticity of the tradition that Jesus did do things that were regarded as miracles.[16]

A few words must also be said about Meier's evaluation of sources. He regards the four canonical Gospels as the essential documents, with "tidbits" supplied occasionally from the writings of Paul or Josephus.[17] This is distinctive in two ways. First, Meier is not automatically dismissive of the Gospel of John, as are many historical scholars. He recognizes that the material in John has undergone more extensive development than that in the other Gospels and must be used with special care, but he does in fact find much in this book that he considers to be historically authentic. One example is that he decides John's Gospel is right in portraying Jesus' ministry as lasting longer than one year and involving multiple trips to Jerusalem (the Synoptic Gospels present a shorter ministry with only one trip to Jerusalem at the end). Another significant point regarding sources is that Meier considers the apocryphal Gospels to be relatively late documents that are virtually worthless as sources for independent historical data about Jesus.[18] No brushstrokes from the Gospel of Thomas can be seen in his portrait of Jesus.

For Meier, historical science demands strict attention to clearly defined criteria and detailed public presentation of evidence to account for even the smallest point of each argument. This, he claims, is why his work is so long. If someone does not agree with his conclusions they can look at his record of how he reached them and try to pinpoint where they believe he went wrong. Indeed, he claims to have done this himself, imaginatively adopting the various persona of those scholars locked in the bowels of Harvard Divinity School and reviewing his work from each perspective:

> Time and time again while writing this volume, I have been constrained to reverse my views because of the weight of the data and the force of the criteria. My own experience has convinced me that, while methodology and criteria may be tiresome topics, they are vital in keeping the critic from seeing in the data whatever he or she already has decided to see. The rules of the road are never exciting, but they keep us moving in the right direction.[19]

MEIER'S PORTRAIT OF JESUS

Like Crossan, Meier chooses words that begin with the letter *m* to shape his presentation of Jesus. Instead of "magic" and "meal," however, we get "mentor," message," and "miracles." To these may be added a prologue concerning Jesus' early years and some projections regarding what is still to come in the unpublished volume.

Jesus' Early Years

Not much can be known with any certainty about Jesus' origins, Meier admits, though the few facts that can be affirmed put him ahead of most historical figures from the ancient world. We have multiple attestation that he was born during the reign of Herod the Great and, therefore, before 4 B.C.E. The most likely time is 7–4 B.C.E. and the most likely place is Nazareth, since he is widely attested to have been from there. The biblical story of a birth in Bethlehem is not impossible, but probably reflects later theological interests rather than historical fact. The claim that his mother was a virgin at the time of his birth has multiple attestation (M, L) but was not open to verification even in Jesus' own lifetime, much less today.

Jesus was Jewish, and was raised as the firstborn son of Joseph and Mary in a family that included at least four brothers (James, Joses, Jude, and Simon) and at least two sisters (who are unnamed). The very names of these family members, as well as Jesus' own name (which is identical to the Hebrew *Joshua*), recall significant figures from Israel's past, suggesting that the family may have nurtured the pious hopes for the restoration of Israel that were common in this environment. Joseph may even have claimed to be of the lineage of David, a fact that would later help to fuel messianic expectations with regard to Jesus.[20] Jesus' mother, brothers, and sisters apparently outlived him, but Joseph probably died before Jesus began his ministry. Reports in the New Testament that seem to be reliable indicate that there was tension between Jesus and his family during his life but that later some of his siblings were prominent leaders in the movement that continued in his name.

In the face of all this information about family members, all sources are completely silent with regard to Jesus having a wife or children. Meier notes that it would have been highly unusual for a man in Jesus' social position to choose a life of celibacy but decides that this nevertheless appears to have been the case. Thus, Jesus would have been marked among his peers as exceptional or odd at an early point.

Like his father, Jesus worked as a carpenter, a trade that involved building parts of houses in addition to the fashioning of furniture. As such, he would have been poor, but not one of the "poorest of the poor." He did not know "the grinding poverty of the dispossessed farmer, the city beggar, the rural day laborer, or the rural slave."[21] He had a trade that involved a fair level of technical skill and—Meier adds incidentally—one that marks him as healthy if not muscular.[22] As a Jew growing up in Nazareth, Jesus would have spoken Aramaic, some Greek, and perhaps some Hebrew. While there is no indication that he received education outside of his home, Meier is inclined to think that he was literate.[23]

Legends abound about the "hidden years" of Jesus' adolescence and early adulthood, but Meier has his own theory as to why the Bible is silent about this time: "nothing much happened." Apart from remaining single, Jesus appears to have been "insufferably ordinary."[24] He did nothing that would earn him religious credentials or gain him a power base.[25] Then, when he was about thirty-three years old, he left home for reasons unknown and traveled to the Judean countryside to be baptized by a man named John.

Mentor

Meier devotes over two hundred pages to a study of John the Baptist, whom he considers to be "the one person who had the single greatest influence on Jesus' ministry."[26] He thinks it possible that John was the only son of a priest who "turned his back on his filial duty of continuing the priestly line and ministering in the Jerusalem temple." He thinks it unlikely, however, that John had any direct connection with the antiestablishment movement at Qumran known to us through the Dead Sea Scrolls.[27]

John was, to use words attributed to Jesus, "a prophet, and more than a prophet" (Matt. 11:9). He stood in the tradition of Israel's prophets but went beyond them in significant ways. Like prophets before him, he proclaimed a message of doom, announcing an imminent fiery judgment that was going to break in upon Israel. But he also related salvation from that judgment to his own person in a way that was not typical of the prophetic tradition. Protection from the coming wrath lay in repentance, which included acceptance of baptism administered by him. This baptism was symbolic: immersion in water signified extinction of flames that would engulf the unrepentant. Yet John also declared that a mysterious "stronger one" was coming after him who would baptize with the Holy Spirit those whom John had marked with his water ritual. There is a paradox, then, in how John saw himself. On the one hand, he pointed away from himself, indicating his own insignificance in light of the coming one, whose sandals he was not worthy to carry (Matt. 3:11). On the other hand, he presented himself as the only one who was able to confer the baptism that prepares people for the salvation that this figure would bring.

John was both eschatological and charismatic, that is, he claimed "direct knowledge of God's will and plans—knowledge unmediated by the traditional channels of law, temple, priesthood, or scribal scholarship."[28] The result of his ministry was the creation of a sectarian community within Israel that was not defined by a particular approach to legal observances or temple worship. Herod noticed the extent of John's influence on people, feared (wrongly in Meier's opinion) that such influence would be used for seditious purposes, and—as Josephus notes—executed him as a "preemptive strike."

Jesus was baptized by John and appears to have joined his circle for a time. Since John offered his baptism for forgiveness of sins and protection against judgment, we must assume that accepting this baptism was for Jesus an act of confession and repentance. Meier warns, however, against construing such repentance in terms of "the introspective conscience of the West."[29] Rather than focusing on individual sins or personal peccadillos, Jesus' repentance would have involved humble admission that he was a member of a sinful people (the rebellious and ungrateful nation of Israel), accompanied by a resolve to be different.

Accepting John's baptism also implied recognition on Jesus' part that he was now, in some sense, a disciple of the Baptist. Thus, he must have accepted the eschatological message that John preached, including the idea that salvation was to be found only through submission to John's ritual washing. At some point, though, Jesus left John's circle and began his own ministry. The break, Meier thinks, was a moderate one. He avoids the idea of apostasy from John, which has been put forward by Paul Hollenbach and picked up in some ways by Borg, Crossan, and others.[30] He also dismisses the suggestion by Hendrikus Boers that Jesus continued throughout his ministry to see John and not himself as the final eschatological figure who would bring in the kingdom of God.[31] Rejecting these "simplistic scenarios,"[32] Meier attempts to delineate the distinctive aspects of Jesus' ministry without obscuring the enduring influence that the Baptist had on him. Jesus was no "carbon copy" of John, but "a firm substratum of the Baptist's life and message" remained with Jesus throughout his ministry.[33]

Thus, Jesus' ministry was different from John's in key respects. It was itinerant rather than localized; he toured villages and towns rather than going out into the wilderness and inviting people to come to him. His preaching also moved in emphasis from God's imminent fiery judgment to God's offer of mercy and forgiveness. This was demonstrated dramatically in his healings and open table fellowship with sinners. And there are other differences. In contrast to Jesus, John was known to be an ascetic. John is never said to have healed the sick. John is depicted as calling people to make themselves acceptable to God, to "bear fruit worthy of repentance" (Luke 3:8) rather than assuring them of their participation in the banquet God was preparing.

Still, Meier insists that Jesus never abandoned John's message of judgment. This eschatological, even apocalyptic notion that the day of divine reckoning was at hand remained one element of Jesus' own preaching. Also, like John, Jesus chose to remain celibate, gathered disciples, and conducted a ministry to Israel. Jesus even imitated John's practice of baptizing and, in Meier's view, probably continued to baptize disciples throughout his ministry. The references to this in the Gospel of John (John 3:22, 26; 4:1) have a strong chance of authenticity due to the criterion of embarrassment, for the Christian church never would have invented this tradition and in fact tried to suppress it, as John 4:2 attests in a rather sloppy way. Meier says, "It is likely that the practice of baptizing flowed like water from John through Jesus into the early church, with the ritual taking on different meanings at each stage of the process."[34]

Thus, Meier thinks Q depicts John and Jesus as "the eschatological odd couple," divergent in accent and style, but united in their effort to prepare unrepentant Israel for a coming crisis involving salvation and judgment (Matt. 11:16–19; Luke 7:31–35).[35] Meier accepts as authentic the Q tradition that John eventually wondered whether Jesus might be "the stronger one" he believed was coming (Matt. 11:2–6), while emphasizing that the tradition does not convey how or whether John resolved that question. He also accepts as authentic the tradition that Jesus declared John to be the greatest person ever born (Matt. 11:7–11), while noting that this tradition also affirms Jesus declaring that "even the most insignificant Israelite who has entered into the eschatological kingdom of God that Jesus announces enjoys a privilege and standing greater than John's."[36]

The greatest similarity of Jesus to John, however, may lie in the paradoxical construal each offered of his own person. On the one hand, Jesus made the kingdom of God, rather than himself, the main focus of his preaching. On the other, what he said about the kingdom involved "a monumental though implicit claim: with the start of Jesus' ministry, a definitive shift has taken place in the eschatological timetable."[37] Thus, what Jesus says about himself in relation to the kingdom has echoes with what John said of himself in relation to "the coming one."

Message

Meier agrees with most historical scholars in affirming that Jesus' teaching and preaching employed the phrase "kingdom of God." He seeks to establish, furthermore, that the use of this phrase was somewhat distinctive for Jesus. While not altogether absent, the words *kingdom of God* do not appear frequently in the Old Testament, in Jewish literature from this period, or in the writings of Paul and other early Christians. Thus, Jesus' use of the term reflects a "conscious, personal choice" and, for that reason, the study of this symbol offers a "privileged way of entering into Jesus' message."[38]

What does the phrase mean? Like Marcus Borg (see page 110), Meier maintains that it is "a tensive symbol," that is, a symbol that "evokes not one meaning but a whole range of meanings."[39] The basic sense is "the dynamic notion of God powerfully ruling over his creation, over his people, and over the history of both." In short, "kingdom of God" is a symbol for "God ruling as king." This concept, as distinct from the precise phrase that Jesus chose, is widespread, appearing in many different contexts and acquiring many facets and dimensions. Thus far, Meier and Borg would be in complete agreement. They part company when Meier insists that one meaning of the phrase (perhaps the dominant one) in the teaching of Jesus involved expectations regarding the imminent future. In the centuries immediately preceding Jesus' life (the intertestamental period), Meier claims, the most prominent use of the "kingdom of God" symbol was in eschatological and apocalyptic contexts, where it conjured up hopes of definitive salvation for Israel in the future.[40]

Meier applies his criteria of authenticity to sayings attributed to Jesus regarding the kingdom and then extrapolates the results of those that meet the test. The Lord's Prayer indicates that Jesus did expect a future, definitive coming of God to rule as king and taught his disciples to pray for this ("Your kingdom come," Luke 11:2). Some of the Beatitudes indicate that this kingdom will bring about a reversal of such unjust conditions as poverty, sorrow, and hunger ("Blessed are you who are hungry now, for you will be filled. . . ." Luke 6:21). Other authentic sayings affirm that the kingdom will include some Gentiles as honored guests alongside Israel's patriarchs (Matt. 8:11–12) and express Jesus' confidence in the face of death that he too will experience a saving reversal and share in the final banquet (Mark 14:25).[41]

Next Meier examines three sayings in which Jesus sets timetables for the kingdom's arrival, apparently stressing that it will come very soon (Matt. 10:23), even during the lifetime of his first followers (Mark 9:1; 13:30). His results here are surprising—they surprised even him.[42] Most scholars, including Sanders (see pages 120–21), have assumed the texts to be authentic, not least because of the embarrassment the church faced when the predictions were not fulfilled. But on further examination, Meier concludes that they do in fact derive from the early church, composed by Christians who were disappointed that the parousia had not come but wanted assurance that it was just around the corner. "Imminent-future eschatology has its origins in Jesus," Meier grants, but "attempts to set time limits for that eschatology have their origin in the church."[43]

Meier also studies some key sayings, which he judges to be authentic, in which Jesus speaks of the kingdom of God as a reality that is already present. The "star witness" here is the Q saying found in Luke 11:20, where Jesus declares, "If it is by the finger of God that I cast out the demons, then the kingdom of God has come to you." Here Jesus presents his exorcisms as "proof that the kingdom of God that he proclaims for the future is in some sense already present."[44] The same basic message is conveyed by the parable Jesus tells in Mark about "binding the strong man" (Mark 3:27). Jesus' response to John the Baptist's question in Matthew 11:2–6 indicates that his miracles and proclamation to the poor are signs that the time he and John have been awaiting has arrived. His rejection of voluntary fasting is grounded in the same vision (Mark 2:18–20). Other sayings that are probably authentic speak of the kingdom as already present in a generic sense, without specific reference to Jesus' ministry as the sign or vehicle of its presence (Luke 10:23; 17:21).[45]

"The precise relationship between the coming and present kingdom remains unspecified," Meier concludes.[46] He notes the tendencies in modern scholarship to resolve the dilemma one way or the other. Crossan, Borg, and the Jesus Seminar deem the "present kingdom" sayings authentic and so rule that Jesus did not speak of the kingdom as something yet to come. Sanders deems the "future kingdom" sayings authentic and tends to disregard any implication that the kingdom is already here.[47] Such concern for logical consistency, says Meier, "may be beside the point when dealing with an itinerant Jewish preacher and miracle worker of 1st-century Palestine."[48] But Meier does not find the "already/not yet" tension to be so contradictory. He (like Sanders) thinks the emphasis in Jesus' message was on the kingdom about to arrive, but he grants that Jesus saw signs that indicated the eschatological drama was already underway and apparently thought that his own ministry constituted "a partial and preliminary realization of God's kingly rule, which would soon be displayed in full force."[49]

Miracles

Meier accepts as a historical fact that Jesus did perform extraordinary deeds that were deemed by himself, his supporters, and his enemies to be miracles. He asserts this defiantly, recognizing that "a miracle-free Jesus has been the holy grail sought by many [historical Jesus] questers from the Enlightenment onwards."[50] The attribution of miracles to Jesus is supported by widespread attestation of sources (Mark, Q, M, L, John, and even Josephus) and coheres well with other information that we know about him, including his claim to offer a preliminary experience of the future kingdom of God and his success at attracting large numbers of followers. Indeed, of all the elements in the mix of what can reliably be attributed to Jesus, Meier thinks that "miracle working probably contributed the most to his prominence and popularity on the public scene—as well as to the enmity he stirred up in high places."[51] The miracle tradition has better historical support than many facts that are commonly accepted, such as that Jesus was a carpenter or that he used the word *Abba* in his prayers. The rejection of this tradition can only be viewed as an imposition of a philosophical concept on objective research. If the tradition that Jesus worked miracles is to be rejected as unhistorical, says Meier, "so should every other Gospel tradition about him."[52]

This is not to say that Jesus actually did work miracles, an affirmation that would also impose a philosophical concept on the evidence. What we can affirm is the attribution of miracles to Jesus *during his own lifetime*. Contrary to the view of Burton Mack (see page 26), the early church did not simply invent this tradition and make up the miracle stories at some point after Jesus' death. At least, it did not make up all of them. Meier devotes some four hundred pages to an exhaustive historical analysis of every miracle story in the Gospels. Some, such as the exorcism of the Syrophoenician woman's daughter (Mark 7:24–30) and most of the so-called nature miracles (walking on water, changing water to wine, stilling storms, cursing the fig tree), serve theological purposes so clearly that they are likely to have developed within the church's preaching to illustrate symbolically some particular point. In such cases, it is impossible for the historian to determine the extent to which an actual event may have served as the catalyst for the story as it appears in the Bible. But many of the individual accounts of miracles do meet criteria for historical authenticity. Reports of miracles that are most likely to go back to the historical Jesus include the exorcism of an epileptic boy (Mark 9:14–29), the exorcism of Mary Magdalene (Luke 8:2), the healing of a paralytic let down through a roof (Mark 2:1–12), the healing of another paralytic by the pool of Bethesda (John 5:1–9), three healings of blind men—Bartimaeus (Mark 10:46–52), the blind man at Bethsaida (Mark 8:22–26), and the man born blind in Jerusalem (John 9), the healing of an official's boy (Matt. 8:5–13; John 4:46–54), and the raising of Jairus's daughter from the dead (Mark 5:21–43). He also inclines to believe that a historical core can be found in such stories as the exorcism of the Gerasene demoniac (Mark 5:1–20), the raising of the widow's son at Nain (Luke 7:11–17), the raising of Lazarus (John 11:1–46), and the feeding of the multitudes (Mark 6:32–44).

A key text for Meier is the passage from Q in which Jesus describes his ministry in generic terms: "the blind receive their sight, the lame walk, the lepers are cleansed, the deaf hear, the dead are raised, the poor have good news brought to them" (Luke 7:22). This logion establishes the types of miracles for which Jesus claimed to be known. The specific accounts that Meier judges to be historical exemplify this general description that Jesus himself offered of his ministry. Although Meier can find no specific accounts of Jesus cleansing lepers or healing the deaf that meet his criteria of authenticity, he believes that Jesus was reputed to have done these things also.

One distinctive feature of Meier's list of authentic miracle accounts is that it contains stories found in John's Gospel, at least three of which concern miracles worked in Jerusalem (the paralytic at Bethesda, the man born blind, and the raising of Lazarus). The majority of historical scholars (following the Synoptic Gospels) do not think Jesus spent any time in Jerusalem but restricted his ministry to Galilee. The working of miracles in Jerusalem adds an element to Meier's portrait of Jesus that differs even from those of scholars such as Borg and Crossan who do assume that Jesus was reputed to work miracles in Galilee. This element derives from Meier's aversion to scholarship's *prima facie* rejection of the Gospel of John as unhistorical. Meier submits individual traditions in John to the same tests he uses for traditions in the other Gospels, though even he is a bit harder on the Johannine accounts. Given the recognizable tradition of theological development in the fourth Gospel, its reports start out with marks against them. It is noteworthy, then, that so many stories in John—miracle stories at that—end up receiving the Meier seal of approval.

More

As this book went to press, the third volume of Meier's *A Marginal Jew* was still in preparation. He has, however, provided some previews of what we will find there.

First, Meier considers the importance of Jesus' selection of twelve disciples.[53] Like Sanders, Meier regards the tradition that Jesus referred to an inner circle of disciples as "the twelve" to be historically authentic. Three factors are determinative for this. First, the tradition has multiple attestation of sources and forms. It receives independent support from Mark, Q, John, Paul, and possibly L. Second, the tradition is supported by the criterion of embarrassment, since the fact that Jesus was handed over by one of the twelve was hardly a matter the church would invent. Finally, the historicity of this tradition is evident in that the concept of the twelve ceased to be important soon after the time of Jesus, as individual leaders (including persons like Paul and James of Jerusalem, who were not among the twelve) came to prominence. Meier further notes that the New Testament tradition distinguishes the twelve from disciples in general (who included many other persons, such as Levi in Mark 2:13–15) and from "the apostles" (among whom Paul includes such relatively unknown persons as Andronicus and Junia in Rom. 16:7). The exact membership of the twelve, Meier notes, may have varied over the course of Jesus' ministry, but maintaining the group intact does not appear to have been important for long in the church after Easter. The book of Acts reports that Judas was replaced by Matthias (Acts 1:15–26) but gives no indication that further appointments were made when other members of the twelve were martyred (Acts 12:2). Whatever the reasons for this, Meier concludes that the concept of the twelve originated with Jesus and that the number twelve itself was significant to him. The clear implication is that Jesus viewed his mission as involving some sort of restoration of the nation of Israel.

Second, Meier recognizes the need to discuss further "Jesus' relation to the Mosaic Law, both in his interpretation and in his praxis of it."[54] The image of Jesus as a teacher of ethical imperatives who gave his disciples concrete directions on how to observe the Mosaic Law must be added to that of the eschatological, miracle-working prophet. But even in relation to the law, Jesus was a charismatic figure. Meier disagrees with Sanders at this point, claiming that Jesus did assume the right to rescind or change parts of the law. What's more, he located his authority to do this not in recognized or traditional channels but in "his own ability to know directly and intuitively what was God's will for his people."[55]

This leads naturally to the question, "Who did this man think he was?"—a subject that Meier intends to explore with reference to the eschatological or messianic designations that existed in Judaism at the time of Jesus. He has said that he thinks "at least some of Jesus' followers believed him to be descended from King David, and that they therefore took him to be the Davidic Messiah."[56]

Finally, Meier has already indicated in part his response to the question of why Jesus was crucified. A variety of factors suggest why he might have been initially viewed as dangerous: he announced the coming of a future kingdom that would soon put an end to the present state of affairs; he claimed to be able to teach the will of God authoritatively, sometimes in ways that ran counter to scripture and tradition; he performed miracles that attracted a large following; and he evinced a freewheeling personal conduct through open fellowship with recognized sinners. If one adds to this "volatile mix" the fact that some Jews took him to be the Davidic Messiah, it becomes "positively explosive," Meier says, and then we must view such events as the staged entry into Jerusalem and the demonstration in the temple as "the match set to the barrel of gasoline."[57]

Convergence

Meier's portrait of Jesus is like that of Marcus Borg in that he understands Jesus to be "a complex figure" who does not fit easily into any known category. The historical Jesus is a 1st-century Jewish eschatological prophet who proclaims an imminent-future coming of God's kingdom, practices baptism as a ritual of preparation for that kingdom, teaches his disciples to pray to God as *abba* for that kingdom's arrival, prophesies the regathering of all Israel (symbolized by the inner circle of his twelve disciples) and the inclusion of the Gentiles when the kingdom comes—but who at the same time makes the kingdom already present for at least some Israelites by his exorcisms and miracles of healing. Hence in some sense he already mediates an experience of the joyful time of salvation, expressed also in his freewheeling table fellowship with toll collectors and sinners and his rejection of voluntary fasting for himself and his disciples. To all this must be added his—at times startling—interpretation of the Mosaic Law.[58]

Notably, Borg's four categories for understanding the historical Jesus do not figure prominently in Meier's equally diverse scheme. Meier does not present Jesus as a mystical holy man who views himself as a channel for the Spirit, or as a subversive sage, movement initiator, or social reformer. Of all the historians reviewed in this book, Meier and Borg are the most eclectic in their collection of images for Jesus, yet there is little overlap in the images that they think apply.

In terms of content, Meier's portrait most closely resembles that of E. P. Sanders. He sees Jesus as an eschatological Jewish prophet who was primarily concerned with announcing and, in some sense, enacting the divine restoration of Israel. Because Meier is less averse than Sanders to what appear to be contradictory impulses, however, his portrait takes in qualities that Sanders rejects. Unlike Sanders, Meier thinks Jesus did engage his contemporaries in conflicts over the law and he affirms that Jesus did regard the coming kingdom as already present in some definitive and significant way.[59] Ultimately, what sets Meier's portrait of Jesus apart from that of Sanders may be its complexity. We have seen that Sanders insists, as a historian, that no aspect of Jesus can truly be regarded as unique (see page 126). Meier contends that the "atypical configuration of Jesus' characteristics" is what marks him as unique:

> At one and the same time he acted as (1) the prophet of the last days, which were soon to come and yet were somehow already present in his ministry; (2) the gatherer of the Israel of the last days, the twelve tribes of Israel being symbolized by the circle of the twelve disciples Jesus formed around himself; (3) the teacher of both general moral truths and detailed directives concerning the observance of the Mosaic Law (e.g., divorce); and last but not least (4) the exorcist and healer of illnesses who was even reputed, like Elijah and Elisha, to have raised the dead. . . . It is the explosive convergence and mutual reinforcement of all these usually distinct figures in the one Jesus of Nazareth that made him stand out.[60]

CRITIQUE OF MEIER'S STUDY OF JESUS

Because Meier's work is recent and incomplete, it has not been subjected to the sort of detailed criticism leveled against some of the other studies discussed in this book.[61] Clearly, though, he has become a major player in the current debate. While he is basically supportive of Sanders's study, his work undermines basic conclusions of everyone else we have discussed so far. Yet few have responded. Perhaps they are still formulating their counterarguments or perhaps they just don't want to tangle with him on his turf (more about that in a moment).

Let us note two specific exceptions that other historical scholars would want to take with Meier's conclusions. First, the suggestion that Jesus was an eschatological prophet announcing an imminent divine intervention in history meets with the same objections brought against Sanders, whom Meier basically follows on this point (see pages 126–27). We need not rehearse the arguments here, but should note as Meier does that many recent historians have disagreed with this emphasis on Jesus' expectation that God was about to act in history to redeem and restore Israel.

Second, the omission of any attribution of a political or social program to Jesus troubles many historical scholars. As we have seen, Borg, Crossan, Fiorenza, Horsley, and others consider Jesus to have been a conscious social reformer in one respect or another. Meier's reluctance to attribute this role to Jesus is related to the previous point about eschatology. He has written elsewhere that "Jesus seems to have had no interest in the great political and social questions of his day. He was not interested in the reform of the world because he was prophesying its end."[62] Borg quotes this sentence as evidence of why the "eschatological prophet" model does not do justice to the historical Jesus.[63] Borg would claim that many of Jesus' sayings and deeds do point to political and social reform and that (following Meier's own logic) this argues against the proposition that Jesus was expecting the world to end soon.

In general, critiques of Meier's project seem to be more sweeping, focusing either on its specific methodological premises or on its fundamental presupposition as to how one ought to do history. The best example of the former may be illustrated by comparing Meier to the Jesus Seminar. At times, Meier appears to function as a one-man Jesus Seminar, applying criteria of authenticity to individual sayings and deeds attributed to Jesus and determining whether or not they are likely to be historical. Reading his second volume in particular, one can imagine him casting red, pink, gray, and black marbles in his mind as he decides that *this* bit of data is definitely authentic, *that* one might be but probably isn't, and so forth. Still, his conclusions differ radically from theirs. Why? I discern two reasons (and there may be more).

First, Meier studies the sayings and the deeds together. The Jesus Seminar separated sayings from deeds and studied them independently, as two different types of tradition passed along separately in the church to serve different functions (*Sitze im Leben*). Thus, when the Jesus Seminar gave black type (meaning "unauthentic") to the Q saying in Luke 7:22 where Jesus speaks of the blind seeing, the lame walking, and the dead being raised, they apparently did not consider the coherence of this saying with the stories in the Gospel tradition about these things happening. For Meier, that coherence, with the implicit multiple attestation of forms, becomes a major reason for deciding in favor of the authenticity of the Q saying as well as for that of some of the individual accounts that describe deeds illustrative of the works it mentions.

Second, Meier dismisses the apocryphal Gospels (including those attributed to Peter and Thomas) as late documents that are dependent on canonical writings, and credits the Gospel of John with preserving independent worthwhile testimony. The Jesus Seminar decided exactly the opposite: the Gospel of Thomas, at least, is a valuable early source, while John is late and so intrinsically flawed that it hardly counts at all. Both Meier and the Jesus Seminar allowed these early decisions about the relative value of source materials to guide their decisions. The issue in evaluating them, then, becomes "Who has the better premises?" But some scholars think it should not come to that.

A fundamental critique of both Meier and the Jesus Seminar arises from philosophical debate as to the best way to study history. Both Meier and the Jesus Seminar pursue a time-honored approach of accumulating and evaluating data piece by piece until a reasonable interpretation of that data can be offered. They claim that they do not want to impose any conception of Jesus on these data. Instead, they want to determine first which sayings or deeds are historical and then construct a portrait of Jesus faithful to these determinations. To many people, this would seem to be the only objective or fair way to go about it. Indeed, as we have noted, one major criticism of the Jesus Seminar has been that they did not in fact do as they claimed. They *did* start with a conception of Jesus (albeit an unstated one) and this influenced their decisions about the evidence. Not surprisingly, similar charges are whispered against Meier.[64] Skeptics find his Jesus to be conveniently amenable to Christianity, even to Catholicism.[65] Some question whether it is possible for anyone to begin with no conception of Jesus and then blandly accumulate information regarding him until they are able to construct a disinterested portrait. Others question whether it would be desirable to do so.

N. T. Wright proposes another way of doing history, a model he calls "critical realism."[66] This will be discussed in more detail in the next chapter, but for now let us note that Wright suggests the proper starting point is a hypothesis (a conception of Jesus), which one then seeks to verify by sifting through the evidence. Wright is one who thinks the Jesus Seminar's purported claim to have arrived at conclusions based on objective analysis of individual passages is only a ruse. In fact, the Seminar provides an assessment of the historicity of materials based on a particular (prior) view of Jesus that they propose to be correct. Ironically, though, Wright says this is the proper way to do history. He happens to think the Jesus Seminar has a bad hypothesis, which cannot ultimately be sustained, but he does not fault them for trying.[67] Accordingly, he might encourage Meier to come up with a hypothesis about Jesus first, state it, and then work through the materials to see if it holds up.

The difference in approaches will become more evident in the next chapter when we look at Wright's work on Jesus. But, to a lesser extent, we can see a difference already by comparing Meier's approach to data with that of Sanders.[68] Sanders begins with the hypothesis that Jesus was a Jewish prophet of restoration eschatology. He works through the Jesus tradition, applying criteria of authenticity, to determine how much of the material fits his hypothesis. But he does not feel compelled to make everything fit. Some material that has reasonably good support may need to be rejected as not fitting with the overall hypothesis, or at least reinterpreted so that it does fit (sayings regarding the presence of the kingdom are an example). Meier espouses a building-block approach to history, which Wright denounces as "pseudo-atomistic work on isolated fragments."[69] He wants to sift data, accumulate evidence, and see where it leads. The result, predictably, is that materials that point in diverse if not contradictory directions are judged to be authentic. With no macrohypothesis to guide him, he is committed by his method to use *all* the apparently historical blocks in his final construction. It is only two-thirds complete and already the bottom line is that Jesus was "a complex figure." Meier maintains that the convergence of diverse factors and images in the historical figure of Jesus marks him as unique. Sanders has said that any portrait of Jesus that presents him as historically unique is almost by definition incorrect.[70] It is not impossible that Jesus was all the things that potentially authentic materials portray him as being, but it seems more likely that he was only some of them. So, also, Crossan alleges that Meier's method does not allow him to discriminate adequately between layers of tradition with the result that "he ends up honestly unable to combine what are not only divergent but even opposing strata of the Jesus tradition."[71]

In time, scholars will probably debate individual judgments that Meier offers: Did Jesus really baptize? Does the theological tale of the raising of Lazarus go back to an actual event in Jesus' life? For now, though, such discussion is stalled. Those who are potentially his biggest critics seem to think that he and they have reached a methodological impasse. They do not want to quibble with the arguments he reaches in any way that respects his terms of engagement. They object to the terms themselves. Some, like the Jesus Seminar, accept his general approach but deny foundational premises that influence his judgments as to what material should be deemed historical. Others, like Wright, challenge the approach itself as embodying a naive positivism that simply does not work in practice.

Meier is well aware of the problem of inherent subjectivity. "There is," he says, "no neutral Switzerland of the mind in Jesus research."[72] Still,

> the solution to this dilemma is neither to pretend to an absolute objectivity that is not to be had nor to wallow in total relativism. The solution is to admit honestly one's own standpoint, to try to exclude its influence in making scholarly judgments by adhering to certain commonly held criteria, and to invite the correction of other scholars when one's vigilance inevitably slips.[73]

Crossan, we recall, regards objectivity as "spurious" and "unattainable." Meier disagrees with the "spurious" part. He considers objectivity, even in the so-called naive positivist sense, to be an "asymptotic goal," that is "a goal we have to keep pressing toward, even though we never fully reach it."[74] But don't lessons of the past reveal the futility of this? Meier responds:

> I often remember a philosophy professor who taught me years ago asking my class why anyone should struggle with the question of whether or how we can

know truth, when the greatest minds down through the centuries have come up with contradictory answers to that question. Why bother to try when the best and brightest have floundered? One thoughtful student replied that no one thinks that we should stop the quest for and practice of love, just because our forebears have made a mess of that subject.[75]

9

N. T. WRIGHT

Jesus was a herald, the bringer of an urgent message that could not wait, could not become the stuff of academic debate. He was issuing a public announcement, like someone driving through a town with a loudhailer. He was issuing a public warning, like a man with a red flag heading off an imminent railway disaster. He was issuing a public invitation, like someone setting up a political party and summoning all and sundry to sign up and help create a new world.

—N. T. Wright[1]

Wright makes a sustained argument that the New Testament gospels' depictions of the sayings, ministry, and crucifixion of Jesus are fundamentally reliable. . . . Jesus prophetically foresaw and symbolically enacted in his death a very specific, albeit religiously cataclysmic, first century event (and was proven quite right): the Roman destruction of the Temple in Jerusalem (A.D. 70) and its replacement by a renewed people of God. . . . Jesus also understood himself as the bearer of God's own presence in the midst of God's people.

—Mary Knutsen[2]

Jesus saw himself as a prophet announcing and inaugurating the kingdom of [God]; he believed himself to be Israel's true Messiah; he believed that the kingdom would be brought about by means of his own death at the hands of the pagans.

—N. T. Wright[3]

N T. Wright has burst upon the scene of historical Jesus studies rather unex
. pectedly and threatens now to take that stage by storm. A well-published
scholar in Great Britain who has taught at both Cambridge and Oxford, he was not
particularly well known in the United States until recently.

Other scholars don't quite know what to make of him yet. This is evident even
from comments on the back cover of his major book, *Jesus and the Victory of God,*
solicited by the publisher as endorsements of the volume: "Wright is one of the most
formidable of traditionalist Bible scholars," writes one critic.[4] "Wright has established himself as the leading British Jesus scholar of his generation," says another
(Marcus Borg, in fact). The praise is attended by caveats: he is notable among *traditionalist* scholars or *British* scholars. Actually, as we will see, Wright is not always
traditional in his views, though he is certainly formidable in his arguments. And,
though he may be a notable Briton, he has established himself in the minds of many
as the leading Jesus scholar, period. He has become "the force to be reckoned with"
(or to use traditionalist, British grammar: "the force with which to be reckoned").

The most conspicuous aspect of his work is probably its least significant. Even
those who have never read any of Wright's volumes may know him as the scholar
who spells *god* with a lowercase *g*. The traditional spelling, Wright complains,
"sometimes amounts to regarding 'God' as the proper name of the Deity" and "implies that all users of the word are monotheists and, within that, that all monotheists believe in the same god."[5] He also sometimes refers to the god of Israel as
YHWH, following a scholarly convention that is more widely accepted. In the Hebrew Old Testament, God's name (rendered either Yahweh or Jehovah in English
Bibles) is given as a tetragrammaton, four consonants that cannot be pronounced.
It was considered sacrilegious to speak the name of God aloud.

An Anglican priest, Wright currently serves as dean of Lichfield and canon of
Coventry Cathedral. His main contribution to historical Jesus studies is *Jesus and
the Victory of God,* published in 1996. It is actually the second volume in a pro-
jected five-volume series on the broad subject of "Christian Origins and the Question of God." The first volume in this series was *The New Testament and the
People of God,* published in 1992.[6] That book dealt primarily with reconstruction
of the Jewish world in which Jesus lived and in which the New Testament was produced and so laid the foundations for the study of Jesus himself.

WRIGHT'S METHOD
FOR STUDYING JESUS

In *The New Testament and the People of God,* Wright lays out a method for historical research that he calls "critical realism."[7] This model involves an overt
process of hypothesis and verification. Rather than beginning with a supposedly
objective analysis of data, he suggests beginning with a stated hypothesis that may
or may not be substantiated through analysis of the data. The vindication of a hypothesis depends on three things: its inclusion of data without distortion, its essential simplicity of line, and its ability to shed light elsewhere.[8] These elements,

especially the first two, can be in tension with each other. Historians can often find simple hypotheses that explain some of the data (for example, "Jesus was a Cynic philosopher") while ignoring the rest. Historians can also concoct elaborate, complex portraits that take everything into account but ascribe wildly diverse if not contradictory impulses to their subject. The trick is to come up with an inherently consistent picture that includes as much of the data as possible. Then if the hypothesis is sound, it should also help to explain related developments, such as (in the case of the historical Jesus) developments in the history of early Christianity. More specifically, Wright suggests that with regard to Jesus any hypothesis must provide reasonable answers to five major questions: (1) How does Jesus fit into Judaism? (2) What were Jesus' aims? (3) Why did Jesus die? (4) How and why did the early church begin? and (5) Why are the Gospels what they are?[9]

Wright eschews the sort of microscopic study of individual sayings evident in the work of the Jesus Seminar and John Meier. He does not see the task fundamentally as reconstructing traditions about Jesus but rather as advancing hypotheses that account for the traditions we have. In this, he claims to be suggesting "no more than that Jesus be studied like any other figure of the ancient past."[10] When historians study, say, Alexander the Great or Julius Caesar, they do not make lists of all the things the subject is reported to have said or done and then consider each of these individually, asking, "Did this really happen?" or "Did the person really say this?" Trying to "peel the historical onion back to its core," Wright says, is "the way of tears and frustration."[11]

Of course, Wright must make some judgments as to what data are most relevant. His account of Jesus' life does not incorporate as much material from John's Gospel as does that of Meier, nor does Wright's Jesus reflect the image presented in the apocryphal gospels to the degree that Crossan's Jesus does.[12] Rather, Wright appears to draw most heavily on the traditions of the Synoptic Gospels, but he does not seem to be particular about differentiating between what might be ascribed to Mark, Q, M, or L. With regard to the Synoptic material, at least, he does manage to include more data than other scholars we have discussed.

Any solid hypothesis about Jesus, Wright continues, must make historical sense of him with reference to what we know about two contexts that can be related to him. The outside limits for understanding Jesus "are pre-Christian Judaism and the second-century church; and the puzzle involves fitting together the bits in the middle to make a clear historical sequence all the way across."[13] This leads Wright to propose a somewhat refined criterion for authenticity, what he calls the "double criterion of similarity and dissimilarity":

> When something can be seen to be credible (though perhaps deeply subversive) within first-century Judaism, *and* credible as the implied starting point (though not the exact replica) of something in later Christianity, there is a strong possibility of our being in touch with the genuine history of Jesus.

Wright admits that first-century Judaism and second-century Christianity are themselves difficult to describe. The task can be "like climbing from one moving boat into another" and the "history of research indicates how easy it is to fall into the water."[14] Still, the historical quest is to understand Jesus as the necessary link between these two movements.

Wright is more pronounced than any other Jesus scholar in regarding the beliefs of early Christianity not as a problem to be overcome (in order to get back to the real or historical Jesus) but as part of the phenomenon to be explained. He asks, "How do we account for the fact that, by A.D. 110, there was a large and vigorous international movement, already showing considerable diversity, whose founding myth . . . was a story about one Jesus of Nazareth, a figure of the recent past?"[15] Or, more specifically, "How did it come about that Jesus was *worshipped* . . . in very early, very Jewish, and still insistently monotheist Christianity?"[16] What was there about the person and mission of this man that, historically, would explain such developments?

We may take just one example: the meaning of Jesus' death. As we have seen, many scholars address the question of what Jesus did that led to his execution, focusing, for instance, on political implications of his ministry that might have antagonized the Romans or on his opposition to the temple cult, which might have aroused the ire of Jewish high priests. This is all well and good, says Wright, but we also have the fact that a few years after the crucifixion, Christians such as Paul were affirming that Jesus had died for their sins. Whether we personally embrace this theological interpretation or not, Wright argues, we need to account for it. The historian should ask what there was about Jesus, and especially about his execution, that could prompt such belief.[17]

Wright's most innovative work so far, however, has concerned the other outside limit for understanding Jesus: first-century Judaism. He approaches this with reference to discerning what he calls "worldview" and "mindset."[18] The term *worldview* applies to the perspective of a society and the term *mindset* applies to the perspective of a particular individual. Both imply convictions so fundamental as to be taken for granted: "If challenged, a worldview generates the answer, 'that's just the way things are,' and a mindset replies to critics with 'that's just the sort of person I am.'"[19] Both are revealed through the study of four things: characteristic stories, fundamental symbols, habitual praxis, and answers to a set of basic questions (who are we? where are we? what's wrong? what's the solution? what time is it?).

The model gets more complex. Wright goes on to suggest that worldviews and mindsets generate a set of "basic beliefs" and "aims," which in turn are expressed through "consequent beliefs" and "intentions." The detailed distinctions between these are not necessary for our survey. Basically, Wright wants to recover the mindset of Jesus, which he assumes must be set within the worldview of first-century Judaism. So he suggests that where some action or activity of Jesus is securely established, we can ask what beliefs, aims, and intentions it reveals, granted the prevailing Jewish worldview whose basic shape, it is assumed, he shared.[20] Of course, he realizes it is also possible to make the reverse move, to determine that some reported saying or activity is not likely to be authentic because it does not fit within the "mindset-within-worldview" that otherwise seems to hold. He is cautious about doing this, however, because "most historical characters worth studying are so because they held mindsets that formed significant variations on the parent worldview."[21]

One section of *The New Testament and the People of God* is devoted to describing the worldview of first-century Judaism. Two points are especially important for the later study of Jesus. First, Wright holds that most first-century Jews believed they were still in exile. Numerous texts from the period focus on retelling the story of Israel in a way that indicates this.[22] The Jewish people in the first century cherished the memory of how their god had delivered them from captivity in Egypt. This high point, however, was paired with the devastating memory of how the Babylonians had destroyed the temple several hundred years later. The latter event, which precipitated the exile, was a catastrophe of unspeakable proportion. Israel viewed the temple as the dwelling of their god, as the place where heaven and earth met. The destruction meant that their god had abandoned the temple, and so had abandoned them to their enemies. Of course, a new temple had been built, but the fact that the people of Israel were still in bondage to a hostile foreign power was evidence to many Jewish people that their god had not returned to dwell in it. The hope—kept alive through retellings of the exodus story—was that Israel's god would return and the exile would finally end.[23]

A second key point Wright develops in this first book is that although eschatological expectation was widespread in first-century Judaism, the apocalyptic imagery it employed did not refer literally to the end of the world. It referred, symbolically, to the end of *a* world.[24] Jesus, then, was eschatological not in the sense that he expected the end of the space-time universe, but in the sense that he expected the end of the present world order. Thus, his "warnings about imminent judgment were intended to be taken as denoting (what we would call) socio-political events."[25]

Chart 6. Historical Facts about Jesus according to N. T. Wright

- born in 4 B.C.E.
- grew up in Nazareth of Galilee
- spoke Aramaic, Hebrew, and probably some Greek
- was initially associated with John the Baptist, but emerged as a public figure in his own right around 28 C.E.
- summoned people to repent
- used parables to announce the reign of Israel's god
- conducted itinerant ministry throughout villages of Galilee
- effected remarkable cures, including exorcisms, as enactments of his message
- shared in table fellowship with a socioculturally diverse group
- called a close group of disciples and gave twelve of them a special status
- performed a dramatic action in the temple
- incurred the wrath of some elements in Judaism, especially among the high-priestly establishment
- was handed over by this powerful Jewish element to the Romans to be crucified as an insurrectionist
- was reported by his followers to have been raised from the dead

WRIGHT'S PORTRAIT OF JESUS

Wright begins, as does Sanders, with "a brief list of things that few will deny about Jesus' life and public activity" (see chart 6).[26] A few of the items are in fact disputed by other scholars we have discussed in this book. Sanders doubts that Jesus was a preacher of repentance. Crossan does not think Jesus accorded any special status to twelve of his disciples; he also plays down the role of any significant Jewish element in handing Jesus over to be crucified. But Wright thinks that such points are well enough established in the sources to allow them to stand. He also adds to his outline a few details about Jesus that he regards as "comparatively non-controversial," including a devotion to prayer and a relaxed stance toward family commitments.[27]

Jesus as Prophet

Taking all these facts together, Wright proceeds to argue that the best initial model for understanding Jesus is that of a prophet, specifically, "a prophet bearing an urgent eschatological, and indeed apocalyptic, message for Israel."[28] From the above discussion, it should be clear that for Wright to call Jesus an eschatological or apocalyptic prophet does not mean to imply that Jesus was predicting the imminent end of the world. Rather,

> Jesus was seen as, and saw himself as . . . a prophet like the prophets of old, coming to Israel with a word from her covenant god, warning her of the imminent and fearful consequences of the direction she was travelling, urging and summoning her to a new and different way.[29]

Part of the evidence for this identification of Jesus as a prophet consists of the many sayings throughout the Gospels that refer to Jesus as a prophet.[30] Some of these, such as Mark 6:4, use the term as Jesus' own self-designation. The sayings are likely to be authentic, Wright reasons, since the early church thought this was too weak a title for Jesus and would not have invented such traditions. In fact, apart from Acts 3:22, Jesus is never referred to as a prophet in any New Testament writing other than the Gospels.

What type of prophet was Jesus? Wright notes that traditions in the Gospels model his ministry after a wide variety of Old Testament prophets: Micaiah ben Imlah (1 Kings 22), Ezekiel, Jeremiah, Jonah, Amos, and, above all, Elijah and Elisha. In ways reminiscent of all these figures, Jesus sought to embody the ideal of a popular "oracular prophet," delivering a message through spoken words and symbolic actions. But Jesus combined this image with that of the "leadership prophet"; he started a renewal movement consisting of a group that claimed to represent a reconstitution of Israel. Wright admits that John the Baptist had probably combined these two prophetic models before Jesus, but Jesus took the new model further and with greater effect. This was at least in part because he was itinerant while John was localized, and because his message both conveyed greater urgency and was accompanied by the remarkable healings.[31]

Wright offers us "a Jesus who engaged in that characteristically Jewish activity of subversively retelling the basic Jewish story."[32] The message that this Jesus proclaimed and ultimately enacted had three main components: (1) Israel's god was about to bring the exile to an end at last, (2) Israel's god was going to act decisively to defeat Israel's enemies, and (3) Israel's god was going to return to Zion to dwell with the people again. Wright says that these components were commonplace in Jewish eschatological expectation. These were the things for which the Jewish people longed. Jesus promised them but also redefined them in subversive ways; the promises would be fulfilled—indeed, *were being* fulfilled—in ways that people had not anticipated.

Return from Exile

As we have seen, Wright describes the Jewish people of the first century as a people who believed they were still in exile, held captive by foreign powers, and enamored of a hope that someday their god would return to deliver them. Jesus, says Wright, announced that this was about to happen. This is the meaning that should be attached to such statements as "Repent, for the kingdom of heaven has come near" (Matt. 4:17). It is also the central notion that informs many of Jesus' parables. Wright suggests, for instance, that the so-called parable of the prodigal son (Luke 15:11–32) retells the story of Israel (as the prodigal) being separated from god (the father) and then—after a period spent with swine—being welcomed back to the good life again. The story of the sower (Mark 4:1–9) likewise proclaims that the time of lost seed is over and the time of fruit has dawned: Israel's god "was returning to his people, to 'sow' his word in their midst, as he promised, and so restore their fortunes at last."[33]

Similarly, the mighty works that Jesus performed were prophetic acts accompanying this announcement. Wright agrees with Meier that "Jesus' contemporaries, both those who became his followers and those who were determined not to become his followers, certainly regarded him as possessed of remarkable powers."[34] The mighty works were presented as signs that prophecy was being fulfilled. Healings, in particular, worked to support the notion of a restored Israel, for now those who had been excluded as sick or unclean could be included. Exorcisms demonstrated the defeat of the true enemy—the satan—and power over nature illustrated the new harmony that Jesus said was coming into the world as Israel's god took charge. Thus, all of the actions that are typically called "miracles of Jesus" may be understood as prophetic signs, announcing that Israel's god was bringing the exile to an end.

It is this announcement that marks Jesus as an eschatological prophet. So stated, Wright's view of Jesus is very similar to that of Sanders, who accentuates Jesus as a prophet of "Jewish restoration eschatology." As we continue our sketch, however, significant differences will emerge. Some of these begin to come out in what Wright presents as implications of Jesus' announcement.

First, Jesus' announcement included an *invitation* to repentance and faith (Mark 1:15). Repentance in this instance involved abandoning a way of life, a way of being Israel, and awaiting a different sort of vindication than had been expected. It did not mean primarily "moral repentance" and it did not involve the usual practices of restitution or temple sacrifices. Similarly, faith meant believing that Israel's god was acting climactically in Jesus himself. It did not mean subscribing to a particular religious system or body of doctrine.[35]

Second, Jesus' announcement included a *welcome* to sinners, evidenced dramatically by his practice of sharing meals with those who were thought to be excluded from Israel. Wright thinks that Jesus associated with both those who would have been viewed as sinners by the Pharisees (because they did not follow particular regulations) and those who would have been viewed as sinners by just about everybody (because they participated in what was widely regarded as wicked behavior). In any case, Jesus offered such people forgiveness, which is to say, inclusion in the restored people of Israel, and he did so on his own authority, outside the official structures.[36]

Third, Jesus' announcement included a *challenge* to live as a community that behaves in a distinctive way. In this sense, Jesus was announcing a "new covenant," which, like all covenants, would shape the society that adopts it. Specific expectations of this new covenant are laid out in the Sermon on the Mount (Matt. 5—7), but one fundamental principle is forgiveness. To elevate this as the central characteristic of those loyal to Jesus was to eschew the climate of the times with its emphasis on resistance to Roman tyranny. The people whom Jesus invited and welcomed as part of the new, restored Israel would be renewed in their hearts. They would love their enemies.

Fourth, Jesus' announcement included a *summons* to join him in proclaiming the kingdom. Some (but not all) of the people who believed his message were expected to follow him by taking up his task. They would assist him in his work of announcement even if it involved personal suffering and sacrifice. Thus, Jesus was in a very real sense the founder of a renewal movement and the instigator of a social revolution.

Stories of Jesus' controversies with the Pharisees are likely to be historical, but once again Wright thinks their meaning is not what has typically been assigned to them. "They were about eschatology and politics, not religion or morality."[37] At issue was Jesus' proclamation of the coming kingdom of god in a way that undermined the antipagan revolutionary zeal of certain Pharisees. The point of such Pharisaic practices as sabbath observance and purity codes regarding meals was not (as Christian interpreters sometimes assume) to establish a means by which individuals could earn their salvation by keeping the law. The point, rather, was to guarantee a distinctive identity for the people of Israel while they were in exile. Rigorous application of the law was a defense against assimilation into the pagan Gentile world. But Jesus declared that the time of exile was ending, and "now that the moment for fulfillment had come, it was time to relativize those god-given markers of Israel's distinctiveness."[38] In fact, for Jesus, these practices had become "a symptom of the problem rather than part of the solution. The kingdom of the one true god . . . would be characterized not by defensiveness, but by Israel's being the light of the world, not by paying the Gentiles back . . . but by turning the other cheek."[39] Thus,

> the clash between Jesus and his Jewish contemporaries must be seen in terms of *alternative political agendas* generated by *alternative eschatological beliefs and expectations*. Jesus was announcing the kingdom in a way which did not reinforce, but rather called into question, the agenda of revolutionary zeal which dominated the horizon of, especially, the dominant group within Pharisaism.[40]

In some ways, Jesus' conflict within Judaism can be understood as a clash of symbols. Jesus replaced key symbols appropriate to preserving Israel's distinctiveness during exile with symbols appropriate for the new reign of god. Feasting replaced fasting; since the exile was ending, life could now be viewed as a celebration (Mark 2:18–19). Open table fellowship replaced segregating purity codes as a more appropriate symbol of life in the postexile reign of god. Likewise, healing the sick (as opposed to quarantining them) symbolized the restoration of creation that was taking place. But, above all, forgiveness replaced retribution, blessing replaced cursing, love replaced hatred. The restored Israel would seek not to conquer her enemies but to become a light to the nations.

How radical such a message would have been is difficult for us to grasp. People in living memory had died, Wright reminds us, for refusing to eat pork. Now Jesus was saying that it didn't matter or wouldn't matter in the kingdom that was dawning: "The traditions which attempted to bolster Israel's national identity were out of date and out of line."[41] Jesus "was offering the return from exile, the renewed covenant, the eschatological 'forgiveness of sins' . . . to all the wrong people, and on his own authority. This was his real offense."[42]

Jesus was announcing a message that ultimately focused on his own self. "Jesus was replacing adherence to Temple and Torah with allegiance to himself," says Wright. "He was declaring, on his own authority, that anyone who trusted in him and in his kingdom-announcement was within the kingdom."[43] Conversely, those who did not heed him and accept his message would be excluded from the kingdom, from the restored Israel. Wright therefore disagrees with Sanders and a number of others who think that Jesus was not a prophet of judgment. He cannot be contrasted with John the Baptist in this regard. The tradition simply contains too many items, a "devastating catalogue of threats and warnings"[44] attributed to Jesus and spread over a wide variety of sources (Mark, Q, M, L, and Thomas). He predicted an impending national disaster, "a coming political, military, and social nightmare"[45] that would bring about the total destruction of Jerusalem and the temple. This would come upon the Jewish people who rejected Jesus' message of peace and chose to pursue war instead. It is to such a cataclysm that the apocalyptic language in Jesus' speech points; the darkening of the sun and the falling of stars (Mark 13:24–25) are symbolic ways of indicating the transforming nature of the event, similar perhaps to what people today mean when they describe something as "earth-shattering."

Much of this judgment talk employed traditional images and language, but

Jesus added his own new twist: he and his people would escape and be vindicated. The form that this vindication would take is striking. Wright accepts the authenticity of Gospel texts in which Jesus speaks of the coming of the Son of Man, but interprets these in a nontraditional way. They do not reveal Jesus speaking of a descent of some figure from heaven to earth, but the opposite: the Son of Man travels from earth to heaven, as one who has been vindicated by god and, so, is welcomed on clouds into the heavenly kingdom.[46] Jesus uses this biblical image as a symbol for how he and his followers will be vindicated by god, welcomed into the reign of god as the newly restored people of Israel. The sign that this has happened will be twofold: Jerusalem and the temple will be destroyed by the Romans, but Jesus' followers—warned of what was to come—will flee the city before this actually occurs. This, in itself, will symbolize a return from exile.[47] Furthermore, Wright suggests that Jesus predicted only the destruction of the temple, not its rebuilding. Whereas Sanders presents Jesus as claiming God is about to build a new temple of bricks and mortar, Wright thinks that "Jesus saw himself, and perhaps his followers with him, as the new Temple."[48]

There is more, but we should pause already to consider the implications of this construal. First, Wright is able, like Sanders, to present Jesus as an eschatological prophet, predicting what was to come upon his generation in the near future. Unlike Sanders, however, Wright is able to say that Jesus was right! Jesus' predictions were not subsequently shown to be mistaken, for he never said that he would return to earth in some glorified state while his followers were still alive. In fact, he never said he would return in such a fashion at all. Rather, he predicted that Jerusalem and the temple would be destroyed but that his followers would escape the conflagration, and that these events would be signs that vindicated his (and their) message about the reign of god. Historically, these events did occur, pretty much as Jesus said they would, which for Wright helps to explain why the Christian movement was able to sustain itself and gain momentum in those early years.

Another implication of Wright's construal of this part of Jesus' message is that it subverts the traditional thinking about how Israel's god would deliver his people from their enemies. Jesus foresaw no holy war through which Israel's god would deliver Jerusalem from the Romans. Rather, as it turns out, Jerusalem and the temple *were* the enemies, and Israel's god would use the Romans to bring judgment upon them.[49] But actually the matter is even more complicated. In a fundamental sense, Israel's real enemy is "the satan and his hordes, who are deceiving Israel into thinking that Rome is the real enemy so that she [Israel] will not notice the reality."[50] Ultimately, the satan must be defeated and this brings us to consideration of another aspect of Jesus' career—his crucifixion.

Defeat of Enemies

Wright accepts as entirely credible the biblical account that Jesus was crucified as the result of a convergence of Jewish and Roman interests. In the latter case, though, it was primarily a matter of self-interest on the part of one particular Roman, Pontius Pilate. As the Gospels indicate, the governor probably realized that Jesus was not an ordinary sort of revolutionary leader and that he posed no real threat to the empire. He knew the Jewish leaders wanted him dead for other reasons (what he would have regarded as "religious" concerns, not "political" ones), but he caved in to their demands for fear that failure to execute a would-be king could be interpreted as disloyalty to Caesar. Pilate "not only put cynical power-games before justice (that was normal), but also, on this occasion, put naked self-interest before both."[51]

Jewish leaders, Wright thinks, wanted Jesus put to death for the crime of leading Israel astray, a capital offense according to Deuteronomy 13. They viewed him as a false prophet. As such, Wright accepts the biblical record that hostile Pharisees would have wanted Jesus dead even before he came to Jerusalem. His actions in that city, however, particularly the temple incident, sealed his fate. The leaders conducted a hearing at which they hoped he would incriminate himself with regard to Roman law. Apparently, he did so, admitting—or at least refusing to deny—that he viewed himself as a king acting on behalf of Israel's god. Thus, the Jewish leaders could add blasphemy to their charges against Jesus and, more to the point, hand him over to Pilate as a claimant to the throne:

> The leaders of the Jewish people were thus able to present Jesus to Pilate as a seditious trouble-maker; to their Jewish contemporaries (and later generations of rabbinic Judaism) as a false prophet and a blasphemer, leading Israel astray; and to themselves as a dangerous political nuisance. On all counts, he had to die.[52]

Wright also considers the death of Jesus from another angle, as a symbolic action that can be understood within the context of Jesus' message and work. In contrast to most other historical scholars (with notable exceptions such as Albert Schweitzer), Wright thinks that for Jesus death might have been part of the plan. Sanders, we have seen, thinks the notion that Jesus sought to orchestrate his own death amounts to a presentation of him as "weird."[53] But Wright notes that what might seem weird to a comfortable modern western scholar would not be regarded as such within the worldview of first-century Judaism. Jesus is described as referring to death as his purpose or destiny numerous times and in a wide variety of ways. Aside from explicit predictions (such as Mark 8:31), there are parables (Mark 12:1–12), and riddle sayings ascribed to material from various sources (Matt. 23:37–39; Luke 23:27–31). He describes a baptism that he must undergo (Luke 12:49–50) and a cup that he must drink (Mark 10:38–40), he speaks of being anointed beforehand for his burial (Mark 14:3–9; John 12:1–8), and he eats a "last supper" with his disciples. In short, a rich theme throughout much of the tradition holds that Jesus believed death was his vocation; he was *supposed* to die and somehow his death would serve to accomplish the redemption of Israel.[54]

Wright tries to figure out how such a concept would fit with Jesus' message as described above. First, he relates it to the notion of "messianic woes." There was a widespread conviction among Jews of this period that the deliverance from exile would be accompanied by intense suffering.[55] The suffering of individual righteous persons could be interpreted within this framework; prophets would suffer for the truth that they spoke and a true king would be willing to share the suffering of his people. A number of scripture texts from Daniel, Psalms, Zechariah, Ezekiel, and especially Isaiah 40—55 could be (and were) interpreted as expressive of such suffering. Wright theorizes that, informed by such scripture, Jesus believed he was called to suffer as the representative of Israel, to take upon himself the divine wrath that must conclude the exile. The thinking seems to have been that this would somehow hasten the moment when Israel's tribulation would be complete. Based on his understanding of scripture, Jesus decided that his vocation was to assume the fate of Israel in exile and to undergo symbolically the fate that he had announced for Jerusalem as a whole. The wrath of god against Israel (appropriate for her sins) would be spent, and judgment would remain only for those who had excluded themselves from the Israel that he had constituted around himself. In other words, "Jesus intended that his death should in some sense function sacrificially."[56] Such a construal, Wright contends, meets the double criteria of similarity and dissimilarity. It derives from Jewish interpretation of Hebrew scripture *and* explains the development of Christian atonement theology, but is not identical to either.

Wright expands this proposal to include the notion of conflict and the defeat of enemies. Jesus identified the true enemy of Israel as the satan. He also taught his disciples that the victory of god will come not through armed resistance but by going the second mile and turning the other cheek. "Fighting the battle of the kingdom with the enemy's weapons meant that one had already lost it in principle, and would soon lose it, and lose it terribly, in practice."[57] Granted this, Jesus could overcome the satan only by allowing himself to be overcome. The only way to defeat evil, he had taught, was to allow it to do its worst. This he intended to do by bearing his cross, going to an unjust death without insults or threats, suffering either in silence or with words of forgiveness. This, Wright says, was "a startling innovation in the martyr tradition," one that sent echoes throughout early Christianity.[58] Normally, "followers of a Messiah who was crucified knew beyond question that they had backed the wrong horse," but somehow "the earliest Christians regarded Jesus' achievement on the cross as the decisive victory over evil."[59]

Return of the King

One more element remains. The Jewish hope was not only that the exile would end and Israel's enemies be defeated. This would count for little unless their god returned to dwell with them. Jesus, according to Wright, "was not content to announce that YHWH was returning to Zion. He intended to enact, symbolize and personify that climactic event."[60]

He spoke of it first in parables. We have already seen that Wright does not think Jesus predicted his own return to earth from heaven in clouds of glory. The texts that seem to refer to such an event he thinks describe a trip in the opposite direction—a coming of the vindicated Son of Man from earth to heaven. If this is so, then, what of the parables that Christians usually interpret with reference to Jesus' second coming? Are they all creations of the early church? Wright accepts their authenticity but thinks the subject of these parables is not Jesus' own return but the return of YHWH, Israel's god. The famous story of the talents or pounds (Matt. 25:14–30; Luke 19:11–27), for instance, speaks of a master or king returning after a time of absence to reward his faithful servants and punish the unfaithful ones. According to Wright, through this parable and others like it, Jesus was announcing that YHWH was returning to Zion while also warning that this return would bring judgment as well as blessing.[61]

Jesus also dramatized this return of God through the acted parable of his own journey to Jerusalem. He rode into the city on a donkey, an image the prophet Zechariah had used to describe the coming of Israel's god as an offer of peace. He enacted, symbolically, a judgment upon the temple, such as Jesus had said Israel's god would do. He summoned those who represented the true Israel to participate in a banquet replete with eschatological and messianic overtones. All these elements indicate to Wright that Jesus "saw his journey to Jerusalem as the symbol and embodiment of YHWH's return to Zion."[62] The word *embodiment* is key here. Jesus, in Wright's view, did not think his actions were but one more symbolic representation of what Israel's god would someday do. Rather, through Jesus' actions, it was actually taking place:

> As [Jesus] was riding over the Mount of Olives, celebrating the coming kingdom, and warning Jerusalem that it would mean judgment for those who rejected him and his way of peace, so YHWH was returning to his people, his city, and his Temple.[63]

The Mindset of Jesus

Wright goes beyond most historical studies of Jesus in an effort to reconstruct not only what Jesus said and did, but what he believed. He does not attempt to analyze Jesus from a psychologist's point of view, suggesting ulterior motives or subconscious complexes that might have driven him to be what he was. Rather, he tries to discern the historical aims and intentions of Jesus and, on the basis of these, to hypothesize what Jesus thought about his world, his god, and himself.

By way of summary, we may indicate how Wright thinks Jesus would have answered the five basic questions of worldview mentioned above (page 152):[64]

Who are we? The people of Israel, chosen by god not for our own sake, but for the sake of the world.

Where are we? In exile, still, but soon to be released.

What's wrong? The satan has made its home in Israel, taken over the temple, and deceived the people into embracing an idolatrous nationalism.

What's the solution? Israel's god will at last become king through Jesus' own life and work, and, indeed, through his death—an ultimate act of obedience by which the satan will be defeated.

What time is it? Time to recognize *now* that these things are happening and to begin to live as the restored people of God.

Beyond all this, however, Wright also tries to get at what Witherington has provocatively called "the christology of Jesus." "Jesus applied to himself the three central aspects of his own prophetic kingdom announcement: the return from exile, the defeat of evil, and the return of YHWH to Zion."[65] Who, then, did Jesus think he was? Wright answers that he thought he was the Messiah. He "saw himself as the leader and focal point of the true, returning-from-exile Israel" and as the king through whose work Israel's god was bringing about this restoration.[66] In these terms, which are compatible with first-century Jewish messianic expectation, he would have accepted the designation Messiah and applied it to himself. Wright finds evidence that he did so in certain sayings (which he regards as "royal riddles") and, especially, in actions associated with the last week of Jesus' life. The entry to Jerusalem was staged with messianic overtones, the final meal with his disciples was presented as a messianic banquet, and the trial before Caiaphas focused on messianic claims. Indeed, "if Jesus did *not* want to be thought of in any way as Messiah, the Entry and the action in the Temple were extremely unwise things to undertake."[67] To assert that Jesus presented himself as the Messiah explains why he would have been charged with blasphemy by the Jews and executed as a royal pretender by the Romans. Wright grants, however, that Jesus was in some ways redefining the concept of Messiah even as he embraced it. As Messiah, he thought that he was Israel's rightful king but he defined that role in terms of his own understanding of the kingdom of god. Another way of answering this question, then, would be to affirm that Jesus thought he was "Israel-in-person, Israel's representative, the one in whom Israel's destiny was reaching its climax." For that, Wright says, is what Jesus believed it meant to be Messiah.[68]

There is still more. Jesus, as Wright depicts him, was one who spoke and acted for the god of Israel. We see this, first, in his offer of forgiveness. Such a practice had the effect, Wright says, of "a private individual approaching a prisoner in jail and offering him a royal pardon, signed by himself."[69] Jesus took upon himself to offer what only god could grant. Even more important are those scenes at the end of his life in which he appears to have maintained that his visit to Jerusalem fulfilled the hopes of Israel regarding the return of her god. In all, Jesus seems to have applied to himself numerous categories traditionally reserved for YHWH. He spoke of himself as "the bridegroom" and invoked for himself the image of a shepherd, both images that scripture used for Israel's god. He spoke of himself as the new lawgiver, giving new instructions to his followers as YHWH did to Moses. He "acted as if he thought he were the reality to which the Temple pointed . . . as if he were in some sense the replacement for Torah . . . the spokesman of the divine Wisdom."[70] In calling followers to abandon possessions and family to follow him, he indicated that "loyalty to Israel's god, astonishingly, would now take the form of loyalty to Jesus."[71]

What are we to make of this? It fits, Wright says, as the middle element between certain aspects of first-century Judaism and early Christian theology. Some texts of scripture (Ezekiel 1, Daniel 7) seem to have been interpreted as indicating that "when YHWH acted in history, the agent through whom he acted would be vindicated, exalted, and honoured in a quite unprecedented manner."[72] This figure, who might be identified with the Messiah, would in fact be allowed to share the throne of Israel's god. The fact that Jesus saw himself and was seen by his followers as assuming such a role fits with the indisputable fact that early, monotheistic Christians worshiped him as divine. Did Jesus think he was God? Or a god? Wright does not engage that question, on those terms. But he does claim that the historical Jesus "believed he had to do and be, for Israel and the world, that which according to scripture only YHWH himself could do and be."[73] This is why Christians came to call him God. And if Jesus really did believe that he was doing what only God could do, then why should he "not also come to hold the strange and risky belief that the one true God, the God of Israel, was somehow present and active in him and even *as* him?"[74]

CRITIQUE OF WRIGHT'S STUDY OF JESUS

Wright's work on Jesus is the most recent of those surveyed in this book and has not yet been subjected to detailed published critique.[75] We may, however, note where his work differs markedly from that of others and so indicate where criticisms are most likely to be made.

First, with regard to method, Wright makes some moves that are sure to lose him the support of some scholars at the outset. His decision that the Gospel of Thomas belongs to a later, derivative stage of the tradition is a feature he shares with Sanders and Meier, yet scholars associated with the Jesus Seminar (including Funk and Crossan) are certain to find this disheartening. Beyond this, Wright appears to treat almost all of the material in the Synoptic Gospels as though it is on an equal footing. In this regard, he is the mirror opposite of Crossan, who develops an elaborate hierarchy for weighing the relative value of different sources. He also differs markedly from Meier, who painstakingly checks for multiple attestation of sources. Indeed, Wright thinks the best hypothesis will be the one that can incorporate the most data, including matters that have only single attestation in the Synoptic Gospels, even matters that are found only in M or L, but not Mark or Q.

With regard to the Gospel of Thomas, Wright is in line with the majority of scholars, avoiding what he considers to be the excesses of idiosyncratic scholarship. But with regard to the Synoptic tradition, Wright himself sometimes becomes the minority voice. Two examples may suffice. First, Wright accepts the eschatological discourse of Mark 13 as having "a strong claim to go back, in some form or other, to Jesus himself," though he acknowledges that this material is commonly ascribed to the early church.[76] Second, Wright explains differences between common traditions in the Gospels by allowing that Jesus may have spoken on the same topic more than once:

> My guess would be that we have two versions of the great supper parable, two versions of the talents/pounds parable, and two versions of the beatitudes, not because one is adapted from the other, or both from a single common written source, but because these are two out of a dozen or more possible variations that, had one been in Galilee with a tape recorder, one might have "collected."[77]

Most Gospel scholars would not agree with this supposition. Jesus probably did say similar things in somewhat different versions, but the Synoptic Gospels seem to be based on common streams of tradition that in most cases would have preserved only one version. Most scholars do not think that Matthew or Luke would have had access to the numerous versions of the accounts cited above, such as might have been collected fifty years earlier by someone with a tape recorder. Rather, most Gospel scholars think that both of these evangelists had access to only one version of these accounts, namely, that preserved in the Q source. Accordingly, the differences in their accounts would not represent independent memories of different original versions but redactional variations on the only version that had been preserved.[78]

We noted in chapter 4 that the Jesus Seminar's emphasis on the criterion of dissimilarity seems to guarantee a non-Christian Jesus. Wright faults them for this, but his own emphasis on including a maximum amount of data seems to guarantee a biblical Jesus (since, after all, most of the data is found in biblical materials). More precisely, his intention to include the maximum amount of data that fits with his hypothesis of Jesus as an eschatological figure seems to guarantee an image of Jesus similar to that presented in the Synoptic Gospels, since these are the writings that attribute eschatological and apocalyptic language to Jesus (the Gospel of John and the Gospel of Thomas do not). Wright wants to present the general reliability of the Synoptic tradition as a result rather than a presupposition of his work, but to those who have challenged the reliability of that tradition (Mack, Funk, Crossan), it is not likely to appear that way. To them, Wright's work may seem reactionary, almost a throwback to Jesus scholarship of another era before the gains of source criticism. The problem of constructing a portrait that includes a maximum amount of data, these scholars aver, is that *most* of the data is late and unreliable. A portrait based on the data in Q (or even, for some, an early recension of Q) yields a portrait of the historical Jesus; one that incorporates "most of the data" provides a composite portrait of Christian christology.[79]

This criticism, of course, reflects the climate of post-Wrede skepticism described in the first chapter of this book (see pages 24–25). Wright denounces that climate as tendentious and simplistic, setting the study of Jesus into a context that would not apply for most historians working in most other fields.[80] Nevertheless, it remains part of the context in which his work will be evaluated. Wright contends that there are two basic streams in Jesus research, one harking back to the "thoroughgoing skepticism" of Wrede, and the other to the "thoroughgoing eschatology" of Schweitzer:

> Do we know rather little about Jesus, with the gospels offering us a largely misleading portrait (Wrede)? Or was Jesus an apocalyptic Jewish prophet, with the gospels reflecting, within their own contexts, a good deal about his proclamation of the kingdom (Schweitzer)?[81]

In short, if one determines to understand Jesus eschatologically, one will get a historically plausible reading of the Synoptic tradition. Wright views this as a mark of the success of the eschatological hypothesis. But those who do not view Jesus eschatologically see that hypothesis as a means of asserting the reliability of a tradition that is more representative of Christian theology than historical reporting.

In response, two further points might be made. First, Wright reacts forcefully against the tendency in scholarship to attribute theological ideas to the authors of the Gospels rather than to Jesus himself. In much scholarship, he complains, it seems that "Jesus must remain an unreflective, instinctive, simplistic person, who never thought through what he was doing."[82] This, he maintains, is intrinsically unlikely. We are on surer ground when we assume that the great ideas (including christological conceptions) that underscore the various Gospels go back to Jesus himself. The church revered Jesus, not Matthew, Mark, or Luke as the originator of its faith and, "the authors of at least the synoptic gospels . . . intended to write about Jesus, not just about their own churches and theology."[83] Second, Wright does employ a *double* criterion that demands dissimilarity as well as similarity. Hypothetically, at least, this should acquit him of sneaking in some sort of conservative confessionalism under the guise of historical scholarship. In fact, his portrait of Jesus differs significantly in some ways from that of confessional Christianity. For instance, while Wright does attribute the material in Mark 13 to the historical Jesus, he also interprets it such that Jesus is not talking about his own second coming, as the church has usually thought.

The proposal of this double criterion may well be Wright's most enduring contribution to the methodological enterprise. To most critics, it simply makes sense to say that while authentic material may be distinctive, it also ought to exhibit a logical connection to what preceded it and derived from it. It will be difficult in the future for any historian to present a portrait of Jesus that differs radically from what is in the Gospels without at least accounting for that discrepancy. Simply to say, "The church misrepresented him," will no longer do. But even as Wright's double criterion is being applauded as a hedge against those who would abuse the criterion of dissimilarity, Wright himself is being viewed as one who may have overcompensated to err on the side of similarity. Still, it may be too soon to tell. Wright's Jesus book is but volume two of a five-volume work. Subsequent volumes will address the development of Jesus' ideas in the early church and further instances of dissimilarity may surface.

Beyond the concerns with method, a few specific points in Wright's proposal have been contested. Maurice Casey argues against the interpretation of Daniel 7 as involving an ascent rather than descent of the Son of Man.[84] The latter interpretation provides the basis for Wright's controversial claim that the Gospels present Jesus as predicting only that he will be vindicated after death, not that he will return to earth. Witherington echoes Casey's argument and notes that Paul appears to have understood both Daniel and Jesus as predicting a future descent of the Son of Man (1 Thess. 4:16–17).[85]

Other criticisms focus on elements of Wright's representation of first-century Judaism. First, as we have seen, he believes the heart of Jesus' controversy with the Pharisees concerned his rejection of their policies that would increase alienation from the Gentile environment and lead ultimately to war with Rome. But were the Pharisees really revolutionaries? Wright argues that one sect, the Shammaite Pharisees, were, and that these were dominant. On this, he has the support of a number of scholars, but the issue is debated. Both Jacob Neusner and E. P. Sanders, though differing widely on other points, would present the Pharisees as devoted almost exclusively to religious pursuits, not political ones.[86] Second,

Wright's insistence that most first-century Jews thought of themselves as being still in exile is regarded as "most dubious" by James D. G. Dunn. He suggests that this might have been true for diaspora Jews (those living outside of Palestine) but thinks there is little evidence that the Essenes at Qumran or, for that matter, Paul thought in such a fashion.[87]

More troubling to some is Wright's insistence that Jewish authorities were primarily responsible for the crucifixion of Jesus. The trend in scholarship has been toward disassociation with Christian condemnations of Jews for killing Jesus, often by placing the onus for Jesus' death on the Romans. Wright sees his view as an alternative to two typical ideas, that Jesus was executed either as a political figure who offended the Romans or as a religious leader whose ideas were unpopular with Jews. Wright envisions a *political* Jesus who offended *Jews*.[88] But, whatever the motives, Jewish leaders get the blame: the Romans crucified thousands of people in the first century, but "few if any were handed over by Jewish authorities, as Jesus seems to have been."[89] Though Sanders would agree, many contemporary scholars would contest the tradition that Jesus was handed over by Jewish authorities. Still, Wright is sensitive about allowing current sensibilities to determine the writing of history. There is no antidefamation league operating on behalf of Romans today, nor is attribution of responsibility for the death of Jesus to them marred by centuries of pogroms and holocausts against their descendants. The concern, clearly, is not to establish who should get the blame, but to define Jesus' relationship with Judaism. The role that Wright believes the Jewish authorities played in bringing about the death of Jesus serves to confirm the subversive nature of the retelling of the Jewish story that he attributes to Jesus.

On a final note, we may ask what Wright makes of the resurrection. It is almost completely missing from his sketch, though he intends to devote generous space to the subject in his next volume.[90] He does not deny its occurrence, as does Crossan, or bracket it out as a topic unsuited for historical discussion, as does Meier. He identifies it clearly with the vindication that Jesus expected to receive from Israel's god.[91] If Jesus was raised, then his prophetic vision and self-claims would seem to be substantiated. If not, then in an important sense his vision would have to be regarded as mistaken. But was he raised? Did it happen? The closest Wright comes to making a commitment as a historian is to agree with that earlier quote from E. P. Sanders (see page 125): "Without the resurrection, would [Jesus'] disciples have endured longer than did John the Baptist's? We can only guess, but I would guess not."[92] Of course, for Wright, that's what history is about—making guesses—hypothesis and verification.

Wright is an unabashed theologian. He is explicitly interested in studying Jesus as a historical figure in order to reflect upon his continuing significance for today. History may be the means, theology or christology the end.[93] What does Wright make of Jesus today? Should we call him Messiah? God? Or god? The project is only two-fifths done, but already Wright (hardly the traditionalist!) offers this clue:

> If it is true that Jesus ultimately fits no known pattern within the first century, it is more or less bound to be true that he fits none within the twentieth.[94]

10

THE QUEST CONTINUES:
ISSUES AND CONCERNS

I'm not in that academic, seminary-trained world, and I think my faith is strong enough that the debate going on in that world doesn't frighten me. . . . I trust in the staying power of Christianity. Some really goofy things have happened in the past 2,000 years, but somehow, the core, the essence of the Christian religion has survived.

—Gene Janssen[1]

I realize much of what we know about Jesus is novelistic, but I act as if it isn't.

—Peter A. Bien, professor of English at Dartmouth College[2]

You can study the scriptures till your eyes fall out, and without the gift of faith, you're not going to believe Christ was the Son of God. The miracle is faith itself.

—Archbishop John Cardinal O'Connor[3]

Here's what I imagine. If you were in Galilee, let's say in the 30s, you would have seen a person called Jesus. Let's imagine three different people responding to that same person. One says, "This guy's a bore. Let's leave him." The second one says, "This guy's dangerous. Let's kill him." The third one says, "I see God here. Let's follow this guy." Now each of these, in its own way is an act of faith.

—John Dominic Crossan[4]

A thousand years ago not many people seemed to be very interested in writing history. In fact, between the work of the Venerable Bede (c. 672–735) and the flourishing of the Renaissance lay a span when the discipline went largely untried. A hundred years ago, the historical quest for Jesus had run itself ragged and waited only for Albert Schweitzer to call attention to that fact. But today that quest is alive and well, pursued with vibrancy and conviction as never before.

The confusion that results from so many voices all speaking at once can disguise the common commitments historical scholars share, just as their quibbles over various matters can obscure the large areas of consensus. A hundred and fifty years ago a fairly well respected scholar named Bruno Bauer maintained that the historical person Jesus never existed.[5] Anyone who says that today—in the academic world at least—gets grouped with the skinheads who say there was no Holocaust and the scientific holdouts who want to believe the world is flat.

Just fifty years ago, Rudolf Bultmann allowed that Jesus had existed but claimed this bare fact was the only thing about him that mattered for faith. Not many theologians would be likely to hold that position any longer either. Jesus did more than just exist. He said and did a great many things that most historians are reasonably certain we can know about today. And though we can know these things apart from faith, most theologians would grant that what we can know is significant for faith and ought to shape our faith.

This book is a report of a work in progress, a quest that will continue. Of the six major historical studies we have examined, four are incomplete. The Jesus Seminar, John Dominic Crossan, John Meier, and N. T. Wright have all announced future volumes that may fill out or revise their current understanding of Jesus. Other important scholars will also enter the fray. Nevertheless, enough has been done already to warrant this report. We conclude, therefore, with a summary of key issues in the debate.

METHOD

The survey undertaken in this book has brought to the fore an ongoing debate over method. Three issues here seem to be paramount:

First, there are questions regarding *sources*. The value of the apocryphal gospels, particularly the Gospel of Thomas, continues to be argued. Some scholars, such as Crossan, treat Thomas as a primary source for their research, while others, including Sanders and Meier, effectively ignore the book. Even more significant, however, is the argument over the relative weight assigned to Q and to Mark. Crossan and the Jesus Seminar regard material in Mark as generally less reliable than the sayings tradition of Q. Most other scholars put the Markan narratives more on a par with Q. Other questions also remain unresolved, concerning, for instance, the value of material in John or the discernment of recensions in Q.

Second, there are questions regarding the use of *criteria*. The criterion of dissimilarity, on which all scholars rely, has proved to be the most controversial. At issue is whether this standard for judgment should be used to exclude data that present Jesus as similar to Palestinian Judaism or early Christianity, or whether it should be used only to include data that present him as dissimilar. On the one hand, the Jesus Seminar has readily applied the criterion in both senses to produce a minimalist portrait of a Jesus who would not have fit easily into either environment. On the other hand, Wright has proposed a new "double criterion of similarity and dissimilarity" that will uncover a Jesus who bridges these two environments. Similarly, distinctions may be observed with regard to the degree of respect scholars show for what is sometimes called a "criterion of explanation," namely, the ability for material to explain why Jesus' life had the impact that it did. Meier explicitly appeals to such a criterion in that he says no historical portrait of Jesus can be convincing unless it explains why Jesus disturbed and threatened people, to the point that he met with a violent and hostile death. Wright seems to apply such a criterion often, seeking to affirm within the Jesus tradition matters that explain developments in early Christianity. But other scholars, such as Burton Mack, explicitly reject this criterion, denying the need or ability for historians to explain such subsequent developments: Jesus' death could be just a historical accident.

Third, we have the general question of *approach,* that is, of how historical research ought to proceed at a basic level. One major issue to be decided is whether the best approach is to construct a portrait of Jesus that takes into account a maximum amount of historical data concerning him (Wright, Sanders) or to construct a portrait based only on the minimum amount of data that seems to be most reliable (Crossan, Jesus Seminar). Beyond this is the question of where to begin. One scheme, exemplified by critics as diverse as Meier and the Jesus Seminar, favors a relatively piecemeal approach to the data, considering the merits of each saying or fact on its own terms and then, finally, attempting to form a hypothesis that accounts for what has been deemed authentic. The opposite strategy, favored by Sanders and Wright, is to begin with an overall hypothesis and interpret the data in light of this to see if a fairly consistent and reasonable accounting can be offered for the authenticity of what fits and the subsequent development of what does not fit. The former strategy appears to be biased against simplicity, and the latter against complexity. In other words, the first approach is at least hypothetically open to discovering the sort of multifaceted portraits of Jesus unveiled by Borg and Meier. The second approach strives for a dominant paradigm that helps to insure internal consistency for the more narrowly focused image of Jesus that is presented.

JESUS AND JUDAISM

Everyone agrees that Jesus was Jewish, but what sort of a Jew was he and how well did he fit into the Jewish religion of his day? Scholars try to explain both his commitment to Jewish identity and his critique or neglect of certain themes or practices that were significant to at least some Jews in his day. The former may be evident, for instance, in his respect for the Jewish scriptures; the latter, in the mere fact that within a generation his following had developed into a distinct religion. Ben Witherington describes the dilemma this way:

> The difficulty for any historian is in achieving the right balance between Jesus' continuity and discontinuity with early Judaism. Insist on too much discontinuity, and it becomes impossible to explain why Jesus had an exclusively Jewish following during his lifetime and why so many different kinds of Jews were interested in giving him a hearing. Insist on too much continuity, and differences of the church from Judaism, even in the church's earliest days, become very difficult to explain.[6]

The debate is an old one. At the beginning of this century, Schweitzer criticized most of the historical Jesus studies that had preceded him for neglecting the Jewish matrix for understanding Jesus on his own terms, but his insistence on doing so seemed to produce a figure so foreign to modern Christians that historical interest in him waned considerably for fifty years. When the New Quest recaptured that interest, scholars tended once more to deemphasize aspects of Jesus that were particularly Jewish.

Arguments over this issue are central to Jesus studies today. E. P. Sanders, whose understanding is closest to that of Schweitzer, insists on a thoroughly Jewish Jesus, one so steeped in covenantal nomism and committed to restoration eschatology that he would appear typical for the Jews of his day. Meier steers away from the word *typical* to call Jesus "a marginal Jew," but he clearly does not mean to suggest that Jesus was "marginally Jewish." Rather, the phrase itself serves as a riddle, posing the questions: How did Jesus relate to Palestinian Judaism and how was he different from other Palestinian Jews?

The issue is complicated by a wonderful problem that now confronts historians: the wealth of information that has come to the fore concerning first-century Palestine. Archaeological excavations, the discovery of the Dead Sea Scrolls, refinement of social-scientific methods for studying ancient cultures, and other factors have combined to broaden our view of Jesus' world. It was a more diverse world than we once thought. Indeed, most scholars are reluctant to speak of Judaism as a monolithic entity at all for this period. Rather, there were varieties of "Judaisms," developing trajectories, and competing ways of being Jewish. Crossan, for instance, maintains that Jesus was representative of an inclusive stream of Judaism that stood in contradiction to the more conservative (and exclusive) variety that ultimately became identified as rabbinic Judaism. Thus, Jesus appears non-Jewish to us only because he differed from what later became a dominant identification for Judaism.

With regard to Jesus as a Jew, at least three perspectives can be discerned among historical scholars.

A Hellenistic Jew

Many historians now see Jesus as a Jew who had been deeply influenced by Greco-Roman culture. We know that the influx of this culture was great for the time and place where Jesus lived. Josephus tells us, for instance, that some Jews in Roman Palestine were willing to pay for a surgical procedure that would undo their circumcision (he spares us the details of exactly what this entailed). Apparently, many Jews wanted to be like everyone else, to define their identity with primary reference to the whole human race rather than to a specific ethnic group. Some scholars think that the impact of Hellenism was especially strong in Galilee, noting that Jesus' territory is even called "Galilee of the Gentiles" at one point (Matt. 4:15). They claim, further, that Jesus' hometown of Nazareth was essentially a suburb of the great Roman city Sepphoris, which would have offered Jesus a full panoply of Greek and Roman society, a society where there would have been Cynics but probably not many Pharisees. We need to note, however, that many historical scholars do not accept this description of Galilee as historically accurate.[7]

Scholars who think Jesus may have been heavily influenced by Hellenism include Gerard Downing, Burton Mack, John Dominic Crossan, and the Jesus Seminar. Opponents to this view often accuse them of favoring "a non-Jewish image of Jesus," but that is not quite accurate. They favor a Hellenistic Jewish image. Jesus was a Jew, yes, but like many Jews in his environment, he had come to have more in common with the Greek philosophers than the Hebrew prophets. The evidence for this view comes largely from the Q source, where a generous portion of the early sayings attributed to Jesus reflect an ethnically generic outlook on life similar to that of the Cynics.

A Charismatic Jew

Another proposal holds that Jesus may be differentiated from other Jews of his day not so much by geographical or cultural affiliations as by spiritual ones. Immersed in a stream of Jewish mysticism, he believed himself to be endowed with the divine Spirit in a way that authenticated his words and deeds apart from the usual structures of authority. This explains why he could consider himself to be faithful to the Jewish religion while other leaders of that religion might consider him hostile or dangerous. The image of Jesus as a "spirit person" or "holy man" does not cast him in a totally unique mold. It describes him as fitting a paradigm that existed within his culture but which would have granted him a certain ambiguous status within that culture. Geza Vermes and Marcus Borg are two scholars who have tried to set Jesus within this charismatic strain of Judaism. Borg also stresses the dichotomy between Jewish peasants and the ruling urban elites in Jesus' society. As a charismatic Jew, Jesus related specifically to the peasant culture, on whose behalf he believed the Spirit of God was moving. The appeal to the Spirit became in essence an invocation of an alternative authority, distinct from the traditional bases of authority that preserved the hierarchy of power favoring the elite. Thus, for Borg, this category of "charismatic Jew" overlaps with that which follows.

A Jewish Prophet

A third possibility distinguishes Jesus from other Jews primarily in terms of his vocation. He believed he was called by God to be a prophet, like the biblical prophets of old. Most who hold this view do not think Jesus was overly Hellenized, nor do they find it necessary to place him in a particular stream of Jewish diversity. As a peasant, he and his family remained somewhat oblivious to the allure that foreign culture might have exercised on city folk. They may also have been somewhat oblivious to the controversies that divided educated Jews into sects: Pharisees, Sadducees, Essenes, and the like. Jesus would have been a typical Jew insofar as he embraced the basic elements of that religion as it was practiced by common people: worship, ethics, and a vision of life informed by the stories in the Bible. He became atypical only in his career as a prophet, as he came to a particular understanding of what God wanted to happen and of how this would come to pass. Thus, when Meier calls Jesus "a marginal Jew," he means in part that he was marginalized in the same sense that most Jews who lived in Palestine were at this time. But he also means to suggest that Jesus marginalized himself still further by remaining celibate and adopting a vocation and lifestyle that marked him as odd and eventually aroused hostility. In one way or another, not only Meier but also Sanders, Wright, and Borg hold to this view. They think that, as a prophet, Jesus fit into an established Jewish mold and yet one that by definition would set him apart from other Jews in key respects.

JESUS AND ESCHATOLOGY

The one issue over which historical scholars currently appear to be most divided concerns Jesus' stance toward the future.[8] This concern is closely related to the foregoing discussion because, usually, scholars who emphasize the Jewishness of Jesus (as understood in traditional terms) also emphasize his eschatological vision regarding some sort of imminent divine intervention. Those who construe Jesus as more influenced by Hellenism usually view him as less constrained by a vision of the future. Borg is an exception, the "bridge" figure who emphasizes Jesus' Jewishness while describing him as basically noneschatological.

Again, the argument goes back to the First Quest and continues to be affected by the dynamics of that movement. Schweitzer insisted that Jesus must be viewed as a mistaken eschatological prophet, one who went to his death maintaining that God was about to act for the deliverance of Israel in a way that God never did. The New Questers, influenced by their mentor Rudolf Bultmann, emphasized the existential component of Jesus' teaching, often interpreting sayings about the kingdom of God as applicable to life "here and now." For example, Bornkamm took Jesus' message as being about "making the reality of God present."[9] Still, Bornkamm insisted that Jesus' sayings about the kingdom of God had a range of meanings, some present in application and some future. This has been the dominant view in New Testament studies. For recent historical Jesus scholars, the questions have become, Which group of sayings (present or future) should receive the emphasis? Which of the sayings are authentic? Two abruptly diverse perspectives may be discerned.

A Noneschatological Jesus

A prominent view among recent Jesus scholars has been that Jesus did not expect or announce any imminent divine intervention in history. The Gospel texts that Schweitzer took to be so representative of Jesus' attitude have been understood as developments of the church prompted by such crises as the persecution of Christians and the destruction of the Jerusalem temple. Jesus' interests are taken to have been decidedly this-worldly. The Jesus Seminar, for example, has deemed all sayings that speak of the kingdom as a future reality to be unauthentic, as well as all sayings that speak of a coming Son of Man or future judgment. In their view, shared by Mack and Crossan, Jesus was primarily a sage, concerned with dispensing advice for making the most of life in this world. Crossan says Jesus spoke of the kingdom of God "not as an apocalyptic event in the imminent future but as a mode of life in the present."[10] Gerald Downing differs only slightly. Rather than denying the authenticity of eschatological sayings, he reinterprets them. Even the Cynics, Downing maintains (in what has been one of the least accepted aspects of his proposal), used eschatological language, but they used it in a metaphorical sense, applying imagery of the afterlife to life on earth. Richard Horsley also thinks that Jesus spoke of the kingdom only in present terms, but he construes the phrase "kingdom of God" as a metaphor for a social-political phenomenon.

Whether they view Jesus as a sage or a political activist, all these scholars think Jesus' words and his deeds were directed at improving the lot of people in the present. His efforts and his counsel in this regard would have been largely pointless if the world were about to end, or if things were so bad that only God could fix them. Scholars who hold to this orientation in their work on Jesus cannot imagine that he ever would have taught his followers to wait for God to put things right. "Simply translated," says Mack, "Jesus' message seems to have been, 'See how it's done? You can do it also.'"[11]

Marcus Borg allows that Jesus may have predicted political crises that would come soon upon Israel, and that he might have used end-of-the-world metaphors for this. He also grants that the phrase "kingdom of God" is a tensive symbol that may have a wide range of meaning (see page 110), but he wants to redefine the expectations of Jesus away from imminence. Thus, Borg prefers to think of Jesus as noneschatological, unless, he says, one uses the term *eschatological* in such a broadened sense "that the affirmation becomes virtually meaningless, given the variety of meanings it encompasses."[12] This raises the problem of semantics. Crossan wants to say that Jesus' message *was* eschatological even though it did not involve predicting any imminent divine intervention. For him, Jesus espoused an *ethical* eschatology but not an *apocalyptic* or *ascetical* eschatology.

Borg also notes, in his own survey of historical Jesus studies, that the eschatological image for Jesus (that is, as a figure who did anticipate some sort of imminent divine intervention) succeeded in dominating most scholarship in the twentieth century. In recent years, said Borg, writing in 1988, the old consensus to this effect disappeared and was replaced by "a growing conviction [that] the mission and message of Jesus were 'non-eschatological.'"[13] If Borg thought a "new consensus" was emerging, he spoke too soon. The old view did not go quietly into the night but, suddenly, has enjoyed a revival.

An Eschatological Jesus

Many historical scholars think that Jesus had a powerful future orientation with specific ideas about what God was going to do soon. For them this does not remove the need for humans to work for God's will here and now but accentuates it. The day of salvation and judgment is at hand, creating a crisis of decision: the need to live now as God has always wanted people to live is imperative. These scholars think that the so-called apocalyptic material in the Gospels represents some of the most historically certain tradition. The church did not always know what to make of this material but preserved it because it had been so central to Jesus' message. He claimed that God was about to do something momentous through the Son of Man, something that would change the world forever. Meier, Sanders, and Wright all follow this line of thought, though they differ on particulars. Even some scholars who emphasize Jesus' role as a sage want to preserve the eschatological element in his teaching. Witherington, for instance, sees no contradiction in seeing Jesus as an eschatological prophet and as a wandering Jewish sage; he affirms the authenticity of material associated with both strains.

Sanders revives Schweitzer's notion that Jesus was mistaken in his view that God was about to establish a heavenly kingdom on earth. Wright, however, insists that Jesus predicted the end of a social world, not the space-time universe, and, further, suggests that Jesus was shown to be right. Sanders also differs from some other scholars in this camp over the authenticity of particular sayings. First, he is less inclined to accept the authenticity of present-oriented kingdom sayings than is Meier, who is more open to affirming the both/and character of present and future kingdom references. Sanders also insists that the sayings in which Jesus predicted events that would occur within the span of his own generation (for example, Mark 9:1; 13:30) must be authentic, whereas Meier attributes all date-setting references to the later church. Meier wants to affirm that Jesus spoke of an imminent divine intervention that would bring in the kingdom without setting specific times for this occurrence. Witherington takes the latter point a step further, insisting that Jesus proclaimed only that the kingdom was *possibly* imminent, not that it was *necessarily* so.

JESUS AND POLITICS

With regard to Jesus' stance toward politics, scholars seem to be moving closer to consensus, such that discussion is not as disparate as it once was. For a time, the issue seemed to be whether Jesus should be viewed as a religious figure (the traditional concept) or as the leader of a political movement. Today, the dichotomy seems unnecessary, an anachronism imposed, perhaps, by Western scholars reared in societies that pride themselves on (supposedly) being able to separate church

and state.[14] Even today, especially in the Mideast, the line between politics and religion is indistinct. This was certainly true in Jesus' situation as well. Nevertheless, some disparity of perspective among scholars is observable with regard to
where they place the emphasis in Jesus' mission and message.

Reimarus is thought by many to have initiated the quest for the historical Jesus
with his postmortem publications in the late eighteenth century. He was also the
first to challenge the pious assumption that Jesus was primarily a spiritual or religious leader. As Reimarus had it, Jesus was a political claimant who thought that
God was going to establish him as the new king of an earthly realm. He was, in effect, a madman, a presentation that served Reimarus's ulterior purpose of discred-
iting Christianity quite nicely. But even scholars who see through the tendentious
aspects of Reimarus' construal often grant that he was onto something. He was able
to make his case as well as he did because the Gospel narratives do indeed show
Jesus speaking and acting in ways that must have had powerful political implications. Jesus entered a highly charged, politically sensitive environment (Roman-
occupied Jerusalem), demonstrated against the principal political institution (the
temple), and was subsequently executed by order of the governor, charged with
treason or rebellion against the state.

Nevertheless, as Borg indicates, the political dimension of Jesus' life and message has not been emphasized in the two hundred years since Reimarus. But now
Borg sees this as "an emerging majority position."[15] Still, there are streams of Jesus
scholarship that contend against such a view. First, the image of Jesus as a Jewish
sage or (especially) as a Cynic philosopher moves, for some, in another direction.
The Jesus Seminar appears to resolve the old question of whether Jesus was motivated by religious or political concerns in the opposite manner of most contemporary scholars; instead of affirming commitment to both spheres, they deny that
Jesus had much interest in *either* religion or politics, save to denounce them. But
Crossan accepts the Cynic philosopher model for Jesus and still makes considerable room for sociopolitical concerns in his description of Jesus' ideas, and both
Borg and Witherington have no problem wedding the image of Jesus as a Jewish
sage with that of a politically oriented prophet.

The diversity that does attend modern analyses of Jesus' relationship to politics reflects disagreement as to his primary goal or orientation. For convenience, I
offer here two categories of thought, but we should recognize that these are not
necessarily mutually exclusive. Even the terms I use to label them are problematic, deriving from ways of viewing the situation that, as I have indicated, are
somewhat outmoded.

Social-Political Liberation

A number of scholars have suggested over the years that Jesus was primarily
concerned with liberating Israel from Roman rule. He has been cast in the role of
a Zealot or in some other way depicted as a political revolutionary.[16] This view has
not fared well of late and, in fact, is not endorsed by any of the scholars we have
discussed in this book. In its place have arisen various theories in keeping with

Richard Horsley's supposition that Jesus instituted a revolution from the bottom up rather than from the top down. Jesus sought to teach the common people a better way to live, one that did not depend upon the disposition of their rulers. As Borg puts it, Jesus "did not seek a position of governmental power or to reform governmental policy," yet he was political in that he "both challenged the existing social order and advocated an alternative."[17] Thus, Borg claims that Jesus challenged the politics of holiness in his day with an unconventional wisdom that gave new priority to compassion. More to the point, he challenged the mindset of the ruling urban elites in a way that offered new vision to the peasant class. Similarly, Crossan believes that Jesus facilitated the reconstitution of peasant communities by demonstrating a shared egalitarianism that defied the unjust system of brokerage. By encouraging and enacting social transformation, Jesus posed a real threat to the political system of his day, indeed, a greater threat ultimately than those who thought they would change society by overthrowing this or that particular tyrant.

Spiritual Renewal

Another view that has not fared well in recent scholarship is the understanding of Jesus as a teacher of timeless spiritual truth that had little to do with the concrete situation in which he worked. In place of this idea, however, many scholars would insist that for Jesus, the concern for social justice or political liberation was specifically a religious or spiritual matter. As a preacher and a prophet, he believed that God would establish justice for those who accepted God's rule. Accordingly, he called people to live in accord with God's will and to trust in God for vindication. He sought to inspire a spiritual renewal of faith and obedience among the people of Israel. Sanders and Meier emphasize this aspect to the point that they doubt Jesus was overtly concerned with the reform of existing earthly institutions (which he expected would soon come to an end). But both Meier and Sanders are nevertheless careful to relate Jesus' message to the hopes and aspirations of Israel. They do not, for instance, present him as primarily addressing individuals with regard to how they might personally obtain peace with God. The context for Jesus' ministry concerns the eschatological hope for the kingdom of God, the divine creation of a social order in which righteousness will prevail and the fortunes of Israel will be restored. Wright likewise stresses that Jesus' vision was very political and this-worldly: a transformation of society through which Israel will at last be returned from exile and set free from her enemies. But, Wright adds, this deliverance will be accomplished by God, not Zealots, and the enemy to be defeated is Satan, not the Romans.

JESUS AND THE SUPERNATURAL

Perhaps the thorniest issue of all in historical studies of religious figures is what in common parlance would be called "supernatural" forces or events. The very use of the term *supernatural* raises a host of philosophical problems[18] (some theologians prefer *supranatural;* most don't like either word), but at a basic level the term points us toward what we need to discuss. In the Gospel traditions there are, first, miracles—reports of observable events that would have no reasonable explanation according to the laws of nature. The issue here is not just whether certain events may have been *perceived* as supernatural by people who did not know all the laws of nature, but whether they may be understood as such even by historians. In the nineteenth century the problem was almost inevitably construed as one of perception. Assuming that supernatural events did not actually occur, historians would inquire as to what might have happened that was subsequently interpreted in this way. Thus, Paulus developed elaborate rational explanations for most of the miracle stories in the Bible: raisings from the dead were actually arousals from comas or "deliverances from premature burial."[19] Renan entertained the notion that some of the miracles were hoaxes, staged events to draw attention to Jesus and his message. But Strauss's position became the dominant one: the miracle stories are mythological reports, poetic accounts that used symbolic imagery to convey meaning to a primitive audience that lacked categories for truth that we possess today. Such stories may convey what we would call philosophical truth rather than what we would call historical or scientific fact. The story of Jesus changing water into wine, for example, signifies the transformative impact that his word has on human lives.

This mythological understanding of miracle became best associated with the work of Rudolf Bultmann in the twentieth century. Bultmann sought to "demythologize" the New Testament stories in order to uncover the kernel of existential engagement that each story sought to convey. Such demythologizing is necessary, Bultmann maintained, because the modern worldview does not allow for miracles in a literal sense. John Meier reacts sharply to that assumption in his study of Jesus. In fact, a Gallup poll revealed that in 1989 about 82 percent of Americans surveyed believed that "even today, miracles are performed by the power of God." Thus, as far as Meier is concerned, "the academic creed of 'no modern person can believe in miracles' should be consigned to the dustbin of empirically falsified hypotheses."[20] The fact is, most people, including most well-educated people, including (when he removes his historian's hat) Meier himself, do believe that what are popularly called supernatural events have occurred. If the majority of modern people do not view the world in line with what is called "the modern worldview," the accuracy of that label must be questioned.

Miracle stories may offer the prime example for the problem historians face in dealing with material that refers to the supernatural, but the issue for Jesus studies is broader than this. The Gospels also contain accounts that may be termed "mythological" because they involve interaction of humans and supernatural beings (that is, beings whose existence has not been confirmed in the world of nature as analyzed through modern science). The story of Jesus' temptation by Satan in the wilderness (Matt. 4:1–11) provides a good example. The question of whether this is a *historical* event involves consideration of what occurred on a level that would have been empirically observable to neutral bystanders. If a camera crew from a modern television network had been on hand the day that Jesus was tempted in the wilderness, what would they have been able to document regarding his encounter with Satan? Of course, in a sense, any story that assumes the existence of God is mythological. Eventually the question becomes whether a historian—speaking *as a historian*—can acknowledge the existence or activity of God. Can a historian ever say, "God did this"?

We will delineate three general stances that historical Jesus scholars seem to take with regard to this issue, allowing again for some overlap of positions.

Objective Neutrality

Most historians adopt a position of official silence when confronted with religious claims concerning anything that might be regarded as supernatural. John Meier, despite his reaction against the Bultmannian description of a "modern worldview," thinks it is "inherently impossible for historians working with empirical evidence within the confines of their own discipline" to attribute anything in history to God. To clarify this, he supposes that two historians, one a Christian and the other an atheist, might both conclude that an event "cannot be explained by any human ability or action, by any known force in the physical universe, or by fraud or self-delusion." Still, the atheist might maintain that "even in the absence of an explanation, I am sure that this is not a miracle." The Christian might decide that "this is a miracle worked by God." In either case, for Meier, the judgment is evaluative in such a way that it cannot be made by a person acting within "his or her capacity as a professional historian."[21] For Meier, historical investigation is a field that "stubbornly restricts itself to empirical evidence and rational deductions or inferences from such evidence."[22] Thus, even though Meier insists that Jesus did things that were considered to be miracles by his contemporaries (both supporters and opponents), he refrains from saying that Jesus did things that historians ought to regard as miracles. Invoking the supernatural is a matter of interpretation that goes beyond historical science.

Denial

Some scholars renounce this hands-off approach as a cop-out. Historical science need not be cowed into supposedly objective silence regarding such matters, but has a responsibility to speak. The leaders of the Jesus Seminar have in general endorsed this stance, though the membership of that group has not always followed suit. At one meeting of the Seminar, participants were asked to vote on the statement "Mary conceived of the Holy Spirit." After some discussion, they determined to revise the statement to read "The question of whether Mary conceived of the Holy Spirit is a matter that historical science cannot determine." Robert Funk was disappointed with this move. "I think they're just a bunch of cowards," he told the press. "Jesus had a human father."[23]

The Jesus Seminar did decide by a large majority that Jesus' "resurrection" (whatever is meant by that term) did not involve "the resuscitation of a corpse."[24] Gerd Lüdemann, a member of the Seminar who delivered a paper at the meeting where that vote was taken, has written two entire books on this subject. He maintains that the resurrection appearances all have psychological explanations: for Peter, a subjective vision produced by his overwhelming guilt for having denied Jesus when he was arrested; for Paul, the resolution of an unconscious "Christ complex"; for the five hundred followers mentioned in 1 Corinthians 15:6, mass hysteria. For Lüdemann himself, the resurrection is simply "an empty formula" that must be rejected by anyone holding "a scientific world view."[25] Note how this approach is different from the neutrality advocated by Meier. In keeping with Meier's position, Marcus Borg (also a member of the Jesus Seminar) maintains that "we cannot say, on historical grounds," whether anything happened to the corpse of Jesus.[26] But Lüdemann thinks we *can* say. On historical grounds, he told *Newsweek* magazine, we may affirm that Jesus' body "rotted away" in the tomb.[27] John Dominic Crossan almost agrees, but not quite. Jesus' body, he claims, never made it to the tomb; it was left without burial and devoured by dogs.[28]

If the occurrences can be explained in natural ways, stories of healings and exorcisms are sometimes accepted by scholars who deny the historical reality of miracles. Crossan thinks Jesus healed people by relieving the negative social connotations attached to their physical condition without altering the condition itself.[29] Burton Mack actually translates Jesus' command for his disciples, "Heal the sick," as "Pay attention to the sick."[30] Many of these scholars will also grant the possibility of psychosomatic healings. Exorcisms, in particular, are interpreted this way.[31] Thus, for Crossan (following Morton Smith), Jesus effected some genuine cures by working what the people of his day regarded as a form of folk magic, though what actually happened could now be explained from an informed understanding of the interrelationship of mental, emotional, and physiological well-being.

The so-called nature miracles, however, are another matter. Crossan agrees with David Aune's conclusion that these are "creations out of whole cloth by the early church."[32] He also objects on ethical grounds to Meier's attempt to bracket from discussion the historicity of supernatural events. He questions, for instance, whether Meier *as a historian* would take this stance with regard to reports of figures other than Jesus. Meier says that historians must keep silent regarding whether Jesus was actually born to a virgin. Would he say the same about Caesar Augustus, whose mother is said to have been impregnated by a serpent in the temple of Apollo? Crossan has no trouble stating his own position "as a historian trying to be ethical": "I do not accept the divine conception of *either* Jesus *or* Augustus as factual history."[33]

Scholars who deny the historicity of Jesus' miracles often point out that such miracles are not reported in Q or referred to by Paul. Mack is the most extreme, claiming not only that Jesus did no miracles but, further, that he was not even thought to have done miracles during his lifetime.

Critique the Paradigm

A third perspective on how historians deal with this sort of material involves the allowance for (if not advocacy of) a critique of the traditional paradigm for historical research. In short, some scholars believe it is responsible, as historians, to challenge the strictures of historical-critical method when these do not appear to account for reality. Even Meier agrees that this may be done *philosophically,* but when historians write history, he thinks they must operate with set principles of empirical research and rational deduction that are standard for those who work within the field. But what Meier calls "the confines of the discipline," some regard as artificially confining. Why should scholars have to impose a particular vision of reality on the evidence when (as even Meier admits may happen) some of the data do not fit neatly into the resultant grid? If there is substantial evidence that reality is not or has not always been the way post-Enlightenment scientific analysis suggests, then that evidence should be allowed to stand in critical disjuncture with historical description rather than being arbitrarily dismissed or ignored.

N. T. Wright questions how "scientific" any method can really be if it is not open to having its own presuppositions challenged. "To insist at the beginning of an enquiry . . . that some particular contemporary worldview is the only possible one . . . is to show that all we want to do is to hear the echo of our own voices."[34] He calls for "suspension of judgment," which is not the same thing as maintaining neutrality:

> It is prudent, methodologically, to hold back from too hasty a judgment on what is actually possible and what is not within the space-time universe. There are more things in heaven and earth than are dreamed of in post-Enlightenment philosophy.[35]

Wright, for instance, dismisses as naive the notion that Jesus' contemporaries were prone to believe in miracles because they did not understand the laws of nature. For Wright, the simplest and best explanation for the widespread report that Jesus did such things is that "it was more or less true."[36] Wright seems to think that historians *as historians* can and should affirm this. If the best historical reconstruction of reality and the best post-Enlightenment scientific description of reality are incongruous, that may be a problem. But why should this problem be solved by requiring the historians to fudge their discipline for the sake of the scientists?

Ben Witherington also raises this issue pointedly. He sees the suggestion that Jesus may have healed people by manipulating presently unknown natural causes as begging the question of why only explanations that are considered "natural" are to be allowed:

> Are we to attribute to Jesus a scientific knowledge of cures and *natural* healing principles that have escaped other doctors in the last two thousand years? Is it not easier to believe that perhaps God does intervene in human lives in ways we would call miraculous? In view of how little we know about our universe, do we really know that nothing can happen without a "natural" cause?[37]

Marcus Borg affirms *as a historian* the reality of what he calls the "world of spirit." This world might correlate with what some would regard as a supernatural realm. Borg himself probably does not consider it supernatural, but an often unrecognized or poorly understood part of nature. Still, he admits that the world of spirit is not visible or tangible, that it cannot be studied in the same way as the visible world, and that it does not necessarily follow what are traditionally called "the laws of nature." With regard to Jesus' miracles, Borg does not want to affirm absolutely that they did occur as historical events, but he is willing to bend the discipline of historical science to allow for that possibility. "We simply do not know if there are limits to the powers of a charismatic mediator," he says. It remains at least hypothetically possible that the power from the spirit world did enable Jesus to walk on water or to resuscitate genuinely dead people.[38]

THE SELF-CONSCIOUSNESS
AND INTENTION OF JESUS

What did Jesus believe about himself? What was he trying to do? What did he hope to accomplish? These questions are related to all of the points discussed so far, but by way of summary, we may identify some of the answers that have been given. These answers might be arranged along a continuum that recognizes varying degrees of continuity between the views of Jesus and views that became normative for the early church.

At one end of the spectrum are those scholars who think Jesus saw himself and his mission quite differently than the Christians who later invoked his name. The most extreme viewpoint (again) would probably be that of Burton Mack, for whom the historical Jesus really had no sense of purpose or mission, but was essentially aimless.[39] Without going this far, many other scholars—including Crossan, Funk, and Vermes—contrast the historical Jesus with the figure who replaced him in the creeds of Christianity. For them, Jesus was primarily a teacher, and his goal was to teach people a different way of life. In addition, Horsley emphasizes Jesus' political interests and insists that he saw himself as a prophet of social change. But all of these scholars doubt that Jesus ever viewed himself as the Messiah or that he would have applied exalted titles such as Son of God or Son of Man to himself. Most of them would also doubt that he ever intended for his own death to serve any particular purpose, although Christians within a generation would come to view this as the primary means through which he accomplished his purpose in life (now construed as saving people from sin). Rather, his crucifixion is viewed, at best, as a martyrdom that he was willing to suffer for the sake of his ideas or, at worst, as an unfortunate accident that befell him when he miscalculated the social impact of his actions.

In contrast, Meier and Wright see far more continuity between Jesus' own perception and goals and those of his later followers. It is quite possible for them that Jesus did come to see himself as the Messiah or at least believe that he was called to live out prophecies of scripture that were applied to that figure. He saw himself as more than a teacher, as a prophet who was divinely inspired to reveal God's will in a sense that was definitive and authoritative for Israel. Wright's work (which is more complete than Meier's at this point) even suggests that Jesus believed he was called to do and be what only God could do and be, establishing a major point of continuity between Jesus' historical self-consciousness and the church's confession of him as divine. His death, furthermore, was part of the plan and may have been linked in his own mind to some notion of atonement for Israel.

Somewhere between these perspectives are the views of most other scholars, including Borg and Sanders. The former grants that Jesus saw himself as a Spirit-filled agent of God and that his primary mission was that of a teacher and prophet of social change. Sanders claims that Jesus saw himself as *the* end-time prophet responsible for inaugurating God's kingdom, and sees a relatively easy transition from this self-perception as "king of the messianic kingdom" to the church's confession of him as the Messiah. But neither Borg nor Sanders thinks that Jesus intended to die. Also, for Borg and Sanders, Jesus' vision appears to have gone unfulfilled, at least in the sense that he himself intended. In Borg's case, the revitalization of Israel's peasant culture did not occur; in Sanders's, the divine intervention that would bring about an eschatological restoration of Israel did not happen. Rather, for both Borg and Sanders, and for the majority of historical scholars, reports of Jesus' subsequent resurrection caused his followers to think of him and his mission in new categories. His ultimate significance, then, took on dimensions that transcended anything that he himself may ever have imagined.

NOW WHAT?

Thomas Long, editor of the journal *Theology Today,* says that he can identify with the experience of Cullen Murphy, managing editor of the popular magazine *The Atlantic*. Some years ago Murphy did an article on historical Jesus studies for his magazine. He spent one long day in Chicago interviewing several scholars about their quest. "At times," he says of that day, "I had the distinct impression of being present at some sort of clinical procedure." At the end of the day, as he departed the building to find snow lightly falling, he was met outside by a Salvation Army band. Just as he approached, they began to play "O Little Town of Bethlehem." Murphy confesses, "I must say that it was quite a thrill."[40]

Murphy (and Long, who passed on this anecdote) is not, presumably, a person given easily to sentiment. If anything, I suspect both would meet the "hardened journalist" stereotype of persons who have pretty much heard everything and are surprised by little. But both find the specter of Bible scholars dissecting the Jesus tradition to be somewhat daunting. Just what sort of "clinical procedure" is it? Surgical? To see if faith can be repaired, reconstituted to last another century? Or is it an autopsy? To find out why it died?

For many who have made their way this far in a survey of Jesus scholarship, the discipline may seem to lack the vibrancy, the power, and even the sentiment that a simple hymn can evoke. But it isn't that way for all. Marcus Borg affirms that "one can be a Christian without historical knowledge of Jesus,"[41] but goes on to confess that for himself, the work of historians "has made it possible to be a Christian again."[42] Frederick Gaiser relates the study of the historical Jesus to the unflinching honesty that authenticates Christian faith. He finds permission to ask historical questions about Jesus and the Bible to be "magnificently liberating" and maintains that he has never "felt the need to leave the classic Christian faith in order to pursue honesty." In fact, he adds (sounding very Borgian), "it would not be putting it too strongly to say that such honesty permitted me to remain a Christian."[43] Paula Fredriksen goes so far as to say that Christianity's own claims necessitate historical study of Jesus. Specifically, the doctrine of the Incarnation (that, in Jesus, God became a human being) begs the historical question. By confessing this doctrine, the church "lays upon itself the obligation to do history." Otherwise, Christians will be docetists, believing in Jesus only as a divine figure, not as the human (historical) representation of God.[44]

Thus, many witnesses maintain that, "clinical" or not, the quest is necessary for the theological confession of the Christian church and/or for their personal faith. But historical Jesus studies may also have a usefulness to theology apart from their effect on faith. John Meier notes that these studies offer "a constant stimulus to theological renewal" in that they reveal a figure who "refuses to be held fast by any given school of thought," who evinces "strange, off-putting, embarrassing contours, equally offensive to right and left wings."[45] For others, though, all this may be beside the point. The issue, simply, is the advancement of knowledge. If we can learn more about Jesus—a significant figure in history—we should, and if what we learn troubles the believers or the unbelievers, so be it. The truth will out, if we let it.

Whether these studies feed one's faith or threaten it, whether they reveal profound insights or merely satisfy idle curiosity, they will continue. A century ago, their death knell was supposedly sounded by Schweitzer, but here we are, questing still. The secular view that Jesus is only important to religion and the theological position that the Jesus of history is not significant for faith have both eroded away. Secular and theological authorities agree: Jesus matters. Whether we are Christians or not, then, we appear to be destined to share a planet with people who think Jesus is important but who do not believe the same things about him that we do. As long as encyclopedias include articles on Jesus and public school textbooks devote space to him, someone will have to decide what counts as historical knowledge regarding him. It seems certain, then, that the quest will continue.

Something else seems certain. It may be comforting to some, frustrating to others, but it seems certain. Whatever the historical scholars decide about Jesus, Christians are not going to quit confessing creeds concerning him or offering prayers to him. Evangelists are not going to quit imploring people to call upon him for salvation and the evangelized are not going to quit asking him to come into their hearts.

Salvation Army bands are not my personal cup of tea, but not long ago I attended an outdoor concert by the rock group Jars of Clay. This group's members, young from my perspective, are openly Christian. Their audience, equally young and younger, appeared to be also. The group led some fifteen to twenty thousand of these young people in a moving hymn to Jesus, singing one line over and over:

> I want to fall in love with you . . .
> I want to fall in love with you . . .
> I want to fall in love with you . . .
> I want to fall in love with you.

There they were, the next generation, swaying their hands in the air, on a quest for Jesus—but a different quest than the one this book describes. Is their quest simply to know—indeed to *love*—the one whom Borg calls "the post-Easter Jesus"? Then why do they clutch in their hands those books that tell what Jesus did before Easter? Their quest, I think, is for the Jesus of a story, a story of which history is but a part, sometimes but a shadow. Stories, unlike history, cannot always be divided neatly along a chronological axis. Good stories often involve so many anachronies—foreshadowings, predictions, flashbacks, memories—that we lose track of what was post- and what was pre-, what was then and what was now, and finally, we don't care. We just let the story take us wherever it is going. The quest for the Jesus of history is two hundred years old now; the quest for the Jesus of story, almost two thousand. People have been challenged by both—invigorated, frightened, angered, renewed, intrigued. I think the two quests can and should overlap (since the latter includes the former), but often they don't.

For better or worse, the story will have the last word. The hymns will make sure of that. Philip Brooks, the composer of "O Little Town of Bethlehem," was born the same year that David Friedrich Strauss published the first edition of his *Life of Jesus* (1835). Not many read Strauss anymore. But, oh, that hymn! Jars of Clay may not have that kind of staying power, but some of my students were in that audience, and I know they are more affected by that music than by any of my books. So am I. A bit old for this sort of thing, I can still sing and sway with the best of them, and I do. I fell in love with *this* Jesus a long time ago, the Beautiful Savior, the Lover of my soul, the Jesus of story and song.

This has little to do with the historians' quest, but from a historical standpoint the endurance of the hymns may be appropriate, because, as most Jesus scholars will grant, the hymns came first. Before the Gospels, before the Epistles, before Josephus, even before Q, Christians were writing hymns about Jesus. A few of them even get quoted in the Bible. The hymns were there before anyone tried to write a narrative of Jesus' life or reflect systematically about his identity or message. They were inspired by a story that was beginning to emerge, a story that defied simple chronological distinctions between past and present, then and now. Jesus scholars argue over which came first: history or theology. For what it's worth, I think a story preceded them both—and that worship consisted of hymns directed to the Jesus known and experienced through this story.

The bands aren't going to quit playing. But still, the quest continues.

> Jesus went on with his disciples to the villages of Caesarea Philippi; and on the way he asked his disciples, "Who do people say that I am?" And they answered him, "John the Baptist; and others, Elijah; and still others, one of the prophets." He asked them, "But who do you say that I am?"
>
> *(Mark 8:27–29)*

NOTES

Introduction

1. Crossan, *Historical Jesus*, xi.
2. Sanders, *Historical Figure of Jesus*, 1.
3. Hollenbach, "Historical Jesus Question," 20.
4. Frederick J. Gaiser, "The Quest for Jesus and the Christian Faith: Introduction," in *The Quest for Jesus and the Christian Faith*, ed. Frederick J. Gaiser (St. Paul: Luther Seminary, 1997), 7. Gaiser is paraphrasing Hans Walter Wolff.
5. Kähler, *So-Called Historical Jesus*.
6. Borg, *Jesus in Contemporary Scholarship*, 195. John Dominic Crossan gives a theological critique of this dichotomy in *Birth of Christianity*.
7. See the discussion on pages 137–38.

1. Historians Discover Jesus

1. Schweitzer, *Quest of the Historical Jesus*, 403.
2. Bultmann, *Jesus and the Word*, 8.
3. Bornkamm, *Jesus of Nazareth*, 13.
4. Wright, *Jesus and the Victory of God*, 123. The preceding three quotes from Schweitzer, Bultmann, and Bornkamm are all cited by Wright on page 3 of this same volume.
5. Cited in Schweitzer, *Quest of the Historical Jesus*, 13.
6. See, for instance, the Gospel harmony of Osiander (1498–1552), discussed in Schweitzer, *Quest of the Historical Jesus*, 13. The hapless daughter of Jairus also ends up being raised from the dead several times.
7. Harold Lindsell, *The Battle for the Bible* (Grand Rapids: Zondervan Publishing House, 1976). Lindsell also reconciles apparent discrepancies in the biblical accounts of Peter's denials by having Peter deny Jesus *six* times (174–76).
8. John Calvin, *A Harmony of the Gospels of Matthew, Mark, and Luke*, trans. A. W. Morrison, 3 vols. (Grand Rapids: Wm. B. Eerdmans Publishing Co., 1972).
9. This work is summarized in Schweitzer, *Quest of the Historical Jesus*, 13–26.
10. Reimarus, *Fragments*, 151.
11. Schweitzer, *Quest of the Historical Jesus*, 15.
12. Heinrich Eberhard Gottlob Paulus, *Das Leben Jesu als Grundlage einer reinen Geschichte des Urchristentums*, 2 vols. (Heidelberg: C. F. Winter, 1828). For an English summary, see Schweitzer, *Quest of the Historical Jesus*, 48–87.
13. For a summary, see Schweitzer, *Quest of the Historical Jesus*, 78–120.
14. For a summary, see Schweitzer, *Quest of the Historical Jesus*, 181–92.
15. Though the concept is Renan's, this oft-cited phrase (actually, "Galilaean spring-

tide") appears to have been first used by another scholar, Theodor Keim. See Schweitzer, *Quest of the Historical Jesus,* 211.

16. Schweitzer says, "There is scarcely any other work on the subject which so abounds in lapses of taste. . . . Nevertheless, there is something magical about it. It offends and yet it attracts" (*Quest of the Historical Jesus,* 182).

17. Schweitzer, *Quest of the Historical Jesus,* 398.

18. On form criticism see the classic volume by Edgar McKnight, *What Is Form Criticism?* (Philadelphia: Fortress Press, 1969), or the shorter description in Mark Allan Powell, *A Fortress Introduction to the Gospels* (Minneapolis: Fortress Press, 1998), 15–23.

19. Weiss, *Jesus' Proclamation of the Kingdom of God.*

20. Schweitzer, *Quest of the Historical Jesus,* 370–71.

21. Wright, *Jesus and the Victory of God,* 4.

22. Schweitzer, *Quest of the Historical Jesus,* 399.

23. See two essays collected in Bultmann, *Faith and Understanding:* "Liberal Theology and the Latest Theological Movement" (1924), 28–52, and "The Significance of the Historical Jesus for the Theology of Paul" (1929), 220–46, especially 238, 241.

24. Schweitzer, *Quest of the Historical Jesus,* 401.

25. Wright, *Jesus and the Victory of God,* 14.

26. Ibid., 4–5.

27. Tatum, *In Quest of Jesus,* 73.

28. An English translation of the lecture can be found in Ernst Käsemann, *Essays on New Testament Themes* (Naperville, Ill.: Alec R. Allenson, 1964), 15–47.

29. Originally published in German in 1956. Numerous English editions exist.

30. Bornkamm, *Jesus of Nazareth,* 62.

31. Perrin, *Rediscovering the Teaching of Jesus,* 39.

32. Perrin, *Jesus and the Language of the Kingdom,* 41.

33. Bornkamm, *Jesus of Nazareth,* 62.

34. N. T. Wright, "Quest for the Historical Jesus," *Anchor Bible Dictionary* 3.796–802.

35. Wright, *Jesus and the Victory of God,* 84. Pride of place on the list goes to an influential scholar we do not discuss, George B. Caird, who was the first to publish in the area of what Wright calls "the Third Quest" and might, from our perspective, be viewed as the inaugurator of it. See his *Jesus and the Jewish Nation.*

36. John Dominic Crossan says Wright's efforts at categorization fall "somewhere between the tendentious and the hilarious." See "Straining Gnats, Swallowing Camels: A Review of *Who Was Jesus?* by N. T. Wright," *Bible Review* 9 (August 1993): 10–11. See also Crossan, *Birth of Christianity,* 44.

37. Schweitzer, *Quest of the Historical Jesus,* 84.

38. See, for example, James L. Blevins, *The Messianic Secret in Markan Research, 1901–1976* (Washington: University Press of America, 1981), Christopher Tuckett, ed., *The Messianic Secret* (Philadelphia: Fortress Press, 1983), Jack Dean Kingsbury, *The Christology of Mark's Gospel* (Philadelphia: Fortress Press, 1983), and Heikki Räisänen, *The "Messianic Secret" in Mark's Gospel,* rev. ed., trans. C. Tuckett (Edinburgh: T. & T. Clark, 1990).

39. In another book, *The Lost Gospel,* Mack turns his attention to the Q source to try to salvage from scripture some of the truth about Jesus that may remain hidden there. He has also written a more popular treatment, *Who Wrote the New Testament?*

40. Mack, *Myth of Innocence,* 78–123. I am simplifying here. Actually, Mack discusses a variety of Jesus movements and Christ cults, but these two types of development in the tradition can be distinguished from each other.
41. Ibid., 96.
42. Ibid. (here describing what Jesus was *not* for the Jesus movement).
43. Ibid., 111.
44. Ibid., 322–23.
45. Ibid., 349.
46. Mack, *Who Wrote the New Testament?* 47.
47. Mack, *Myth of Innocence,* 368–76 (quotation on 372). He cites works by Scott Johnson and Robert Jewett.
48. Ibid., 376.
49. Charlotte Allen, "The Search for a No-Frills Jesus," *Atlantic Monthly* (December 1996): 57.
50. Mack, *Myth of Innocence,* 55.
51. Ibid., 56.
52. Adela Yarbro Collins, "Review of *A Myth of Innocence* by Burton Mack," *Journal of Biblical Literature* 108 (1989): 728.
53. Borg, *Jesus in Contemporary Scholarship,* 38. Compare Allen, "No-Frills Jesus," 55.
54. Mack, *Myth of Innocence,* 23.
55. For more on this theory, see Fiorenza, *Jesus—Miriam's Child, Sophia's Prophet.*
56. For a fairly harsh critique by one who is sympathetic to many of Fiorenza's views, see Witherington, *Jesus Quest,* 163–85; 242–44. He cites the work of another feminist scholar who holds that while Jesus "in no way reinforced patriarchy, there's also no evidence that he did anything radical to overthrow it" (Judith Plaskow, "Blaming Jews for Inventing Patriarchy," *Lilith* 7 [1980]: 11–12).
57. Fiorenza, "Jesus of Piety," 90–99.
58. Cited in Josh Simon, "Who Was Jesus?" *Life* (December 1994): 67–82, citation on 72.

2. Sources and Criteria

1. Meier, *Marginal Jew,* 2:1–2.
2. Sanders, *Historical Figure of Jesus,* 8.
3. Crossan, *Historical Jesus,* xxviii.
4. On this subject, see especially Walter F. Taylor, Jr., "Jesus within His Social World: Insights from Archaeology, Sociology, and Cultural Anthropology," in Gaiser, *Quest for Jesus and the Christian Faith,* 49–71.
5. The translation and reconstruction is from Meier, who gives details on the textual problems. See *Marginal Jew,* Vol. 1:56–92. Three passages are usually omitted as Christian interpolations at the spots marked by superscripted letters:
    ᵃif indeed one should call him a man
    ᵇHe was the Messiah.
    ᶜFor he appeared to them on the third day, living again, just as the divine prophets had spoken of these and countless other wondrous things about him.
6. Unfortunately, the portion of Tacitus's *Annals* dealing with the years 29–31 C.E. is missing from our manuscripts. We don't know for sure whether he described the life or death of Jesus further in the missing portion of his book.

7. Meier has a good discussion of the problems involved in *Marginal Jew*, 1:93–98.

8. One study of Paul's possible use of quotations of Jesus is Dungan, *Sayings of Jesus in the Churches of Paul.*

9. For fuller discussion on the authorship of all four Gospels, see Mark Allan Powell, *A Fortress Introduction to the Gospels* (Minneapolis: Fortress Press, 1998).

10. This alternative proposal is known as the Two-Gospel hypothesis or the Griesbach hypothesis. See William R. Farmer, *The Synoptic Problem: A Form-Critical Analysis* (New York: Macmillan Publishing Co., 1964).

11. See, for instance, Craig Blomberg, *Jesus and the Gospels: An Introduction and Survey* (Nashville: Broadman and Holman, 1997), 122–23.

12. Mack, *Lost Gospel*, 4.

13. Charlotte Allen, "The Search for a No-Frills Jesus," *Atlantic Monthly* (December 1996): 57.

14. Siegfried Schulz, *Q Die Spruchquelle der Evangelisten* (Zurich: Theologischer Verlag, 1972).

15. See Christopher M. Tuckett, "Q (Gospel Source)," *Anchor Bible Dictionary* 5:567–72.

16. Meier, *Marginal Jew*, 2:179.

17. Ibid., 2:153.

18. The arguments for early dates are summarized in Blomberg, *Jesus and the Gospels*, 134–35, 150–52.

19. These lists are based on ones that I developed for publication in *Fortress Introduction to the Gospels.*

20. See, for example, Robert T. Fortna, *The Gospel of Signs: A Reconstruction of the Narrative Source Underlying the Fourth Gospel* (New York: Cambridge University Press, 1970); *The Fourth Gospel and Its Predecessor: From Narrative Source to Present Gospel* (Philadelphia: Fortress Press, 1988); Urban C. Von Wahlde, *The Earliest Version of John's Gospel: Recovering the Gospel of Signs* (Wilmington: Michael Glazier, 1989).

21. For the texts of several significant works, see Miller, ed., *The Complete Gospels;* Robinson, *Nag Hammadi Library;* Wilhelm Schneelmelcher, ed., *New Testament Apocrypha,* vol. 1, *Gospels and Related Writings,* rev. ed., trans. R. McL. Wilson (Louisville: Westminster/John Knox Press, 1990). Quotations of documents in this chapter are from Miller.

22. The process through which writings came to be regarded as canonical was complex and, at times, remains unclear. It involved the eventual coherence of both acceptance at a grassroots level (which books got used the most) and sanction by official authorities. See H. Von Campenhausen, *The Formation of the Christian Bible* (Philadelphia: Fortress Press, 1972). Other Gospels were used, especially in the Eastern church, but by the beginning of the third century, collections of Matthew, Mark, Luke, and John were being widely circulated and appear to have achieved definitive scriptural standing as a group.

23. For one assessment of these works and their significance, see Koester, *Ancient Christian Gospels.*

24. Gnosticism evinced a radically dualistic vision of reality that contrasted the goodness of the spiritual realm with the evil of the material world. Gnostic Christians claimed that Jesus was a spirit-being who had imparted a secret knowledge that would free people's spirits from the earthly prisons of their physical bodies. See Pheme Perkins, *Gnosticism and the New Testament* (Minneapolis: Fortress Press, 1993); Pagels, *Gnostic Gospels.*

25. The text from Matthew is rendered in the Scholar's Version for purpose of comparison with the text from Thomas, which is also in that version. Here and in the preceding citations I have omitted the square, pointed, and parenthetical brackets used in the Scholar's Version to indicate degrees of textual certainty since these are unnecessary for our purpose.
26. Miller, *Complete Gospels*, 302–3.
27. See Crossan, *Cross That Spoke*. The argument is updated somewhat in his *Four Other Gospels*, 85–127. See also Koester, *Ancient Christian Gospels*, 216–40.
28. Wright, *Jesus and the Victory of God*, 51.
29. Russell Shorto, "Who Put the *Hell* in *Hellenism*?" *The Fourth R* 10, no. 5 (1997): 5.
30. Ibid.

3. Snapshots:
Contemporary Images of Jesus

1. Taylor, "New Quests for the Historical Jesus," 69.
2. Cited in Josh Simon, "Who Was Jesus?" *Life* (December 1994): 76.
3. Yarbrough, "Modern Wise Men Encounter Jesus," 38.
4. Horsley, *Spiral of Violence*, 246–73.
5. Ibid., 231–45.
6. Ibid., 286–306, citation on 287.
7. Ibid., 320.
8. Ibid., 160–64.
9. Ibid., 157–60, 321–22.
10. Ibid., 255–73. See also Horsley, "Ethics and Exegesis."
11. Horsley, *Spiral of Violence*, 170.
12. Borg, *Jesus in Contemporary Scholarship*, 28.
13. See, for example, the complaints offered in Wright, *Jesus and the Victory of God*, 156–59.
14. Witherington, *Jesus Quest*, 150, 153.
15. Wright, *New Testament and the People of God*, 179–80.
16. Wink, "Neither Passivity nor Violence" and "Counter-Response to Richard Horsley," both in Willard M. Swartley, *The Love of Enemy and Nonretaliation in the New Testament* (Louisville: Westminster/John Knox Press, 1992), 102–25; 133–36. See also Wright, *Jesus and the Victory of God*, 290.
17. Horsley, *Spiral of Violence*, 212–17.
18. Kaylor, *Jesus the Prophet*, 142–43.
19. The intriguing story is recounted in an interview with Vermes conducted by Hershel Shanks in "Escape and Rescue," *Bible Review* (June 1994): 30–37.
20. Vermes, *Jesus the Jew*, 79.
21. Ibid., 80.
22. Ibid., 79.
23. Meier, *Marginal Jew*, 2:587.
24. Crossan, *Historical Jesus*, 142–56; Borg, *Jesus: A New Vision*, 25–75, esp. 30–32.
25. Sanders, *Historical Figure of Jesus*, 138–40.
26. Twelftree, *Jesus the Exorcist*, 157–65, citation on 165.
27. Ibid., 228.
28. Smith, *Jesus the Magician*, 69.
29. Ibid., vii.

30. Ibid., 94–139.

31. Ibid., 96.

32. Ibid., 132.

33. Ibid., 146.

34. Ibid., 110–11. Smith quotes an intriguing passage from Origen, who also thought Satan entered Judas through the bread.

35. Ibid., vii.

36. Meier, *Marginal Jew*, 2:12. This is a summary of the argument found on 509–75.

37. On these and other similar points, see Witherington, *Jesus the Sage*, 147–208, plus Witherington's summary of his own views in *Jesus Quest*, 185–94.

38. The specific reference is *b. B. Bat.* 12a. See Witherington, *Jesus the Sage*, 158.

39. Instead, he uses the formula, "Amen, I say to you . . ." See Witherington, *Christology of Jesus*, 186–89.

40. Witherington, *Jesus Quest*, 189–90.

41. For discussion of this text, see Witherington, *Christology of Jesus*, 45–53.

42. Witherington, *Christology of Jesus*, 221–28.

43. Witherington, *Jesus Quest*, 192–93.

44. See Borg, *Jesus: A New Vision*, 97–124; Witherington, *Jesus the Sage*, 52–74.

45. Borg, *Jesus in Contemporary Scholarship*, 47–68. Compare Witherington, *Jesus Quest*, 94–98, 101.

46. Sanders, *Jesus and Judaism*, 7.

47. Wright, *Jesus and the Victory of God*, 312, 315.

48. Two recent articles debating the validity of the image are Eddy, "Jesus as Diogenes?" and Seeley, "Jesus and the Cynics Revisited."

49. See especially Vaage, *Galilean Upstarts,* the works of Burton Mack, and the works cited in note 11 on page 69 of Mack's *Myth of Innocence.* For parallels between Cynics and Paul, see Abraham J. Malherbe, *Paul and the Popular Philosophers* (Minneapolis: Fortress Press, 1989).

50. Some would trace the line back still further to Antisthenes, a pupil of Socrates. After Diogenes, famous Cynics included Crates of Thebes (c. 360–280 B.C.E.), whose student Zeno was the founder of Stoicism.

51. On *chreiai,* see Burton L. Mack and Vernon K. Robbins, *Patterns of Persuasion in the Gospels* (Sonoma, Calif.: Polebridge Press, 1989) and Vernon K. Robbins, *Ancient Quotes and Anecdotes: From Crib to Crypt* (Sonoma, Calif.: Polebridge Press, 1989). Cynics are also said to have developed (along with their cousins, the Stoics) the rhetorical form of speech called *diatribe* (argument with an imaginary partner), which is used by Paul. See Malherbe, *Paul and the Popular Philosophers.*

52. Laertius puts it delicately: he did "everything in public, the works of Demeter and Aphrodite alike." On shamelessness, see also Diogenes Laertius, *Lives* 6.32, 46, 58, 61, and the discussion in Downing, *Cynics and Christian Origins,* 50–53.

53. Crossan, *Historical Jesus,* 74. Wright suggests a different reason for the derivation: "The Cynics barked at society, snapped at its heels" (*Jesus and the Victory of God,* 66–67).

54. Crossan, *Historical Jesus,* 421 and elsewhere.

55. Crossan notes the irony of the aristocratic, multimillionaire Seneca's attraction to the simple life (*Historical Jesus,* 75).

56. For his reckoning of Cynic themes not addressed in Christian materials, see Downing, *Christ and the Cynics,* 196–203.

57. Downing, *Christ and the Cynics,* vii.

58. See Downing, *Cynics and Christian Origins*, 154–62. Actually, this book expands the proposed range for Cynic influence in two directions. A full half of the book traces the continuation of Cynic tradition throughout church history from the second century to the dawn of the medieval period. The "Cynic strand" evident in such luminaries as Tertullian, Origen, and Eusebius forms the background for the development of Christian asceticism. Downing had begun to show this movement beyond the Gospel tradition already in *Christ and the Cynics* by presenting five pages of parallels to Pauline and Deutero-Pauline writings and *twenty-five* to the epistle of James.
59. See Tuckett, "A Cynic Q?"
60. Downing, *Cynics and Christian Origins*, 141.
61. See Downing, *Jesus and the Threat of Freedom*, a popular treatment that calls modern Christians to consider the message of Cynic radicalism.
62. In *Cynics and Christian Origins*, Downing devotes a whole chapter to the subject of dating and another chapter to the question of definition: "Who or What Counts as Cynic?"
63. Crossan says, "Cynicism was practical and radical Stoicism; Stoicism was theoretical and moderate Cynicism" (*Historical Jesus*, 74). Thus, the Stoics may have admired the Cynics and relayed stories about them without actually emulating their lifestyle.
64. Downing, *Cynics and Christian Origins*, 30.
65. Downing, *Christ and the Cynics*, 1.
66. Gerd Theissen, "Wanderradikalismus: Literatursoziologische Aspekte der uber-lieferung von Worten Jesu im Urchristentum," *Zeitschrift für Theologie und Kirche* 70 (1973): 259.
67. Leif Vaage has said, "The standard uniform of the Cynics was a cloak, a wallet [bag], a staff" (*Q: The Ethos and Ethics*, 374–75). Downing attempts to adduce examples of variety in dress in *Cynics and Christian Origins*, 10–11, 32–33.
68. Witherington, *Jesus Quest*, 59–63.
69. Henry Chadwick, "Review of *Cynics and Christian Origins* by F. Gerard Downing," *Journal of Theological Studies* 45 (1994): 210. Actually, there is some confusion over whether the sexual acts that Diogenes and company performed in public involved copulation or masturbation. (Yes, scholars really do debate such matters.) Chadwick's point holds either way.
70. Downing, *Cynics and Christian Origins*, 26–56, 124.
71. He may have visited the city of Gadara itself, but the manuscripts that report this story are corrupt. Some locate the story that begins in Mark 5:1 in Gadara, others in Gerasa, and still others in Gergesa.
72. Leif Vaage, "Review of *Cynics and Christian Origins* by F. Gerald Downing," *Catholic Biblical Quarterly* 56 (1994): 587–89.
73. Taylor, "New Quests for the Historical Jesus," 81.
74. Simon, "Who Was Jesus?" 67–82.
75. Docetism is the belief, officially rejected by most Christian bodies, that while Jesus *seemed* to be human, he did not really experience the pain or hardship of being mortal.

4. The Jesus Seminar

1. Funk, *Honest to Jesus*, 302–3.
2. Funk et al., *Five Gospels*, 33.

3. Borg, *Jesus in Contemporary Scholarship*, 178. Borg is referring specifically to publication of *Five Gospels*.

4. The film is tentatively titled *Fully Human* and has been in development since 1986. Verhoeven has shared his script ideas off and on with the Seminar members, submitting them for critique. See Paul Verhoeven, "Christ the Man (with responses by Roy W. Hoover, Bruce Chilton, and Arthur J. Dewey)," *The Fourth R* 4, no. 1 (1991): 5–14. There has been some debate, for Verhoeven has planned to include things about Jesus that the Seminar rejected. He says, "You'd have a man walking about from marketplace to marketplace saying aphorisms. That isn't much of a movie." See Charlotte Allen, "Away with the Manger," *Lingua Franca* (January-February 1995): 1, 22–30, esp. 28.

5. James M. Robinson, Afterword to "The Gospel according to the Jesus Seminar" by Birger A. Pearson, Institute for Antiquity and Christianity Occasional Paper 35 (Claremont, Calif.: Institute for Antiquity and Christianity, 1996), 45.

6. Funk, "Issue of Jesus," 7.

7. See Funk et al., *Five Gospels*, 533–37; *The Acts of Jesus: What Did Jesus Really Do?* (San Francisco: HarperSanFrancisco, 1998), 537–42.

8. Statistics are based on the official voting records of the Jesus Seminar published in *Forum* 6, no.1 (1990): 3–55. Slightly different numbers may be obtained by counting colored sayings as they appear in *Five Gospels*.

9. Funk et al., *Five Gospels*, 36.

10. Borg, *Jesus in Contemporary Scholarship*, 163.

11. Funk et al., *Five Gospels*, 37.

12. Borg, *Jesus in Contemporary Scholarship*, 163.

13. See the periodic reports in the journal *The Fourth R*, some of which are cited in the notes below.

14. Even here, there appears to have been some modification of definition as the process went along. For instance, at one point the Westar Institute's journal said the black type indicated that a deed "seems to be a fabrication," but the final published report in *The Acts of Jesus* says black type indicates a deed "is largely or entirely fictive." Compare *The Fourth R* 7, no. 1 (1994): 12; Funk et al., *Acts of Jesus*, 36–37.

15. Released in March 1998, this time without media sensation.

16. "The Jesus Seminar Fall 1994 Meeting: The Birth and Family of Jesus," *The Fourth R* 7, no. 6 (1994): 11–16.

17. "The Jesus Seminar Fall 1993 Meeting," *The Fourth R* 7, no. 1 (1994): 15.

18. "The Jesus Seminar Spring 1995 Meeting," *The Fourth R* 8, no. 2 (1995): 12.

19. Bultmann, "Primitive Christian Kerygma," 42.

20. Cited in David Van Biema, "The Gospel Truth?" *Time* (April 8, 1996): 59, 55.

21. Much of this sketch is based on Funk, "Jesus of Nazareth: A Glimpse." See also the summary, "What Do We Really Know about Jesus?" in Funk et al., *Acts of Jesus*, 527–34.

22. W. Barnes Tatum, *Jesus at the Movies: A Guide to the First Hundred Years* (Santa Rosa, Calif.: Polebridge Press, 1997).

23. Allen, "Away with the Manger," 26.

24. Charlotte Allen, "The Search for a No-Frills Jesus," *Atlantic Monthly* (December 1996): 52, 55.

25. Cited in the *Atlanta Journal-Constitution* (September 30, 1989). Vaage may have

been alluding to behavior and attitudes attributed to Jesus in such biblical passages as Mark 2:15–19; Luke 7:34; 14:26.

26. Cited in Russell Watson, "A Lesser Child of God," *Newsweek* (April 4, 1994): 53.

27. Cited in Jeffery L. Sheler et al., "In Search of Jesus," *U.S. News and World Report* (April 8, 1996): 49.

28. Ibid.

29. Cited in Gustav Niebuhr, "The Jesus Seminar Courts Notoriety," *Christian Century* (November 23, 1988): 1061.

30. Cited in Sheler et al., "In Search of Jesus," 49.

31. Funk, *Honest to Jesus,* 304.

32. Ibid.

33. Ibid., 305.

34. Ibid., 302.

35. Ibid., 303.

36. Ibid., 300.

37. Ibid., 305–14.

38. Borg, *Jesus in Contemporary Scholarship,* 143–200.

39. Ibid., 172.

40. Ibid., 195.

41. Cited in Allen, "No-Frills Jesus," 51.

42. Ibid., 51, 67.

43. Van Biema, "Gospel Truth?" 58. Blomberg joined a number of other conservative scholars in a collection of essays responding to claims of the Jesus Seminar and other modern studies of the historical Jesus. His contribution to that volume goes beyond a confessional appeal to divine inspiration to offer academic arguments for the reliability of the Gospel tradition. See Blomberg, "Where Do We Start Studying Jesus?" 21.

44. Johnson, *Real Jesus,* 166. See also Van Biema, "Gospel Truth?" 58.

45. Wright, "Five Gospels but No Gospel," 120–21.

46. Cited in Van Biema, "Gospel Truth?" 54.

47. Letter to the editor, *Los Angeles Times,* March 30, 1991.

48. Hays, "Corrected Jesus," 47.

49. Johnson, *Real Jesus,* 1, 8.

50. See, for example, Allen, "Away with the Manger," 26, 30. One difference worth noting is that Funk's comments seem to have been made in informal in-house settings on occasions when reporters happen to have been present; those of his opponents cited here were all premeditated, offered in writing and *intended* for publication.

51. Allen, "Away with the Manger," 25.

52. An ordained Disciples of Christ minister, Funk discusses his years as "a teenage evangelist" in *Honest to Jesus* under the heading "Youthful Discretions and Indiscretions" (3–5). He claims now to have had at that time "a string of beliefs and very little faith."

53. Crossan still considers himself "a Catholic through and through," though he does not attend mass regularly. "If you are empowered by Jesus' life," he says, "in my judgment that makes you a Christian" (Sheler et al., "In Search of Jesus," 52). The Seminar's premier critic, Luke Johnson, is also a former Roman Catholic cleric. He too exchanged the collar for a wedding band.

54. Wright, "Five Gospels but No Gospel," 121.

55. Robert W. Funk, *A Greek Grammar of the New Testament and Other Early Christian Literature*, 5th ed. (Chicago: University of Chicago Press, 1973); Crossan, *In Parables; Finding Is the First Act* (Missoula, Mont.: Scholars Press, 1979).

56. Hardly worth mentioning is the charge that Seminar members are "in it for the money" or for status, or some other aspect of career enhancement. Projects ought not be condemned simply because they are successful.

57. Watson, "A Lesser Child," 54; Van Biema, "Gospel Truth," 55.

58. Cited in Niebuhr, "Jesus Seminar Courts Notoriety," 1061.

59. Ibid., 1060.

60. Hays, "Corrected Jesus," 47.

61. Fourteen from Claremont, nine from Vanderbilt, eight from Harvard, five from Chicago, and four from Union. The count is based on the 1993 roster provided in *Five Gospels*.

62. "What Did Jesus Really Say?" *U.S. News and World Report* (July 1, 1991): 55.

63. Cited in Van Biema, "Gospel Truth," 57.

64. Cited in Sheler et al., "In Search of Jesus," 48. Compare Funk, *Honest to Jesus*, 300.

65. Borg, *Jesus in Contemporary Scholarship*, 162.

66. Blomberg, "Where Do We Start Studying Jesus?" 21.

67. Wright, "Five Gospels but No Gospel," 135.

68. Meier, *Marginal Jew*, 1:177.

69. Robert W. Funk, "Beyond Criticism in Quest of Literacy: The Parable of the Leaven," *Interpretation* 25 (1971): 151.

70. Jesus Seminar, *The Gospel of Mark: Red Letter Edition* (Sonoma, Calif.: Polebridge Press, 1991), 1–26.

71. Wright, *Jesus and the Victory of God*, 32.

72. These words were actually used in the initial flyer advertising the group. The basic idea that an unbiased application of scholarly criteria can lead to the discovery of objective "facts" or "truth" is alluded to in much of the Seminar's literature. See the discussion in Wright, "Five Gospels but No Gospel," 125–27.

73. Niebuhr, "Jesus Seminar Courts Notoriety," 1061.

74. Cited in "Scholars Vote on Sayings of Jesus," *The Lutheran* (January 15, 1986): 14.

75. Wright, *Jesus and the Victory of God*, 33.

76. Funk et al., *Five Gospels*, 34–35.

5. John Dominic Crossan

1. Borg, *Jesus in Contemporary Scholarship*, 34.

2. Charlotte Allen, "Away with the Manger," *Lingua Franca* (January-February 1995): 26.

3. Keck, "Second Coming of the Liberal Jesus?" 785.

4. Wright, *Jesus and the Victory of God*, 44.

5. Witherington, *Jesus Quest*, 76–77.

6. Major publications by Crossan on these topics include *In Parables, Finding Is the First Act* (Missoula, Mont.: Scholars Press, 1979), *In Fragments, The Dark Interval: Toward a Theology of Story*, 2d ed. (Sonoma, Calif.: Polebridge Press, 1988), and *Cross That Spoke*.

7. See *Birth of Christianity*, 17–46; citations on 30, 44.

8. In the second book, Crossan often responds to criticisms of the first.

9. Wright, *Jesus and the Victory of God*, 44.

10. Crossan, *Historical Jesus*, xxxiv. This comment has sparked response. "Unlike objectivity," writes Ben Meyer, "honesty, be it ever so flawless, will not secure the validity of historical judgments" ("Review of *The Historical Jesus* by John Dominic Crossan," *Catholic Biblical Quarterly* 55 [1993]: 575). Others note that Crossan's careful attention to methodology suggests that he *is* concerned with at least an attempt at or appearance of objectivity. Says Witherington, "He is not simply staring at an inkblot and stating what he thinks he sees in it" (*Jesus Quest*, 82). To clarify this, perhaps, Crossan later added to "honesty" a quality he calls "interactivism." He now offers the following "working definition of history": "History is the past reconstructed interactively by the present through argued evidence in public discourse" (*Birth of Christianity*, 20, 42–43).

11. "The Historical Jesus: An Interview with John Dominic Crossan," *Christian Century* 108 (1991): 1200–24. Also cited in *Jesus: A Revolutionary Biography*, xiv.

12. To facilitate his system of classification, Crossan groups similar sayings or stories into "complexes." The sayings about kingdom and children are not identical, but probably reflect different versions of the same idea.

13. Ben Meyer calls Crossan's dating of sources "eccentric and implausible" ("Review of *The Historical Jesus*," 575). He cites also Brown, "Gospel of Peter," and Meier, *Marginal Jew*, 1:114–23, 142–52.

14. Wright, *Jesus and the Victory of God*, 48. Wright himself regards the Gospel of Thomas as a relatively late, secondary work and is far more generous than Crossan in accepting the authenticity of material found in the canonical Gospels. He has expressed their conflict wittily for those who know that he, like Crossan, goes by his middle name (Thomas): "There will come a man called Dominic who will claim that most Jesus-material comes from Thomas; and he will be opposed by a man called Thomas who will claim that most Jesus-material is Dominical" (N. T. Wright, "Taking the Text with Her Pleasure: A Post-Modernist Response to J. Dominic Crossan's *The Historical Jesus: The Life of a Mediterranean Jewish Peasant*," *Theology* 96 [1993]: 305).

15. Crossan, *Birth of Christianity*, 119–20.

16. Crossan, *Historical Jesus*, 218–24, drawing on the work of Robert Gurr.

17. Crossan, *Historical Jesus*, 72. He describes seven possible responses.

18. This question is raised, for instance, with regard to the system of patrons, brokers, and clients that looms large in Crossan's third level of analysis. Witherington says, "It is a mistake to ascribe the sort of Greco-Roman patronage system we find in Rome or Corinth . . . to Lower Galilee" (*Jesus Quest*, 83).

19. In *Birth of Christianity*, 346–50, Crossan adopts the term *peasant artisan*, insisting that policies of rural commercialization in the first century were forcing rural artisans (such as carpenters) into a situation only semantically different from that of the landless laborer.

20. John Dominic Crossan, "The Search for Jesus," in *The Search for Jesus: Modern Scholarship Looks at the Gospels*, ed. Hershel Shanks (Washington, D.C.: Biblical Archaeology Society, 1994), 132.

21. Crossan, *Historical Jesus*, 304.

22. Ibid., 422.

23. Ibid., 300.

24. Ibid., 266–82.

25. Ibid., 319–20, 336–37. He also entertains Allan Young's triadic distinction between disease, illness, and sickness as three components of "unhealth."

26. Crossan, *Jesus: A Revolutionary Biography*, 82.
27. Ibid., 84–88.
28. Crossan, *Historical Jesus*, 304–10.
29. Ibid., 323–25.
30. Ibid., 313–18. He cites Mark 5:1–17 only to illustrate this point, without maintaining that it records an authentic act of the historical Jesus.
31. Ibid., 341–44.
32. Ibid., 341.
33. Ibid., 344.
34. Ibid., 227–60, 282–92; citations are on 259. On the concept of ethical eschatology, see *Birth of Christianity*, 273–89.
35. Crossan, *Historical Jesus*, 345–48.
36. Crossan, *Birth of Christianity*, 336.
37. Crossan, *Historical Jesus*, 360.
38. Crossan, "Passion Narrative," 5. These examples are more precise than the complex example of the two goats in Leviticus 16 discussed in *Historical Jesus*, 376–83.
39. Crossan, *Historical Jesus*, 372.
40. Crossan, *Birth of Christianity*, 573, drawing on Kathleen Corley and Marianne Sawicki.
41. Crossan, *Jesus: A Revolutionary Biography*, 145. Crossan's emphasis.
42. Crossan, *Historical Jesus*, 383–91; citation is on 389.
43. Crossan, *Jesus: A Revolutionary Biography*, 163.
44. Ibid., 161.
45. Ibid., 155.
46. Ibid., 152.
47. Ibid., 127.
48. Crossan, *Historical Jesus*, 393.
49. Crossan, *Birth of Christianity*, xxxi.
50. Crossan, *Jesus: A Revolutionary Biography*, 124.
51. Crossan, *Birth of Christianity*, 407–17.
52. Ibid., 257–89; citations on 283–84.
53. Ibid., 363–406.
54. Ibid., 444. Crossan's emphasis.
55. Witherington, *Jesus Quest*, 80. Crossan discusses the function of memory in oral cultures extensively in *Birth of Christianity*, 59–89.
56. Burton Mack, as we noted above (see pages 25–28) is another exception.
57. Wright, *Jesus and the Victory of God*, 55. See also Keck, "Second Coming of the Liberal Jesus?": "The brokerless Jesus is himself thoroughly brokered by this biographer" (785).
58. Robin Scroggs, "Review of *The Historical Jesus* by John Dominic Crossan," *Interpretation* 47 (1993): 301.
59. Crossan, *Historical Jesus*, 434.
60. Witherington, *Jesus Quest*, 89–90.
61. The charge by Luke Timothy Johnson that Crossan's method is "fixed" (*Real Jesus*, 47) offers its criticism in language that has not proved helpful. Crossan responds, "It is very, very serious to charge that another scholar has 'fixed' his research methodology. . . . 'Fixing data' entails a deliberate intention to deceive" (*Birth of Christianity*, 114).

62. Crossan, *Jesus: A Revolutionary Biography*, 122. This is a more nuanced view than was presented in *Historical Jesus* (see, for example, page 421).

63. Wright, *Jesus and the Victory of God*, 59.

64. Witherington, *Jesus Quest*, 84. The charge may hold for Crossan's recent works on the historical Jesus, but would not be true of his earlier studies on parables, such as *Finding Is the First Act*.

65. Crossan, *Historical Jesus*, 417.

66. Ibid., 417–22.

67. Crossan, *Birth of Christianity*, 303.

68. Meier, *Marginal Jew*, 2:269–70. Meier later evaluates Crossan's idea that Jesus proclaimed a sapiential kingdom that "imagines how one could live here and now within an already or always available divine dominion" (*Historical Jesus*, 292). Says Meier, "At this point we are indeed not far from a gnostic Jesus" (2:488 n. 164).

69. Meier, *Marginal Jew*, 2:350.

70. Sanders, *Jesus and Judaism*, 329.

71. Witherington, *Jesus Quest*, 65.

72. Wright, *Jesus and the Victory of God*, 59.

73. Crossan, *Historical Jesus*, 424.

6. Marcus J. Borg

1. Borg, "From Galilean Jew to the Face of God," 10.

2. Wright, *Jesus and the Victory of God*, 75.

3. Borg, *Meeting Jesus Again*, 8.

4. Ibid.

5. Ibid., 12.

6. Ibid., 13.

7. Ibid., 15.

8. Ibid., 137.

9. Borg, *Jesus: A New Vision*, 15.

10. Ibid.

11. Ibid., 16.

12. Borg, *Jesus in Contemporary Scholarship*, 83.

13. His ideas are updated somewhat in *Jesus in Contemporary Scholarship* (1994), *Meeting Jesus Again* (1994), and *The God We Never Knew* (1997).

14. Borg, *Jesus and Contemporary Scholarship*, 40–41 n. 59.

15. Borg, *Jesus: A New Vision*, 25–26.

16. Ibid., 25–27.

17. Ibid., 40–43.

18. This intimate sense of "Abba" is disputed by James Barr, "Abba Isn't 'Daddy,'" *Journal of Theological Studies* 39 (1988): 28–47.

19. Borg, *Jesus: A New Vision*, 43–45.

20. Ibid., 46.

21. Ibid., 51.

22. Ibid., 61.

23. Ibid., 71.

24. Ibid., 66.

25. Ibid., 97.

26. Ibid., 81.

27. Ibid., 100.

28. Ibid., 114.
29. Ibid., 99.
30. Ibid., 116.
31. Ibid., 99. Borg's emphasis.
32. Ibid., 103.
33. Ibid., 125.
34. Ibid., 126–27.
35. Ibid., 83–93. See also *Conflict, Holiness, and Politics*, 51–72.
36. Borg, *Jesus in Contemporary Scholarship*, 26. Borg contrasts here Leviticus 19:2 with Luke 6:36.
37. Borg, *Jesus: A New Vision*, 150.
38. Ibid., 161.
39. Lenski, *Power and Privilege*. See also John H. Kautsky, *The Politics of Aristocratic Empires* (Chapel Hill: University of North Carolina Press, 1982).
40. Borg, *Jesus in Contemporary Scholarship*, 101–5.
41. Ibid., 110.
42. Ibid., 111. Some movement in Borg's thought can be discerned here from his earlier representation (for instance, in *Jesus: A New Vision*) of the purity system as the conventional wisdom of Israelite society.
43. Borg, *Jesus: A New Vision*, 174. The symbolism of the image derives from Zechariah 9:9–10.
44. Ibid., 175.
45. Ibid., 178–84.
46. Borg, *Jesus in Contemporary Scholarship*, 47–68.
47. Borg's views on Jesus and eschatology, however, have undergone some development. In a recent work, he nuances his position, struggles with semantics, and concedes that Jesus' message could have included a peripheral eschatological component. See Borg, "Jesus and Eschatology," 207–18.
48. Borg, *Jesus in Contemporary Scholarship*, 55, drawing on Norman Perrin.
49. Ibid., 87–88. Borg admits that this part of his work is still somewhat undeveloped, and presents these options as "promising possibilities."
50. Borg, *Meeting Jesus Again*, 16.
51. Borg, *Jesus: A New Vision*, 184–85, 189 n. 44.
52. Wright, *Jesus and the Victory of God*, 75.
53. Mack, *Myth of Innocence*, 53–77.
54. Sanders, *Jesus and Judaism*, 61–76. Witherington thinks that since the eschatological sayings about a coming Son of Man meet certain historical criteria (multiple attestation, dissimilarity), Borg deems them unauthentic simply because they do not fit into his overall view of the pre-Easter Jesus. He further notes that, ironically, this is because Borg misconstrues the sayings as proclaiming an end that is necessarily imminent as opposed to possibly imminent (Witherington, *Jesus Quest*, 94–95). Wright agrees with Borg's interpretation of eschatological language as referring to the end of a social order, but fears he takes this so generally that he loses the sense of God "actually *doing* something climactic and unique" (*Jesus and the Victory of God*, 77). Meier says that Borg fails to grasp that "Jesus' message of future eschatology and a future kingdom does not rise or fall with Jesus' statements about a Son of Man" (*Marginal Jew*, 2:350, 396 n. 233).
55. Sanders, *Jesus and Judaism*, 180–82, 210.
56. Borg, "Portraits of Jesus," 87.

57. Wright, *Jesus and the Victory of God*, 77.
58. Ibid. I say *must* instead of *might* on the assumption that Wright's series of questions (leading up to and including "Is he not . . . a failure?") is rhetorical.
59. Borg, "Historian, the Christian, and Jesus," 16.

7. E. P. Sanders

1. Sanders, *Jesus and Judaism*, 334.
2. Borg, *Jesus in Contemporary Scholarship*, 19–20.
3. Sanders, *Jesus and Judaism*, 319.
4. E. P. Sanders, *Paul and Palestinian Judaism: A Comparison of Patterns of Religion* (Philadelphia: Fortress Press, 1977).
5. See especially *Judaism: Practice and Belief*.
6. Sanders, *Judaism: Practice and Belief*, 275.
7. Ibid., 275–78.
8. Sanders, *Paul and Palestinian Judaism*, 422.
9. Sanders, *Judaism: Practice and Belief*, 277. Sanders's emphasis.
10. Sanders, *Paul and Palestinian Judaism*, 420.
11. Sanders, *Jesus and Judaism*, 336.
12. Sanders, *Judaism: Practice and Belief*, 277.
13. For more on this subject, see Sanders, *Jesus and Judaism*, 77–119.
14. Sanders, *Jesus and Judaism*, 336. The wording of the three elements is my own, as is the interpretation of the chronological markers given. Rabbinic materials are notoriously difficult to date. I use the earliest estimate (second century C.E.) for key documents cited by Sanders.
15. Sanders, *Historical Figure of Jesus*, 54.
16. Ibid., 64.
17. Sanders, *Jesus and Judaism*, 11; *Historical Figure of Jesus*, 10–11.
18. This is due in part to the more popular style of *Historical Figure of Jesus*, in which Sanders does not nuance judgments as precisely as in *Jesus and Judaism*. In the latter volume, he actually stratifies knowledge about Jesus into six categories: "virtually certain," "highly probable," "probable," "possible," "conceivable," and "incredible" (for a summary list of some key items, see 326–27). This system is similar to the Jesus Seminar's four color-coded categories, but the Seminar would not always agree with Sanders as to where individual items belong.
19. Sanders, *Jesus and Judaism*, 321.
20. Burton Mack may be the only exception. See pages 25–28.
21. Sanders, *Jesus and Judaism*, 61–76.
22. Wright objects to the assumption that if Jesus expected the temple to be destroyed, he must also have expected it to be replaced. See *Jesus and the Victory of God*, 425–28.
23. Crossan is skeptical of traditions regarding "the twelve," partly because the theme is not significant for Q (*Historical Jesus*, 334). He regards the selection of twelve disciples (Mark 3:13–19) to be from the second stratum of tradition (60–80 C.E.) with only single attestation (444).
24. Arguments to establish this point "beyond reasonable doubt" are laid out already in Sanders, *Jesus and Judaism*, 98–106.
25. Sanders, *Jesus and Judaism*, 101.
26. Sanders, *Historical Figure of Jesus*, 120.
27. Ibid.

28. Ibid., 120, 184–88.
29. Sanders, *Jesus and Judaism*, 99.
30. Ibid., 153.
31. See Sanders, *Jesus and Judaism*, 123–56, 222–41, and *Historical Figure of Jesus*, 169–88.
32. Meier rejects this reasoning. See *Marginal Jew*, 2:338–48.
33. Sanders, *Historical Figure of Jesus*, 181.
34. Ibid., 180.
35. See Sanders, *Jesus and Judaism*, 157–73, and *Historical Figure of Jesus*, 132–68.
36. He does think that some of the miracle stories (especially what are called nature miracles) are exaggerated, or else their impact would have been greater than that reported. See *Historical Figure of Jesus*, 154–57.
37. Sanders, *Historical Figure of Jesus*, 164.
38. Ibid., 168.
39. Sanders, *Jesus and Judaism*, 330.
40. Sanders, *Historical Figure of Jesus*, 238.
41. Ibid., 239–48.
42. Ibid., 238.
43. Ibid., 248.
44. Sanders, *Jesus and Judaism*, 307–8.
45. See Sanders, *Jesus and Judaism*, 245–69, and *Historical Figure of Jesus*, 205–24.
46. Sanders, *Jesus and Judaism*, 336.
47. Ibid., 55.
48. Ibid., 336.
49. Sanders, *Historical Figure of Jesus*, 192. Elsewhere he says that though Jesus did not institute a Gentile mission, he did start "a movement which came to see the Gentile mission as a logical extension of itself" (*Jesus and Judaism*, 220).
50. Sanders, *Jesus and Judaism*, 199.
51. Ibid., 319.
52. Sanders, *Historical Figure of Jesus*, 233.
53. Ibid., 234.
54. Ibid., 235.
55. Sanders, *Jesus and Judaism*, 322.
56. Ibid.
57. Sanders, *Historical Figure of Jesus*, 218.
58. Sanders, *Jesus and Judaism*, 331.
59. Ibid., 333.
60. Ibid., 331.
61. Sanders, *Historical Figure of Jesus*, 269.
62. Ibid., 273–74.
63. Sanders, *Jesus and Judaism*, 333.
64. Sanders, *Historical Figure of Jesus*, 274–75.
65. Ibid., 275.
66. Ibid., 280.
67. Sanders, *Jesus and Judaism*, 240.
68. Sanders details some differences between his conception of Jesus and that of Schweitzer in *Jesus and Judaism*, 327–29.
69. Meier, *Marginal Jew*, 1:173.
70. Sanders, *Jewish Law from Jesus*, 28.

71. James D. G. Dunn, "Review of *Jesus and Judaism* by E. P. Sanders," *Journal of Theological Studies* 37 (1986): 513.
72. Borg, *Jesus in Contemporary Scholarship*, 20–21.
73. Sanders, *Jesus and Judaism*, 319–20.
74. Ibid., 320.
75. Borg, *Jesus in Contemporary Scholarship*, 76–77.
76. Ibid., 82.
77. Meier takes him to task for this several times in *Marginal Jew*, 2:398–506. But when writing that volume (published in 1994), Meier apparently did not have access to Sanders's *Historical Figure of Jesus* (1993), where the discomfort with present eschatology is less evident.
78. Witherington, *Jesus Quest*, 128.
79. Borg, *Jesus in Contemporary Scholarship*, 21.
80. Sanders, *Historical Figure of Jesus*, 183.
81. See Horsley, *Jesus and the Spiral of Violence*; Theissen, *Sociology of Early Palestinian Christianity* and *Gospels in Context*; Yoder, *Politics of Jesus*.
82. Witherington, *Jesus Quest*, 132.
83. Sanders, *Historical Figure of Jesus*, 188.
84. Crossan, *Birth of Christianity*, 337–42, citations on 341–42. Crossan is referring to other polemical descriptions of Jesus offered by his enemies in biblical traditions.
85. Sanders, *Historical Figure of Jesus*, 202.
86. Ibid., 196–98, 203.
87. Meier, *Marginal Jew*, 2:149. See also 212 n. 154 and 431, with the caveat on 485 n. 152.
88. Witherington, *Jesus Quest*, 127. See also 211 for a compelling critique of Sanders's argument regarding Mark 3:1–6 (probably Witherington's best argument against Sanders, but hidden in the chapter on Meier).
89. Wright, *Jesus and the Victory of God*, 379.
90. Ibid., 382.
91. Ibid., 378
92. Reginald H. Fuller, "Searching for the Historical Jesus," *Interpretation* 41 (1987): 301–3.
93. Meier, *Marginal Jew*, 2:464–65 n. 52.
94. Ibid., 2:473–74 n. 97.
95. Sanders, *Historical Figure of Jesus*, 201. See similar comments on 178, 247.
96. Ibid., 280–81.

8. John P. Meier

1. Meier, *Marginal Jew*, 2:453–54.
2. Witherington, *Jesus Quest*, 197, 207.
3. Sheler et al., "In Search of Jesus," 50. Crossan was "the ground shaker" and Borg "the mystic." Less cute, but accurate.
4. Meier, *Marginal Jew*, 1:6, 7. He suggests six aspects of Jesus' life and ministry that the term *marginal* may be expected to conjure.
5. Ibid., 1:7.
6. Ibid., 1:8.
7. Ibid., 1.9.
8. Ibid.

9. Crossan, *Historical Jesus,* xxxiv.

10. Meier, *Marginal Jew,* 1:1.

11. Meier, *Marginal Jew,* 2:4. For the full discussion, see 1:21–40.

12. Sheler et al., "In Search of Jesus," 52.

13. Witherington has complained that, so stated, this distinction is not helpful because it seems to imply that the things about Jesus that cannot be recovered through historical analysis are "real" in some sense other than being grounded in history. He suggests a distinction between "the historical Jesus" (Meier's "real Jesus") and "the Jesus that we can recover by means of the historical-critical method" (Meier's "historical Jesus"). In either case, the latter is viewed as a subset of the former. See Witherington, *Jesus Quest,* 199.

14. Feminist and third world scholars often claim that the interpretation of data is as likely to be affected by *social location* as it is by confessional commitments. See, for instance, Corley, *Gender and Jesus.*

15. Meier, *Marginal Jew,* 1:167–77. These are discussed in chapter 2 of this book. I group "embarrassment" and "discontinuity" together under what some call "dissimilarity," and I place Meier's fifth criterion, "Jesus' rejection and death," in the broader category of "explanation."

16. Ibid., 2:619–22.

17. Meier's work includes a more extensive study of certain Josephus passages than has been undertaken by any other historical Jesus scholar (*Marginal Jew,* 1:66–88). He eventually decides that, like Paul, Josephus offers "little more than tidbits" (2:5), yet what he does offer is "of monumental importance" (1:68). The presentation in chapter 2 of this book of what may be regarded as authentic in Josephus's comments on Jesus (see 32–33) reflects Meier's research.

18. Meier, *Marginal Jew,* 1:112–66.

19. Ibid., 2:6.

20. Ibid., 1:205–52.

21. Ibid., 1:351.

22. Ibid., 1:278–85.

23. Ibid., 1:268–78.

24. Ibid., 1:352.

25. Ibid., 1:351.

26. Ibid., 2:7.

27. Ibid., 2:27.

28. Ibid., 2:40.

29. Ibid., 2:113, quoting Krister Stendahl.

30. See Hollenbach, "Conversion of Jesus."

31. Boers, *Who Was Jesus?* 31–53.

32. Meier, *Marginal Jew,* 2:9.

33. Ibid., 2:124.

34. Ibid., 2:9.

35. Ibid., 2:127.

36. Ibid., 2:144.

37. Ibid.

38. Ibid., 2:265

39. Ibid., 2:241. The language derives from Perrin, *Jesus and the Language of the Kingdom* (though Perrin, in turn, draws on literary critic Philip Wheelwright).

40. Ibid., 2:243–70.

41. Ibid., 2:291–337.
42. Ibid., 2:6.
43. Ibid., 2:348.
44. Ibid., 2:423.
45. Ibid., 2:398–454.
46. Ibid., 2:451.
47. Sanders has become increasingly open to recognizing the validity of some "present kingdom" sayings. See page 201 n. 77.
48. Meier, *Marginal Jew,* 2:452.
49. Ibid., 2:453.
50. Ibid., 2:617–18.
51. Ibid., 2:4. Here he cites Evans, "Life of Jesus Research," 29.
52. Ibid., 2:630.
53. See Meier, "The Circle of the Twelve."
54. Meier, *Marginal Jew,* 2:1046.
55. Ibid.
56. Ibid., 2:628; compare 1:216–19.
57. Ibid.
58. Ibid., 454.
59. Meier also disagrees with Sanders in affirming that Jesus did call people to personal and national repentance, though Sanders's rejection of this point is based on exegetical arguments rather than a sense that it would contradict the portrait he has sketched.
60. Meier, *Marginal Jew,* 2:3.
61. The most extensive critique so far is that of Witherington, offered in *Jesus Quest,* 198–218. Wright, in *Jesus and the Victory of God,* simply footnotes Meier a half-dozen times, always on matters where they agree. Borg appears to have added a few notes belatedly to his *Jesus in Contemporary Scholarship,* noting Meier's objection to the views that he presents without engaging him in debate over these. Most of the other works discussed in this book came out before Meier's tomes.
62. Meier, "Reflections on Jesus-of-History Research," 92.
63. Borg, *Jesus in Contemporary Scholarship,* 32, 43 n. 85.
64. One significant difference between Meier and the Jesus Seminar at this point is that Meier offers detailed accounts of his reasoning, facilitating evaluation of his arguments. The Jesus Seminar publishes only conclusions with brief summaries indicating factors affecting each vote.
65. See, for instance, the comment in *U.S. News and World Report:* "Some criticize his work as unimaginative and too beholden to official Catholic doctrine" (Sheler et al., "In Search of Jesus," 52). I have not found any reference in which a major scholar offers such a charge in print. It is more the sort of thing that is said in hallways and elevators.
66. See Wright, *New Testament and the People of God,* 81–120.
67. Wright, *Jesus and the Victory of God,* 33.
68. I think Meier's approach exemplifies what Wright polemically calls "chastened positivism." Somewhat ironically for my argument, Wright actually says that he detects "more than a hint of this" in Sanders (*New Testament and the People of God,* 82 n. 3). With Meier, one doesn't have to worry about detecting hints; he wears the charge with pride.
69. Wright, *Jesus and the Victory of God,* 33. While Wright denounces this sort of ap-

proach, he does not specifically denounce Meier for approaching history in this way.

70. Sanders, *Jesus and Judaism*, 320. Again, while Sanders does not say this with reference to Meier, I am suggesting that what Sanders says in another context might apply as a critique of Meier's work.
71. Crossan, *Birth of Christianity*, 146.
72. Meier, *Marginal Jew*, 1:5.
73. Ibid., 1:5–6.
74. Ibid., 1:4. The scary word *asymptotic* derives from geometry, where it is used to refer to the tendency for a curve always to approach becoming a straight line without ever quite becoming one. It is applied as a theological metaphor in the work of Karl Rahner.
75. Ibid., 1:3–4.

9. N. T. Wright

1. Wright, *Jesus and the Victory of God*, 172.
2. Mary Knutsen, "Review of *Jesus and the Victory of God*," *Augsburg Fortress Book Newsletter* 571 (1997): 1–3.
3. Wright, *Jesus and the Victory of God*, 612. Where I have placed the word *God* in brackets, Wright uses the tetragrammaton, YHWH, a transliteration of Hebrew letters used in the Old Testament in place of the divine name.
4. Richard N. Ostling of *Time* magazine.
5. Wright, *New Testament and the People of God*, xiv. To be faithful to Wright's views on this subject, the word *god* will be spelled with a lowercase *g* throughout this chapter when discussing Wright's work.
6. Like Crossan, Wright has also produced a popular version of his Jesus biography, *The Original Jesus*, a slim volume augmented by photos and artwork. See also Wright, *Who Was Jesus?*
7. This method is described with fullest detail in 81–120. It is indebted in key respects to the work of Ben F. Meyer, especially as presented in *The Aims of Jesus*.
8. Wright, *Jesus and the Victory of God*, 133 and *New Testament and the People of God*, 98–109.
9. Wright, *Jesus and the Victory of God*, 89–121.
10. Ibid., 88.
11. Ibid., 133.
12. Wright believes that the Gospel of Thomas represents a later, derivative stage of the tradition. See *New Testament and the People of God*, 442–43.
13. Wright, *Jesus and the Victory of God*, 5.
14. Ibid., 93.
15. Ibid., 90.
16. Ibid., 612.
17. Ibid., 109.
18. Wright, *New Testament and the People of God*, 109–12, 122–26. See also the summary in *Jesus and the Victory of God*, 137–44.
19. Wright, *Jesus and the Victory of God*, 138.
20. Ibid., 139.
21. Ibid.

22. Wright, *New Testament and the People of God*, 268–70. See also *Jesus and the Victory of God*, xvii.
23. Wright, *Jesus and the Victory of God*, 204–6.
24. Wright, *New Testament and the People of God*, 280–338. He is dependent at this point on the views of his mentor, George B. Caird. See Caird, *Language and Imagery of the Bible*.
25. Wright, *Jesus and the Victory of God*, 97.
26. Ibid., 147–48. Wright's "list" is not a literal one. I have developed this list from the narrative paragraph in his book; the precise wording of items is sometimes my own.
27. Ibid., 148–49.
28. Ibid., 150.
29. Ibid., 163.
30. As he notes, none of the sayings comes from Q (or from Thomas), which may explain why the Jesus Seminar has not made more of this image for Jesus.
31. On all of this, see Wright, *Jesus and the Victory of God*, 162–70. The typologies of prophets are drawn from Horsley and Hanson, *Bandits, Prophets, and Messiahs* and, especially, Webb, *John the Baptizer and Prophet*.
32. Wright, *Jesus and the Victory of God*, 201.
33. Ibid., 239. For discussion of the prodigal son story, see 125–31.
34. Ibid., 187.
35. Ibid., 246–64.
36. Ibid., 268–74.
37. Ibid., 372.
38. Ibid., 389.
39. Ibid.
40. Ibid., 390.
41. Ibid., 398.
42. Ibid., 272.
43. Ibid., 274.
44. Ibid., 184.
45. Ibid., 320.
46. Ibid., 361. See also *New Testament and the People of God*, 280–338. The argument is based in part on interpretation of Daniel 7, and on recognition that the Greek word (*erchomenon*) often translated "coming" in Mark 13:26 can actually mean either "coming" or "going." Similarly, the Greek word *parousia* (Matt. 24:3, 27, 37, 39), which Christians often invoke when speaking of the "return" of Christ, literally means "presence."
47. Wright, *Jesus and the Victory of God*, 343–67.
48. Ibid., 426.
49. Ibid., 359. In a fundamental sense, though, the true enemy is "the satan," as indicated below.
50. Ibid., 196.
51. Ibid., 547.
52. Ibid., 552.
53. Sanders, *Jesus and Judaism*, 333.
54. Wright, *Jesus and the Victory of God*, 553–76.
55. Wright, *New Testament and the People of God*, 277–78; *Jesus and the Victory of God*, 577–79.
56. Wright, *Jesus and the Victory of God*, 604.

57. Ibid., 595.
58. Ibid., 607.
59. Ibid., 609, 607.
60. Ibid., 615.
61. Ibid., 632–39.
62. Ibid., 639.
63. Ibid.
64. Ibid., 443–72.
65. Ibid., 477.
66. Ibid.
67. N. T. Wright, "Jesus, Israel, and the Cross," in *SBL 1985 Seminar Papers,* ed. K. H. Richards (Atlanta: Scholars Press, 1985), 87.
68. Wright, *Jesus and the Victory of God,* 538.
69. Ibid., 435.
70. Ibid., 647.
71. Ibid., 646.
72. Ibid., 624.
73. Ibid., 653.
74. Wright, *Who Was Jesus?* 103.
75. The most extensive critique so far is in Witherington, *Jesus Quest,* 219–32. But this was written before *Jesus and the Victory of God* was published, and so responds only to Wright's ideas as presented in *New Testament and the People of God* and in various articles and papers.
76. Wright, *Jesus and the Victory of God,* 339.
77. Ibid., 170.
78. See Crossan, *Birth of Christianity,* 104.
79. Crossan in particular has criticized Wright's approach, which he says tries to rely upon hypothesis and verification "without any prior judgments about sources and traditions" (*Birth of Christianity,* 98–101, citation on 98).
80. Wright, *Jesus and the Victory of God,* 16–21, 28–32.
81. Ibid., 21.
82. Ibid., 479.
83. Ibid., 89.
84. See Casey, *Son of Man.*
85. Witherington, *Jesus Quest,* 230–31.
86. See Jacob Neusner, *From Politics to Piety* (Englewood Cliffs, N.J.: Prentice-Hall, 1973), and Sanders, *Paul and Palestinian Judaism.* Wright's own view is most clearly stated in *New Testament and the People of God,* 181–203.
87. James D. G. Dunn, "Review of *The New Testament and the People of God* by N. T. Wright," *Journal of Theological Studies* 46 (1995): 242–45, citation on 244. Wright maintains that there *is* evidence that both the Essenes and Paul thought this way. On the Essenes, see Michael Knibb, *The Qumran Community* (Cambridge: Cambridge University Press, 1987), 20. On Paul (with reference to Gal. 3:10–14), see N. T. Wright, *The Climax of the Covenant: Christ and the Law in Pauline Theology* (Minneapolis: Fortress Press, 1991), 141–48.
88. Wright, *Jesus and the Victory of God,* 370.
89. Ibid., 86.
90. Thus, Luke Timothy Johnson's criticism of Wright on this point may prove to be premature. Johnson says Wright downplays the disruptive character of the res-

urrection for the early church and fails to recognize its role as a "generative matrix for interpretations of Jesus." See his "Review of *The New Testament and the People of God* by N. T. Wright," *Journal of Biblical Literature* 113 (1994): 536–38.
91. Wright, *Jesus and the Victory of God*, 131.
92. Sanders, *Jesus and Judaism*, 240; cited in Wright, *Jesus and the Victory of God*, 110.
93. See the preface to *New Testament and the People of God*, esp. xiv.
94. Wright, *Jesus and the Victory of God*, 144.

10. The Quest Continues:
Issues and Concerns
1. Cited in Van Biema, "The Gospel Truth," 59. Janssen is reference librarian and archivist for the Publishing House of the Evangelical Lutheran Church in America.
2. Cited in Josh Simon, "Who Was Jesus?" *Life* (December 1994): 68. Bien is the translator of Nikos Kazantzakis's novel *The Last Temptation of Christ*.
3. Ibid., 71.
4. Crossan, "Infancy and Youth of the Messiah," 80.
5. Bruno Bauer, *Kritik der Evangelien und Geschichte ihres Ursprungs*, 2 vols., 2d ed. (Berlin: Hempel, 1850–51). Bauer's work is summarized in Schweitzer, *Quest of the Historical Jesus*, 137–60.
6. Witherington, *Jesus Quest*, 122.
7. See especially Freyne, *Galilee, Jesus, and the Gospels*.
8. Wright offers a sevenfold description of how different scholars have construed the eschatological stance of Jesus. See *Jesus and the Victory of God*, 208.
9. Bornkamm, *Jesus of Nazareth*, 62.
10. Crossan, *Historical Jesus*, 304.
11. Mack, *Myth of Innocence*, 73.
12. Borg, *Jesus in Contemporary Scholarship*, 73.
13. Ibid., 7–8.
14. Borg gives five reasons why the social location of contemporary Jesus scholars (primarily, church-related academic institutions) has discouraged recognition of the sociopolitical dimension of Jesus' activity and message. See *Jesus in Contemporary Scholarship*, 99.
15. Borg, *Jesus in Contemporary Scholarship*, 97.
16. See, for instance, Brandon, *Jesus and the Zealots*.
17. Borg, *Jesus in Contemporary Scholarship*, 98.
18. For example, Wright notes that the biblical concept of a miracle is not the work of a force alien to nature, but an unanticipated work by a force within the natural world, enabling nature "to be more truly itself." See *Jesus and the Victory of God*, 188.
19. See Schweitzer, *Quest of the Historical Jesus*, 53.
20. Meier, *Marginal Jew*, 2:520–21.
21. Ibid., 2:513–14.
22. Ibid., 2:511.
23. Cited in Charlotte Allen, "Away with the Manger," *Lingua Franca* (January-February 1995): 25.
24. "The Jesus Seminar Spring 1995 Meeting," *The Fourth R* 8, no. 2 (1995): 10, 12.
25. Cited in Kenneth L. Woodward, "Rethinking the Resurrection," *Newsweek* (April 8, 1996): 62.
26. Borg, *Jesus: A New Vision*, 185.

27. Cited in Woodward, "Rethinking the Resurrection," 62.
28. Crossan, *Jesus: A Revolutionary Biography* 123–58.
29. Crossan, *Historical Jesus*, 319–20, 336–37.
30. Cited in Charlotte Allen, "The Search for a No-Frills Jesus," *Atlantic Monthly* (December 1996): 67.
31. See, for instance, Crossan, *Jesus: A Revolutionary Biography*, 84–88.
32. Crossan, *Historical Jesus*, 320. Compare Aune, "Magic in Early Christianity," 1538.
33. Crossan, *Birth of Christianity*, 26–29, citation on 29. He does add that "as a Christian trying to be faithful" he *believes* that "God is incarnate in the Jewish peasant poverty of Jesus and not in the Roman imperial power of Augustus" (29).
34. Wright, *Jesus and the Victory of God*, 187.
35. Ibid.
36. Ibid., 194. See also 186 n. 160.
37. Witherington, *Jesus Quest*, 124. He attributes the view that he is contesting to Sanders, but I do not see Sanders actually saying this on the page to which Witherington refers (*Historical Figure of Jesus*, 159; Sanders simply notes that "some of the miracle stories cannot be explained on the basis of today's scientific knowledge").
38. Borg, *A New Vision*, 67. But elsewhere (and later) Borg has said, "In common with the majority of mainline scholars, I see the nature miracles as not historical, but as symbolic narratives." The context for this comment included a specific reference to "walking on the water" (Borg, "From Galilean Jew to the Face of God," 18).
39. This is how Borg describes Mack's Jesus in *Jesus in Contemporary Scholarship*, 23.
40. Thomas G. Long, "Stand Up, Stand Up for (the Historical) Jesus," *Theology Today* 52, no. 1 (1995): 4–5. The original article to which Long refers was Cullen Murphy, "Who Do Men Say That I Am?" *The Atlantic* 258 (December 1986).
41. Borg, "The Historian, the Christian, and Jesus," 7.
42. Ibid., 16.
43. Frederick J. Gaiser, "The Quest for Jesus and the Christian Faith: Introduction," in *The Quest for Jesus and the Christian Faith*, ed. Frederick J. Gaiser (St. Paul: Luther Seminary, 1997), 6.
44. Fredriksen, *From Jesus to Christ*, 214–15.
45. Meier, *Marginal Jew*, 1:200.

BIBLIOGRAPHY
SELECTED WORKS IN ENGLISH

Those desiring a more extensive list of works will find the single most useful volume to be Craig A. Evans's *Life of Jesus Research* (listed below).

Allison, Dale C. "The Contemporary Quest for the Historical Jesus." *Irish Biblical Studies* 18 (1996): 174–93.

———. *The End of the Ages Has Come: An Early Interpretation of the Passion and Resurrection of Jesus.* Philadelphia: Fortress Press, 1985.

———. "Jesus and the Covenant: A Response to E. P. Sanders." In *The Historical Jesus: A Sheffield Reader,* ed. Craig A. Evans and Stanley E. Porter, 61–82. Sheffield: Sheffield Academic Press, 1995.

———. "A Plea for Thoroughgoing Eschatology." *Journal of Biblical Literature* 113 (1994): 651–58.

Alsup, John. *The Post-Resurrection Appearances of the Gospel Tradition,* Stuttgart: Calwer Verlag, 1975.

Anderson, Hugh, ed. *Jesus.* Englewood Cliffs, N.J.: Prentice-Hall, 1967.

Anderson, Norman. *The Teaching of Jesus.* The Jesus Library. Downers Grove, Ill.: InterVarsity Press, 1983.

Antwi, Daniel J. "Did Jesus Consider His Death to Be an Atoning Sacrifice?" *Interpretation* 45 (1991): 17–28.

Aulen, Gustaf. *Jesus in Contemporary Historical Research.* Philadelphia: Fortress Press, 1976.

Aune, David. "Magic in Early Christianity." *Aufstieg und Niedergang der römischen Welt* 2.23.1507–57.

———. *Prophecy in Early Christianity and the Ancient Mediterranean World.* Grand Rapids: Wm. B. Eerdmans Publishing Co., 1983.

Avis, Paul, ed. *The Resurrection of Jesus Christ.* London: Darton, Longman & Todd, 1993.

Bammel, Ernst, and C. F. D. Moule, eds. *Jesus and the Politics of His Day.* Cambridge: Cambridge University Press, 1984.

Banks, Robert J. "Setting 'The Quest for the Historical Jesus' in a Broader Framework." In *Gospel Perspectives 2: Studies of History and Tradition in the Four Gospels,* ed. Richard J. France and David Wenham, 61–82. Sheffield: JSOT Press, 1981.

Barnett, Paul W. "The Jewish Sign Prophets—A.D. 40–70: Their Intentions and Origin." *New Testament Studies* 27 (1980–81): 679–97.

Barrett, C. K. *Jesus and the Gospel Tradition.* London: SPCK, 1967.

Bartsch, Hans. "The Historical Problem of the Life of Jesus." In *The Historical Jesus and the Kerygmatic Christ,* ed. Carl E. Braaten and Roy A. Harrisville, 106–43. Nashville: Abingdon Press, 1964.

Bauckham, Richard J. "The Brothers and Sisters of Jesus: An Epiphanian Response to John P. Meier." *Catholic Biblical Quarterly* 56 (1994): 686–700.

———. "Jesus' Demonstration in the Temple." In *Law and Religion: Essays on the Place of the Law in Israel and Early Christianity,* ed. B. Lindars, 72–89, 171–76. Cambridge: James Clarke, 1988.

———. "The Parting of the Ways: What Happened and Why." *Studia theologica* 47 (1993): 135–51.

———. "The Son of Man: 'A Man in My Position' or 'Someone'?" In *The Historical Jesus: A Sheffield Reader,* ed. Craig A. Evans and Stanley E. Porter, 245–55. Sheffield: Sheffield Academic Press, 1995.

———. "The Study of Gospel Traditions outside the Canonical Gospels: Problems and Prospects." In *Gospel Perspectives 5: The Jesus Tradition outside the Gospels,* ed. David Wenham, 369–404. Sheffield: JSOT Press, 1985.

Beasley-Murray, George R. *Jesus and the Kingdom of God.* Grand Rapids: Wm. B. Eerdmans Publishing Co., 1986.

Becker, Jürgen. *Jesus of Nazareth.* Hawthorne, N.Y.: Walter de Gruyter, 1998.

Betz, Hans Dieter. "Jesus and the Cynics: Survey and Analysis of a Hypothesis." *Journal of Religion* 74 (1994): 453–75.

Betz, Otto. *What Do We Know about Jesus?* Philadelphia: Westminster Press, 1968.

Blackburn, Barry L. "The Miracles of Jesus." In *Studying the Historical Jesus: Evaluations of the State of Current Research,* ed. Bruce Chilton and Craig A. Evans, 353–94. Leiden: E. J. Brill, 1994.

Blomberg, Craig. *The Historical Reliability of the Gospels.* Downers Grove, Ill.: InterVarsity Press, 1987.

———. "The Parables of Jesus: Current Trends and Needs in Research." In *Studying the Historical Jesus: Evaluations of the State of Current Research,,* ed. Bruce Chilton and Craig A. Evans, 231–54. Leiden: E. J. Brill, 1994.

———. "Where Do We Start Studying Jesus?" In *Jesus under Fire: Modern Scholarship Reinvents the Historical Jesus,* ed. Michael J. Wilkins and J. P. Moreland, 17–51. Grand Rapids: Zondervan Publishing House, 1995.

Bock, Darrell L. "The Words of Jesus in the Gospels: Live, Jive, or Memorex?" In *Jesus under Fire: Modern Scholarship Reinvents the Historical Jesus,* ed. Michael J. Wilkins and J. P. Moreland, 73–100. Grand Rapids: Zondervan Publishing House, 1995.

Bockmuehl, Markus. *This Jesus: Martyr, Lord, Messiah.* Edinburgh: T. & T. Clark, 1994.

Boers, Hendrikus. *Who Was Jesus? The Historical Jesus and the Synoptic Gospels.* San Francisco: Harper & Row, 1989.

Bokser, Baruch M. "Wonder-Working and the Rabbinic Tradition: The Case of Hanina ben Dosa." *Journal for the Study of Judaism* 16 (1985): 42–92.

Borg, Marcus J. *Conflict, Holiness, and Politics in the Teaching of Jesus.* New York: Edwin Mellen Press, 1984.

———. "From Galilean Jew to the Face of God: The Pre-Easter and Post-Easter Jesus." In *Jesus at 2000,* ed. Marcus J. Borg, 7–20. Boulder, Colo.: Westview Press, 1997.

———. *The God We Never Knew: Beyond Religion to a More Authentic Contemporary Faith.* San Francisco: HarperSanFrancisco, 1997.

———. "The Historian, the Christian, and Jesus." *Theology Today* 52 (1995): 6–16.

———. "The Historical Study of Jesus and Christian Origins." In *Jesus at 2000,* ed. Marcus J. Borg, 121–47. Boulder, Colo.: Westview Press, 1997.

————. "Jesus and the Buddha." *The Fourth R* 10, no. 6 (1997): 11–13, 15–17.

————. "Jesus and Eschatology: A Reassessment." In *Images of Jesus Today,* ed. James H. Charlesworth and W. P. Weaver. Valley Forge, Pa.: Trinity Press International, 1994.

————. *Jesus: A New Vision.* San Francisco: Harper & Row, 1988.

————. *Jesus in Contemporary Scholarship.* Valley Forge, Pa.: Trinity Press International, 1994.

————. "The Jesus Seminar and the Passion Sayings." *Foundations and Facets Forum* 3, no. 2 (1987): 81–95.

————. *Meeting Jesus Again for the First Time: The Historical Jesus and the Heart of Contemporary Faith.* San Francisco: HarperSanFrancisco, 1994.

————. "An Orthodoxy Reconsidered: The End-of-the-World Jesus." In *The Glory of Christ in the New Testament,* ed. L. D. Hurst and N. T. Wright. Oxford: Clarendon Press, 1987.

————. "The Palestinian Background for a Life of Jesus." In *The Search for Jesus: Modern Scholarship Looks at the Gospels,* ed. Hershel Shanks, 37–58. Washington, D.C.: Biblical Archaeology Society, 1994.

————. "Portraits of Jesus." In *The Search for Jesus: Modern Scholarship Looks at the Gospels,* ed. Hershel Shanks, 83–108. Washington, D.C.: Biblical Archaeology Society, 1994.

————. "Reflections on a Discipline: A North American Perspective." In *Studying the Historical Jesus,* ed. Bruce Chilton and Craig A. Evans, 9–32. Leiden: E. J. Brill, 1994.

Borg, Marcus J., ed. *Jesus at 2000.* Boulder, Colo.: Westview Press, 1997.

Borg, Marcus J., with Ray Riegert, eds. *Jesus and the Buddha: The Parallel Sayings.* Berkeley, Calif.: Ulysses, 1997.

Boring, M. Eugene. "Criteria of Authenticity: The Lucan Beatitudes as a Test Case." *Foundations and Facets Forum* 1 no. 4 (1985): 3–38.

————. *The Continuing Voice of Jesus: Christian Prophecy and the Gospel Tradition.* Louisville: Westminster/John Knox Press, 1991.

————. "The 'Third Quest' and the Apostolic Faith." *Interpretation* 50 (1996): 341–54.

Bornkamm, Günther. *Jesus of Nazareth.* New York: Harper & Row, 1960.

Bowden, John. *Jesus: The Unanswered Questions.* London: SCM Press, 1988.

Bowker, John. *Jesus and the Pharisees.* Cambridge: Cambridge University Press, 1993.

Boyce, James. "The Quest for Jesus and the Church's Proclamation." In *The Quest for Jesus and the Christian Faith,* ed. Frederick J. Gaiser, 175–90. St. Paul: Luther Seminary, 1997.

Boyd, Gregory A. *Cynic Sage or Son of God? Recovering the Real Jesus in an Age of Revisionist Replies.* Wheaton, Ill.: Bridgepoint, 1995.

Braaten, Carl E. "Martin Kähler on the Historic Biblical Christ." In *The Historical Jesus and the Kerygmatic Christ: Essays on the New Quest of the Historical Jesus,* ed. Carl E. Braaten and Roy A. Harrisville, 79–105. Nashville: Abingdon Press, 1964.

Braaten, Carl E., and Roy A. Harrisville, eds. *The Historical Jesus and the Kerygmatic Christ: Essays on the New Quest of the Historical Jesus.* Nashville: Abingdon Press, 1964.

Brandon, S. G. F. *Jesus and the Zealots: A Study of the Political Factor in Primitive Christianity.* New York: Charles Scribner's Sons, 1967.

Braun, Herbert. "The Significance of Qumran for the Problem of the Historical Jesus." In *The Historical Jesus and the Kerygmatic Christ: Essays on the New Quest of the Historical Jesus,* ed. Carl E. Braaten and Roy A. Harrisville, 69–78. Nashville: Abingdon Press, 1964.

Breech, James. *The Silence of Jesus: The Authentic Voices of the Historical Man.* Philadelphia: Fortress Press, 1983.

Brown, Colin. *Jesus in European Protestant Thought, 1778–1860.* Grand Rapids: Baker Book House 1988.

————. *Miracles and the Critical Mind.* Grand Rapids: Wm. B. Eerdmans Publishing Co., 1984.

Brown, Raymond E., *The Death of the Messiah: From Gethsemane to the Grave: A Commentary on the Passion Narratives in the Four Gospels.* Anchor Bible Reference Library. New York: Doubleday, 1994.

————. "The Gospel of Peter and Canonical Gospel Priority." *New Testament Studies* 33 (1987): 321–43.

Bruce, F. F. "The Background to the Son of Man Sayings." In *Christ the Lord: Studies in Christology Presented to Donald Guthrie,* ed. Harold Rowdon, 50–70. Downers Grove, Ill.: InterVarsity Press, 1982.

Bryan, Christopher. "Discerning Our Origins: The Words and Works of the Jesus Seminar." *Sewanee Theological Review* 39 (1996): 339–48.

Buchanan, George W. *Jesus: The King and His Kingdom.* Macon, Ga.: Mercer University Press, 1984.

Büchler, A. *Types of Jewish-Palestinian Piety from 709 B.C.E.–70 C.E.: The Ancient Pious Man.* New York: Ktav, 1968 (original 1922).

Bultmann, Rudolf. *Faith and Understanding.* London: SCM Press, 1969.

————. *History and Eschatology: The Presence of Eternity.* New York: Harper and Brothers, 1957.

————. *Jesus and the Word.* New York: Charles Scribner's Sons, 1958 (original 1926).

————. *Jesus Christ and Mythology.* New York: Charles Scribner's Sons, 1958.

————. *The History of the Synoptic Tradition.* New York: Harper & Row, 1968 (original 1921).

————. "The Primitive Christian Kerygma and the Historical Jesus." In *The Historical Jesus and the Kerygmatic Christ: Essays on the New Quest of the Historical Jesus,* ed. Carl E. Braaten and Roy A. Harrisville, 15–42. Nashville: Abingdon Press, 1964.

Burridge, Richard A. *What Are the Gospels? A Comparison with Graeco-Roman Biography.* Cambridge: Cambridge University Press, 1992.

Butts, James R. "Probing the Polling: Jesus Seminar Results on the Kingdom Sayings." *Foundations and Facets Forum* 3, no. 1 (1987): 98–128.

Cadbury, Henry A. *The Peril of Modernizing Jesus.* New York: Charles Scribner's Sons, 1962 (original 1937).

Caird, George B. *Jesus and the Jewish Nation.* London: Athlone Press, 1965.

————. *The Language and Imagery of the Bible.* Philadelphia: Westminster Press, 1980.

Calvert, David G. A. "An Examination of the Criteria for Distinguishing the Authentic Words of Jesus." *New Testament Studies* 18 (1971–72): 209–19.

Cameron, Ronald D. *The Other Gospels: Non-Canonical Gospel Texts.* Philadelphia: Westminster Press, 1982.

Carlson, Jeffrey. "Crossan's Jesus and Christian Identity." In *Jesus and Faith: A Conversation on the Work of John Dominic Crossan,* ed. Jeffrey Carlson and Robert A. Ludwig, 31–43. Maryknoll, N.Y.: Orbis Books, 1994.

Carlson, Jeffrey, and Robert A. Ludwig, eds. *Jesus and Faith: A Conversation on the Work of John Dominic Crossan.* Maryknoll, N.Y.: Orbis Books, 1994.

Casey, Maurice. *From Jewish Prophet to Gentile God: The Origins and Development of New Testament Christology.* Louisville: Westminster/John Knox Press, 1991.

————. *Son of Man: The Interpretation and Influence of Daniel 7*. London: SPCK, 1979.

Cassels, Louis. *The Real Jesus: How He Lived and What He Taught*. New York: Double-day, 1968.

Catchpole, David R. *The Quest for Q*. Edinburgh: T. & T. Clark, 1993.

Charlesworth, James H. "The Dead Sea Scrolls and the Historical Jesus." In *Jesus and the Dead Sea Scrolls*, ed. James H. Charlesworth, 1–74. New York: Doubleday, 1992.

————. "The Foreground of Christian Origins and the Commencement of Jesus Research." In *Jesus' Jewishness: Exploring the Place of Jesus within Early Judaism*, ed. James H. Charlesworth, 63–83. New York: Crossroad, 1991.

————. "From Messianology to Christology: Problems and Prospects." In *The Messiah: Developments in Earliest Judaism and Christianity*, ed. James H. Charlesworth, 3–35. Minneapolis: Fortress Press, 1992.

————. "Jesus, Early Jewish Literature, and Archaeology." In *Jesus' Jewishness: Exploring the Place of Jesus within Early Judaism*, ed. James H. Charlesworth, 177–98. New York: Crossroad, 1991.

————. "Jesus Research Expands with Chaotic Creativity." In *Images of Jesus Today*, ed. James H. Charlesworth and W. P. Weaver, 1–41. Valley Forge, Pa.: Trinity Press International, 1994.

————. *Jesus within Judaism: New Light from Exciting Archaeological Discoveries*. Garden City, N.Y.: Doubleday, 1988.

Charlesworth, James H., ed. *Jesus and the Dead Sea Scrolls*. Anchor Bible Reference Library. New York: Doubleday, 1992.

————. *Jesus' Jewishness: Exploring the Place of Jesus within Early Judaism*. New York: Crossroad, 1991.

————. *The Messiah: Developments in Earliest Judaism and Christianity*. Minneapolis: Fortress Press, 1992.

Charlesworth, James H., and Craig A. Evans. "Jesus in the Agrapha and Apocryphal Gospels." In *Studying the Historical Jesus: Evaluations of the State of Current Research*, ed. Bruce Chilton and Craig A. Evans, 479–534. Leiden: E. J. Brill, 1994.

Charlesworth, James H., and W. P. Weaver, eds. *Images of Jesus Today*. Valley Forge, Pa.: Trinity Press International, 1994.

Chilton, Bruce. *A Galilean Rabbi and His Bible*. Wilmington, Del.: Michael Glazier, 1984.

————. "The Gospel according to Thomas as a Source for Jesus' Teaching." In *Gospel Perspectives 5: The Jesus Tradition outside the Gospels*, ed. David Wenham, 155–76. Sheffield: JSOT Press, 1985.

————. "The Kingdom of God in Recent Discussion." In *Studying the Historical Jesus: Evaluations of the State of Current Research*, ed. Bruce Chilton and Craig A. Evans, 255–80. Leiden: E. J. Brill, 1994.

————. *The Kingdom of God in the Teaching of Jesus*. Philadelphia: Fortress Press, 1984.

————. *God in Strength: Jesus' Announcement of the Kingdom*. Sheffield: JSOT Press, 1987.

————. "Jesus and the Repentance of E. P. Sanders." *Tyndale Bulletin* 39 (1998): 1–18.

————. *Pure Kingdom: Jesus' Vision of God*. Grand Rapids: Wm. B. Eerdmans Publishing Co., 1996.

————. *The Temple of Jesus: His Sacrificial Program within a Cultural History of Sacrifice*. University Park, Pa.: Pennsylvania State University Press, 1992.

Chilton, Bruce, and Craig A. Evans. "Jesus and Israel's Scriptures." In *Studying the Historical Jesus: Evaluations of the State of Current Research*, ed. Bruce Chilton and Craig A. Evans, 281–336. Leiden: E. J. Brill, 1994.

———. *Jesus in Context: Temple, Purity, and Restoration*. Leiden: E. J. Brill, 1997.

Chilton, Bruce, and Craig A. Evans, eds. *Studying the Historical Jesus: Evaluations of the State of Current Research*. New Testament Tools and Studies 19. Leiden: E. J. Brill, 1994.

Chilton, Bruce, and J. I. H. MacDonald. *Jesus and the Ethics of the Kingdom*. London: SPCK, 1987.

Cohen, Shaye J. D. *Josephus in Galilee and Rome: His Vita and Development as a Historian*. Columbia Studies in the Classic Traditions 8. Leiden: E. J. Brill, 1979.

———. *From the Maccabees to the Mishnah*. Library of Early Christianity. Philadelphia: Westminster Press, 1987.

Conzelmann, Hans. *Jesus*. Philadelphia: Fortress Press, 1973.

———. "The Method of the Life-of-Jesus Research." In *The Historical Jesus and the Kerygmatic Christ: Essays on the New Quest of the Historical Jesus,* ed. Carl E. Braaten and Roy A. Harrisville, 54–68. Nashville: Abingdon Press, 1964.

Corley, Kathleen. *Gender and Jesus: History and Lament in Gospel Tradition*. New York: Oxford University Press, forthcoming.

Cornfeld, Gaalyahu. *The Historical Jesus: A Scholarly View of the Man and His World*. New York: Macmillan Publishing Co., 1982.

Craig, William Lane. *Assessing the New Testament Evidence for the Historicity of the Resurrection*. Lewiston, N.Y.: Edwin Mellen Press, 1989.

———. "The Bodily Resurrection of Jesus." In *Gospel Perspectives 1: Studies of History and Tradition in the Four Gospels,* ed. Richard T. France and David Wenham, 47–74. Sheffield: JSOT Press, 1980.

———. "Did Jesus Rise from the Dead?" In *Jesus under Fire: Modern Scholarship Reinvents the Historical Jesus,* ed. Michael J. Wilkins and J. P. Moreland, 141–76. Grand Rapids: Zondervan Publishing Co., 1995.

———. *The Historical Argument for the Resurrection of Jesus*. Lewiston, N.Y.: Edwin Mellen Press, 1985.

———. "The Problem of Miracles: A Historical and Philosophical Perspective." In *Gospel Perspectives 6: The Miracles of Jesus,* ed. David Wenham and Craig Blomberg, 9–48. Sheffield: JSOT Press, 1986.

Crossan, John Dominic. "Aphorism in Discourse and Narrative." *Semeia* 43 (1988): 121–40.

———. *The Birth of Christianity*. San Francisco: HarperSanFrancisco, 1998.

———. *The Cross That Spoke: The Origins of the Passion Narrative*. San Francisco: Harper & Row, 1988.

———. *The Essential Jesus: Original Sayings and Earliest Images*. San Francisco: HarperSanFrancisco, 1994.

———. "Exile: Stealth and Cunning." *Foundations and Facets Forum* 1, no.1 (1985): 59–61.

———. *Four Other Gospels: Shadows on the Contours of Canon*. Sonoma, Calif.: Polebridge Press, 1992.

———. *The Historical Jesus: The Life of a Mediterranean Jewish Peasant*. San Francisco: HarperSanFrancisco, 1991.

———. "The Historical Jesus in Earliest Christianity." In *Jesus and Faith: A Conversation on the Work of John Dominic Crossan,* ed. Jeffrey Carlson and Robert A. Ludwig, 1–21. Maryknoll, N.Y.: Orbis Books, 1994.

———. "The Infancy and Youth of the Messiah." In *The Search for Jesus: Modern Scholarship Looks at the Gospels,* ed. Hershel Shanks, 59–82. Washington, D.C.: Biblical Archaeology Society, 1994.

————. *In Fragments: The Aphorisms of Jesus.* San Francisco: Harper & Row, 1983.

————. *In Parables: The Challenge of the Historical Jesus.* New York: Harper & Row, 1973.

————. "Jesus and the Kingdom: Itinerants and Householders in Earliest Christianity." In *Jesus at 2000,* ed. Marcus J. Borg, 21–54. Boulder, Colo.: Westview Press, 1997.

————. *Jesus Parallels: A Workbook for the Jesus Tradition.* 2d ed. Philadelphia: Fortress Press, 1991.

————. *Jesus: A Revolutionary Biography.* San Francisco: HarperSanFrancisco, 1994.

————. "The Passion, Crucifixion, and Resurrection." In *The Search for Jesus: Modern Scholarship Looks at the Gospels,* ed. Hershel Shanks, 109–34. Washington, D.C.: Biblical Archaeology Society, 1994.

————. "The Passion Narrative." *The Fourth R* 9, nos. 5–6 (1996): 3–8.

————. "Thoughts on Two Extracanonical Gospels." *Semeia* 49 (1990): 155–68.

————. *Who Killed Jesus? Exposing the Roots of Anti-Semitism in the Gospel Story of the Death of Jesus.* San Francisco: HarperSanFrancisco, 1995.

————. "Why Christians Must Search for the Historical Jesus." *Bible Review* 12, no. 2 (1996): 34–39, 42–45.

Crossan, John Dominic, with R. G. Watts. *Who Is Jesus? Answers to Your Questions about the Historical Jesus.* San Francisco: HarperSanFrancisco, 1996.

Dalman, Gustav H. *The Words of Jesus Considered in the Light of Post-Biblical Jewish Writings and the Aramaic Language.* Edinburgh: T. & T. Clark, 1903.

Davaney, Sheila Greeve. "A Historicist Model for Theology." In *Jesus and Faith: A Conversation on the Work of John Dominic Crossan,* ed. Jeffrey Carlson and Robert A. Ludwig, 44–56. Maryknoll, N.Y.: Orbis Books, 1994.

Davids, Peter H. "The Gospels and Jewish Tradition: Twenty Years after Gerhardsson." In *Gospel Perspectives 1: Studies of History and Tradition in the Four Gospels,* ed. Richard T. France and David Wenham, 75–100. Sheffield: JSOT Press, 1980.

Davies, Stevan L. *The Gospel of Thomas and Christian Wisdom.* New York: Seabury Press, 1983.

————. "Whom Jesus Healed and How." *The Fourth R* 6, no. 2 (1993): 1–11.

Davis, Stephen T. *Risen Indeed: Making Sense of the Resurrection.* London: SPCK, 1993.

deHaven-Smith, L. *The Hidden Teachings of Jesus: The Political Meaning of the Kingdom of God.* Grand Rapids: Phanes, 1994.

de Jonge, Marinus. *Jesus, the Servant Messiah.* New Haven: Yale University Press, 1991.

————. *Jewish Eschatology, Early Christian Christology and the Testaments of the Twelve Patriarchs: Collected Essays of Marinus de Jonge.* Leiden: E. J. Brill, 1991.

den Heyer, C. J. *Jesus Matters: 150 Years of Research.* Valley Forge, Pa.: Trinity Press International, 1997.

DeRosa, Peter. *Jesus Who Became Christ.* London: Collins, 1974.

Derrett, J. D. M. *Jesus's Audience: The Social and Psychological Environment in Which He Worked.* New York: Seabury Press, 1973.

————. *Law in the New Testament.* London: Darton, Longman & Todd, 1970.

Dimont, M. I. *Appointment in Jerusalem: A Search for the Historical Jesus.* New York: St. Martin's Press, 1991.

Downing, F. Gerald. *Christ and the Cynics: Jesus and Other Radical Preachers in First-Century Tradition.* Sheffield: Sheffield Academic Press, 1988.

————. *Cynics and Christian Origins.* Edinburgh: T. & T. Clark, 1992.

————. "Cynics and Christians." *New Testament Studies* 30 (1984): 584–93.

————. "Deeper Reflections on the Jewish Cynic Jesus." *Catholic Biblical Quarterly* 117 (1998): 97–104.

————. *Jesus and the Threat of Freedom.* London: SCM Press, 1987.

————. "Words as Deeds and Deeds as Words." *Biblical Interpretation* 3, no. 2 (1995): 129–43.

Duling, Dennis C. *Jesus Christ through History.* New York: Harcourt Brace Jovanovich, 1979.

Dungan, David L. *The Parting of the Ways between Christianity and Judaism and Their Significance for the Character of Christianity.* Philadelphia: Trinity Press International, 1991.

————. "Pharisees, Sinners, and Jesus." In *The Social World of Formative Christianity and Judaism: Essays in Tribute to Howard Clark Kee,* ed. J. Neusner et al., 264–89. Philadelphia: Fortress Press, 1988.

————. *The Sayings of Jesus in the Churches of Paul: The Use of the Synoptic Tradition in the Regulation of Early Church Life.* Oxford: Basil Blackwell Publisher, 1971.

Dunn, James D. G. *Christology in the Making.* Philadelphia: Westminster Press, 1980.

————. *The Evidence for Jesus.* Philadelphia: Westminster Press, 1985.

————. "The Historicity of the Synoptic Gospels." In *Crisis in Christology: Essays in Quest of Resolution,* ed. William R. Farmer, 199–216. Livonia, Mich.: Dove Booksellers, 1995.

————. *Jesus and the Spirit: A Study of the Religious and Charismatic Experience of Jesus and the First Christians as Reflected in the New Testament.* Philadelphia: Westminster Press, 1975.

————. "Jesus Tradition in Paul." In *Studying the Historical Jesus: Evaluations of the State of Current Research,* ed. Bruce Chilton and Craig A. Evans, 155–78. Leiden: E. J. Brill, 1994.

————. "The Making of Christology—Evolution of Unfolding?" In *Jesus of Nazareth: Lord and Christ,* ed. Joel B. Green and Max Turner, 437–52. Grand Rapids: Wm. B. Eerdmans Publishing Co., 1994.

Eckardt, A. Roy. *Reclaiming the Jesus of History.* Minneapolis: Fortress Press, 1992.

Eddy, Paul Rhodes, "Jesus as Diogenes? Reflections on the Cynic Jesus Thesis." *Journal of Biblical Literature* 115 (1996): 449–69.

Edersheim, Alfred. *The Life and Times of Jesus the Messiah.* Peabody, Mass.: Hendrickson Publishers, 1993 (original 1883).

Edwards, David L. *The Real Jesus.* London: HarperCollins, 1992.

Ellis, E. Earle. "Gospels Criticism." In *The Gospel and the Gospels,* ed. Peter Stuhlmacher, 237–53. Grand Rapids: Wm. B. Eerdmans Publishing Co., 1991.

————. "The Synoptic Gospels and History." In *Crisis in Christology: Essays in Quest of Resolution,* ed. William R. Farmer, 83–92. Livonia, Mich.: Dove Booksellers, 1995.

Ellis, Marc H. "The Brokerless Kingdom and the Other Kingdom: Reflections on Auschwitz, Jesus, and the Jewish-Christian Establishment." In *Jesus and Faith: A Conversation on the Work of John Dominic Crossan,* ed. Jeffrey Carlson and Robert A. Ludwig, 100–114. Maryknoll, N.Y.: Orbis Books, 1994.

Evans, Craig A. "The Recently Published Dead Sea Scrolls and the Historical Jesus." In *Studying the Historical Jesus: Evaluations of the State of Current Research,* ed. Bruce Chilton and Craig A. Evans, 547–65. Leiden: E. J. Brill, 1994.

————. *Jesus.* Grand Rapids: Baker Book House, 1992.

————. "Jesus' Action in the Temple: Cleansing or Portent of Destruction?" *Catholic Biblical Quarterly* 51 (1989): 237–70.

————. "Jesus and the 'Cave of Robbers': Toward a Jewish Context for the Temple Action." *Bulletin of Biblical Research* 3 (1993): 93–110.

————. *Jesus and His Contemporaries: Comparative Studies.* Leiden: E. J. Brill, 1995.

————. "Jesus in Non-Christian Sources." In *Studying the Historical Jesus: Evaluations of the State of Current Research,* ed. Bruce Chilton and Craig A. Evans, 443–78. Leiden: E. J. Brill, 1994.

————. *Life of Jesus Research: An Annotated Bibliography.* 2d ed. Leiden: E. J. Brill, 1996.

————. "Life of Jesus Research and the Eclipse of Mythology." *Theological Studies* 54 (1993): 3–36.

————. *Non-canonical Writings and New Testament Interpretation.* Peabody, Mass.: Hendrickson Publishers, 1992.

————. "Opposition to the Temple: Jesus and the Dead Sea Scrolls." In *Jesus and the Dead Sea Scrolls,* ed. James H. Charlesworth, 235–53. New York: Doubleday, 1992.

————. "What Did Jesus Do?" In *Jesus under Fire: Modern Scholarship Reinvents the Historical Jesus,* ed. Michael J. Wilkins and J. P. Moreland, 101-16. Grand Rapids: Zondervan Publishing House, 1995.

Evans, Craig A., and Stanley E. Porter, eds. *The Historical Jesus: A Sheffield Reader.* Sheffield: Sheffield Academic Press, 1995.

Evans, C. Stephen. *The Historical Christ and the Jesus of Faith: The Incarnational Narrative as History.* Oxford: Clarendon Press, 1996.

Falk, Harvey. *Jesus the Pharisee: A New Look at the Jewishness of Jesus.* Mahwah, N.J.: Paulist Press, 1985.

Farmer, William R. "The Historical Perimeters for Understanding the Aims of Jesus." In *Crisis in Christology: Essays in Quest of Resolution,* ed. William R. Farmer, 175–98. Livonia, Mich.: Dove Booksellers, 1995.

————. *Jesus and the Gospel: Tradition, Scripture, and Canon.* Philadelphia: Fortress Press, 1982.

Farmer, William R., ed. *Crisis in Christology: Essays in Quest of Resolution.* Livonia, Mich.: Dove Booksellers, 1995.

Fiorenza, Elisabeth Schüssler. *In Memory of Her: A Feminist Theological Reconstruction of Christian Origins.* New York: Crossroad, 1987.

————. *Jesus—Miriam's Child, Sophia's Prophet: Critical Issues in Feminist Christology.* New York: Continuum, 1994.

————. "The Jesus of Piety and the Historical Jesus." *Catholic Theological Society of America Proceedings* 49 (1994): 90–99.

Flusser, David. "Jesus, His Ancestry, and the Commandment of Love." In *Jesus' Jewishness: Exploring the Place of Jesus within Early Judaism,* ed. James H. Charlesworth, 153–76. New York: Crossroad, 1991.

Fortna, Robert T. "The Gospel of John and the Historical Jesus." *The Fourth R* 8, nos. 5–6 (1995): 12–16.

France, Richard T. *Divine Government: God's Kingship in the Gospel of Mark.* London: SPCK, 1990.

————. *The Evidence for Jesus.* Downers Grove, Ill.: InterVarsity Press, 1986.

————. *Jesus and the Old Testament.* London: Tyndale, 1971.

————. "Jewish Historiography, Midrash, and the Gospels." In *Gospel Perspectives 3: Studies in Midrash and Historiography,* ed. Richard T. France and David Wenham, 99–128. Sheffield: JSOT Press, 1983.

————. "The Worship of Jesus: A Neglected Factor in Christological Debate?" In *Christ the Lord: Studies in Christology Presented to Donald Guthrie,* ed. Harold Rowdon, 17–36. Leicester: Inter Varsity Press, 1982.

France, Richard T., and David Wenham, eds. *Gospel Perspectives 1: Studies of History and Tradition in the Four Gospels.* Sheffield: JSOT Press, 1980.

———. *Gospel Perspectives 2: Studies of History and Tradition in the Four Gospels.* Sheffield: JSOT Press, 1981.

———. *Gospel Perspectives 3: Studies in Midrash and Historiography.* Sheffield: JSOT Press, 1983.

Fredriksen, Paula. "Did Jesus Oppose the Purity Laws?" *Bible Review* (June 1995): 20–47.

———. *From Jesus to Christ: The Origins of the New Testament Images of Jesus.* New Haven, Conn.: Yale University Press, 1988.

———. "What You See Is What You Get: Context and Content in Current Research on the Historical Jesus." *Theology Today* 52 (1995): 75–97.

Freyne, Sean. *Galilee from Alexander the Great to Hadrian: A Study of Second Temple Judaism.* Wilmington, Del.: Michael Glazier, 1980.

———. *Galilee, Jesus, and the Gospels: Literary Approaches and Historical Investigations.* Philadelphia: Fortress Press, 1988.

———. "The Geography, Politics, and Economics of Galilee and the Quest for the Historical Jesus." In *Studying the Historical Jesus: Evaluations of the State of Current Research,* ed. Bruce Chilton and Craig A. Evans, 75–122. Leiden: E. J. Brill, 1994.

———. "The Quest for the Historical Jesus: Some Theological Reflections." *Concilium* 1 (1997): 37–51.

Fuller, Reginald. *The Formation of the Resurrection Narratives.* Philadelphia: Fortress Press, 1980 (original 1971).

———. *The Foundations of New Testament Christology.* London: Lutterworth Press, 1965.

Funk, Robert W. *Honest to Jesus: Jesus for a New Millenium.* San Francisco: HarperSanFrancisco, 1996.

———. "The Issue of Jesus." *Foundations and Facets Forum* 1, no. 1 (1985): 7–12.

———. *Jesus as Precursor.* Rev. ed. Ed. E. Beutner. Sonoma, Calif.: Polebridge Press, 1993.

———. "Jesus of Nazareth: A Glimpse." *The Fourth R* 9, nos. 1, 2 (1996): 17–20.

———. "On Distinguishing Historical from Fictive Narrative." *Foundations and Facets Forum* 9, nos. 3–4 (1993): 179–216.

———. "Unraveling the Jesus Tradition: Criteria and Criticism." *Foundations and Facets Forum* 5, no. 2 (1989): 31–62.

Funk, Robert W., Roy W. Hoover, and the Jesus Seminar. *The Five Gospels: The Search for the Authentic Words of Jesus.* New York: Macmillan, 1993.

Funk, Robert W., and the Jesus Seminar. *The Acts of Jesus: The Search for the Authentic Deeds of Jesus* (San Francisco: HarperSanFrancisco, 1998).

Gager, John G. "The Gospels and Jesus: Some Doubts about Method." *Journal of Religion* 54 (1974): 244–72.

Gaiser, Frederick J., ed. *The Quest for Jesus and the Christian Faith. Word and World* Supplement Series 3. St. Paul: Luther Seminary, 1997.

Gallagher, Eugene V. *Divine Man or Magician? Celsus and Origen on Jesus.* Society of Biblical Literature Dissertation Series 64. Chico, Calif.: Scholars Press, 1982.

Galvin, John P. "'I Believe . . . in Jesus Christ, His Only Son, Our Lord': The Earthly Jesus and the Christ of Faith," *Interpretation* 50 (1996): 373–82.

Gammie, John G., and Leo G. Purdue. *The Sage in Israel and the Ancient Near East.* Winona Lake, Ind.: Eisenbrauns, 1990.

Geisler, Norman L. "In Defense of the Resurrection: A Reply to Criticisms." *Journal of the Evangelical Theological Society* 34 (1991): 243–61.

Geivett, R. Douglas. "Is Jesus the Only Way?" In *Jesus under Fire: Modern Scholarship Reinvents the Historical Jesus,* ed. Michael J. Wilkins and J. P. Moreland, 177–206. Grand Rapids: Zondervan Publishing House, 1995.

Georgen, Donald. *A Theology of Jesus.* Vol. 1, *The Mission and Ministry of Jesus.* Wilmington, Del.: Michael Glazier, 1986.

———. *A Theology of Jesus.* Vol. 2, *The Death and Resurrection of Jesus.* Wilmington, Del.: Michael Glazier, 1986.

Gerhardsson, Birger. *The Gospel Tradition.* Lund: Gleerup, 1986.

———. *Memory and Manuscript: Oral Tradition and Written Transmission in Rabbinic Judaism and Early Christianity.* Uppsala: Gleerup, 1961.

———. *The Origins of the Gospel Tradition.* London: SCM Press, 1979.

———. *Tradition and Transmission in Early Christianity.* Uppsala: Gleerup, 1964.

Goetz, S. C., and Craig Blomberg. "The Burden of Proof." *Journal for the Study of the New Testament* 11 (1981): 39–83.

Goodman, Martin. *The Ruling Class of Judea.* Cambridge: Cambridge University Press, 1987.

Goppelt, Leonhard. *Theology of the New Testament.* Vol. 1, *The Ministry of Jesus in Its Theological Significance.* Grand Rapids: Wm. B. Eerdmans Publishing Co., 1981 (original 1975).

Grant, Frederick C. "The Authenticity of Jesus' Sayings." In *Neutestamentliche Studien für Rudolf Bultmann,* Beihefte zur ZNW, 137–43. Berlin: Töpelmann, 1954.

Grant, Michael. *Jesus: A Historian's Review of the Gospels.* New York: Macmillan, 1992 (original 1977).

Grant, Robert. *Gnosticism and Early Christianity.* 2d ed. New York: Columbia University Press, 1966.

Gray, Rebecca. *Prophetic Figures in Late Second Temple Jewish Palestine.* Oxford: Oxford University Press, 1993.

Green, Joel B., and Max Turner, eds. *Jesus of Nazareth, Lord and Christ: Essays on the Historical Jesus and New Testament Christology.* Grand Rapids: Wm. B. Eerdmans Publishing Co., 1994.

Guillet, Jacques. *The Consciousness of Jesus.* New York: Newman Press, 1971.

Habermas, Gary R. *Ancient Evidence for the Life of Jesus: Historical Records of His Death and Resurrection.* Nashville: Thomas Nelson, 1984.

———. "Did Jesus Perform Miracles?" In *Jesus under Fire: Modern Scholarship Reinvents the Historical Jesus,* ed. Michael J. Wilkins and J. P. Moreland, 117–41. Grand Rapids: Zondervan Publishing House, 1995.

———. "Resurrection Claims in Non-Christian Religions." *Religious Studies* 25 (1989): 167-77.

Hagner, Donald A. *The Jewish Reclamation of Jesus: An Analysis and Critique of Modern Jewish Study of Jesus.* Grand Rapids: Zondervan Publishing House, 1984.

Hahn, Ferdinand. "Methodological Reflections on the Historical Investigation of Jesus." In *Historical Investigation and New Testament Faith: Two Essays,* 35–105. Philadelphia: Fortress Press, 1983.

Haight, Roger. "The Impact of Jesus Research on Christology." *Louvain Studies* 21 (1996): 216–28.

Harrington, Daniel J. "The Jewishness of Jesus: Facing Some Problems." *Catholic Biblical Quarterly* 49 (1987): 1–13.

Harrisville, Roy A. "Representative American Lives of Jesus." In *The Historical Jesus and the Kerygmatic Christ: Essays on the New Quest of the Historical Jesus,* ed. Carl E. Braaten and Roy A. Harrisville, 172–96. Nashville: Abingdon Press, 1964.

Harvey, Anthony E. *Jesus and the Constraints of History: The Bampton Lectures, 1980.* London: Duckworth, 1982.

————. *Strenuous Commands: The Ethic of Jesus.* Philadelphia: Trinity Press International, 1990.

Harvey, Van A., and Schubert M. Ogden. "How New Is the 'New Quest of the Historical Jesus'?" In *The Historical Jesus and the Kerygmatic Christ: Essays on the New Quest of the Historical Jesus,* ed. Carl E. Braaten and Roy A. Harrisville, 197–242. Nashville: Abingdon Press, 1964.

Hays, Richard B. "The Corrected Jesus." *First Things* 43 (1994): 43–48.

Hebblethwaite, Brian. "Jesus Christ—God and Man: The Myth and Truth Debate." In *Crisis in Christology: Essays in Quest of Resolution,* ed. William R. Farmer, 1–12. Livonia, Mich.: Dove Booksellers, 1995.

Hengel, Martin. *The Atonement: The Origins of the Doctrine in the New Testament.* Philadelphia: Fortress Press, 1981.

————. *The Charismatic Leader and His Followers.* Edinburgh: T. & T. Clark, 1996 (original 1968).

————. *Crucifixion in the Ancient World and the Folly of the Message of the Cross.* Philadelphia: Fortress Press, 1977.

————. *The Hellenization of Judea in the First Century after Christ.* Philadelphia: Trinity Press International, 1989.

————. "Jesus, the Messiah of Israel." In *Crisis in Christology: Essays in Quest of Resolution,* ed. William R. Farmer, 217–40. Livonia, Mich.: Dove Booksellers, 1995.

————. *Judaism and Hellenism.* 2 vols. Philadelphia: Fortress Press, 1974.

————. *Victory over Violence: Jesus and the Revolutionists.* Philadelphia: Fortress Press, 1973.

————. *Was Jesus a Revolutionist?* Philadelphia: Fortress Press, 1971.

————. *The Zealots: Investigations into the Jewish Freedom Movement in the Period from Herod I until 70 A.D.* Edinburgh: T. & T. Clark, 1995.

Hennecke, Edgar, and Wilhelm Schneemelcher, eds. *New Testament Apocrypha.* 2 vols. Philadelphia: Fortress Press, 1963, 1965.

Herzog, William R. *Parables as Subversive Speech: Jesus as Pedagogue of the Oppressed.* Louisville: Westminster John Knox Press, 1994.

Hobsbawm, Eric J. *Bandits.* London: Penguin Books, 1985 (original 1969).

————. "The Passion Narratives and Historical Criticism." *Theology* 75 (1972): 58–71.

————. *Primitive Rebels: Studies in Archaic Forms of Social Movement in the Nineteenth and Twentieth Centuries.* New York: W. W. Norton and Co., 1965.

Hoehner, Harold W. *Chronological Aspects of the Life of Christ.* Grand Rapids: Zondervan Publishing House, 1977.

Hofius, Otfried. "Unknown Sayings of Jesus." In *The Gospel and the Gospels,* ed. Peter Stuhlmacher, 336–60. Grand Rapids: Wm. B. Eerdmans Publishing Co., 1991.

Höistad, Ragnar. *Cynic Hero and Cynic King.* Uppsala: Bloms, 1948.

Hollenbach, Paul. "The Conversion of Jesus: From Jesus the Baptizer to Jesus the Healer." Aufstieg und Niedergang der römischen Welt 2.25. 196–219.

————. "The Historical Jesus Question in North America Today." *Biblical Theology Bulletin* 19 (1989): 11–22.

Hooker, Morna D. "On Using the Wrong Tool." *Theology* 75 (1972): 570–81.

Hoover, Roy W. "Answering the Critics: A Scholar Responds to *Jesus under Fire*." *The Fourth R* 8, nos. 5–6 (1995): 17–20.

———. "The Work of the Jesus Seminar." *The Fourth R* 9, nos. 5–6 (1996): 9–15.

Horbury, William. "The Messianic Associations of 'The Son of Man.'" *Journal of Theological Studies* 36 (1985): 34–53.

———. "The Passion Narratives and Historical Criticism." *Theology* 75 (1972): 58–71.

Horsley, Richard A. "Archaeology of Galilee and the Historical Context of Jesus." *Neotestamentica* 29 (1995): 211–29.

———. "The Death of Jesus." In *Studying the Historical Jesus: Evaluations of the State of Current Research,* ed. Bruce Chilton and Craig A. Evans, 395–423. Leiden: E. J. Brill, 1994.

———. "Ethics and Exegesis: 'Love Your Enemy' and the Doctrine of Nonviolence." In *The Love of Enemy and Nonretaliation in the New Testament,* ed. W. M. Swartley, 72–101. Louisville: Westminster/John Knox Press, 1992 (original 1986).

———. *Jesus and the Spiral of Violence: Popular Jewish Resistance in Roman Palestine.* San Francisco: Harper & Row, 1973.

———. "Jesus, Itinerant Cynic or Israelite Prophet?" In *Images of Jesus Today,* ed. James H. Charlesworth and W. P. Weaver, 68–97. Valley Forge, Pa.: Trinity Press International, 1994.

———. "Messianic Figures and Movements in First-Century Palestine." In *The Messiah: Developments in Earliest Judaism and Christianity,* ed. James H. Charlesworth, 276–95. Minneapolis: Fortress Press, 1992.

———. *Sociology and the Jesus Movement.* New York: Crossroad, 1989.

———. "What Has Galilee to Do with Jerusalem? Political Aspects of the Jesus Movement." *Hervormde Teologiese Studies* 52 (1996): 88–104.

Horsley, Richard A., and John S. Hanson. *Bandits, Prophets, and Messiahs: Popular Movements at the Time of Jesus.* Minneapolis: Winston Press, 1985.

Houlden, J. Leslie. *Jesus: A Question of Identity.* London: SPCK, 1992.

Hull, John M. *Hellenistic Magic and the Synoptic Tradition.* Studies in Biblical Theology 2/28. Naperville, Ill.: Alec R. Allenson, 1974.

Hultgren, Arland. "Jesus of Nazareth: Prophet, Visionary, Sage, or What?" *Dialog* 33 (1994): 263–73.

———. "The Use of Sources in the Quest for Jesus: What You Use Is What You Get." In *The Quest for Jesus and the Christian Faith,* ed. Frederick J. Gaiser, 33–48. St. Paul: Luther Seminary, 1997.

Hurst, L. D. "The Neglected Role of Semantics in the Search for the Aramaic Words of Jesus." In *The Historical Jesus: A Sheffield Reader,* ed. Craig A. Evans and Stanley E. Porter, 219–36. Sheffield: Sheffield Academic Press, 1995.

Hurtado, Larry. *One God, One Lord: Early Christian Devotion and Ancient Jewish Monotheism.* Grand Rapids: Wm. B. Eerdmans Publishing Co., 1988.

Jacobson, Arland. *The First Gospel: An Introduction to Q.* Sonoma, Calif.: Polebridge Press, 1992.

Jacobson, Diane. "Jesus as Wisdom in the New Testament." In *The Quest for Jesus and the Christian Faith,* ed. Frederick J. Gaiser, 72–93. St. Paul: Luther Seminary, 1997.

Jeremias, Joachim. *Jesus' Promise to the Nations.* Studies in Biblical Theology 24. London: SCM Press, 1958.

———. *New Testament Theology.* Vol. 1, *The Proclamation of Jesus.* New York: Charles Scribner's Sons, 1971.

Johnson, Elizabeth A. *Consider Jesus: Waves of Renewal in Christology.* New York: Crossroad, 1992.

Johnson, Luke Timothy. *The Real Jesus: The Misguided Quest for the Historical Jesus and the Truth of the Traditional Gospels.* San Francisco: HarperSanFransisco, 1996.

Johnson, Paul. "An Historian Looks at Jesus." In *Crisis in Christology: Essays in Quest of Resolution,* ed. William R. Farmer, 25–38. Livonia, Mich.: Dove Booksellers, 1995.

Juel, Donald H. *Messianic Exegesis: Christological Interpretation of the Old Testament in Early Christianity.* Philadelphia: Fortress Press, 1988.

———. "The Trial and Death of the Historical Jesus." In *The Quest for Jesus and the Christian Faith,* ed. Frederick J. Gaiser, 33–48. St. Paul: Luther Seminary, 1997.

Kähler, Martin. *The So-Called Historical Jesus and the Historic, Biblical Christ.* Philadelphia: Fortress Press, 1964 (original 1892).

Käsemann, Ernst. "Blind Alleys in the 'Jesus of History' Controversy." In *New Testament Questions of Today,* 23–65. Philadelphia: Fortress Press, 1969.

———. "The Problem of the Historical Jesus." In *Essays on New Testament Themes,* 15–47. Naperville, Ill.: Alec R. Allenson, 1964.

Kasper, Walter. *Jesus the Christ.* New York: Paulist Press, 1977.

Kaylor, R. David. *Jesus the Prophet: His Vision of the Kingdom on Earth.* Louisville: Westminster John Knox Press, 1994.

Kealy, Sean P. *Jesus and Politics.* Zacchaeus Studies. Collegeville, Minn.: Liturgical Press, 1990.

Keck, Leander E. *A Future for the Historical Jesus: The Place of Jesus in Preaching and Theology.* Nashville: Abingdon Press, 1971.

———. "The Second Coming of the Liberal Jesus." *Christian Century* 111 (1994): 784–87.

Kee, Howard C. "A Century of Quests for the Culturally Compatible Jesus." *Theology Today* 52 (1995): 17–28.

———. *Jesus in History.* 2d ed. New York: Harcourt Brace Jovanovich, 1977.

———. *Medicine, Miracle, and Magic in New Testament Times.* Society for New Testament Studies Monograph Series 55. Cambridge: Cambridge University Press, 1986.

———. *Miracle in the Early Christian World.* New Haven, Conn.: Yale University Press, 1983.

———. *What Can We Know about Jesus?* Cambridge: Cambridge University Press, 1990.

Keeley, Robin, ed. *Jesus 2000.* Oxford: Lion, 1989.

Keller, Catherine. "The Jesus of History and the Feminism of Theology." In *Jesus and Faith: A Conversation on the Work of John Dominic Crossan,* ed. Jeffrey Carlson and Robert A. Ludwig, 71–82. Maryknoll, N.Y.: Orbis Books, 1994.

Kelly, J. Landrum. *Conscientious Objections: Towards a Reconstruction of the Social and Political Philosophy of Jesus of Nazareth.* Toronto Studies in Theology 68. Lewiston, N.Y.: Edwin Mellen Press, 1994.

Kilpatrick, G. D. "Jesus, His Family, and His Disciples." In *The Historical Jesus: A Sheffield Reader,* ed. Craig A. Evans and Stanley E. Porter, 13–28. Sheffield: Sheffield Academic Press, 1995.

Kim, Seyoon. *The Son of Man as the Son of God.* Tübingen: Mohr, 1983.

King, Karen L. "Kingdom in the Gospel of Thomas." *Foundations and Facets Forum* 3, no. 1 (1987): 48–97.

Kissinger, W. S. *The Lives of Jesus: A History and Bibliography.* New York: Garland, 1985.

Klausner, Joseph. *Jesus of Nazareth: His Life, Times, and Teaching.* London: George Allen & Unwin, 1947 (original 1925).

Kloppenborg, John S. "Alms, Debt, and Divorce: Jesus' Ethics in Their Mediterranean Context." *Toronto Journal of Theology* 6 (1990): 182–200.

―――――. *The Formation of Q: Trajectories in Ancient Wisdom Collections.* Philadelphia: Fortress Press, 1987.

―――――. *Q Parallels: Synopsis, Critical Notes, and Concordance.* Sonoma, Calif.: Polebridge Press, 1988.

Kloppenborg, John S., ed. *The Shape of Q: Signal Essays on the Sayings Gospel.* Minneapolis: Fortress Press, 1994.

Kloppenborg, John, Marvin Meyer, Stephen Patterson, and Michael Steinhauser. *The Q-Thomas Reader.* Sonoma, Calif.: Polebridge Press, 1990.

Knibb, Michael. "The Exile in the Literature of the Intertestamental Period." *Heythrop Journal* 17 (1976): 253–72.

―――――. *The Qumran Community.* Cambridge: Cambridge University Press, 1987.

Knutsen, Mary M. "The Third Quest for the Historical Jesus: Introduction and Bibliography." In *The Quest for Jesus and the Christian Faith,* ed. Frederick J. Gaiser, 13–32. St. Paul: Luther Seminary, 1997.

Koch, Klaus. *The Rediscovery of Apocalyptic: A Polemical Work on a Neglected Area of Biblical Studies and Its Damaging Effects on Theology and Philosophy.* Studies in Biblical Theology 2.22. London: SCM Press, 1972.

Koester, Helmut. *Ancient Christian Gospels: Their History and Development.* Philadelphia: Trinity Press International, 1990.

―――――. "The Historical Jesus and the Cult of the *Kyrios Christos.*" *Harvard Divinity Bulletin* 24 (1995): 13–18.

―――――. "The Historical Jesus and the Historical Situation of the Quest: An Epilogue." In *Studying the Historical Jesus: Evaluations of the State of Current Research,* ed. Bruce Chilton and Craig A. Evans, 535–46. Leiden: E. J. Brill, 1994.

―――――. "Jesus the Victim." *Journal of Biblical Literature* 111 (1992): 3–15.

Leivestad, Ragnar. *Jesus in His Own Perspective: An Examination of His Sayings, Actions, and Eschatological Titles.* Minneapolis: Fortress Press, 1987.

Lenski, Gerhard. *Power and Privilege: A Theory of Social Stratification.* New York: McGraw-Hill, 1966.

Levine, Amy-Jill. "Who's Catering the Q Affair? Feminist Observations on Q Paraenesis." *Semeia* 50 (1990): 145–61.

Levine, Lee I., ed. *The Galilee in Late Antiquity.* New York: Jewish Theological Seminary, 1992.

Lieu, Judith. "'The Parting of the Ways': Theological Construct or Historical Reality?" *Journal for the Study of the New Testament* 56 (1994): 101–19.

Lohfink, Gerhard. *Jesus and Community.* Philadelphia: Fortress Press, 1984.

Luck, Georg. *Arcana Mundi: Magic and the Occult in the Greek and Roman Worlds.* Baltimore: Johns Hopkins, 1985.

Lüdemann, Gerd. *The Resurrection of Jesus: History, Experience, Theology.* Minneapolis: Fortress Press, 1994.

―――――. *What Really Happened to Jesus? A Historical Approach to the Resurrection.* Louisville: Westminster John Knox Press, 1996.

Ludwig, Robert A. "Reconstructing Jesus for a Dysfunctional Church: Crossan's Christology and Contemporary Spirituality." In *Jesus and Faith: A Conversation on the Work of John Dominic Crossan,* ed. Jeffrey Carlson and Robert A. Ludwig, 57–70. Maryknoll, N.Y.: Orbis Books, 1994.

Lunny, William J. *The Jesus Option.* Mahwah, N.J.: Paulist Press, 1994.

Maccoby, Hyam. *The Mythmaker: Paul and the Invention of Christianity.* London: Weidenfeld & Nicolson, 1980 (original 1973).

Mack, Burton L. *The Lost Gospel: The Book of Q and Christian Origins*. San Francisco: HarperSanFrancisco, 1993.

———. *A Myth of Innocence: Mark and Christian Origins*. Philadelphia: Fortress Press, 1988.

———. *Who Wrote the New Testament? The Making of the Christian Myth*. San Francisco: HarperSanFrancisco, 1995.

Maier, Paul L. *In the Fullness of Time: A Historian Looks at Christmas, Easter, and the Early Church*. San Francisco: HarperSanFrancisco, 1991.

Malina, Bruce J. *The Social World of Jesus and the Gospels*. New York: Routledge & Kegan Paul, 1996.

Manson, T. W. *The Servant-Messiah: A Study of the Public Ministry of Jesus*. Cambridge: Cambridge University Press, 1953.

———. *The Teaching of Jesus: Studies of Its Form and Content*. Cambridge: Cambridge University Press, 1931.

Marsh, John T. *Jesus in His Lifetime*. London: Sidgwick & Jackson, 1981.

Marshall, I. H. *The Origins of New Testament Christology*. Downers Grove, Ill.: Inter-Varsity Press, 1990.

Martin, David. "Jesus Christ and Modern Sociology." In *Crisis in Christology: Essays in Quest of Resolution,* ed. William R. Farmer, 29–46. Livonia, Mich.: Dove Booksellers, 1995.

Martin, Raymond A. *Studies in the Life and Ministry of the Historical Jesus*. New York: University Press of America, 1995.

McArthur, Harvey K. *The Quest through the Centuries: The Search for the Historical Jesus*. Philadelphia: Fortress Press, 1966.

McArthur, Harvey K., ed. *In Search of the Historical Jesus: A Source Book*. New York: Charles Scribner's Sons, 1969.

McAteer, Michael R., and Michael G. Steinhauser. *The Man in the Scarlet Robe: Two Thousand Years of Searching for Jesus*. Etobicoke, Ont.: United Church Publishing House, 1996.

McCann, Dennis P. "Doing Business with the Historical Jesus." In *Jesus and Faith: A Conversation on the Work of John Dominic Crossan*, ed. Jeffrey Carlson and Robert A. Ludwig, 132–41. Maryknoll, N.Y.: Orbis Books, 1994.

McCown, C. C. *The Search for the Real Jesus: A Century of Historical Study*. New York: Charles Scribner's Sons, 1940.

McGaughy, Lane C. "The Search for the Historical Jesus: Why Start with the Sayings?" *The Fourth R* 9, nos. 5–6 (1996): 17–26.

McKnight, Scott. "Who Is Jesus? An Introduction to Jesus Studies." In *Jesus under Fire: Modern Scholarship Reinvents the Historical Jesus,* ed. Michael J. Wilkins and J. P. Moreland, 51–72. Grand Rapids: Zondervan Publishing House, 1995.

Meier, John P. "The Circle of the Twelve: Did It Exist during Jesus' Public Ministry?" *Journal of Biblical Literature* 116 (1997): 635–72.

———. "Dividing Lines in Jesus Research Today: Through Dialectical Negation to a Positive Sketch." *Interpretation* 50 (1996): 355–72.

———. *A Marginal Jew: Rethinking the Historical Jesus*. Vol. 1, *The Roots of the Problem and the Person*. New York: Doubleday, 1991.

———. *A Marginal Jew: Rethinking the Historical Jesus*. Vol. 2, *Mentor, Message, and Miracles*. New York: Doubleday, 1994.

———. "On Retrojecting Later Questions from Later Texts: A Reply to Richard Bauckham." *Catholic Biblical Quarterly* 59 (1997): 511–27.

————. "Reflections on Jesus-of-History Research Today." In *Jesus' Jewishness: Exploring the Place of Jesus within Early Judaism,* ed. James H. Charlesworth, 84–107. New York: Crossroad, 1991.

Mendels, Doron. "Jesus and the Politics of His Day." In *Images of Jesus Today,* ed. James H. Charlesworth and W. P. Weaver, 98–112. Valley Forge, Pa.: Trinity Press International, 1994.

Meyer, Ben. *The Aims of Jesus.* London: SCM Press, 1979.

————. "Appointed Deed, Appointed Doer: Jesus and the Scriptures." In *Crisis in Christology: Essays in Quest of Resolution,* ed. William R. Farmer, 271–310. Livonia, Mich.: Dove Booksellers, 1995.

————. *Christus Faber: The Master Builder and the House of God.* Princeton Theological Monograph Series 29. Allison Park, Pa.: Pickwick Publications, 1992.

————. *Critical Realism and the New Testament.* Princeton Theological Monograph Series 17. Allison Park, Pa.: Pickwick Publications, 1989.

————. "Jesus' Ministry and Self-Understanding." In *Studying the Historical Jesus: Evaluations of the State of Current Research,* ed. Bruce Chilton and Craig A. Evans, 337–52. Leiden: E. J. Brill, 1994.

————. "'Phases' in Jesus' Mission." *Gregorianum* 73 (1992): 5–17.

Michaels, J. Ramsey. "The Kingdom of God and the Historical Jesus." In *The Kingdom of God in Twentieth Century Interpretation,* ed. Wendell Willis, 109–18. Peabody, Mass.: Hendrickson Publishers, 1987.

Miller, Robert J. "Historical Method and the Deeds of Jesus: The Test Case of the Temple Demonstration." *Foundations and Facets Forum* 8, nos. 1–2 (1992): 5–30.

————. "The Jesus Seminar and Its Critics: What Is Really at Stake?" *The Fourth R* 10, nos. 1–2 (1997): 17–27.

Miller, Robert J., ed. *The Complete Gospels: Annotated Scholars Version.* Rev. ed. San Francisco: HarperSanFrancisco, 1994.

Miller, Robert J., and Ben Witherington III. "Battling over the Jesus Seminar." *Bible Review* 13 (April 1997): 18–26.

Mitchell, Stephen. *The Gospel according to Jesus: A New Translation and Guide to His Essential Teachings for Believers and Unbelievers.* New York: HarperCollins, 1990.

Moltmann, Jürgen. *The Way of Jesus Christ: Christology in Messianic Dimensions.* San Francisco: HarperSanFrancisco, 1990.

Moo, Douglas J. "Jesus and the Authority of the Mosaic Law." In *The Historical Jesus: A Sheffield Reader,* ed. Craig A. Evans and Stanley E. Porter, 83–130. Sheffield: Sheffield Academic Press, 1995.

Moule, C. F. D. "The Gravamen against Jesus." In *Jesus, the Gospels, and the Church,* ed. E. P. Sanders, 177–95. Macon, Ga.: Mercer University Press, 1987.

————. *The Origin of Christology.* Cambridge: Cambridge Univesity Press, 1977.

Neil, John C. *Messiah: Six Lectures on the Ministry of Jesus.* Cambridge: Cochrane Press, 1980.

————. *Who Did Jesus Think He Was?* Leiden: E. J. Brill, 1995.

Neirynck, Frans. "The Historical Jesus: Reflections on an Inventory." *Ephemerides theologicae lovanienses* 70 (1994): 221–34.

Neusner, Jacob, William S. Green, and Ernst Frerichs, eds. *Judaisms and Their Messiahs at the Turn of the Era.* Cambridge: Cambridge University Press, 1987.

Nolan, Albert. *Jesus before Christianity.* Rev. ed. Maryknoll, N.Y.: Orbis Books, 1992.

Oakman, Douglas E. *Jesus and the Economic Questions of His Day.* Studies in the Bible and Early Christianity 8. Lewiston, N.Y.: Edwin Mellen Press, 1986.

O'Collins, Gerald. *Christology: A Biblical, Historical, and Systematic Study of Jesus.* Oxford: Oxford University Press, 1995.

———. *The Resurrection of Jesus Christ: Some Contemporary Issues.* Milwaukee: Marquette University Press, 1993.

O'Neill, John C. *Who Did Jesus Think He Was?* Leiden: E. J. Brill, 1995.

Osiek, Caroline. "Jesus and Galilee." *Bible Today* 34 (1996): 153–59.

Ott, Heinrich. "The Historical Jesus and the Ontology of History." In *The Historical Jesus and the Kerygmatic Christ: Essays on the New Quest of the Historical Jesus,* ed. Carl E. Braaten and Roy A. Harrisville, 142–71. Nashville: Abingdon Press, 1964.

Pagels, Elaine. *The Gnostic Gospels.* New York: Random House, 1980.

Pals, D. L. *The Victorian "Lives" of Jesus.* Trinity University Monograph Series. San Antonio: Trinity University Press, 1982.

Parrinder, E. Geoffrey. *Son of Joseph: The Parentage of Jesus.* Edinburgh: T. & T. Clark, 1992.

Patterson, Stephen J. "The End of the Apocalypse: Rethinking the Eschatological Jesus." *Theology Today* 52 (1995): 29–48.

———. *The Gospel of Thomas and Jesus.* Sonoma, Calif.: Polebridge Press, 1993.

———. "Sources for a Life of Jesus." In *The Search for Jesus: Modern Scholarship Looks at the Gospel,* ed. Hershel Shanks, 9–36. Washington, D.C.: Biblical Archaeology Society, 1994.

Pearson, Birger. "The Gospel according to the Jesus Seminar." Institute for Antiquity and Christianity Occasional Paper 35. Claremont, Calif.: Institute for Antiquity and Christianity, 1996.

Perelmuter, H. Goren. "Jesus the Jew: A Jewish Perspective." *New Theology Review* 7 (1994): 27–36.

Perkins, Pheme. *Jesus as Teacher.* Cambridge: Cambridge University Press, 1990.

———. "The Resurrection of Jesus of Nazareth." In *Studying the Historical Jesus: Evaluations of the State of Current Research,* ed. Bruce Chilton and Craig A. Evans, 423–42. Leiden: E. J. Brill, 1994.

Perrin, Norman. *Jesus and the Language of the Kingdom: Symbol and Metaphor in New Testament Interpretation.* Philadelphia: Fortress Press, 1976.

———. *The Kingdom of God in the Teaching of Jesus.* Philadelphia: Fortress Press, 1963.

———. *Rediscovering the Teaching of Jesus.* New York: Harper & Row, 1967.

Petersen, W. L. *Tatian's Diatessaron: Its Creation, Dissemination, Significance, and History in Scholarship.* Supplements to Vigilae Christianae 25. Leiden: E. J. Brill, 1994.

Piper, Ronald A., ed. *The Gospel behind the Gospels: Current Studies on Q.* Novum Testamentum Supplements 75. Leiden: E. J. Brill, 1995.

Pokorny, Petr. *The Genesis of Christology.* Edinburgh: T. & T. Clark, 1987.

Porter, Stanley E. "Jesus and the Use of Greek in Galilee." In *Studying the Historical Jesus: Evaluations of the State of Current Research,* ed. Bruce Chilton and Craig A. Evans, 123–54. Leiden: E. J. Brill, 1994.

Powell, Evan. *The Unfinished Gospel: Notes on the Quest for the Historical Jesus.* Westlake Village, Calif.: Symposium Books, 1994.

Powelson, M., and R. Riegert, eds. *The Lost Gospel Q: The Original Sayings of Jesus.* Berkeley: Ulysses, 1996.

Rajak, Tessa. *Josephus: The Historian and His Society.* London: Duckworth, 1983.

Reimarus, *Fragments.* Ed. C. H. Talbert. Lives of Jesus Series. Philadelphia: Fortress Press, 1970 (original 1778).

Reiser, Marius. *Jesus and Judgment: The Eschatological Proclamation in Its Jewish Context.* Minneapolis: Fortress Press, 1997.

Remus, Harold E. *Pagan-Christian Conflict over Miracle in the Second Century.* Patristic Monograph Series 10. Cambridge, Mass.: Philadelphia Patristic Foundation, 1983.

Renan, Ernst. *The Life of Jesus.* New York: Random House, 1972 (original 1863).

Reumann, John. *Jesus in the Church's Gospels: Modern Scholarship and the Earliest Sources.* Philadelphia: Fortress Press, 1968.

Riches, John K. *Jesus and the Transformation of Judaism.* London: Darton, Longman & Todd, 1980.

————. "The Social World of Jesus." *Interpretation* 50 (1996): 383–93.

Riesner, Rainer. "Jesus as Preacher and Teacher." In *Jesus and the Oral Gospel Tradition,* Journal for the Study of the New Testament Monograph Series 64, ed. Henry Wansbrough, 185–210. Sheffield: Sheffield Academic Press, 1991.

Rivkin, Ellis. *What Crucified Jesus? The Political Execution of a Charismatic.* Nashville: Abingdon Press, 1984.

Robinson, James M. "Jesus from Easter to Valentinus (or to the Apostles' Creed)." *Journal of Biblical Literature* 101 (1982): 5–37.

————. *The Nag Hammadi Library.* 3d ed. San Francisco: Harper & Row, 1990.

————. *A New Quest of the Historical Jesus.* Studies in Biblical Theology 25. London: SCM Press, 1959.

Robinson, James M., and Helmut Koester. *Trajectories through Early Christianity.* Philadelphia: Fortress Press, 1971.

Robinson, John A. T. *Jesus and His Coming: The Emergence of a Doctrine.* Philadelphia: Westminster Press, 1979.

Rowdon, Harold, ed. *Christ the Lord: Studies in Christology Presented to Donald Guthrie.* Downers Grove, Ill.: InterVarsity Press, 1982.

Sacchi, Paolo. "Recovering Jesus' Formative Background." In *Jesus and the Dead Sea Scrolls,* ed. James H. Charlesworth, 123–39. New York: Doubleday, 1992.

Sanders, E. P. "Defending the Indefensible." *Journal of Biblical Literature* 110 (1991): 463–77.

————. *The Historical Figure of Jesus.* London: Penguin Press, 1993.

————. *Jesus and Judaism.* Philadelphia: Fortress Press, 1985.

————. "Jesus and the First Table of the Jewish Law." In *Jews and Christians Speak of Jesus,* ed. Arthur E. Zannoni, 55–76. Minneapolis: Fortress Press, 1994.

————. "Jesus and the Sinners." In *The Historical Jesus: A Sheffield Reader,* ed. Craig A. Evans and Stanley E. Porter, 29–60. Sheffield: Sheffield Academic Press, 1995.

————. "Jesus in Historical Context." *Theology Today* 50 (1993): 429–48.

————. *Jewish Law from Jesus to the Mishnah: Five Studies.* Philadelphia: Trinity Press International, 1990.

————. *Judaism: Practice and Belief, 63 B.C.E.–66 C.E.* Philadelphia: Trinity Press International, 1992.

Schaberg, Jane. "A Feminist Experience of Historical Jesus Scholarship." *Continuum* 3 (1994): 266–85.

————. *The Illegitimacy of Jesus: A Feminist Theological Interpretation of the Infancy Narratives.* Sheffield: Sheffield Academic Press, 1995.

Schiffman, Lawrence. "The Jewishness of Jesus: Commandments concerning Interpersonal Relations." In *Jews and Christians Speak of Jesus,* ed. Arthur E. Zannoni, 37–54. Minneapolis: Fortress Press, 1994.

Schillebeeckx, Edward. *Jesus: An Experiment in Christology.* New York: Seabury Press, 1979.

Schmidt, Daryl D. "The Witness of Gospel Fragments." *The Fourth R* 9, nos. 1–2 (1996): 3–8, 21.

Schnabel, Eckhard J. "Jesus and the Beginnings of the Mission to the Gentiles." In *Jesus of Nazareth, Lord and Christ: Essays on the Historical Jesus and New Testament Christology,* ed. Joel B. Green and Max Turner, 37–58. Grand Rapids: Wm. B. Eerdmans Publishing Co., 1994.

Schnackenburg, Rudolf. *Jesus in the Gospels: A Biblical Christology.* Louisville: Westminster John Knox Press, 1995.

Schweitzer, Albert. *The Kingdom of God and Primitive Christianity.* Ed. U. Neuenschwander. London: A & C Black, 1968.

———. *The Mystery of the Kingdom of God.* London: A & C Black, 1925 (original 1901).

———. *The Quest of the Historical Jesus: A Critical Study of the Progress from Reimarus to Wrede.* New York: Macmillan, 1968 (original 1906).

Schweizer, Eduard. *Jesus Christ: The Man from Nazareth and the Exalted Lord.* Macon, Ga.: Mercer University Press, 1987.

———. *Jesus the Parable of God: What Do We Really Know about Jesus?* Allison Park, Pa.: Pickwick Publications, 1994.

Scott, Bernard Brandon. "From Reimarus to Crossan: Stages in a Quest." *Currents in Research: Biblical Studies* 2 (1994): 253–80.

———. "The Reappearance of Parables." *The Fourth R* 10, nos. 1–2 (1997): 3–14.

———. "to impose is not/To Discover: Methodology in John Dominic Crossan's *The Historical Jesus.*" In *Jesus and Faith: A Conversation on the Work of John Dominic Crossan,* ed. Jeffrey Carlson and Robert A. Ludwig, 22–30. Maryknoll, N.Y.: Orbis Books, 1994.

Seeley, David. "Jesus and the Cynics Revisited." *Journal of Biblical Literature* 116 (1997): 704–12.

———. "Jesus' Death in Q." *New Testament Studies* 38 (1992): 222–34.

Segal, Alan F. "Jesus and First-Century Judaism." In *Jesus at 2000,* ed. Marcus J. Borg, 55–73. Boulder, Colo.: Westview Press, 1997.

———. "Jesus the Revolutionary." In *Jesus' Jewishness: Exploring the Place of Jesus within Early Judaism,* ed. James H. Charlesworth, 199–225. New York: Crossroad, 1991.

Segundo, Juan Luis. *The Historical Jesus of the Synoptics.* Maryknoll, N.Y.: Orbis Books, 1985.

Senior, Donald. "The Never Ending Quest for Jesus." *Bible Today* 34 (1996): 141–47.

Shanks, Hershel, ed. *The Search for Jesus: Modern Scholarship Looks at the Gospels.* Washington, D.C.: Biblical Archaeology Society, 1994.

Sheehan, Thomas. *The First Coming: How the Kingdom of God Became Christianity.* New York: Random House, 1988.

———. "The Resurrection: An Obstacle to Faith?" *The Fourth R* 8, no. 2 (1995): 3–9.

Shorto, Russell. *Gospel Truth: The New Image of Jesus Emerging from Science and History, and Why It Matters.* New York: Riverhead Books, 1997.

Sloyan, Gerard S. *The Crucifixion of Jesus: History, Myth, Faith.* Minneapolis: Fortress Press, 1995.

Smith, Huston. "Jesus and the World's Religions." In *Jesus at 2000,* ed. Marcus J. Borg, 107–20. Boulder, Colo.: Westview Press, 1997.

Smith, Morton. *Jesus the Magician.* New York: Harper & Row, 1978.

Sobrino, Jon. *Jesus the Liberator: A Historical-Theological Reading of Jesus of Nazareth.* Maryknoll, N.Y.: Orbis Books, 1993.

Sommer, Benjamin D. "Did Prophecy Cease? Evaluating a Reevaluation." *Journal of Biblical Literature* 115 (1996): 31–47.

Spong, John S. *Born of a Woman: A Bishop Rethinks the Birth of Jesus.* San Francisco: HarperSanFrancisco, 1992.

———. *Resurrection: Myth or Reality? A Bishop's Search for the Origins of Christianity.* San Francisco: HarperSanFrancisco, 1994.

Stanton, Graham N. *Gospel Truth? New Light on Jesus and the Gospels.* Valley Forge, Pa.: Trinity Press International, 1995.

———. "Jesus of Nazareth: A Magician and a False Prophet Who Deceived God's People?" In *Jesus of Nazareth: Lord and Christ: Essays on the Historical Jesus and New Testament Christology,* ed. Joel B. Green and Max Turner, 164–80. Grand Rapids: Wm. B. Eerdmans Publishing Co., 1994.

Stauffer, Ethelbert. *Jesus and His Story.* London: SCM Press, 1960.

———. "The Relevance of the Historical Jesus." In *The Historical Jesus and the Kerygmatic Christ: Essays on the New Quest of the Historical Jesus,* ed. Carl E. Braaten and Roy A. Harrisville, 43–53. Nashville: Abingdon Press, 1964.

Stein, Robert H. "The 'Criteria' for Authenticity." In *Gospel Perspectives 1: Studies of History and Tradition in the Four Gospels,* ed. Richard T. France and David Wenham, 253–63. Sheffield: JSOT Press, 1980.

———. *Jesus the Messiah: A Survey of the Life of Christ.* Downers Grove, Ill.: InterVarsity Press, 1996.

———. *The Method and Message of Jesus' Teachings.* Rev. ed. Louisville: Westminster John Knox Press, 1994.

Strain, Charles R. "Sapiential Eschatology and Social Transformation: Crossan's Jesus, Socially Engaged Buddhism, and Liberation Theology." In *Jesus and Faith: A Conversation on the Work of John Dominic Crossan,* ed. Jeffrey Carlson and Robert A. Ludwig, 115–31. Maryknoll, N.Y.: Orbis Books, 1994.

Strauss, David Friedrich. *The Life of Jesus Critically Examined.* Philadelphia: Fortress Press, 1972 (original 1835–36).

Strecker, Georg. "The Historical and Theological Problem of the Jesus Question." *Toronto Journal of Theology* 6 (1990): 201–23.

Stroker, William D., ed. *Extracanonical Sayings of Jesus.* Atlanta: Scholars Press, 1989.

Strudum, J. M. "The 'Unconventionality' of Jesus from the Perspective of a Diverse Audience: Evaluating Crossan's Historical Jesus." *Neotestamentica* 29 (1995): 313–23.

Stuhlmacher, Peter. *Jesus of Nazareth—Christ of Faith.* Peabody, Mass.: Hendrickson Publishers, 1993.

———. "Jesus of Nazareth—The Christ of Our Faith." In *Crisis in Christology: Essays in Quest of Resolution,* ed. William R. Farmer, 1–12. Livonia, Mich.: Dove Booksellers, 1995.

Stuhlmacher, Peter, ed. *The Gospel and the Gospels.* Grand Rapids: Wm. B. Eerdmans Publishing Co., 1991 (original 1983).

Talbert, Charles H. "Political Correctness Invades Jesus Research." *Perspectives in Religious Studies* 21 (1994): 245–52.

Tatum, W. Barnes. *In Quest of Jesus: A Guidebook.* Atlanta: John Knox Press, 1982.

———. *John the Baptist and Jesus: A Report of the Jesus Seminar.* Sonoma, Calif.: Polebridge Press, 1993.

Taussig, Hal. "The Jesus Seminar and Its Public." *Foundations and Facets Forum* 2, no. 2 (1986): 69–78.

Taylor, Walter F. "Jesus within His Social World: Insights from Archaeology, Sociology, and Cultural Anthropology." In *The Quest for Jesus and the Christian Faith,* ed. Frederick J. Gaiser, 49–71. St. Paul: Luther Seminary, 1997.

———. "New Quests for the Historical Jesus." *Trinity Seminary Review* 15 (1992): 69–83.

Telford, William R. "Major Trends and Interpretive Issues in the Study of Jesus." In *Studying the Historical Jesus: Evaluations of the State of Current Research,* ed. Bruce Chilton and Craig A. Evans, 33–75. Leiden: E. J. Brill, 1994.

Thatcher, Adrian. "Resurrection and Rationality." In *The Resurrection of Jesus Christ,* ed. Paul Avis, 171–86. London: Darton, Longman & Todd, 1993.

Theissen, Gerd. *The Gospels in Context: Social and Political History in the Synoptic Tradition.* Minneapolis: Fortress Press, 1991.

———. *Sociology of Early Palestinian Christianity.* Philadelphia: Fortress Press, 1978.

Theissen, Gerd, and Annette Metz. *The Historical Jesus: A Comprehensive Guide.* Minneapolis: Fortress Press, 1998.

Torjeson, Karen Jo. "'You Are the Christ': Five Portraits of Jesus from the Early Church." In *Jesus at 2000,* ed. Marcus J. Borg, 73–88. Boulder, Colo.: Westview Press, 1997.

Tuckett, Christopher M. "A Cynic Q?" *Biblica* 70 (1989): 349–76.

———. *Q and the History of Earliest Christianity: Studies on Q.* Edinburgh: T. & T. Clark, 1996.

Twelftree, Graham. *Jesus the Exorcist: A Contribution to the Study of the Historical Jesus.* Peabody, Mass.: Hendrickson Publishers, 1993.

———. "Jesus in Jewish Traditions." In *Gospel Perspectives 5: The Jesus Tradition outside the Gospels,* ed. David Wenham, 289–343. Sheffield: JSOT Press, 1985.

Vaage, Leif. *Galilean Upstarts: Jesus' First Followers according to Q.* Valley Forge, Pa.: Trinity Press International, 1994.

———. *Q: The Ethos and Ethics of an Itinerant Intelligence.* Ann Arbor, Mich.: University Microfilms, 1987.

———. "Q¹ and the Historical Jesus: Some Peculiar Sayings (7:33–34; 9:57–58; 59–60; 14:26–27)." *Foundations and Facets Forum* 5, no. 2 (1989): 159–76.

van Beeck, Frans Jozef. "The Quest of the Historical Jesus: Origins, Achievements, and the Specter of Diminishing Returns." In *Jesus and Faith: A Conversation on the Work of John Dominic Crossan,* ed. Jeffrey Carlson and Robert A. Ludwig, 83–99. Maryknoll, N.Y.: Orbis Books, 1994.

Vermes, Geza. *The Gospel of Jesus the Jew.* Newcastle: University of Newcastle upon Tyne, 1981.

———. *Jesus and the World of Judaism.* London: SCM Press, 1983.

———. *Jesus the Jew: A Historian's Reading of the Gospels.* London: Collins, 1973.

———. *The Religion of Jesus the Jew.* Minneapolis: Fortress Press, 1993.

Viviano, Benedict T. "The Historical Jesus in the Doubly Attested Sayings: An Experiment." *Revue Biblique* 103 (1996): 367–410.

Wallis, Ian G. *The Faith of Jesus Christ in Early Christian Traditions.* Society for New Testament Studies Monograph Series 84. Cambridge: Cambridge University Press, 1995.

Wansbrough, Henry, ed. *Jesus and the Oral Gospel Tradition.* Journal for the Study of the New Testament Supplement Series 64. Sheffield: Sheffield Academic Press, 1991.

Watson, Alan. *The Trial of Jesus.* Athens: University of Georgia Press, 1995.

Webb, Robert L. *John the Baptizer and Prophet: A Socio-Historical Study.* Journal for the Study of the New Testament Supplement Series 62. Sheffield: Sheffield Academic Press, 1991.

————. "John the Baptist and His Relationship with Jesus." In *Studying the Historical Jesus: Evaluations of the State of Current Research,* ed. Bruce Chilton and Craig A. Evans, 179–230. Leiden: E. J. Brill, 1994.

Weiss, Johannes. *Jesus' Proclamation of the Kingdom of God.* Philadelphia: Fortress Press, 1972 (original 1892).

Wells, G. A. *Did Jesus Exist?* London: Prometheus Books, 1975.

————. *The Historical Evidence for Jesus.* Buffalo, N.Y.: Prometheus Books, 1982.

Wengst, Klaus. *Pax Romana and the Peace of Jesus Christ.* Philadelphia: Fortress Press, 1987.

Wenham, David. "Paul's Use of the Jesus Tradition: Three Samples." In *Gospel Perspectives 5: The Jesus Tradition outside the Gospels,* ed. David Wenham, 7–38. Sheffield: JSOT Press, 1985.

Wenham, David, ed. *Gospel Perspectives 5: The Jesus Tradition outside the Gospels.* Sheffield: JSOT Press, 1985.

Wenham, David, and Craig Blomberg, eds. *Gospel Perspectives 6: The Miracles of Jesus.* Sheffield: JSOT Press, 1986.

Wiebe, B. *Messianic Ethics: Jesus' Proclamation of the Kingdom of God and the Church in Response.* Waterloo, Ont.: Herald, 1992.

Wilkins, Michael J., and J. P. Moreland, eds. *Jesus under Fire: Modern Scholarship Reinvents the Historical Jesus.* Grand Rapids: Zondervan Publishing House, 1995.

Willis, Wendell, ed. *The Kingdom of God in Twentieth Century Interpretation.* Peabody, Mass.: Hendrickson Publishers, 1987.

Wilson, Ian. *Jesus: The Evidence—The Latest Research and Discoveries.* 2d ed. San Francisco: HarperSanFrancisco, 1997.

Wink, Walter. *John the Baptist in the Gospel Tradition.* Society for New Testament Monograph Series 7. Cambridge: Cambridge University Press, 1968.

————. "Neither Passivity nor Violence: Jesus' Third Way Out (Matt. 5.38–42 par.)." In *The Love of Enemy and Nonretaliation in the New Testament,* ed. Willard M. Swartley, 102–25. Louisville: Westminster/John Knox Press, 1992.

Winter, Paul. *On the Trial of Jesus.* Berlin: Walter de Gruyter, 1974 (original 1961).

Winton, Alan P. *The Proverbs of Jesus.* Journal for the Study of the New Testament Supplement Series 35. Sheffield: Sheffield Academic Press, 1990.

Witherington III, Ben. *The Christology of Jesus.* Minneapolis: Fortress Press, 1990.

————. *Jesus, Paul, and the End of the World: A Comparative Study in New Testament Eschatology.* Downers Grove, Ill.: InterVarsity Press, 1992.

————. *The Jesus Quest: The Third Search for the Jew of Nazareth.* Downers Grove, Ill.: InterVarsity Press, 1995.

————. *Jesus the Sage: The Pilgrimage of Wisdom.* Minneapolis: Fortress Press, 1994.

Wrede, William. *The Messianic Secret.* London: James Clarke, 1971 (original 1901).

Wright, N. T. "Five Gospels but No Gospel: Jesus and the Seminar." In *Crisis in Christology: Essays in Quest of Resolution,* ed. William R. Farmer, 115–58. Livonia, Mich.: Dove Booksellers, 1995.

————. "How Jesus Saw Himself." *Bible Review* 12 (June 1996): 22–29.

————. "Jesus." In *Early Christian Thought in Its Jewish Context,* ed. J. P. M. Sweet and J. M. G. Barclay, 43–58. Cambridge: Cambridge University Press, 1996.

————. *Jesus and the Victory of God.* Christian Origins and the Question of God 2. Minneapolis: Fortress Press, 1996.

————. *The New Testament and the People of God.* Christian Origins and the Question of God 1. Minneapolis: Fortress Press, 1992.

————. *The Original Jesus.* Grand Rapids: Wm. B. Eerdmans Publishing Co., 1996.

————. *Who Was Jesus?* Grand Rapids: Wm. B. Eerdmans Publishing Co., 1992.

Yamauchi, Edwin M. "Jesus outside the New Testament: What Is the Evidence?" In *Jesus under Fire: Modern Scholarship Reinvents the Historical Jesus,* ed. Michael J. Wilkins and J. P. Moreland, 207–30. Grand Rapids: Zondervan Publishing House, 1995.

————. "Magic or Miracle? Disease, Demons, and Exorcisms." In *Gospel Perspectives 6: The Miracles of Jesus,* ed. David Wenham and Craig Blomberg, 89–184. Sheffield: JSOT Press, 1986.

Yarbrough, Robert W. "Modern Wise Men Encounter Jesus." *Christianity Today* (December 12, 1994): 38–45.

Yoder, John H. *The Politics of Jesus: Agnus Noster.* 2d ed. Grand Rapids: Wm. B. Eerdmans Publishing Co., 1994.

Young, Brad H. *Jesus and His Jewish Parables: Rediscovering the Roots of Jesus' Teaching.* Mahwah, N.J.: Paulist Press, 1989.

————. *Jesus the Jewish Theologian.* Peabody, Mass.: Hendrickson Publishers, 1995.

Young, Norman H. "Jesus and the Sinners: Some Queries." *Journal for the Study of the New Testament* 24 (1985): 73–75.

Zannoni, Arthur E., ed. *Jews and Christians Speak of Jesus.* Minneapolis: Fortress Press, 1994.

Zeitlin, Irving M. *Jesus and the Judaism of His Time.* Oxford: Basil Blackwell Publisher, 1988.

INDEX OF SCRIPTURE AND ANCIENT SOURCES

This index does not include the biblical references cited in the list *Contents of Q, M, and L* on pages 39–42.

BIBLICAL TEXTS

OLD TESTAMENT

Leviticus
16   196 n. 38
16:7–10   98
16:21–22   98
19:2   108, 198 n. 36

Deuteronomy
13   159

1 Kings
22   154

Job
28   60

Psalms
22   125
22:18   92

Proverbs
1 9   29
1   60
3   60
8–9   59
8   60
8:14 -36   59
9   60

Isaiah
11:1–3   59
20:3   120
40–55   160

Jeremiah
19:1–13   120
27:1–7   120

Ezekiel
1   162

Daniel
1   162
7   165, 205 n. 46

Amos
8:9   92

Zechariah
9:9   120
9:9–10   198, n. 43

APOCRYPHA

Sirach
1   60
23:1   58
23:4   58
24   60
51:10   58

Wisdom of Solomon
2.13   59
2:16   59
4:10–15   59
8–9   59
10:10   58
14:3   58

NEW TESTAMENT

Matthew
3:10–12   121
3:11   136
3:13–15   47
4:1–11   177
4:15   171
4:17   123, 155
5–7   156
5:5   48
5:11–12   62
5:13   68
5:21–28   129
5:34–37   35
5:38–48   35
5:39   48, 53, 68
5:39–41   21
5:40   68
5:41   68
5:42   52
5:44   52
5:44–48   21
5:45   106
6:9   57
6:25–33   59, 63
6:26   61, 106
7:3–5   48
7:13–14   21
8:5–13   12, 141
8:8–9   12
8:11–12   139
10:9 -10   63
10:10   34
10:17–22   17
10.23   17, 139
10:37   52
11,2–6   120, 138, 139
11:7–11   138
11:9   136
11:12   21
11:16–19   21, 59, 138
11:19   59, 123
11:25–27   59
12:27   57, 105
12:28   56, 105, 120
13:24–30   54, 89
13:31–32   45
13:33   89
13:44   7, 103
13:44–46   21
16:27–28   120
18:3   86
18:23–35   21, 52
19:3–9   59
19:28   119
20:1–16   21, 106, 128
21:12–17   12
21:28–32   21

Matthew (*continued*)

21:28–31	70
21:31	122
22:1–10	128
22:1–4	21
22:34–40	36
23:8–9	52
23:9	28
23:24	48
23:37–39	59 (2x), 159
24:3	205 n. 46
24:27	205 n. 46
24:37	205 n. 46
24:39	205 n. 46
25:14–30	161
26:11	4
27:37	14
27:46	14
27:57–61	93
28:11–15	14
28:20	4

Mark

1:10	104
1:11	55
1:15	17, 123, 155
1:23–25	24
1:34	25
1:43–44	24
1:45	24
2:1–3:6	38
2:1–12	89,141
2:13–15	142
2:13–17	47
2:17	123
2:18–19	63, 157
2:18–20	139
2:23–28	122
3:1–6	201 n. 88
3:11–12	24
3:20–30	106
3:22	57
3:24–26	21
3:27	21, 56, 139
3:35	52
4–8	38
4:1–9	155
4:3–8	21
4:11	24, 104
4:26–29	21
4:30–32	21
5:1	191 n. 71
5:1–13	90
5:1–17	196 n. 30
5:1–20	71, 141
5:13	57

5:21–43	141
5:27–32	111
5:41	57
5:43	24
6:4	48, 154
6:8–9	62
6:8–10	63
6:13	15
6:14	57
6:32–44	141
7:15	21, 126
7:19	122
7:24–30	140
7:34	57
7:36	24
8:11–12	121
8:22–26	57, 141
8:23	15
8:27–29	184
8:27–30	121
8:30	24
8:31	159
8:31–33	17
8:34	68, 107
8:35	21
9:1	139, 174
9:2–4	105
9:9	24
9:1	174
9:14–29	140
9:38–39	105
9:49	49
10:2–9	34
10:11–12	49
10:13–15	89
10:13–16	86
10:17–26	62
10:23	21
10:25	21
10:31	21
10:32	105
10:38–40	159
10:43–44	52
10:45	98
10:46–52	141
11:1–10	120
11:15	118
11:15–19	12, 92
12:1–12	21, 159
12:17	45, 68
12:28–34	36
12:34	49
13	38, 163, 165
13:1–2	118
13:24–25	157
13:24–30	109, 120

13:26	205 n. 46
13:30	139, 174
14–16	38
14:3–9	159
14:22–25	120
14:25	125, 139
14:32–42	35
14:36	47, 105
14:57–59	118
14:58	92
14:61	105
14:62	68
15:24	92
15:33	92
15:34	68
15:42–47	93

Luke

2:41–51	23, 30
3:8	137
4:1–13	104
5:32	123
6:12	105
6:20	52, 54, 68, 109
6:21	139
6:24	52, 109
6:26	61
6:27	68
6:30	62
6:34–35	52
6:36	198 n. 36
7:1–10	12, 55, 105
7:6–8	12–13
7:11–17	141
7:22	141, 144
7:28	91
7:31–34	123
7:31–35	138
7:33–34	63
7:35	28–29
8:2	141
9:3	63
9:60	21
9:62	21
10:17–18	104
10:17–20	121
10:19	105
10:23	139
10:25–28	36
10:29–37	21
10:30–37	39
11:2	139
11:2–4	21
11:4	52
11:5–8	21
11:20	21, 139

11:27–28	89	**Acts**		**NON-CANONICAL**		
12:8–9	109	1:15–26	142	**GOSPELS**		
12:49–50	159	3:22	154			
12:51–53	89	5:36–37	112	**Gospel of Peter**		
13:20–21	21	12:2	142	6:21–22	93	
14:7–11	90	18:2	33	10:2–4	46	
14:11	21	21:38	112			
14:16–24	21			**Gospel of Thomas**		
14:21–23	90	**Romans**		20:2–3	45	
14:25–26	89	1:3	35	22:1–2	86	
14:28–32	21	3:25	98	22:4–7	44	
15:3–32	21	12:14	35	54	45	
15:11–32	106, 155	12:17–20	35	71	92	
16:1–9	21	14	122	82	49	
16:15	21	14:17	18, 98	82:3–13	21	
17:20–21	21, 120	16:7	142	85:15–19	21 (2x)	
17:21	139			92:10–35	21	
18:1–18	21	**1 Corinthians**		93:1–18	21	
18:9–14	21	7:10	34	97:1–4	45, 68	
19:11–27	161	9:14	34	97:2–6	21	
19:45–48	12	11:23–25	34	98:1–3	45, 68	
23:27–31	159	11:24–26	120	100:2	45	
23:34	68	14:34–35	29	109:1–3	45	
23:43	68	15:1–11	92			
23:46	68	15:3–4	88	**RABBINIC WRITINGS**		
		15:5	35, 119			
John		15:6	179	*Babylonian*		
1:1	86	15:8	34	*Talmud*		
1:17	114	15:8–10	119			
2:1–12	43	15:9	128	*Baba Batra*		
2:13–17	12	15:50	98	12a	190 n 38	
2:18–22	118					
3:1–10	86	**Galatians**		*Berakoth*		
3:3	68	1:13–14	128	17b	55	
3:22	5, 138	3:10–14	206 n. 87	34b	55	
3:26	5, 138					
4:1	138	**1 Thessalonians**		*Hullin*		
4:1–2	5	4:2	35	17a	55	
4:2	138	4:15–17	121			
4:44	68	4:16–17	165	*Sanhedrin*		
4:46–54	43, 141			43a	34	
5:1–9	43	**1 Timothy**				
6:1–13	43	2:11–15	29	*Taanith*		
6:15–25	43			24b	55	
8:12	43	**Hebrews**				
9:1–7	43	5:7–8	35	*Jerusalem Talmud*		
9:6	15	7:14	35	*Berakoth*		
11:1–44	43	9:11–14	98	9d	55	
11:1–46	141					
12:1–8	159	**James**		**GRECO-ROMAN**		
13:21–30	57	5:12	35	**LITERATURE**		
14:6	43, 68					
19:26–30	68	**2 Peter**		*Cicero*		
19:38–42	93	3:3–8	121			
21:1–6	43			*Tusculan Disputations*		
21:24	43	**1 John**		5.92	61	
		2:2	98			

Dio Chrysostum

Orations
6:15   62

Epictetus

Discourses
2:14.14   62
2:14.18–24   62

Josehus

Antiquities
18.3.3   33
20.9.1   32

Diogenes Laertius

Lives of Eminent Philosophers
6   62
6.29   62

6.69   61
6.8   61

Lucian of Samosata

Demonax
11   62

Peregrinus
11–13   34

Musonius Rufus

Fragment
15   61
19   61

Pliny the Younger

Letter to Trajan
10.96   33

Pseudo-Anacharsis
5   61

Seneca

Epistulae Morales
90.14–16   61

Suetonius

The Twelve Caesars
25.4   33

Tacitus

Annals
15.44   33

INDEX OF AUTHORS

This index does not cover the Bibliography. Names in the endnotes are listed only when they are not also listed for the pages in the main text to which the notes refer.

Allen, Charlotte, 39, 73, 76, 82–83, 187 nn.49, 53; 192 n.4, 193 nn. 41, 42, 50; 207 n. 23, 208 n.30
Aune, David, 179

Barr, James, 197 n.18
Bauer, Bruno, 168
Beyer, Barry, 6
Bien, Peter, 167
Blevins, James, 186 n.38
Blomberg, Craig, 75–76, 78, 188 nn.11, 18
Boers, Hendrikus, 137
Borg, Marcus, 4, 8, 9, 22–23, 53, 55–56, 60, 65, 69, 74–75, 82–83, 101–12, 109, 113, 126–27, 137–39, 142–44, 150, 169, 171–73, 175–76, 179–80, 182, 187 n.53, 192 n.12, 194 n.64, 201 nn.3, 79; 203 n.61, 207 nn.14, 39
Bornkamm, Günther, 11, 20, 22, 172
Brandon, S. G. F., 207 n.16
Brooks, Philip, 184
Brown, Raymond, 195 n.13
Bultmann, Rudolf, 9, 11, 18–19, 71, 168, 172, 177–78

Caird, George, 186 n.35
Calvin, John, 13
Carson, Don, 77
Casey, Maurice, 165
Castenada, Carlos, 102
Chadwick, Henry, 63
Chilton, Bruce, 192 n.4
Collins, Adela, 27
Corley, Kathleen, 196 n.40, 202 n.13
Crossan, John Dominic, 1, 31, 37, 46, 53, 55, 58, 60–61, 71, 76–77, 83–99, 103, 105–6, 109, 110–11, 116, 124, 126, 128, 132–33, 135, 137, 139, 144, 146, 151, 153, 163–64, 166–69, 171, 173, 175–76, 179, 181, 185 n.6, 186 n.36, 190 nn.53, 55; 191 n. 63, 199 n.23, 201 n.3, 204 n.6, 206 nn.78, 79

Dewey, Arthur, 73, 192 n.4
Douglas, Mary, 90
Downing, F. Gerald, 60–63, 96, 106, 111,

126, 171, 173, 190 n.52, 191 n. 69
Dungan, David, 188 n.8
Dunn, James D. G., 126, 166

Eddy, Paul, 190 n.48

Falwell, Jerry, 64
Farah, Mounir, 7
Farmer, William, 188 n.10
Fiorenza, Elizabeth S., 9, 28–29, 106, 110, 144
Fortna, Robert, 188 n.20
Fredriksen, Paula, 183
Freyne, Sean, 207 n.7
Fuller, Reginald, 128
Funk, Robert, 65–66, 71, 73–74, 76–77, 79–81, 163–64, 178, 181

Gaiser, Frederic, 3, 182
Graham, Billy, 9, 19
Gurr, Robert, 195 n.16

Hanson, John, 205 n.31
Hays, Richard, 76–77
Hind, James, 64
Hollenbach, Paul, 3, 137
Hoover, Roy, 192 n.4
Horsley, Richard, 22, 52–54, 88, 110, 127, 144, 173, 176, 205 n.31

Janssen, Gene, 167
Jesus Seminar, 37, 44–45, 65–81, 86, 97, 102, 109, 111, 116, 124, 126, 129, 134, 139, 144–46, 151, 163–64, 168–69, 171, 178, 203 n.64
Jewett, Robert, 187 n.47
Johnson, Luke T., 75–77, 193 n.53, 196 n.61, 206 n.90
Johnson, Scott, 187 n.47

Kähler, Martin, 4, 8, 9
Karls, Andrea, 7
Käsemann, Ernst, 19–20
Kautsky, John, 198 n.39
Kaylor, R. David, 54

Keck, Leander, 82–83, 196 n.57
Kee, Howard Clark, 76
Keim, Theodor, 186 n.15
Kingsbury, Jack Dean, 186 n.38
Kloppenborg, John, 38–39
Knibb, Michael, 206 n.87
Knutsen, Mary, 149
Koester, Helmut, 46, 188 n.23

Lenski, Gerhard, 87, 109
Lindsell, Harold, 185 n.7
Long, Thomas, 182
Lüdemann, Gerd, 178–79
Luther, Martin, 12

Mack, Burton, 25–28, 29, 37–38, 49, 60, 75,
    106, 111, 126, 140, 164, 169, 171, 173, 179,
    181, 190 nn.49, 51; 196 n.56, 199 n.20
Malherbe, Abraham, 190 nn.49, 51
McKnight, Edgar, 186 n.18
Meier, John, 5, 9, 22, 31, 37, 39, 53, 55, 58,
    76, 78, 97–98, 103, 111, 126–29, 131–47,
    151, 163, 166, 168–70, 172, 174, 176–81,
    183, 187 n.5, 188 n.7, 195 n.13, 198 n.54,
    200 n.32, 203 nn. 59, 68
Meyer, Ben, 195 nn.10, 13; 204 n.7
Miller, Robert, 188 n.21, 189 n.28
Murphy, Cullen, 182
Murray, Jon, 64

Neusner, Jacob, 165
Niebuhr, Gustav, 193 n.29, 194 nn.58, 59

Ostling, Richard, 204 n.4
O'Connor, John, 167

Pagels, Elaine, 188 n.24
Paulus, Heinrich, 14–15, 23, 177
Pelikan, Jaroslav, vii, 30
Perkins, Pheme, 188 n.24
Perrin, Norman, 20–22, 202 n.39
Plaskow, Judith, 187 n.56
Powell, Mark Allan, 186 n.18, 188 n.9

Rahner, Karl, 204 n.74
Räisänen, Heikki, 186 n.38
Reimarus, Hermann, 13–14, 175
Renan, Ernst, 15–16, 177
Robbins, Vernon, 77, 190 n.51
Roberts, Tyler, 51
Robinson, James, 66, 188 n.21

Sanders, E. P., 1, 22, 31, 37, 53, 55, 60, 98,
    111, 113–29, 132, 139–40, 142–44, 153,
    155, 158–59, 163, 165–66, 169–70, 172,
    174, 176, 182, 203 nn.59, 68; 207 n.37
Sawicki, Marianne, 196 n.40

Schneelmelcher, Wilhelm, 188 n.21
Schulz, Siegfried, 39
Schwarz, Donald, 6
Schweitzer, Albert, 11, 14–20, 22–24, 125,
    159, 164, 168, 170, 174, 183, 185 nn.5, 9,
    12, 13, 14; 186 nn.15, 16; 207 n. 19
Scroggs, Robin, 96
Seeley, David, 190 n.48
Shanks, Hershel, 189 n.19
Sheler, Jeffrey, 193 nn. 27, 28, 30; 194 n. 64,
    201 n.3; 202 n. 12, 203 n.65
Shorto, Russell, 50
Simon, Josh, 187 n.58, 189 n.2, 191 n.74,
    207 nn.2, 3
Smith, Morton, 56–58, 89, 97, 179
Stearns, Peter, 6
Strauss, David, 15–16, 23, 177, 184

Tatum, W. Barnes, 186 n.27
Taussig, Hal, 73
Taylor, Walter, 51, 64, 187 n.4
Theissen, Gerd, 127, 191 n.66
Tuckett, Christopher, 186 n.38, 188 n.15,
    191 n.59
Twelftree, Graham, 56

Vaage, Leif, 63, 68, 73, 190 n.49, 191 n.67
Van Biema, David, 192 n.20, 193 nn. 43, 44,
    46; 194 nn. 57, 63, 73; 207 n.1
Verhoeven, Paul, 66
Vermes, Geza, 22, 54–56, 110, 171, 181
Von Campenhausen, Hans, 188 n.22
Von Wahlde, Urban, 188 n.20

Watson, Russell, 193 n. 26, 194 n. 57
Webb, Robert, 205 n.31
Weiss, Johannes, 17
Wilson, Bryan, 87
Wink, Walter, 54
Witherington, Ben, 9, 22, 53, 58–60, 84, 95,
    106, 111, 127–28, 131, 161, 165, 170, 174,
    180, 187 n.56, 191 n.68, 195 n.10, 196 n.60,
    198 n.54, 202 n.13, 203 n.61, 206 n.75
Wolff, Hans W., 185 n.4
Woodward, Kenneth, 207 n. 25, 208 n.27
Wrede, William, 24–25, 28–29, 37, 164
Wright, N. T., 11, 22–23, 37, 47, 49, 53–54,
    60, 76, 78, 80–81, 84, 86, 97–98, 101, 103,
    110–12, 127–28, 134, 145–46, 149–66,
    168–69, 172, 174, 176, 180–81, 186 nn.21,
    25, 26; 189 nn.13, 16; 194 n.72, 195 n.14,
    198 n.54, 199 nn. 57, 22; 203 nn.61, 68; 207
    nn. 8, 18

Yarborough, Robert, 51
Yoder, John H., 127
Young, Allan, 195 n.25